# International Trade Policy Formation

## Theory and Politics

## World Scientific Studies in International Economics

(ISSN: 1793-3641)



---

*Published**

Vol. 18 Quantitative Analysis of Newly Evolving Patterns of International Trade: Fragmentation, Offshoring of Activities, and Vertical Intra-Industry Trade
*edited by Robert M Stern (University of Michigan and University of California-Berkeley, USA)*

Vol. 19 The World Economy after the Global Crisis: A New Economic Order for the 21st Century
*edited by Barry Eichengreen (University of California-Berkeley, USA) & Bokyeong Park (Korea Institute for International Economic Policy, Korea)*

Vol. 20 Trade, Development and Agriculture: Essays in Economic Policy Analysis
*edited by Kym Anderson (University of Adelaide, & Australian National University, Australia)*

Vol. 21 Regulations of Foreign Investment: Challenges for International Harmonization
*edited by Zdenek Drabek (Charles University, Czech Republic) & Petros Mavroidis (Columbia University, USA)*

Vol. 22 International Trade Policy Formation: Theory and Politics
*by Wolfgang Mayer (University of Cincinnati, USA)*

*Forthcoming*

Globalizing Information: The Economics of International Technology Trade
*by Keith E Maskus (University of Colorado at Boulder, USA)*

Globalizing Trade and Investment: India Arrives
*edited by Rajesh Chadha (National Council of Applied Economic Research (NCAER), India)*

*The complete list of the published volumes in the series can be found at
http://www.worldscientific.com/series/wssie

22 World Scientific Studies in International Economics

# International Trade Policy Formation

## Theory and Politics

**Wolfgang Mayer**
University of Cincinnati, USA

World Scientific

NEW JERSEY · LONDON · SINGAPORE · BEIJING · SHANGHAI · HONG KONG · TAIPEI · CHENNAI

*Published by*

World Scientific Publishing Co. Pte. Ltd.
5 Toh Tuck Link, Singapore 596224
*USA office:* 27 Warren Street, Suite 401-402, Hackensack, NJ 07601
*UK office:* 57 Shelton Street, Covent Garden, London WC2H 9HE

**British Library Cataloguing-in-Publication Data**
A catalogue record for this book is available from the British Library.

**World Scientific Studies in International Economics — Vol. 22**
**INTERNATIONAL TRADE POLICY FORMATION**
**Theory and Politics**



ISBN 978-981-4434-76-8

In-house Editor: Monica Lesmana

Typeset by Stallion Press
Email: enquiries@stallionpress.com

Printed in Singapore.

# Preface

This volume consists of a collection of previously published articles which are representative of my research in international economics over the last four decades and which remain highly relevant for the ongoing study and future development of international trade theory.

Part I of this collection deals with the pure theory of international trade. It explores the robustness of the Heckscher-Ohlin framework and its core propositions — the Stolper-Samuelson and Rybczynski theorems — by relaxing its underlying assumptions in four different ways: limiting the inter-industry mobility of factors of production; allowing for industry economies of scale; introducing uncertainty of commodity prices; and endogenizing a country's supply of labor.

Part II addresses economic policy issues which had gained prominence during the period of multilateral trade liberalization under the auspices of the GATT, such as: the scope and limits of negotiated tariff agreements; first-best policy justifications for import restrictions and export promotions; and the use of import-quality standards as a substitute for tariffs. The models of Part II have in common that the government's policy choice aims at maximizing its people's overall welfare.

Part III is a response to the observation that, in spite of wide agreement on which policies maximize a country's welfare, sizable gaps persist between actually adopted and social welfare-maximizing policies. The political-economy models of Part III explicitly account for the political environment in which governments operate, emphasizing that individuals' policy interests are far from homogeneous. The general public is allowed to be heterogeneous with respect to its ownership of factors of production, resulting in significant differences of trade-policy preferences across the population. The first five chapters of Part III consider direct democracy as the vehicle for transforming divergent individual policy preferences into majority-supported actual policies. After modeling tariff-policy formation under majority voting in a general framework, specific explanations are offered for the following real-world observations: governments tend to choose tariffs as their preferred instruments to redistribute income rather than more efficient production taxes-*cum*-subsidies; most countries' trade-policies are biased towards import protection rather than export promotion; and the policy preferences of workers who are old tend to differ from those that are young, even if employed in the same industry. The last chapter of Part III deals with trade-policy formation in a representative democracy. It allows for the influence of both the voting public and election-financing interest groups.

Part IV offers a political-economy approach to a specific problem encountered by many International Financial Institutions (IFIs), namely how to design consistently effective conditional assistance programs. Why has the history of conditional assistance — making financial support through loans or grants contingent on the implementation of economic reforms — been one of rather mixed success for organizations such as the International Monetary Fund and the World Bank? Two models are introduced to highlight the need for creating explicit incentives for assistance-receiving governments to engage in reforms when their policy decisions are influenced by special interests and IFIs have limited information on governments' competence and willingness to implement reforms.

# Acknowledgments

My intellectual debt to teachers and peers is substantial. My interest in economics was first stirred by Daniel Hamberg in his macroeconomics course at the Bologna Center of the School of Advanced International Studies. Under the influence of Winston Chang, my curiosity turned towards microeconomics and international trade theory. Throughout my career, my thinking on and approach to topics was considerably influenced by Ronald Jones in the pure theory of trade research of Part I and by Jagdish Bhagwati and Harry Johnson in the trade policy chapters of Part II. The writings of Part III greatly benefited from interactions with Robert Baldwin, Arye Hillman, and Stephen Magee. I am especially grateful to Arye Hillman for his frequent reminders to focus on issues of relevance to actual policy-making. There were many others who shaped my thinking, most notably my co-authors of the Part III research, Raymond Riezman and Jun Li, and my co-author of the Part IV models, Alexandros Mourmouras. I am greatly indebted to all of them. Finally, I wish to express my gratitude to Robert M. Stern, the Series Editor of *World Scientific Studies in International Economics*, for inviting me to publish this collection of research articles.

The following publishers are acknowledged for granting permission to re-use my previously published articles:

American Economic Association for articles:

"The Rybczynski, Stolper-Samuelson, and factor-price equalization theorems under price uncertainty," *American Economic Review*, 66 (5), 1976, pp. 797–808.

"Endogenous tariff formation," *American Economic Review*, 74 (5), 1984, pp. 970–985.

Elsevier for articles:

"The national defense tariff argument reconsidered," *Journal of International Economics*, 7 (4), 1977, pp. 363–377.

"Endogenous choice of trade policy instruments" (with Raymond Riezman), *Journal of International Economics*, 23 (3–4), 1987, pp. 377–381.

"Endogenous labor supply in international trade theory: two alternative models," *Journal of International Economics*, 30 (1–2), 1991, pp. 105–120.

John Wiley and Sons for articles:

"Variable returns to scale in general equilibrium theory: a comment," *International Economic Review*, 15 (1), 1974, pp. 225–235.

"The tariff equivalence of import standards," *International Economic Review*, 23 (3), 1982, pp. 723–734.

"The infant-export industry argument," *Canadian Journal of Economics*, 17 (2), 1984, pp. 249–269.

"Voter preferences for trade policy instruments" (with Raymond Riezman), *Economics & Politics*, 2 (3), 1990, pp. 259–273.

"Interest groups, electoral competition, and probabilistic voting for trade policies" (with Jun Li), *Economics & Politics*, 6 (1), 1994, pp. 59–77.

"International financial assistance: a loan mechanism-design approach" (with Alexandros Mourmouras), *Economics & Politics*, 21 (1), 2009, pp. 126–158.

"Age as a determinant of labor's trade policy interests" (with Jun Li), *Pacific Economic Review*, 1 (2), 1996, pp. 147–167.

"Systematic political grass-root support for tariffs," *Review of International Economics*, 10 (4), 2002, pp. 657–670.

"The political economy of IMF conditionality: a common agency model" (with Alexandros Mourmouras), *Review of Development Economics*, 9 (4), 2005, pp. 449–466.

Oxford University Press for the article:

"Theoretical considerations on negotiated tariff adjustments," *Oxford Economic Papers*, New Series, 33 (1), 1981, pp. 135–153.

University of Chicago Press for the article:

"Short-run and long-run equilibrium for a small open economy," *Journal of Political Economy*, 82 (5), 1974, pp. 955–967.

# Contents

# Introduction

## Part I: International Trade Theory

By the early 1970s, the Heckscher-Ohlin model — in its basic two-commodity, two-factor form — had become the most widely accepted theory on the determinants of a country's factor returns and production pattern, as spelled out by the Stolper-Samuelson (1941) and Rybczynski (1951) theorems. The Stolper-Samuelson theorem states that an increase in one commodity's relative price raises the real return on the factor which is used relatively intensively in its production while lowering the real return on the other factor. The Rybczynski theorem asserts that a rise in one factor's endowment more than proportionately increases output of the industry which uses that factor relatively intensively while reducing output of the other industry. Among the essential building blocks in formulating the model and deriving its core propositions are the following four assumptions: both labor and capital are perfectly mobile between industries; production is subject to constant returns to scale at both firm and industry level; firms make their production decisions with full knowledge of future commodity prices; and each country's factor endowments are fixed. The unifying feature of Part I is the objective to evaluate the robustness of Heckscher-Ohlin's core propositions by relaxing these four assumptions one at a time.

*Chapter 1* limits the inter-industry mobility of capital but retains all other assumptions of the basic Heckscher-Ohlin model, including that of perfect labor mobility. It thereby acquires the characteristics of a short-run model in contrast to the long-run features of Heckscher-Ohlin. The distinction between short- and long-run effects of exogenous price and endowment changes, which dates back at least to Haberler (1936), has drawn renewed interest with the emergence of political economy of trade-policy formation as a major field of research. The public's political support for policymakers depends far more on the immediate rather than long-term impact of their policy choices.

The specific objectives of this chapter are two: first, to examine the short-run effects of exogenous commodity price and factor endowment changes on factor returns and industry output; and second, to trace the economy's adjustment from this initial short-run to its eventual long-run equilibrium. From the perspective of policymakers, it thereby highlights the immediate impact of changes in trade and immigration policies on the welfare of voters, in contrast to the long-run effects known from the Stolper-Samuelson and Rybczynski theorems.

The short-run equilibrium of this small, open economy is analyzed within the standard two-commodity, two-factor trade model. In the short run, labor is allowed to be fully mobile between industries, whereas once-installed capital lacks the ability to instantaneously move from one to the other industry. Accordingly, capital is treated as sector specific, making this short-run specification essentially the same as the one adopted by Jones (1971) in his three-factor, two-commodity model. While both industries' firms pay the same wage, there are inter-industry differences in the return on capital. It is this differential in capital returns which triggers the economy's adjustment from short- to long-run equilibrium. Over time, as capital is gradually reallocated, the capital stock expands in the high- and contracts in the low-return industry. This capital-reallocation process, accompanied by instantaneous re-adjustments in labor's employment, continues until capital returns are equalized between industries and a new long-run equilibrium is established.

To illustrate this time-dependent adjustment process, the analysis traces the country's long- and short-run production possibilities. For each point on the long-run curve — and the corresponding long-run industry allocation of capital — there exists a short-run curve along which only labor is mobile between industries. Each short-run curve is anchored at one point on the long-run curve, but lies inside the latter for all of its other points. Starting at a long-run equilibrium, a price change initiates an immediate output adjustment along the short-run curve, followed by a gradual slide of the entire short-run along the long-run curve until a new long-run equilibrium comes about.

The short-run responses of factor returns to a commodity price change differ greatly from the long-run responses, as known from the Stolper-Samuelson theorem. In the short-run, the return on capital rises in the industry whose relative price increased and declines in the other industry. The wage rate also rises, but at a slower rate than the commodity price. Different from the long-run, the short-run factor-return responses to changes in commodity prices are independent of the two industries' relative factor intensities. But relative factor intensities do matter for the adjustment process towards long-run equilibrium. The short-run inter-industry differential in capital returns sets in motion the gradual reallocation of capital. As old capital wears out, all new capital flows to the high-return industry which, in turn, also attracts more labor. The adjustment process is shaped by opposing influences on the two industries' capital returns: capital's return in the high-return industry declines with the capital build-up, but rises with the accompanying inflow of labor. The direction of the combined effect depends on the two industries' relative factor intensities. Capital returns rise (decline), although at different speeds, in both industries if the expanding industry is relatively capital (labor) intensive. Consequently, the initial short-run factor-return responses revert to the long-run responses on the basis of the same factor-intensity criteria as spelled out in the Stolper-Samuelson theorem.

In the long-run model, with complete inter-industry mobility of both factors, endowment changes have no effect on factor returns as long as the economy remains non-specialized. Consequently, the Heckscher-Ohlin model is poorly suited to shed light on the politics behind changing immigration laws. The short-run model, on the other hand, clearly exposes the conflicting interests in the immigration debate. Relaxing immigration restrictions lowers the wage rate and raises both industries' capital returns. The short-run capital-return gain is, however, greater in the labor- than capital-intensive industry. This newly-created capital-return differential starts the adjustment process to long-run equilibrium. As capital begins to move from the capital- to the labor-intensive industry, accompanied by instantaneously reallocating labor, capital returns decline and wages rise in both industries, eventually returning to pre-immigration levels.

The response of industry output to immigration of labor also differs between short and long run. In the short run, an increase in labor's endowment leads to the expansion of both industries. In the long run, on the other hand, output rises in the labor-intensive industry and declines in the capital-intensive industry. During the adjustment from short- to long-run equilibrium, the short-run capital-return differential again attracts more of both capital and labor to the labor-intensive industry, thereby further expanding labor-intensive at the expense of capital-intensive industry production.

*Chapter 2* addresses the issue of variable returns to scale in the general equilibrium theory of production. The basic Heckscher-Ohlin model yields three unambiguous propositions about the effects of commodity price and endowment changes on factor returns and industry output: the Stolper-Samuelson theorem, the Rybczynski theorem, and the direct relationship between an industry's output and its commodity's relative price. All three propositions are based on a two-commodity, two-factor model in which production takes place under constant returns to scale at both firm and industry level. When Jones (1968) explored the validity of the above-stated propositions in the presence of economies of scale which are external to the firm but internal to the industry, he found that generalizing from constant to variable returns invalidates these most treasured relationships.

The objective of Chapter 2 is to restore the three fundamental propositions' validity by invoking Samuelson's (1947) Correspondence Principle after restricting the analysis to stable markets. In commodity markets, a Marshallian adjustment process is assumed: with commodity prices given in world markets, any deviation of a commodity's world price from domestic average cost leads to adjustments in the domestic industry's output. In factor markets, on the other hand, a Walrasian adjustment process is assumed: with a country's fixed factor endowments, any deviation of the two industries' combined demand for a factor from the economy's fixed endowment leads to adjustments in the factor's return. It is demonstrated that both the Rybczynski theorem and the direct relationship between industry output and its commodity's relative price carry over to variable-returns-to-scale models provided both commodity and factor market equilibriums are stable. These findings hold even if industry production functions are non-homothetic. The Stolper-Samuelson theorem's validity, on the other hand, extends to variable-returns-to-scale models only if all industry-production functions are homothetic. In employing stability properties to obtain comparative statics results, the analysis also demonstrates that there exist speeds of adjustment for which stability of both markets is assured.

*Chapter 3* modifies the standard international trade model by allowing firms to be uncertain about future prices at which they will sell their commodities. A basic assumption of the Heckscher-Ohlin model is that commodity markets are competitive, with individual firms making their production decisions under complete certainty about future commodity prices. Considering the unavoidable time lag between a firm's current production decision and its actual selling of the product, this is a strong assumption. Rothenberg and Smith (1971) and Batra (1974, 1975) were pioneers in drawing the attention of international trade theorists to the impact of price uncertainty on the allocation of resources in neo-classical general-equilibrium production models. Of particular concern were Batra's findings, which questioned the relevance of Heckscher-Ohlin after concluding that both the Stolper-Samuelson and the Rybczynski theorem break down under price uncertainty.

The objective of Chapter 3 is to restore the validity of the Heckscher-Ohlin model's core propositions in the presence of price uncertainty. Employing Sandmo's (1971) model of competitive firm behavior under price uncertainty, our findings contradict Batra by concluding that the introduction of risk-averse firms facing uncertain prices does not alter in any fundamental way the cherished propositions on the influence of commodity prices and endowments on factor returns and industry output.

The conclusion is derived from a standard two-good, two-factor trade model, with the modification that risk-averse firms subjectively perceive commodity prices to be random at the time production decisions are made. Each firm's goal is to maximize its expected utility from profit. The model further assumes that all of an industry's firms not only have the same production function, but also the same utility function and probability-of-price assessment. The key to reclaiming the validity of the Stolper-Samuelson, Rybczynski, and factor-price equalization theorems under price uncertainty is the industry-equilibrium condition for competitive markets. Free entry and exit of firms in the long run imply that an industry is in equilibrium when each firm's expected profit equals its risk premium. Consequently, the expected price must cover not only the firm's average cost of production but also its average risk premium.

The chapter's findings are highly comforting. The Rybczynski theorem holds without modification, as does the Stolper-Samuelson theorem after adding the word 'expected' to the terms price and real return. The factor-price equalization theorem — expressing that unimpeded trade of final commodities between countries leads to equalization of their factor returns — also remains valid under uncertainty provided that, for a given industry, both countries' firms have not only identical production functions but also identical utility functions and probability beliefs.

So how did Batra (1975) come to the conclusion that the core propositions which follow from Heckscher-Ohlin no longer apply in the presence of price uncertainty? The explanation is that Batra fails to account for the condition that, in the long-run, competitive firms are free to enter and exit an industry. Batra's specification contains the implicit assumption that, while individual firms can freely adjust their employment of all factors of production and these factors are fully mobile between industries, the number of firms in each industry remains constant. Batra, thereby, specifies an intermediate-run model with imperfect factor mobility, as only existing firms can adjust their factor employment. In contrast, the long-run model of Heckscher-Ohlin allows for adjustments in the number of firms as well.

*Chapter 4* relaxes the Heckscher-Ohlin model's rather stark assumption that a country's supply of labor services is exogenously given: the economy is populated by a fixed number of workers; each worker supplies a constant number of work hours; and labor services yielded per work hour are constant. Accordingly, the economy's supply of labor services is independent of the prevailing wage, as well as of prices paid for commodities.

This chapter proposes to endogenize a country's supply of labor services in two alternative ways. First, it allows a fixed number of workers to choose the number of hours they work. Second, it offers each individual the choice of either working a fixed number of hours or not working at all. Labor economists have associated the first assumption with the long-run and the second with the short-run. Under both assumptions, workers might also receive income from the ownership of capital and the redistribution of tariff revenues. As this unearned income becomes endogenous, income effects exert an important influence on the direction of adjustments in labor supply and industry output after exogenous shocks to the economy.

Both models have in common that a country's labor-supply response to exogenous price shocks, as in the case of a tariff change, depends on two properties: the relative factor intensities in production and leisure being a substitute or complement for commodities in consumption. Not surprisingly, most Heckscher-Ohlin propositions fail to carry over from fixed to variable labor-supply models. In fact, there exists the potential for several "perverse results" unless more restrictive assumptions are added. For example, in the flexible work-hours model without further restrictions, a rise in the world price of the import good might result in a shrinking rather than expanding import-competing industry. If, however, the export good is relatively capital intensive in production and a substitute for leisure in consumption, this perverse outcome is precluded.

Exogenous capital inflows are shown to cause a decline in the country's labor services in both the flexible work-hours and endogenous work-participation model. The combined effect of exogenous expansion of capital and endogenous adjustment of labor on a country's national income, on the other hand, differs between the two models. National income always rises in the flexible work-hours model, whereas income has the potential to decline in the variable work-participation model. This possibility of declining national income in response to exogenous growth of capital is, however, not a case of immiserizing growth; national welfare, as opposed to national income, always rises.

The assumption of endogenous labor supply can also have implications for a country's trade pattern. In international trade models with fixed labor supply, a country displays a bias towards importing a good if its technology for producing it is inferior to or its propensity to consume it is higher than in the rest of the world. In the flexible work-hours model, on the other hand, one cannot preclude the possibility that inferior technology to produce and higher propensity to consume a good impart a bias to becoming an exporter of that good.

## Part II: International Trade Policy

Multilateral negotiations to lower international trade barriers were the driving force behind the explosion of world trade during the second half of the 20$^{\text{th}}$ century. Article XXVIII of GATT explicitly advocated tariff negotiations as the preferred vehicle to expand trade and to enhance national welfare of GATT member countries. By the end of the 1970s, the Kennedy and Tokyo Round negotiations had indeed succeeded in substantially lowering the tariff barriers of most industrialized countries. At the same time, the final agreements, as well as the arduous negotiations leading up to them, had exposed increasing obstacles to further tariff reductions. In addition, the multilateral push towards freer trade had been counteracted by many countries' unilateral actions to protect their import-competing and promote their export-oriented industries. Part II of this collection of articles starts with the specification of a theoretical model that allows for the characterization of all possible outcomes of tariff negotiations. It is followed by two models which shed light on governments' attempts to counter the effects of multilateral tariff reductions with unilaterally adopted protective measures. One of them demonstrates how the venerable "national defense tariff argument" can be invoked as a legitimate first-best "economic" rather than "political" argument to justify protection of some industries. The other model illustrates how the loss of protection due to negotiated or unilateral tariff reductions can be offset through unilaterally-imposed import quality standards. The final chapter of Part II argues that export promotion, which many developing countries' governments had viewed as their most promising path towards accelerated economic growth, can be justified as a first-best trade policy.

*Chapter 5* proposes a theoretical framework for answering numerous questions which came up in the context of the Kennedy and Tokyo Round tariff negotiations and on which the international trade literature had remained largely silent. What are the essential features of negotiated tariff equilibriums? Will the end-result after several rounds of negotiations be free trade or some combination of trade taxes and subsidies? And how can the application of a tariff-cutting formula, as introduced in both Kennedy and Tokyo Round, affect the final agreement? The fact that the United States and European Economic Community (EEC) fiercely disagreed on which formula to employ suggested that negotiation rules matter a great deal to the participating parties. The United States had pushed for linear tariff cuts, with tariffs on all imports getting reduced by the same percentage, whereas the EEC insisted on harmonizing cuts, requiring larger percentage reductions on goods with initially higher tariffs.

The model specifies a two-country, two-commodity world in which tariffs and import subsidies are the only available trade-policy instruments. Assuming conditions that assure unique trading equilibriums, each country's welfare can be expressed as a function of the two countries' respective tariff and import-subsidy rates. When tariff negotiations are not constrained by a previously agreed-upon tariff-cutting formula, the negotiated agreement must satisfy two conditions: each country must be at least as well off as in a state of tariff war and any further tariff or subsidy change cannot improve one country's welfare without hurting the other. These two conditions determine the set of possible outcomes of unconstrained negotiations. Two general properties of the resulting tariff agreements are noteworthy. First, negotiations lead either to free trade for both countries or to a tariff for one and an import subsidy for the other. Second, a free-trade agreement might not be attainable at all, as one cannot preclude situations in which one country is worse off under free trade than in a tariff war.

The Kennedy Round had attempted to widen the scope of negotiated tariff reductions by replacing the item-by-item tariff cutting of earlier GATT-sponsored multilateral negotiations with a tariff-cutting formula that applies the same rate to many goods at the same time. Accordingly, the negotiating parties first had to agree to a tariff-cutting formula before tackling the magnitude of the tariff adjustment. This chapter examines the properties of final tariff agreements when rate negotiations are constrained by either the US-supported linear or the EEC-supported harmonizing tariff-cutting formula. It concludes that, under linear as well as harmonizing constraints, the final agreement must lead to either free trade or positive tariffs for both countries. Importantly, there cannot be a final agreement with a tariff for one and an import subsidy for the other country, as was a possible outcome without a tariff-cutting formula. The paper also demonstrates that the US favoring linear cuts and the EEC favoring harmonizing cuts were no accidental choices. Since the pre-negotiation average tariff was higher for the US than the EEC, the linear tariff adjustment path yielded greater welfare gains for the US while the harmonizing path was more advantageous to the EEC.

Finally, this chapter sketches a model which explicitly recognizes limits to redistributing the gains from trade within a country. Instead of assuming a country's consumption preferences to be represented by a community utility function, distinct interest groups are introduced as a determining influence on negotiated tariff agreements.

*Chapter 6* establishes a first-best economic explanation for the "national defense tariff argument." When Adam Smith (1776; 1904 edition) made his case for free trade between countries, he allowed for one major exception: protection on the basis of national defense considerations. With this endorsement, the national defense tariff argument has been considered a legitimate, non-economic justification for tariffs. It rested on the reasoning that national security considerations override economic efficiency criteria in a country's design of trade policy. Not surprisingly, the national defense tariff argument has been embraced by many different industries of virtually all countries to gain lasting protection from foreign competition.

The objective of Chapter 6 is to demonstrate that clear-cut economic efficiency criteria, rather than vaguely expressed non-economic security considerations, form the basis for the national defense tariff argument. Three conditions must be satisfied for a positive defense tariff to maximize a country's expected welfare. First, the country must trade with the rest of the world in an environment of uncertainty; the probability of a precipitous trade interruption must be positive. Second, after trade is interrupted, adjustments in the country's production must be time-consuming and costly. Third, individual producers and consumers lack perfect foresight. In the absence of government intervention, private economic agents fail to make socially-optimal production and consumption decisions.

A two-commodity, small-economy model serves as the vehicle for justifying the national defense tariff as an efficiency rather than non-economic tariff argument. It deviates from the standard trade model in that it distinguishes between an economy's long-run or potential production possibilities, which are attainable in the absence of adjustment costs, and its short-run or actual production possibilities, to which the economy is constrained for some time after an unanticipated dislocation of production. For each point on a locus of potential production possibilities, there exists a corresponding locus of actual production possibilities. Consequently, a government's choice of long-term trade policy determines not only the country's production pattern in the absence of an interruption, but also its ability to adjust after an interruption has occurred. Given the government's assessment of the risks of trade interruption, it chooses a policy that weighs the benefits from increased specialization in the absence of an interruption against the cost of the economy's reduced adjustment ability in response to an interruption.

The chapter's findings on a government's choice of an efficient trade policy are quite clear-cut. Provided the risk of trade interruption is non-negligible and a tariff is the only available policy instrument, the country's welfare-maximizing policy is a positive import tariff. Furthermore, the first-best national defense tariff is shown to rise with an increase in the probability of trade interruption.

When the choice set of policy instruments is enlarged to include production and consumption taxes-*cum*-subsidies, a national-defense production subsidy alone becomes the first-best policy and the national defense tariff is only second-best. The post-interruption adjustment cost on the production side, combined with imperfect foresight on the part of individual producers, represents a distortion that calls for correction through a production subsidy, as follows from general principles established by Bhagwati (1971).

*Chapter 7* examines a government's ability to attain a desired level of import protection by imposing minimum-quality standards instead of tariffs on imports. Setting minimum standards on the quality of imported goods has become a common practice by many governments. While some countries' quality standards apply to both foreign and domestically produced goods, others have set even higher standards for imports than domestic products. Both practices have been controversial. Domestic governments claim they are justified as an essential tool to shield domestic consumers from inferior foreign products. Foreign governments, on the other hand, argue that they are just another way to protect the importing country's domestic producers.

This chapter introduces a framework for analyzing the effects of import standards on domestic producers and consumers. It demonstrates the existence of a clear-cut trade-off between import standards and tariffs to attain a desired level of protection of an import-competing industry. Consequently, the loss of protection due to unilateral or negotiated tariff reductions can be fully offset by the suitable choice of import standards. The magnitude of the tariff equivalence of import standards is shown to depend on the ability of foreign producers to adjust their product quality and the willingness of domestic consumers to pay for the rise in quality. The more difficult it is for foreign producers and the easier it is for domestic consumers to adjust to the required quality standard, the more effective is an import standard as a tariff substitute. Concerning the controversy of who benefits from import standards, domestic producers or domestic consumers of the import-competing commodity, the analysis yields two conclusions. First, domestic producers always receive some protection as long as the standard raises the quality of the imported good. Second, the tariff equivalence of an import standard is always less than the increase in unit cost to foreign producers. Since consumers benefit from higher quality, the rise in unit cost to foreign firms overstates the true protective effect of the import standard.

The tariff-equivalence of import standards is examined in a model that modifies the usual two-commodity, two-factor, perfect competition trade model by explicitly specifying the quality dimension of a commodity. Production technologies enable firms to adjust not only the quantity but also the quality of output. Tractability of the analysis is retained by assuming that each producer's quality choice exerts a Hicks-neutral impact on input use. Consumers, in turn, value quality. Their preferences are represented by a repackaging utility function, which implies that consumers can trade off a commodity's quantity for its quality to yield the same flow of services. Domestic consumers can purchase either domestic or foreign commodities; and the domestic production technology differs from that of foreign firms.

The degree of protection provided to an import-competing industry by either a tariff or a quality standard is measured by the magnitude of resource reallocation brought about by the interference with free-trade policies. The model first describes a free-trade equilibrium in which the quality of the domestically-produced commodity exceeds that of imports. When a tariff is imposed, factors of production are reallocated towards the import-competing industry. The assumptions of Hicks-neutrality of quality choice in production and of repackaging of quality in consumption conveniently imply that the tariff is neutral with respect to the choice of commodity quality. As an alternative to the tariff, the model next introduces import standards that generate the exact same resource allocation as the previously imposed tariff. Domestic resources move into the import-competing industry as minimum import standards raise the price foreign firms must receive to cover the average cost of their improved-quality export product. A minimum import standard's protection effect is equivalent to that of a tariff when the domestic producers' average cost under the import standard and no tariff is exactly the same as under the tariff and no import standard.

*Chapter 8* formulates a dynamic model to propose the "infant-export industry argument" as a first-best justification for a country's promotion of exports. In the late 1970s, applied trade-policy scholars had started to question the effectiveness and appropriateness of GATT provisions dealing with export subsidization. It became widely accepted that there should be some exceptions to GATT's general principle of prohibiting export subsidies. This position was further strengthened by development economists who provided empirical evidence of a strong, positive relationship between export performance and economic growth in developing countries. The literature on international trade theory, on the other hand, had remained largely silent on the merits of export subsidization even though a decade earlier Bhagwati (1968) had already pointed out that externalities in foreign market cultivation might justify export subsidies as a first-best policy. This chapter's model tries to fill this void by showing in detail how the common practice of subsidizing exports can be rooted in efficiency considerations.

The model's premise is that domestic firms, when trying to enter a foreign market, face foreign-buyer resistance due to unfamiliarity with their product. In order to penetrate a new market, infant-export firms have to incur considerable market-cultivating expenditures. If a firm were a country's sole potential exporter of a well-defined product, the cost of penetrating a new foreign market could be fully internalized. If, on the other hand, there are many domestic firms with equal potential to produce and export the same kind of good, then a single firm's effort at overcoming foreign-buyer resistance benefits not only itself but all other firms as well. Hence, social returns from foreign-market development exceed private returns, and a country's social welfare can be raised by subsidizing the exports of the entire infant-export industry.

Market cultivation is modeled as a dynamic process in which foreign consumers initially lack familiarity with the quality of an export-promoting country's product and in which familiarization requires actual consumption rather than just product inspection. Product familiarization is assumed to take the form of an Arrow-type learning-by-consuming process. Costs and benefits of foreign market cultivation are very unevenly spread over present and future periods. Initial market-cultivating expenditures by the export-promoting country lead to significant short-run welfare losses which over time are gradually offset by welfare gains that become ever more pronounced over time. These short-run welfare losses can be ameliorated by the country's running of a temporary balance-of-trade deficit.

Export subsidization of an infant-export product is shown to be a first-best policy for a two-industry, perfectly competitive domestic economy whose government maximizes society's discounted stream of welfare. Balance of trade constraints are not binding at each instant of time, but must be satisfied over the entire period of market cultivation. During this cultivation phase, the price that foreign consumers are willing to pay rises with the growing degree of product familiarity. A repackaging utility function, in which gaining product familiarity is equivalent to getting more quantity, is implicit in the specification of foreign consumers' behavior.

The presence of externalities in market cultivation calls for government intervention. The government faces an infinite-time-horizon control problem in search of social-welfare-maximizing policies. The infant-export country's first-best policy turns out to be an export subsidy as long as product familiarity on the part of foreign consumers keeps rising. Over time, the optimal export subsidy tends to shrink if the international borrowing rate is relatively low; but the decline may not be monotonic for high borrowing rates.

The government's adoption of optimal export-promoting policies results in two kinds of adjustments: one-time discrete jumps in both domestic production and consumption when the policies are first adopted and gradual adjustments thereafter as the economy moves toward a new long-run equilibrium. During this lengthy adjustment phase, domestic consumption of both import and export goods rises. Foreign consumption of the newly available good, on the other hand, may not rise monotonically during the early phase of the product familiarization process; but it will increase during the entire final phase. On the production side, the infant-export industry always expands at the expense of a shrinking rest-of-the-economy. Finally, the balance of trade path from initial policy action to steady state may go through different phases of deterioration and improvement.

## Part III: Political Economy of Trade Policy Formation

In the 1970s, the international trade-policy literature began to shift its focus from determining "optimal" trade policies, which maximize a country's overall welfare, to explaining "actual" policies as chosen by governments. The impetus for this shift came from the observation that actual policies continued to deviate greatly from optimal prescriptions even though there was general agreement among economists as to what constituted optimal policies. This shift in focus required modeling the effects of trade policies on individuals' economic interests as well as identifying the political process which aggregates individual interests into economy-wide policies.

Economists took note that actual policies reflected the selfish interests of politicians, voters, and interest groups rather than the preferences of a country's benevolent decision-maker. As Baldwin (1976) had pointed out, actual and optimal policies fail to coincide unless highly restrictive conditions are imposed on the political process. He argued that, if a small country's trade policy is determined through majority voting, free trade will not be the outcome unless voters' tastes are homothetic, voting is costless, logrolling is prohibited, and the redistribution of income is not restricted.

The first five chapters of Part III adopt direct democracy as the process through which divergent individual policy preferences are aggregated into majority-supported actual policies. Chapter 9 develops a general model of majority-chosen tariff policies for a country in which individuals differ with respect to ownership of factors of production and each person's wellbeing depends on the country's choice of tariff. Chapters 10 and 11 also assume direct democracy, but focus on voter preferences for the type of policy instrument — tariffs or production subsidies — that best promotes different individuals' economic interests. Chapter 12 is a response to Rodrik's (1995) valid criticism of the political-economy literature that it had failed to address the fundamental issue of why trade policies are biased against rather than for trade. The last of the direct-democracy models, the content of Chapter 13, demonstrates how individual voting preferences change with the age of voters, even if they work in the same industry. The last chapter of Part III considers a representative-democracy process as the mechanism to generate actual trade policies. There are political parties, interest groups, and individual voters, as in Magee, Brock, and Young (1989), and the main objective is to develop the missing micro-foundations for their influential work.

*Chapter 9* presents a general framework for endogenous tariff formation in a direct democracy. It examines a small country's "actual" tariff choice when each person's economic interests are critically dependent on her ownership of factors of production and when majority voting is the political process for aggregating individual interests into actual policies. Each person has three potential sources of income: labor, capital, and tariff revenues. While each person is assumed to own one unit of labor, capital ownership is heterogeneous; it varies across the population from zero to some maximum for the wealthiest capital owner. Tariff revenues, on the other hand, are assumed to be redistributed in a neutral fashion; each person's share of total income is assumed to remain unaffected by the redistribution of tariff revenues, such that individual shares from total income are the same as from factor income alone.

The effect of a tariff or import subsidy on a person's factor income depends on the degree of factor mobility within the economy. The first of this chapter's two models examines tariff formation in a two-industry Heckscher-Ohlin setting, with complete inter-industry mobility of both capital and labor. It thereby sheds light on long-run tariff trends in a direct democracy. The second model addresses tariff formation in a specific-factor model of a multi-industry economy; labor is fully mobile but capital is sector-specific. The narrower goal of the second model is to explain how, in the short run, a single industry can receive protection through a moderate tariff even though this policy fails to provide benefits to the vast majority of people.

In the long-run tariff-formation model, attitudes towards tariff policies vary across the population as each voter is shown to possess her own most-preferred tariff rate. A voter's individually-optimal rate maximizes her share of national income. The relationship between an individual's income share and tariff rates, in turn, hinges on the relative factor intensity of the import-competing industry and on the capital-labor combination owned by that person relative to the capital-labor endowment ratio of the whole economy. If the import good is relatively labor intensive, a voter's most-preferred tariff is positive (negative) if her own capital-labor ownership ratio is less (greater) than the country's capital-labor endowment ratio. Furthermore, the deviation of a voter's individually-optimal tariff from free trade grows with the difference between her factor ownership and the country's endowment ratio.

Under majority voting, it is the median voter's most-preferred tariff rate which determines the actually-adopted rate. The identity of the median voter, in turn, depends on the country's prevailing distribution of factor ownership. If, for example, the capital ownership distribution is asymmetric, with a small fraction of the population owning most of the capital, then the median voter is relatively capital-poor and the democratic process yields a positive tariff on the labor-intensive import good. Apart from the distribution of factor ownership, the median voter's identity is further influenced by the presence of voter participation rules and voting costs. Age, residency, and criminal record exclusions, as well as criteria for voter identification and the ability to access voting booths tend to reduce the fraction of capital-poor voters and shift the identity of the median voter towards a more capital-rich individual.

In contrast to the chapter's first model, which focuses on the long-run trends of a country's tariff policy, its second model illustrates a single industry's short-term ability to gain tariff protection through majority voting even if most eligible voters fail to benefit from the proposed policy. In this short-run general-equilibrium production model, each of many industries employs one specific factor in addition to fully mobile labor. Each eligible voter is assumed to own one unit of labor in addition to one of the country's many specific factors, whereby the amount of specific factor ownership varies across the population. A tariff on a given product potentially affects the income of all individuals no matter the industry in which they own their specific factor. But the distribution of gains and losses is highly asymmetric. The small number of specific-factor owners in the protected industry enjoys substantial individual welfare gains whereas the large number of factor owners in all other industries suffers only small individual losses. In actual voting situations, the presence of voting costs suggests that many of the losers are better off accepting a small loss without voting rather than incurring voting costs to marginally raise the probability of defeating the protective tariff. With all potential winners voting and most potential losers abstaining, the relatively few specific-factor owners of one industry can succeed in gaining protection even when policies are determined through majority voting.

*Chapter 10*, which is coauthored by Raymond Riezman, raises the question of why tariffs, rather than consumption or production taxes-*cum*-subsidies, are adopted to redistribute income. A common feature of the early trade-policy-formation literature — such as the lobbying models of Brock and Magee (1978) and Findlay and Wellisz (1976), as well as the majority-voting models of Baldwin (1976) and Mayer (1984) — is the explicit assumption that policy choices are limited to tariffs and import subsidies. The question of which instrument would be the choice of a majority of voters is not addressed. At issue is whether the median voter's optimal tariff choice can be defeated by a majority of voters who can raise their wellbeing by switching to some other combination of production and consumption taxes-*cum*-subsidies.

This short chapter demonstrates that majority voting on alternative trade-policy instruments results in the adoption of production taxes-*cum*-subsidies rather than tariffs or import subsidies. This conclusion is obtained under the condition that the government's budget is always binding, the impact of income taxes is neutral on individuals' income shares, and consumer preferences are homothetic and identical for all individuals. For a Heckscher-Ohlin model, an individual's optimal production tax (subsidy) is shown to be positive if she is relatively poor (rich) in the factor which is intensively used in the production of the taxed (subsidized) good. As there are no differences in consumer preferences across the entire population, each individual views a zero-consumption tax to be optimal.

The majority-voting choice of production taxes-*cum*-subsidies applies to a small country only. For a country sufficiently large to influence its terms of trade, each voter's trade policy-preference becomes a combination of an import tariff and a production tax-*cum*-subsidy. All voters support the same optimal tariff to take advantage of the country's ability to improve its terms of trade. Individually-optimal production taxes-*cum*-subsidies, on the other hand, vary across the population and serve the purpose of redistributing income.

*Chapter 11*, which also is coauthored by Raymond Riezman, is motivated by the weak empirical evidence of voters preferring production taxes-*cum*-subsidies to import tariffs. Most governments have retained tariffs as their policy instrument of choice to protect domestic industries and to redistribute income. In response to this observation, a variety of arguments have been suggested to reconcile theory with practice. Two of the more widely-accepted arguments are the "transparency argument" of Hillman (1989) and the "public-goods argument" of Rodrik (1986). Chapter 11 proposes three additional arguments for some subset of voters to prefer tariffs to production taxes-*cum*-subsidies.

First, there is the "distribution of tax-revenue argument". A model is formulated for countries whose income tax system, on which production subsidies draw and to which import tariffs contribute, is progressive. Hence, in contrast to Chapters 9 and 10, it no longer is assumed that the distribution of tariff revenues and collection of income taxes leaves each voter's income share unchanged. The income tax rate might be zero or very low for some people and quite high for others. It is shown that a person may prefer a tariff to an equal-value production subsidy if her share of income tax payments exceeds her share of factor income received. Switching from a production subsidy to an equal-value tariff affects a person's real income in two ways. First, real income declines as all consumers must pay a higher price, while factor income shares remain unchanged. Second, each person's after-tax income rises as income tax rates can be reduced when revenues from tariffs replace expenditures on production subsidies. Progressivity of the income tax system implies for many higher-income voters that the second effect overpowers the first. While the cost of a tariff falls more evenly on the entire population, the cost of a production subsidy is disproportionately paid for by high-income consumers.

A second explanation for a person's preference for tariffs over production subsidies is the "uncertainty argument". It applies when voters are asked to choose between two alternative protection regimes, tariffs only or production subsidies only, but are uncertain about the specific rate which will be adopted after a protection regime has been selected. In making her regime choice, each voter is assumed to consider the adoption of a specific protection rate to be more likely the larger the number of people for whom this rate is individually optimal.

The driving force behind differences in individual tariff and production-subsidy preferences is again the unequal distribution of factor endowments. Restoring the assumption that neither the distribution of government revenues nor the collection of taxes alters an individual's income share, each voter is definitely better off under a production subsidy than an equal-value tariff, no matter the rate's value. However, the range of rates of protection from which the eventually adopted rate is chosen is shown to be much narrower for tariffs than production subsidies, as each person's optimal tariff rate is always less extreme than the same person's optimal rate for a production subsidy. This implies that there is less uncertainty for voters under the tariff regime, as possible deviations of eventually-adopted from their own individually optimal rates are less pronounced. This reduction in uncertainty convinces some voters that the tariff regime is preferable.

The third explanation for voters preferring a tariff to a production subsidy is the "large country argument". For a large country, each voter's individually-optimal trade policy is a combination of a tariff, which is the same for all individuals, and a production tax-*cum*-subsidy, which varies with a person's factor ownership. When voters are not able to choose a combination of tariff and production tax-*cum*-subsidy and instead are limited to expressing a preference for either the tariff or the production tax-*cum*-subsidy regime, then many voters might prefer the tariff regime. Specifically, voters whose income shares decline with the degree of protection are shown to prefer a small tariff to an equal-value production subsidy.

*Chapter 12* is motivated by Rodrik's (1995) criticism of the political-economy-of-trade literature that it had failed to address the fundamental question of why trade policies are biased against rather than in favor of trade. He noted that the trade literature was virtually silent on the fact that a systematic anti-trade bias underlies most countries' actual trade policies. In his comprehensive and insightful survey, Rodrik suggests a two-step explanation for the existence of such a bias. Given all governments' revenue needs, infant nations with limited administrative capability adopt trade taxes, as their collection costs are lower than for all other tax instruments. After a nation has matured and its administrative capability has expanded to more efficient tax instruments, trade taxes persist as individuals are uncertain about their personal gains and losses from such drastic tax policy changes. Hence, the initial collection-cost advantage of tariffs relative to other tax instruments turns into a permanent bias in favor of import tariffs.

Chapter 12 offers an alternative explanation for the presence of systematic political grass-root support for tariffs. A model is constructed which adds Rodrik's tax collection-cost feature to Mayer's (1984) Heckscher-Ohlin model with heterogeneous factor owners. Different from Rodrik, however, there is no presumption that tariffs enjoy a collection-cost advantage which would generate a pro-tariff bias; and different from Mayer, any kind of bias in the distribution of factor ownership, which could introduce a bias either for or against trade, is explicitly assumed away. The objective of the analysis is to demonstrate that, in spite of both identical collection costs for all tax instruments and symmetric distribution of factor ownership, more people gain from a small import tariff than a small export subsidy.

In this model, governments collect revenues to provide public goods, as consumers have preferences over both private and public goods. The government has to finance not only import and production subsidies but also the provision of a public good. As potential sources of revenues serve income taxes, import tariffs, and production taxes. Costs are incurred in both the raising of revenues through taxation and the disbursing of payments through subsidization. For the government, costs take the form of tax-collection and subsidy-disbursement costs; for individuals, they take the form of taxpayer-compliance and subsidy-claim costs. The model assumes that both the governmental as well as the personal cost per unit of tax revenue collected and subsidy disbursed is the same for all instruments.

If there were no collection and compliance costs, the political grass-root support of factor owners would favor neither restricting nor expanding trade. With symmetric distribution of factor ownership, the number of beneficiaries from a small tariff would be the same as from a small import-subsidy. If, on the other hand, tax-collection costs for the government and compliance costs for taxpayers are positive, the number of beneficiaries from a small tariff is shown to exceed the number of beneficiaries from a small import subsidy. In addition, there will be a group of factor owners who are hurt by any government interference in free trade, through either taxing or subsidizing imports. Accordingly, the underlying political grass-root support shifts in favor of tariffs when tax-collection costs are made explicit. If there is majority voting and voting costs are non-negligible, this anti-trade bias in grass-root support leads to the actual adoption of an import tariff.

The reason for the political anti-trade bias is that total administrative costs to finance a public good are lower when a tariff rather than an import subsidy is employed to redistribute income. Under free trade, the public good has to be financed entirely by an income tax. When free trade is abandoned and a tariff is imposed, tariff revenues replace income tax revenues without changing the total collection costs for financing the public good. If instead an import subsidy is granted, it has to be financed by additional income taxes, thereby raising government collection and individual compliance costs.

*Chapter 13*, which is coauthored by Jun Li, focuses on age as a crucial determinant of a voter's trade policy preferences. There is overwhelming empirical evidence that older people are far more likely to participate in elections than younger people (Lipset, 1960; Crewe 1981) and that individual policy preferences change with age. This chapter models an economy in which individual trade-policy interests vary both across industries and among age groups within an industry. The traditional specific-factor model is modified by adding temporarily sector-specific labor to permanently sector-specific capital as a factor of production.

All of an economy's individuals are assumed to possess the same innate abilities to train for and engage in work, but actual employability requires industry-specific training in addition to ability. Each person goes through a life-cycle of birth, initial schooling, work, retirement, and death. After birth, a person seeks training for work in a specific industry. Once trained for and employed in one industry, switching to another requires retraining. Whenever the economy experiences an unanticipated external shock that creates inter-industry wage differentials, both initial training and retraining decisions are affected. Over the long run, however, the economy's labor market re-adjusts to any external shock, brought about by the entry of new workers, retraining of current workers, and retirement of old workers.

The economy's labor market is in long-run equilibrium when the wage rate is the same in all industries. A person's life-cycle starts with entry into the labor market to replace retiring workers. In long-run equilibrium, new entries are indifferent about the industry they train for and already-trained workers have no incentive to switch to another industry. Once this long-run equilibrium is disturbed by an unanticipated trade-policy change, the immediate impact on the economy's labor market is the emergence of inter-industry wage differentials. This differential sets in motion an adjustment process in which both new entries and current workers participate. All new entries have an incentive to seek initial training for work in the high-wage industry. Current workers, on the other hand, have to decide whether to stay in their industry of current employment, even if it is the low-wage industry, or to seek retraining for employment in the high-wage industry. Age is the critical factor in making this choice. Over time, as the number of new entries and job switchers exceed that of retirees in the high-wage industry and as workers retiring from and switching out of the low-wage industry are not replaced, the gap between high and low wages narrows and eventually disappears.

Given the specification of each person's life-cycle, older workers are shown to have much stronger incentives to participate in the political process of trade-policy formation than younger workers. Older workers are more affected by policy changes because their ability to retrain and reap the benefits from adjusting their skills to a new policy is more limited. They gain the most from an expansion and lose the most from a contraction of their industry of employment. Younger workers, on the other hand, are far less affected by a policy change. They have a long-life perspective and view labor as almost completely mobile between industries whereas the oldest workers, with a very short-life perspective, view the labor market as highly rigid. Consequently, a given industry's oldest workers push much more actively than its youngest workers for protection of their industry of employment and fight more aggressively against protection of all other industries.

*Chapter 14*, also coauthored by Jun Li, lays out the foundations of a representative-democracy model for the formation of international trade policies. Such representative-democracy models — first introduced to the international trade literature by Brock and Magee (1978) and Findlay and Wellicz (1982) — were criticized by Austen-Smith (1991) and others for a lack of micro-foundations in modeling the political process. Specifically, these models lacked complete characterizations of the identity and interests of general (non-interest group) voters, of the methods (campaign contributions or information transmission) through which lobbies influence the political process, and of the political parties' objectives in competing for the right to choose trade policies. This chapter's goal is to develop the missing micro-foundations for the best-known of these models, namely the one proposed by Magee, Brock, and Young (1989), and to re-assess the validity of their findings with respect to policy formation, lobbying activities, and magnitude of campaign contributions. The model adheres to the basic structure of Magee, Brock, and Young (MBY), but replaces their *ad hoc* formulation of probabilistic voting with an explicit and detailed specification that rests on the extensive probabilistic voting literature.

In contrast to the direct-democracy models of the preceding chapters of Part III, this chapter introduces a representative-democracy model. Individual voters are no longer fully informed and interest groups are explicitly added as independent economic agents. Furthermore, there are political parties each of which aims at maximizing the probability of getting elected. Parties propose policies and use campaign contributions from interest groups to clarify and popularize their policies. The economy is assumed to consist of two industries which employ one industry-specific factor in addition to fully mobile labor. Each potential voter owns one factor only, either one unit of labor or one unit of an industry-specific factor. Both workers and specific-factor owners participate in the political process as voters, but only specific-factor owners are assumed to have the ability to form an interest group. The objective of the interest group is to lobby for a tariff that protects its members' industry. The tariff is chosen by the winner of a two-party election. Each party presents a tariff platform to voters in an environment of uncertainty: the parties are uncertain about the voters' non-policy preferences and the voters are uncertain about the parties' tariff choices once elected. Interest groups provide parties with financial resources which the latter spend to reduce voter uncertainty about their policies.

The chapter's overall conclusion is that putting the MBY model of tariff formation on rigorous micro-foundations calls for substantial adjustments of their specific conclusions, while supporting their overall message. First, their conclusion that each party receives contributions from at most one interest group is not supported; the same party might receive campaign contributions from both interest groups. Second, the MBY assertion that one party's change in its tariff platform alters only the campaign contributions of its supporting interest group is contradicted; both gaining and losing interest group adjust their campaign contributions to a change in one of the parties' platforms. Third, it is not correct that the contribution responses to a policy-platform change are determinate in absolute terms; one only can determine relative changes in contributions, of one interest group relative to the other. Finally, lobbying does not disappear when both parties propose the same tariff.

## Part IV: Designing Conditional Assistance Programs

The success rate of international assistance programs for developing and transition economies, designed by the International Monetary Fund (IMF), the World Bank and other International Financial Institutions (IFIs), has been quite disappointing. Even the more recent conditional-assistance programs, which make aid contingent on economic policy reforms, have led to little more than marginal improvements in assistance effectiveness. From the IMF's extensive conditionality review, conducted between 2000 and 2002, it was concluded that an assistance program's success critically depends on the recipient's "domestic ownership" of the program. Strengthening domestic program ownership, in turn, calls for taking account of the idiosyncrasies of a country's political economy and for the creation of incentives to implement reforms as intended. The political influence of all stakeholders must be considered, especially when conditions for assistance, such as requirements to engage in structural reforms, threaten well-established rents of politically powerful interest groups.

Chapter 15 lays out a model which highlights an IFI's role as designer of an effective economic reform program. It shows how the provision of financial assistance can serve as an incentive to reform when the aid-receiving government is dependent on political support from an interest group. Chapter 16, on the other hand, focuses on the role of information asymmetries in the effective design of conditional assistance programs. IFIs generally lack adequate information about a government's competency to execute economic reforms and its willingness to implement them. Consequently, assistance programs must propose reform conditions that are incentive-compatible while also accounting for the influence of interest groups.

*Chapter 15*, coauthored by Alexandros Mourmouras, presents the design of a conditional assistance program with the help of a common agency model. The objective is to simultaneously determine a government's choice of economic policies and an IFI's offer of financial aid when a domestic interest group is the beneficiary of distorting economic policies. The government's goal is to maximize its political support from both the general public and an interest group, as in Grossman and Helpman (1994). The interest group makes financial contributions to the government in return for policies which benefit its members. The IFI, in turn, offers financial assistance with the objective of maximizing the welfare of the entire world community.

The equilibrium combination of economic policy, adopted by the government, and size of financial assistance, chosen by the IFI, are determined under two alternative assistance schemes, unconditional and conditional. The *unconditional* aid scheme is set up as a Nash game between government and IFI, with the government acting under the influence of a domestic interest group. The government's adoption of economic policy distortions is shown to decline with the magnitude of the IFI's financial assistance. The political impact of the aid program is to benefit the country's general public at the expense of the interest group. In equilibrium, the IFI tends to offer assistance even if government policies are not efficient. The magnitude of assistance is shown to depend on the influence of the interest group: the stronger its influence, the smaller the amount of aid and the more distorted the government's economic policies. The size of the aid package is also influenced by the IFI's opportunity cost of providing assistance; the larger the opportunity cost, the smaller the IFI's aid and the more distorted the government's policies.

*Conditional*-assistance programs are contractual agreements which offer IFI assistance contingent on the government's reform of economic policies. The government faces two competing payment schedules: a financial contribution schedule from the interest group, offering higher payments for more-distorting policies, and a financial assistance schedule from the IFI, offering lower payments for more-distorting policies. The interactions between government, interest group, and IFI are modeled within the political-economy, common-agency framework of Grossman and Helpman (1994). The government is the common agent for both interest group and IFI.

The conditional-aid model demonstrates that adding incentive-compatible conditions enhances the effectiveness of IFI-financed assistance programs. The volume of assistance is enlarged and policy distortions are reduced when conditional aid schemes replace unconditional ones. This switch to conditional aid also raises the economic wellbeing and political influence of the general public at the expense of the domestic interest group. The domestic government, in turn, experiences no loss in the strength of political support, and there are net gains for the world as a whole.

*Chapter 16*, also coauthored by Alexandros Mourmouras, focuses on the relevance of information asymmetries in the design of conditional financial-assistance programs. As stated before, one explanation for the mixed success of these programs has been the IFIs' inadequate accounting for the political realities in the receiving countries. An equally important second explanation is the presence of asymmetric information. Implementation of assistance programs requires both competency and effort on the part of aid-receiving governments. The aid-providing IFI typically possesses only limited information on both accounts.

This chapter presents a model which highlights both the political influence of an interest group and the role of information asymmetries with respect to a government's competency and effort in implementing a conditional loan program. The IFI can observe neither the government's competency prior to nor its effort to implement after the reform program has been instituted. The domestic interest group and government, on the other hand, are fully informed. A successful conditional assistance program requires the IFI to include contractual incentives which, in this model of loan assistance, are tied to the economy's performance, taking the form of rewards and punishments in setting the size of loan repayments.

Incentive mechanisms have the potential to undermine a country's political stability if they threaten punishments for the economy's poor performance. A country's political stability becomes particularly tenuous when its public believes to have been hurt by the reform conditions of the program. To avoid such potentially destabilizing effects of an IFI loan, the model imposes a limited liability constraint for the loan-receiving country; loan repayments can never be so punishing as to make a country's people worse off than if the loan had never been obtained in the first place. There is a second important constraint that determines the feasibility of a loan contract. The IFI's resources are limited. In order to preserve its own financial viability, the IFI must design the loan program in a way that, on average, it does no worse than break even.

In formulating the model, assistance takes the form of a repayable loan; and the government's competency in administering the program is either "good" or "bad". The loan-repayment conditions are contingent on the loan-receiving country's economic performance, which is observable and depends on three influences: the state of nature, which is either "strong" or "weak", the loan's effectiveness in expanding the economy, and the implementation of economic reforms. The impact of successful reforms is to raise the probability of the economy being strong.

The government again chooses its policies to maximize political support from the general public and interest group. When it accepts an IFI loan, the contract specifies the loan's size, the reforms to be implemented, and the amount to be repaid. The latter is made contingent on the observable performance of the economy at the loan due-date. The domestic interest group is the beneficiary of economic rents, created by the government through the adoption of suitable policy distortions. In return, the interest group provides financial support to the government. The third economic agent of this model is an IFI which maximizes the weighted average of the recipient country's net income and its own expected return on the loan. In calculating loan repayments, the IFI is also aware of the possibility that a government might default. Following Eaton and Gersovitz (1995), loan default triggers a penalty whose severity is not known to either IFI or government at the time the loan is offered. However, defaults can be avoided by the IFI renegotiating the terms of repayment.

The IFI's financial viability constraint implies that it will not offer a loan unless it expects at least to break even. The paper shows that the IFI's ability to do so is significantly diminished by its limited information on both the government's competency and loan-implementation effort. Information asymmetry on its competency creates an adverse selection situation. Information asymmetry on its reform effort creates a moral hazard situation. Accordingly, the IFI's loan program must be designed in a way that the government, whatever its competency, is willing to accept the contract designed for its type and that each government type has an incentive to reform the economy. An incentive-compatible loan program is shown to consist of two stochastic contracts, one intended for a "good" and the other for a "bad" government. Each contract spells out the size of the loan and the amounts to be repaid, with the latter being dependent on the observable state of the economy at the loan due-date.

The analysis concludes that an IFI's willingness to offer a loan program with reform incentives critically hinges on the power of the borrowing country's interest group; the more powerful the interest group, the less willing the IFI to offer a loan. However, even a powerful interest group cannot completely eliminate the IFI's influence. While the interest group might be able to block a loan that is contingent on reforms, the mere presence of the IFI as a potential source of assistance reduces the interest group's bargaining position *vis-à-vis* its own government, thereby forcing it to accept partial reforms.

A second force that diminishes the IFI's ability to make reform-contingent loans is the cost of incentive-compatible contracts. The IFI's lack of knowledge of government competency and its inability to observe the government's reform effort require the design of costly incentive schemes. This cost tends to rise with the IFI's concern for the political stability of the loan-receiving country.

The negative influences of a strong interest group and information costs on the IFI's ability to offer a loan is countered by the positive effect of a high-quality loan. The greater is the net income gain generated by the loan, the more likely it is that the IFI is able to offer a reform-contingent assistance program. Provided the IFI has an incentive to offer such a program at all, loans designed for good governments are always efficient, whereas loans to bad governments can lead to either over- or under-investment.

Finally, this chapter examines the IFI's offering of a loan which is not reform-contingent. The IFI considers making an unconditional loan offer when a conditional loan is not viable. This outcome is more likely when the interest group is powerful and the IFI's costs of overcoming information asymmetries are relatively high.

## References

Austin-Smith, David (1987), "Interest groups, campaign contributions, and probabilistic voting," *Public Choice*, 54 (2), pp. 123–139.

Baldwin, Robert E. (1976), "The political economy of postwar U.S. trade policy," *The Bulletin*, Graduate School of Business Administration, New York University.

Batra, Raveendra N. (1974), "Resource allocation in a general equilibrium model of production under uncertainty," *Journal of Economic Theory*, 8 (1), pp. 50–63.

Batra, Raveendra N. (1975), *The Pure Theory of International Trade under Uncertainty*, London: Macmillan.

Bhagwati, Jagdish (1968), *The Theory and Practice of Commercial Policy: Departures from Unified Exchange Rates*, Special Papers in International Economics, Princeton, NJ: Princeton University Press.

Bhagwati, Jagdish (1971), "The generalized theory of distortions and welfare," in J.N. Bhagwati, R.W. Jones, R.A. Mundell, and J. Vanek (eds.), *Trade, Balance of Payments and Growth*, Amsterdam: North-Holland, pp. 69–90.

Brock, William A. and Stephen P. Magee (1978), "The economics of special interest politics: the case of the tariff," *American Economic Review, Papers and Proceedings*, 68 (2), pp. 246–250.

Crewe, Ivor (1981), "Electoral participation," in D. Butler, H.R. Penniman, and A. Ranney (eds.), *Democracy at the Polls: A Comparative Study of Competitive Elections*, Washington DC: American Enterprise Institute for Public Policy Research.

Eaton, Jonathan and Mark Gersovitz (1995), "Some curious properties of a familiar model of debt and default," *Economics Letters*, 48 (3–4), pp. 367–371.

Findlay, Ronald and Stanislaw Wellisz (1982), "Endogenous tariffs, the political economy of trade restrictions, and welfare," in J.N. Bhagwati (ed.), *Import Competition and Response*, Chicago: University of Chicago Press, pp. 223–234.

Grossman, Gene M. and Elhanan Helpman (1994), "Protection for sale," *American Economic Review*, 84 (4), pp. 833–850.

Haberler, Gottfried (1936), *The Theory of International Trade with Its Applications to Commercial Policy*, translated by A. Stonier and F. Benham, London: Hodge.

Hillman, Arye L. (1989), *The Political Economy of Protection*, Chur: Harwood Academic Press.

Jones, Ronald W. (1968), "Variable returns to scale in general equilibrium theory," *International Economic Review*, 10 (3), pp. 261–272.

Jones, Ronald W. (1971), "A three-factor model in theory, trade, and history," in J.N. Bhagwati, R.W. Jones, R.A. Mundell, and J. Vanek (eds.), *Trade, Balance of Payments and Growth*, Amsterdam: North-Holland, pp. 3–21.

Lipset, Seymour M. (1960), *Political Man: The Social Basis of Politics.* Garden City, NY: Doubleday.

Magee, Stephen P., William A. Brock, and Leslie Young (1989), *Black Hole Tariffs and Endogenous Policy Theory: Political Economy in General Equilibrium*, Cambridge: Cambridge University Press.

Mayer, Wolfgang (1984), "Endogenous tariff formation," *American Economic Review*, 74 (5), pp. 970–985.

Rodrik, Dani (1986), "Tariffs, subsidies, and welfare with endogenous policy," *Journal of International Economics*, 21 (3–4), pp. 285–296.

Rodrik, Dani (1995), "Political economy of trade policy," in G. M. Grossman and K. Rogoff (eds.), *Handbook of International Economics*, Vol. 3, Amsterdam: Elsevier Science, pp. 1457–1494.

Rothenberg, Thomas J. and Kenneth R. Smith (1971), "The effect of uncertainty on resource allocation in a general equilibrium model," *Quarterly Journal of Economics*, 85 (3), pp. 440–459.

Rybczynski, Tadeusz M. (1955), "Factor endowment and relative commodity prices," *Economica*, New Series, 22 (88), pp. 336–341.

Samuelson, Paul A. (1947), *Foundations of Economic Analysis*, Cambridge, MA: Harvard University Press.

Sandmo, Agnar (1971), "On the theory of the competitive firm under price uncertainty," *American Economic Review*, 61 (1), pp. 65–73.

Smith, Adam (1904), *An Inquiry into the Nature and Causes of the Wealth of Nations*, edited by E. Cannan, London: Methuen.

Stolper, Wolfgang F. and Paul A. Samuelson (1941), "Protection and real wages," *Review of Economic Studies*, 9 (1), pp. 58–73.

# PART I

# International Trade Theory

# Short-Run and Long-Run Equilibrium for a Small Open Economy

Wolfgang Mayer

*University of Cincinnati*

This paper deals with a small open economy in which capital goods employed by a given industry are temporarily immobile and can be reallocated only gradually over an extended period of time. The short-run responses of employment, factor returns, and output levels to exogenous changes in commodity prices and endowments, as well as the following time-absorbing adjustment process of the endogenous variables to long-run equilibrium, are analyzed. In addition, it is argued that this short-run theory provides a better explanation of factor-owner reactions to trade policies than conventional long-run international trade theory.

## I. Introduction

In many areas of economic theory one distinguishes between the short run, a time period so short that usage of certain inputs cannot be changed, and the long run, a time period long enough to allow for changes in employment of all inputs. The standard models in the theory of international trade, however, do not operate with similar distinction.[1] It

I am much indebted to Jacob Frenkel for his detailed comments, in particular for suggesting the paper's title and for referring me to the works of Haberler (1936) and Jones (1971). I should also like to thank Horst Herberg for his comments. Any errors and shortcomings of the paper are, of course, my sole responsibility. Some conclusions reached in this paper have independently been arrived at by Jorge Marquez–Ruarte in "An Elementary Framework of Inter-Run Analysis," mimeographed (University of Chicago, October 1973), a paper which the associate editor of this *Journal*, Robert Barro, made available to me. No attempt has been made to change my original version on account of this paper.

[1] This is somewhat surprising, since Haberler (1936), in his discussion of international trade theory, already distinguishes between the short and the long run. In fact, he points out that in the short run, when most factors are specific to a given industry, the production-possibility frontier's curvature will be more concave to the origin than in the long run (pp. 178–79). We should add that a long-run concept of a quite different nature has been used by Atsumi (1971). He develops a dynamic trade model in which allowance is made for capital accumulation and population growth.

[*Journal of Political Economy*, 1974, vol. 82, no. 5]

simply is assumed that factors of production are freely mobile within a country and that they are allocated in such a way that the value of a given factor's marginal product is the same in all industries. Clearly, this assumption implies that these models are "long run" in nature.

Two main results of this "long-run" trade theory are the Rybczynski and Stolper-Samuelson theorems. The former is a powerful tool in explaining differences in production patterns between countries with different factor endowments. The latter is helpful in explaining factor-return differentials between countries whose final commodity prices differ because of tariffs, transportation costs, or other forms of trade impediments. In both cases, the explanations are based on comparisons of long-run equilibria. The two theorems are, however, used for other purposes as well. The Rybczynski theorem is applied in attempts to determine the impact of endowment changes—through immigration, capital transfers, or other means—on factor returns and output levels. The Stolper-Samuelson theorem is applied to predict changes in factor rewards as tariffs are imposed or transportation costs change. In both cases, the theorems reveal what eventually is going to happen after enough time has elapsed for reestablishing an optimal, long-run factor-allocation pattern. While there is much value to such long-run predictions, it also is quite obvious that a very substantive vacuum is left by the two theorems. They neither answer any questions concerning the immediate impact of changes in endowment or commodity prices on the economy, nor do they deal with the adjustment of variables between long-run equilibria.

The purpose of our paper is to fill this vacuum. We are going to set up a simple general-equilibrium model and study the short-run effects of varying commodity prices and endowments on factor returns and output levels. Such a short-run theory is based on the assumption that not all factors can move freely between industries as incentives for reallocation arise; some factors are temporarily locked in and cannot be adjusted instantaneously. Only over a longer period of time, if incentives for reallocation continue, the initially locked-in factors will become mobile, and gradual adjustment to long-run equilibrium can take place. Hence, our analysis will not only deal with short-run equilibria, but also with tracing out the adjustment path for factor returns and output levels between different long-run equilibria.

Our results should be of more than theoretical interest. They should help us understand some very important real-world phenomena associated with international trade policies. For example, they illustrate why the liberalization of immigration restrictions is strongly opposed by workers and much favored by capital owners. They also make clear why workers and capital owners of a given industry share a strong common interest when it comes to tariff protection of their industry. Since people work, consume, and earn income in the short run, it is not surprising that such attitudes of factor owners toward trade policies cannot be explained by any long-run theory, such as we find in the standard models of international trade theory.[2] Only a short-run theory can provide meaningful answers to short-run questions.

In the next section, we specify the conditions for short- and long-run equilibrium and compare slope and curvature of the long-run with those of the short-run transformation curve. In Section III, we first study the short-run responses of factor returns and commodity outputs to price changes and then discuss the adjustment path of the variables to long-run equilibrium. Section IV deals with the same questions as the preceding section, except that in Section IV a change in labor endowment is the disturbing force.

## II. Short-Run General Equilibrium

Let us make the usual assumptions of a two-commodity, two-factor economy which is incompletely specialized, in which factors are fully employed, and where perfect competition is prevailing. Factor endowments and final commodity prices are exogenously given. Since the model is a simple two-by-two barter model, only relative prices matter; accordingly, for the remaining analysis the first commodity is chosen as the numeraire. Industry production functions are represented by

$$X_j = X_j(L_j, K_j), \qquad j = 1, 2 \tag{1}$$

where $X_j$ denotes output of commodity $j$, and $L_j$, $K_j$ stand for the amounts of labor and capital, respectively, employed by industry $j$. The functions are assumed to be homogeneous of degree 1, twice differentiable, and strictly quasi-concave; furthermore, $X_{L_j} > 0$ and $X_{K_j} > 0$.

Long-run (LR) equilibrium is established if each factor's marginal product, evaluated in terms of the first commodity, is the same in both industries,

$$\begin{aligned} X_{L_1} &= pX_{L_2}, \\ X_{K_1} &= pX_{K_2}, \end{aligned} \tag{2}$$

and both factors are fully employed,

$$\begin{aligned} L_1 + L_2 &= \bar{L}, \\ K_1 + K_2 &= \bar{K}. \end{aligned} \tag{3}$$

[2] According to the Rybczynski theorem, the inflow of additional labor has no impact on factor returns as long as the economy remains nonspecialized. The Stolper-Samuelson theorem tells us that a protective tariff will raise returns on this factor, which is used relatively intensively in the production of the protected commodity and lower returns on the other factor.

In the preceding equations, $p$ denotes the relative price of the second in terms of the first commodity, and $\bar{L}$ and $\bar{K}$ measure the economy's endowment with labor and capital. With the information contained in equations (1)–(3), we now can trace out the LR transformation locus, denoted by *FF* in figure 1. The locus reflects the economy's production potential, given factor endowments, technology constraints, and no impediments to the optimal allocation of factors. As is well known, the assumptions of perfect competition and production functions homogeneous of degree 1 imply that the LR transformation curve's slope is

$$(dX_2/dX_1)^{\mathrm{LR}} = -(1/p), \quad (4)$$

and that its curvature is convex outward:[3]

$$(d^2X_2/dX_1^2)^{\mathrm{LR}} \leq 0. \quad (5)$$

In the short run (SR), it is assumed, only labor is perfectly mobile between industries.[4] Capital, once installed in a given industry, cannot be transferred instantaneously to uses in the other industry, even though capital returns may differ between industries.[5] Consequently, SR equilibrium is described by the condition that labor's marginal product is the same in both industries,

$$X_{L_1} = pX_{L_2}, \quad (6)$$

and that the following resource constraints are satisfied:

$$\begin{aligned} L_1 + L_2 &= \bar{L}, \\ K_1 &= \bar{K}_1, \quad (7) \\ K_2 &= \bar{K}_2, \end{aligned}$$

where $\bar{K}_j$ is the optimal amount of capital employed by industry $j$ in accordance with a predetermined LR equilibrium. For example, we may choose a point on the *FF* locus, such as $A$, which represents a LR equilibrium position corresponding to the relative price $(1/p)^A$. The optimal factor allocations, based on conditions (2) and (3), are $K_1^A$, $K_2^A$, $L_1^A$, and $L_2^A$. Using $A$ as a reference point, we now can derive the SR transformation curve, denoted by *aa*. Along *aa*, the capital allocation is the same as at point $A$, namely, $K_1^A$, $K_2^A$, but the labor allocation varies in order to satisfy criterion (6). In contrast to the *FF* locus, which describes the economy's ultimate production potential, the *aa* locus expresses the

[3] See, for example, Lancaster (1968).

[4] The assumption of short-run immobility of a certain factor implies that this factor temporarily is specific to a given industry. Hence, our short-run model is basically the same as Jones's (1971) three-factor, two-commodity model, in which each industry uses one factor that is specific to it.

[5] Individual firms within a given industry are still able to choose their optimal capital-labor combinations.

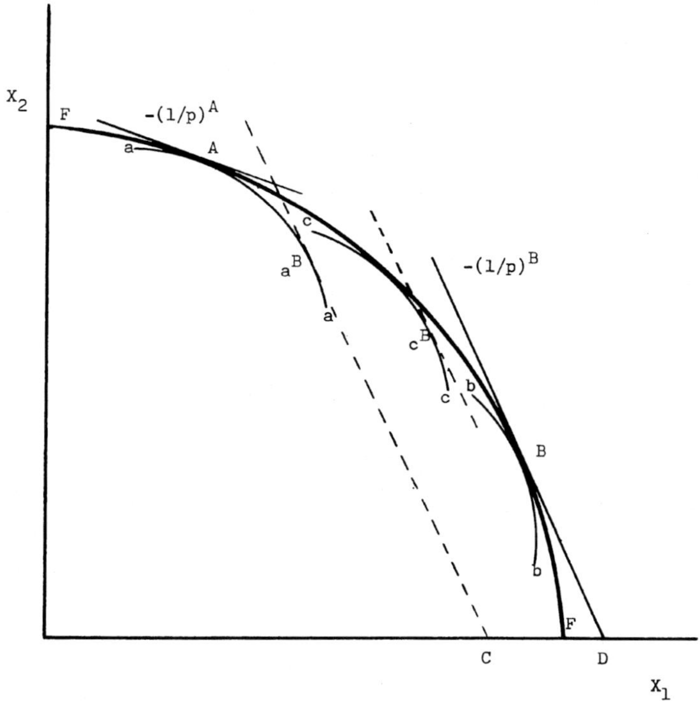


FIG. 1

economy's SR ability to adjust to price changes. If, for instance, the final commodity price ratio changes to $(1/p)^B$, new SR and LR equilibria indicated by points $a^B$ and $B$, respectively, are established. Actual production will change to $a^B$, where the price line is tangent to the *aa* locus. Point $B$, on the other hand, only refers to future output combinations that will become attainable after the passage of sufficient time to allow for optimal reallocation of capital. Stated differently, the price change induces an instantaneous change of outputs from $A$ to $a^B$, and then it brings about a time-dependent adjustment process starting at $a^B$ and terminating at $B$. The SR equilibrium, $a^B$, is characterized by a temporary suboptimal allocation of capital, which is responsible for an income loss, measured in terms of commodity 1 by the distance $CD$ in figure 1.

In the diagram, the SR equilibrium point $a^B$ was determined by drawing the price line tangent to the *aa* locus. That $a^B$ is, in fact, the SR equilibrium can be seen after we take (1), differentiate it totally for both industries while holding $\bar{K}_j$ constant, and set $dL_2$ equal to $-dL_1$. As we divide the expression for $dX_2$ by that for $dX_1$ and use (6) to satisfy the SR conditions we obtain:

$$(dX_2/dX_1)^{SR} = -(X_{L_2}/X_{L_1}) = -(1/p). \tag{8}$$

This proves that, at the point of equilibrium, the slope of the SR and LR transformation curves is the same. Their respective curvatures, however, are not identical. Since from a LR perspective all points on *aa*, except for *A*, represent suboptimal factor allocations, *aa* must lie inside *FF* except for point *A* itself, where *aa* is tangent to *FF*. Furthermore, the *aa* locus must be strictly convex outward.[6]

## III. Short-Run Responses to Price Changes and the Adjustment to Long-Run Equilibrium

Exogenous price changes of final commodities affect factor returns and industry output levels. In this section, we are going to examine these responses in the SR, compare them with the LR results, and describe the adjustment path from the initial to the new LR equilibrium.

First, we will deal with the SR responses of labor and capital returns, both of which are evaluated in terms of commodity 1, and which for industry $j$ are denoted by $w_j$ and $r_j$, respectively. Given these definitions of $w_j$ and $r_j$ and the specification of the SR equilibrium conditions, as stated in (6) and (7), we obtain a system of four equations:

$$\begin{aligned} X_{L_1}(L_1, \bar{K}_1) &= pX_{L_2}(\bar{L} - L_1, \bar{K}_2), \\ X_{L_1}(L_1, \bar{K}_1) &= w, \\ X_{K_1}(L_1, \bar{K}_1) &= r_1, \\ pX_{K_2}(\bar{L} - L_1, \bar{K}_2) &= r_2. \end{aligned} \tag{9}$$

The endogenous variables are $L_1$, $w$, $r_1$, and $r_2$, which are to be evaluated at the initial SR equilibrium point. After differentiating (9) totally, holding labor endowment and capital allocations constant, we can solve for the percentage change in factor returns as a function of the percentage

[6] Total differentiation of (8) with respect to $X_1$ yields

$$(d^2X_2/dX_1^2)^{SR} = -(1/X_{L_1}^2)[X_{L_1}X_{L_2L_2}(dL_2/dL_1) - X_{L_2}X_{L_1L_1}](dL_1/dX_1).$$

Substituting $(dL_2/dL_1) = -1$ and $(dL_1/dX_1) = (1/X_{L_1})$, the above expression can be reduced to:

$$(d^2X_2/dX_1^2)^{SR} = (1/X_{L_1})^3(X_{L_1}X_{L_2L_2} + X_{L_2}X_{L_1L_1}).$$

Since the assumption of production functions that are strictly quasi-concave and homogeneous of degree 1 implies that $X_{L_jL_j} < 0$, we know that $(d^2X_2/dX_1^2)^{SR} < 0$.

change in commodity prices along a given SR transformation curve:

$$\frac{dw}{w} = -\frac{X_{L_1L_1}}{\Delta}\frac{dp}{p}, \tag{10}$$

$$\frac{dr_1}{r_1} = \frac{X_{L_1L_1}}{\Delta}\left(\frac{wL_1}{r_1K_1}\right)\frac{dp}{p}, \tag{11}$$

$$\frac{dr_2}{r_2} = \left[1 - \frac{pX_{L_2L_2}}{\Delta}\left(\frac{wL_2}{r_2K_2}\right)\right]\frac{dp}{p}, \tag{12}$$

where we utilized the relations

$$X_{L_jK_j} = -k_jX_{K_jK_j} = -X_{L_jL_j}/k_j = X_{K_jL_j},^7$$

and where

$$\Delta = -(X_{L_1L_1} + pX_{L_2L_2}) > 0 \quad \text{and} \quad k_j = K_j/L_j.$$

Our results are stated in percentage terms in order to indicate not only directions, but also relative magnitudes of factor-return changes.

From (10), it can be seen that the common wage rate, $w = w_1 = w_2$, is directly related to $p$. As long as relative commodity prices remain unchanged, the wage rate (expressed in terms of commodity 1) will not change either. On the other hand, if $p$ rises, the wage rate will rise as well, although at a slower rate than the relative commodity price; that is, if $dp/p > 0$, then $dp/p > dw/w > 0$. As far as returns on capital are concerned, which in the SR may not be the same in both industries, (11) and (12) reveal that as the price of the second relative to the first commodity rises, the return on capital in the second industry increases at a faster rate than $p$, whereas the return on capital in the first industry declines; that is, if $dp/p > 0$, then $dr_2/r_2 > dp/p > 0 > dr_1/r_1$.

In summary, a tariff structure which leads to a *ceteris paribus* increase in the relative price of a given commodity will, in the SR, raise returns on capital and labor employed in this, the protected industry. In the unprotected industry, only wages will rise, while the capital return will fall. Clearly, there exists an incentive for a given industry to ask for tariff protection relative to other industries, since all factors employed in this industry will be able to raise their earnings.[8] And the more immobile factors employed, the greater the benefits the protected industry can enjoy, and the stronger the incentive for demanding tariff protection.

[7] These relations are implied by the assumption of homogeneity of degree 1 of the production functions.

[8] Since $dp/p > dw/w > 0$, income of workers in terms of commodity 1 will definitely rise. This, however, does not imply that workers are necessarily going to be better off than before. But the smaller the fraction of $X_2$ in the consumption basket of workers, the more likely it is that they are going to gain from the mentioned tariff change.

Our conclusions stand in sharp contrast to those of a LR impact of price changes on factor returns, namely, the Stolper-Samuelson theorem. In the LR, an increase in the relative price of a given commodity will lead to a more than proportionate increase in $w(r)$ and to a decrease in $r(w)$ if this commodity is labor (capital) intensive. Hence, one factor benefits from the price change, while the other factor definitely loses. It is not possible that in the LR all factors employed in a given industry will gain from protection. Consequently, conventional trade theory finds it difficult to explain why lobbyists of a given industry would push for tariff protection and be supported by workers and capital owners.

The LR equilibrium, as specified in (2) and (3), will be reestablished when enough capital has moved from the low to the high capital return industry such as to equate the value of the marginal product of capital in the two productive activities. This change in capital allocation, which in figure 1 amounts to a gradual downward shift of the SR transformation curve from $A$ to $B$, is denoted by $d\bar{K}_1 = -d\bar{K}_2 = dS$; $dS \gtreqless 0$ depending on $r_1 \gtreqless r_2$. If $(1/p)$ rises, than at the new SR equilibrium point, $a^B$, $r_1$ exceeds $r_2$, and capital owners will find it profitable to transfer capital goods from the second to the first industry; the adjustment process to LR equilibrium has started. The adjustment path itself consists of the locus of SR equilibria, where each SR equilibrium point corresponds to a different capital allocation. The impact of the capital-stock adjustment process on the capital return in industry 1 can be traced out by going back to (9), differentiating the four equations totally while holding relative prices and labor endowments constant, and solving for:

$$dr_1/dS = X_{K_1K_1} + X_{K_1L_1}(X_{L_1K_1} + pX_{L_2K_2})/\Delta.$$

The first term on the right side measures the declining value of capital's marginal product in industry 1, whereas the second term represents the rising value of capital's marginal product as more labor is employed; the rise in labor employment is, of course, the consequence of the capital-allocation process.[9] Whether the total effect $(dr_1/dS)$ is positive or negative depends on relative factor intensities, as can be seen after substituting the definition of $\Delta$ and again using $X_{L_jK_j} = -k_jX_{K_jK_j} = -X_{L_jL_j}/k_j = X_{K_jL_j}$:

$$dr_1/dS = -X_{K_1K_1}pX_{L_2L_2}\left(1 - \frac{k_1}{k_2}\right)/\Delta. \tag{13}$$

Equation (13) reveals that during the adjustment process, the return on capital in industry 1 will rise if its production process is relatively capital intensive and fall if it is relatively labor intensive; that is, $dr_1/dS \gtreqless 0$ as $k_1 \gtreqless k_2$.

[9] From (9), we also can derive that $dL_1/dS$, the optimal adjustment in industry one's labor use as capital is reallocated from the second to the first industry, equals

$$(X_{L_1K_1} + pX_{L_2K_2})/\Delta > 0.$$

Values for changes in $r_2$ and $w$ during the capital-adjustment period can be obtained in a similar fashion from (9):

$$dr_2/dS = pX_{K_2K_2}X_{L_1L_1}\left(1 - \frac{k_2}{k_1}\right)/\Delta \gtreqless 0, \tag{14}$$

as $k_1 \gtreqless k_2$; and

$$dw/dS = -X_{L_1K_1}pX_{L_2K_2}(k_1 - k_2)/\Delta \lesseqgtr 0, \tag{15}$$

as $k_1 \gtreqless k_2$.

Equations (13)–(15) describe the adjustment of factor returns during the capital-reallocation process. In both industries capital returns rise and labor returns fall if the first industry is capital intensive.[10] Hence, the LR comparative-statics responses, as expressed in the Stolper-Samuelson theorem, come about through the gradual adjustment of the capital stock in the two respective industries, a process which leads to a rise (decline) in returns on the factor that is used relatively more (less) intensively in the production of the good whose relative price has increased.

Output responses to price changes have already been depicted in figure 1. An increase in $(1/p)$ leads to an immediate SR output effect, indicated by the movement from $A$ to $a^B$. Only labor moves from the second to the first industry, whereas the inability of capital to reallocate instantaneously causes capital-return differentials. Slowly, as long as these differentials persist, capital will be transferred from the low- to the high-return industry, which in figure 1 amounts to a downward sliding of the SR along the LR transformation curve. The output adjustment path between LR equilibria is traced out by connecting all SR production points such as $a^B$ and $c^B$, all of which are determined by the condition that the price line is tangent to a given SR transformation curve.

From the analysis of the previous paragraph, it follows that every LR output effect can be decomposed into an instantaneous SR and a time-absorbing adjustment effect. Stating in terms of elasticities, we can write:

$$\begin{aligned}\left[\frac{(1/p)dX_1}{X_1d(1/p)}\right]^{\text{LR}} &= \left[-\frac{pdX_1}{X_1dp}\right]^{\text{LR}} \\ &= \left[-\frac{pX_{L_1}}{X_1}\frac{dL_1}{dp}\right]^{\text{SR}} \\ &\quad - \left[\frac{pX_{L_1}}{X_1}\frac{dL_1}{dS} + \frac{pX_{K_1}}{X_1}\frac{dK_1}{dS}\right]\frac{dS}{dp}.\end{aligned} \tag{16}$$

[10] In LR equilibrium, $r_1 = r_2$. Since in the SR $r_1$ has risen faster than $r_2$, we also must show that during the adjustment period $r_1$ rises slower than $r_2$ if $k_1 > k_2$, and $r_1$ falls faster than $r_2$ if $k_1 < k_2$. A comparison of (13) with (14) and a few manipulations reveal that $dr_1/dS \gtreqless dr_2/dS$ depending on $(k_2 - k_1)/k_1 \gtreqless (k_2 - k_1)/k_2$.

The LR price elasticity of supply equals the SR plus the adjustment elasticity. Concerning the SR elasticity, we know that it must be positive since $dL_1/dp < 0$, as can be seen utilizing (9). With regard to the adjustment elasticity, the same positive sign must hold since $dS/dp < 0$, $dK_1/dS > 0$, and $dL_1/dS > 0$ as we know from footnote 8. Hence, the LR value of the elasticity of supply always exceeds the SR value as long as at least one factor is not perfectly mobile. *Ceteris paribus*, this implies that import elasticities of demand are smaller in SR than in the LR, a condition that, in turn, enhances the possibility of SR instability of trading systems.[11]

## IV. Short-Run Responses to Changes in Labor Endowments and the Adjustment to Long-Run Equilibrium

Immigration laws, designed to enlarge the existing supply of labor, are in general opposed by workers and favored by capital owners. Workers fear that wages will decline and capital owners expect higher returns per unit of capital employed. Such reaction patterns stand in sharp contrast to predictions expounded by conventional trade theory, namely, that any change in factor endowments has no impact on factor returns at all, provided the economy remains nonspecialized. Again, it is the LR nature of standard trade theory that leads to this apparent contradiction. The divergence between actual anticipations of factor owners and predictions of theory disappear once we apply our SR trading model. In the SR, capital owners in both industries will gain from additional labor supply, whereas workers will lose.

In order to obtain the SR responses of factor returns to changes in labor endowment, we go back to (9), differentiate it totally, and solve for:

$$dr_1/d\bar{L} = (pX_{L_1L_1}X_{L_2L_2})/(\Delta k_1) > 0, \quad (17)$$

$$dr_2/d\bar{L} = (pX_{L_1L_1}X_{L_2L_2})/(\Delta k_2) > 0, \quad (18)$$

$$dw/d\bar{L} = -(pX_{L_1L_1}X_{L_2L_2})/\Delta < 0, \quad (19)$$

where we used the constant returns to scale property

$$X_{K_jL_j} = -X_{L_jL_j}/k_j$$

in order to simplify our results. In the SR, labor is reallocated instantaneously, whereas the capital allocation remains the same as at the initial LR equilibrium. Since both industries absorb more labor, capital returns must rise in both industries and the common wage rate must decline.

[11] Other modifications of the standard two-commodity, two-factor model, such as the introduction of intermediate goods, may lead to greater stability of the trading system; see Chang and Mayer (1973).

A comparison of (17) with (18), furthermore, reveals that the SR rise in returns on capital is greater in the labor- than in the capital-intensive industry; that is, $dr_1/d\bar{L} \gtreqless dr_2/d\bar{L}$, depending on whether $1/k_1 \gtreqless 1/k_2$.

The fact that in the SR capital returns rise in both industries provides a plausible explanation of why capital owners would favor liberalized immigration laws. The fact that SR capital returns in the two industries rise at different rates, on the other hand, provides the starting point for adjustment to LR equilibrium. It creates an incentive to transfer capital from the capital- to the labor-intensive industry; or $dS \gtreqless 0$ as $(1/k_1) \gtreqless (1/k_2)$. During the capital-reallocation period, factor returns again are changing in accordance with the process described in (13)–(15). Capital returns in both industries are declining and the common wage rate is rising.[12] Hence, the SR impact on factor returns, a rise in the return on capital and a fall in the wage rate, is counteracted by the adjustment impact, a decline in capital returns and a rise in the wage rate.[13] Finally, in LR equilibrium, as stated in (2) and (3), returns on capital and labor are again what they were before the inflow of labor occurred.

The total amount of capital that must be transferred before LR equilibrium is attained can be determined by going back to the labor constraint (3) and rewriting it as

$$K_1/k_1 + K_2/k_2 = \bar{L}. \tag{3'}$$

As we remember that in the LR wage-rental ratios and, therefore, capital-labor ratios of the two industries are not affected by endowment changes, we take (3′), differentiate it totally, and set $dk_j = 0$:

$$dK_1/k_1 + dK_2/k_2 = d\bar{L}.$$

After we substitute $dK_1 = -dK_2 = dS$, we solve for:

$$dS = [k_1k_2/(k_2 - k_1)]\ d\bar{L}, \tag{20}$$

which relates the magnitude of capital to be reallocated to the initial change in labor endowment. *Ceteris paribus*, the more similar factor intensities in the two respective industries, the greater the need for extensive capital-stock reallocation.

With respect to changes in output of final commodities, the SR effects differ from the LR effects in a very substantive manner as well. From LR trade theory we know that output of the labor-intensive commodity rises at a faster rate than labor supply, while output of the capital-intensive

[12] If, for example, $k_2$ exceeds $k_1$, the resulting capital adjustment is measured by $dS > 0$. And since, for $k_2 > k_1$, $dr_j/dS < 0$, and $dw/dS > 0$ from (13) to (15), it is implied that both $r_j$ decline and $w$ rises.

[13] By comparing (13) with (14), it can be seen that during the adjustment period returns on capital decrease faster in the labor-than in the capital-intensive industry.

commodity declines.[14] Hence, in the LR one industry expands and the other contracts as more labor is made available to the economy. In the SR, however, the result will be expansion of both industries, as we are going to show next. First, we go back to the industry production functions, stated in (1), and differentiate them with respect to $\bar{L}$, allowing for changes in labor use only:

$$dX_j/d\bar{L} = X_{L_j}(dL_j/d\bar{L}), \qquad j = 1, 2. \tag{21}$$

The SR change in labor employment in industry 1 can be obtained by differentiating (9) and solving for:

$$(dL_1/d\bar{L}) = -(pX_{L_2L_2})/\Delta > 0. \tag{22}$$

The SR change in employment of labor in industry 2 is derived from $(dL_2/d\bar{L}) = 1 - dL_1/d\bar{L}$, into which we substitute (22),

$$(dL_2/d\bar{L}) = -X_{L_1L_1}/\Delta > 0. \tag{23}$$

Combining (22) and (23) with (21) yields:

$$dX_1/d\bar{L} = -X_{L_1}pX_{L_2L_2}/\Delta > 0, \tag{24}$$

$$dX_2/d\bar{L} = -X_{L_2}X_{L_1L_1}/\Delta > 0, \tag{25}$$

which shows that in the SR an increase in the supply of labor leads to expansion of both industries, irrespective of relative factor intensities.

Finally, we decompose the LR output effect, caused by a change in labor endowment, into a SR and an adjustment effect:

$$(dX_j/d\bar{L})^{\mathrm{LR}} = X_{L_j}(dL_j/d\bar{L})^{\mathrm{SR}} + [X_{L_j}(dL_j/dS) + X_{K_j}(dK_j/dS)]\frac{dS}{d\bar{L}}. \tag{26}$$

The first term on the right side, the SR effect, must always be positive as we know from (24) and (25). The second term, the adjustment effect, can have either sign, depending on relative factor intensities. Inspection reveals that the adjustment effect is positive if $X_j$ is relatively labor intensive and negative if $X_j$ is relatively capital intensive. For example, if we set $j = 1$ and then substitute

$$dL_1/dS = -(X_{L_1L_1}/k_1 + pX_{L_2L_2}/k_2)/\Delta$$

from footnote 8, $dS/d\bar{L} = k_1k_2/(k_2 - k_1)$ from (20), and $dK_1/dS = 1$, the adjustment effect of output for commodity one can be described by:

$$-(X_{L_1}X_{L_1L_1}/k_1 + X_{L_1}pX_{L_2L_2}/k_2 + X_{K_1}X_{L_1L_1} + X_{K_1}pX_{L_2L_2})k_1k_2/(k_2 - k_1)\ \Delta.$$

[14] See Rybczynski (1955) or Jones (1965).

Clearly, this expression is positive if $k_2 > k_1$ and negative if $k_2 < k_1$. Hence, the adjustment process leads to expansion of the labor-intensive industry over and above the SR expansion, whereas the capital-intensive industry will contract to offset the initial SR expansionary impact.

As we now continue with our evaluation of the LR output effect for the first industry, we can substitute (24) and the above-obtained expression for the adjustment effect into (26), simplify the terms, and state:

$$\begin{aligned}(dX_1/d\bar{L})^{\mathrm{LR}} &= k_2[(L_1X_{L_1})/L_1 + (K_1X_{K_1})/L_1]/[k_2 - k_1], \\ &= k_2(X_1/L_1)/(k_2 - k_1),\end{aligned} \tag{27}$$

which is positive if the first industry is labor intensive and negative if the first industry is capital intensive.[15]

## References


Atsumi, H. "The Long-Run Offer Function and a Dynamic Theory of International Trade." *J. Internat. Econ.* 1, no. 3 (August 1971): 267–300.

Chang, W., and Mayer, W. "Intermediate Goods in a General EquilibriumTrade Model." *Internat. Econ. Rev.* 14, no. 2 (June 1973): 447–59.

Haberler, G. *The Theory of International Trade, with Its Applications to Commercial Policy.* Translated by A. Stonier and F. Benham. London: Hodge, 1936.

Jones, R. W. "The Structure of Simple General Equilibrium Models." *J.P.E.* 73 (December 1965): 557–72.

———. "A Three-Factor Model in Theory, Trade, and History." In *Trade, Balance of Payments and Growth: Papers in International Economics in Honor of Charles P. Kindleberger,* edited by J. N. Bhagwati, R. W. Jones, R. A. Mundell, and J. Vanek. Amsterdam: North-Holland, 1971.

Kemp, M. C. *The Pure Theory of International Trade and Investment.* Englewood Cliffs, N. J.: Prentice-Hall, 1969.

Lancaster, K. *Mathematical Economics.* New York: Macmillan, 1968.

Rybczynski, T. N. "Factor Endowments and Relative Commodity Prices." *Economica,* n.s. 22 (November 1955): 336–41.


[15] This is precisely the expression given in Kemp's derivation of the output effect in response to endowment changes (1969, p. 14).

INTERNATIONAL ECONOMIC REVIEW
Vol. 15, No. 1, February, 1974

# VARIABLE RETURNS TO SCALE IN GENERAL EQUILIBRIUM THEORY: A COMMENT*

BY WOLFGANG MAYER[1]

## 1. INTRODUCTION

IN HIS SEMINAL ARTICLE on variable returns to scale Jones [4] examines the validity of the Rybczynski and Stolper-Samuelson Theorems in the presence of economies and diseconomies of scale. He assumes that economies and diseconomies are external to the firm and allows for industry production functions which are non-homothetic.[2] Jones' main conclusion is that the Rybczynski and Stolper-Samuelson Theorems as known for constant returns to scale production functions do not carry over to the variable returns to scale case in a straightforward manner. Both theorems break down whereby the factors most instrumental to their breakdown are (a) the degree of economies of scale and (b) the non-correspondence between average and marginal factor intensities, [4, (269)]. The Jones model is presented in simplified form by Kemp [5, (154–167)] who not only assumes that production functions are homothetic[3] but that economies of scale are the same in both industries. Nonetheless, Kemp's simplifications do not restore the validity of the two theorems under discussion for the variable returns to scale case; the obverse of what takes place under constant returns to scale might still occur.

The objective of our comment is to utilize stability analysis and prove that the Rybczynski and Stolper-Samuelson Theorems are valid in the presence of variable returns to scale if the system is *stable* and industry production functions are homothetic. If the stability condition is satisfied but production functions are non-homothetic, only the Rybczynski Theorem carries over to the variable returns to scale case, whereas extension of the Stolper-Samuelson Theorem (in its average factor-intensity form) requires the additional condition that average and marginal factor intensities are the same. We also prove that in a stable system output of a given commodity responds positively to an increase in its relative price.[4]

Application of the correspondence principle enables us to find the sign of the value of a certain determinant which is crucial in extending the two theorems

* Manuscript received March 13, 1973; revised May 14, 1973.

[1] I am much indebted to an anonymous referee who suggested use of the Fisher-Fuller Theorem in order to prove that the stability hypothesis is non-vacuous. Also, I would like to thank Murray C. Kemp for his comments.

[2] Non-homotheticity of production functions implies that for a given input price ratio the expansion path is non-linear. The marginal rate of factor substitution is not independent of the scale of production.

[3] This assumption eliminates the possibility that average and marginal factor-intensities differ.

[4] Kemp [5, (166)], and Herberg and Kemp [3, (409–413)] deal with this question and point out that the obverse result is quite possible when returns to scale are variable.

to the variable returns to scale case. Provided the system is stable, the sign of this determinant's value is known and definite whereas it is unknown in the writings of Jones [4], Herberg and Kemp [3], and Kemp [5].[5]

In Section 2 we restate the Jones model with variable returns to scale and derive relationships between output and endowment changes at constant final commodity prices, and between factor returns and final commodity prices at fixed endowment levels. We also establish the relation between output and price changes of final commodities. In Section 3 we deal with the dynamic properties of the system. The adjustment process of the variables is specified in accordance with the assumptions of the Jones model and the (local) stability problem is examined. Then we go back to the results obtained in Section 2 and interpret them in light of information yielded by stability analysis. Finally, we prove that the stability hypothesis is non-vacuous; i.e., that the assumption of stability does not preclude the existence of either increasing or decreasing returns to scale.

## 2. THE JONES MODEL[6]

Assumed is an economy in which there are two industries producing final commodities $M$ and $F$, their prices being $p_M$ and $p_F$ respectively. The enonomy is endowed with primary factors labor ($L$) and land ($T$) which are used in the production of both final commodities; their returns are denoted by $w$ (wage rate) and $r$ (return on capital) respectively. In addition, it is assumed that returns to scale are variable and external to the firm which allows retention of the assumption of perfect competition. Finally, we note that $a_{ij}$ ($i = L, T$; $j = M, F$) stands for the amount of factor $i$ used per unit of output $j$.

Exogenously given endowments impose the resource constraints

$$a_{LM}M + a_{LF}F = L \tag{1}$$

$$a_{TM}M + a_{TF}F = T\,, \tag{2}$$

and the zero profit condition prevailing under perfect competition states

$$a_{LM}w + a_{TM}r = p_M \tag{3}$$

$$a_{LF}w + a_{TF}r = p_F\,. \tag{4}$$

Differentiation of (1) to (4) yields:

$$\lambda_{LM}\hat{M} + \lambda_{LF}\hat{F} = \hat{L} - \lambda_{LM}\hat{a}_{LM} - \lambda_{LF}\hat{a}_{LF} \tag{5}$$

$$\lambda_{TM}\hat{M} + \lambda_{TF}\hat{F} = \hat{T} - \lambda_{TM}\hat{a}_{TM} - \lambda_{TF}\hat{a}_{TF} \tag{6}$$

[5] Actually, the stability question is touched upon by Jones who writes: "... I shall assume that the economy is incompletely specialized .... In the case of increasing returns, ..., this is not an innocent assumption, for under some set of stability conditions the production point might flee to one axis or another. However, I choose to ignore this question, ..." [4, (262)]. Also Kemp [5, (169–173)] devotes a whole section to the problem of stability of the international equilibrium under variable returns to scale.

[6] Notation, assumptions, and properties of our model are as in [4].

$$(7) \qquad \theta_{LM}\hat{w} + \theta_{TM}\hat{r} = \hat{p}_M - (\theta_{LM}\hat{a}_{LM} + \theta_{TM}\hat{a}_{TM})$$

$$(8) \qquad \theta_{LF}\hat{w} + \theta_{TF}\hat{r} = \hat{p}_F - (\theta_{LF}\hat{a}_{LF} + \theta_{TF}\hat{a}_{TF}),$$

where '$\wedge$' indicates relative changes; e.g., $\hat{M} = dM/M$. $\lambda_{ij}$ $(i = L, T; j = M, F)$ is the fraction of factor $i$ used in industry $j$; e.g., $\lambda_{LM} = L_M/L$, $L_M$ being the amount of labor employed by industry $M$. $\theta_{ij}$ measures the cost share of factor $i$ in industry $j$; e.g., $\theta_{LM} = (wL_M)/(p_M M)$. The $\hat{a}_{ij}$s denote relative changes in input coefficients and can be expressed as

$$(9) \qquad \hat{a}_{LM} = -\theta_{TM}\sigma_M(\hat{w} - \hat{r}) - R_{LM}\hat{M}$$

$$(10) \qquad \hat{a}_{TM} = \theta_{LM}\sigma_M(\hat{w} - \hat{r}) - R_{TM}\hat{M}$$

$$(11) \qquad \hat{a}_{LF} = -\theta_{TF}\sigma_F(\hat{w} - \hat{r}) - R_{LF}\hat{F}$$

$$(12) \qquad \hat{a}_{TF} = \theta_{LF}\sigma_F(\hat{w} - \hat{r}) - R_{TF}\hat{F},$$

where $\sigma_j$ indicates the elasticity of substitution in the $j$-th production process and $R_{ij}$ "is the percentage reduction in $a_{ij}$ corresponding to a one per cent increase in the output of industry $j$ at constant factor prices." [3, (263)]. For later reference we note that $\theta_{Lj}R_{Lj} + \theta_{Tj}R_{Tj} = R_j$ which measures the degree of external economies or diseconomies in industry $j$; for example, a positive $R_j$ indicates the percentage downward shift of industry $j$'s cost curve brought about by a one per cent rise in output of industry $j$. For homothetic production functions $R_{Lj} = R_{Tj} = R_j$.

Next we substitute the $\hat{a}_{ij}$s into (5) to (8), define $\lambda'_{ij} = \lambda_{ij}(1 - R_{ij})$, $\delta_L = \lambda_{LM}\theta_{TM}\sigma_M + \lambda_{LF}\theta_{TF}\sigma_F$, $\delta_T = \lambda_{TM}\theta_{LM}\sigma_M + \lambda_{TF}\theta_{LF}\sigma_F$, and obtain:

$$(5') \qquad \lambda'_{LM}\hat{M} + \lambda'_{LF}\hat{F} - \delta_L\hat{w} + \delta_L\hat{r} = \hat{L}$$

$$(6') \qquad \lambda'_{TM}\hat{M} + \lambda'_{TF}\hat{F} + \delta_T\hat{w} - \delta_T\hat{r} = \hat{T}$$

$$(7') \qquad -R_M\hat{M} + \theta_{LM}\hat{w} + \theta_{TM}\hat{r} = \hat{p}_M$$

$$(8') \qquad -R_F\hat{F} + \theta_{LF}\hat{w} + \theta_{TF}\hat{r} = \hat{p}_F.$$

Equations (5′) to (8′) can be solved for relative changes in output and factor returns in response to relative changes in endowments and final commodity prices. But before we proceed with these derivations, we repeat a set of assumptions made by Jones with the purpose of restricting the variety of possible solutions.[7]

ASSUMPTION 1. At constant factor prices, the expansion of any industry results in an increased demand for each factor of production. This implies that all

$$(13) \qquad \lambda'_{ij} = \lambda_{ij}(1 - R_{ij})$$

are positive.

[7] Although the assumptions limit the classes of production functions under consideration, they do not preclude the existence of either decreasing or increasing returns to scale.

ASSUMPTION 2. In an economy with a fixed set of factor endowments an increase in any factor price must increase the (average) cost of producing each commodity. This implies that each

$$(14)\qquad \begin{aligned} \theta'_{LM} &= \theta_{LM} - R_M\mu_M/|\lambda'|\,, & \theta'_{TM} &= \theta_{TM} + R_M\mu_M/|\lambda'| \\ \theta'_{LF} &= \theta_{LF} + R_F\mu_F/|\lambda'|\,, & \theta'_{TF} &= \theta_{TF} - R_F\mu_F/|\lambda'| \end{aligned}$$

is positive, where $\mu_M = \lambda'_{TF}\delta_L + \lambda'_{LF}\delta_T$, $\mu_F = \lambda'_{TM}\delta_L + \lambda'_{LM}\delta_T$, and $|\lambda'| = \lambda'_{LM}\lambda'_{TF} - \lambda'_{TM}\lambda'_{LF}$.

ASSUMPTION 3. At constant commodity prices the expansion of any industry results in an increased demand for each factor of production. This implies that each

$$(15)\qquad \begin{aligned} \lambda''_{LM} &= \lambda'_{LM} - R_M\delta_L/|\theta|\,, & \lambda''_{LF} &= \lambda'_{LF} + R_F\delta_L/|\theta| \\ \lambda''_{TM} &= \lambda'_{TM} + R_M\delta_T/|\theta|\,, & \lambda''_{TF} &= \lambda'_{TF} - R_F\delta_T/|\theta| \end{aligned}$$

is positive.

The Stolper-Samuelson Theorem states that, given constant returns to scale production functions, a small rise in the price of one commodity will lead to a rise in return on the factor which is used relatively intensively in the prodution of this commodity and to a decline in return on the other factor. In order to examine the validity of this theorem in the presence of variable returns to scale we let $p_M$ change and hold $p_F$ as well as endowments $L$ and $T$ constant. As we solve (5′) to (8′) for $\hat{w}$ and $\hat{r}$, we obtain after substitution of (14):[8]

$$(16)\qquad \hat{w} = \frac{|\lambda'|\theta'_{TF}}{\beta}\hat{p}_M = \frac{\theta'_{TF}}{|\theta|\alpha}\hat{p}_M$$

$$(17)\qquad \hat{r} = \frac{-|\lambda'|\theta'_{LF}}{\beta}\hat{p}_M = \frac{-\theta'_{LF}}{|\theta|\alpha}\hat{p}_M\,,$$

where $\beta$ is the value of the determinant of left-hand coefficients of the equations (5′) to (8′);

$$(18)\qquad \beta = |\lambda'||\theta| - R_F\mu_F - R_M\mu_M = |\lambda'||\theta|\alpha\,,$$

$\alpha$ being equal to

$$1 - \frac{(R_F\mu_F + R_M\mu_M)}{|\lambda'||\theta|}\,.$$

Since each $\theta'_{ij}$ is positive by Assumption 2, it is clear from (16) and (17) that the Stolper-Samuelson Theorem as stated above for constant returns to scale will hold in the variable returns to scale case if and only if $\alpha$ is positive.[9]

[8] Similarly, we can solve for

$$\hat{w} = \frac{-|\lambda'|\theta'_{TM}}{\beta}\hat{p}_F \quad \text{and} \quad \hat{r} = \frac{|\lambda'|\theta'_{LM}}{\beta}\hat{p}_F\,.$$

[9] $|\theta| \gtrless 0$ as $L_M/T_M \gtrless L_F/T_F$.

The Rybczynski Theorem states that, given constant returns to scale production functions, a positive change in endowment with a given factor will, at constant final commodity prices, lead to a rise in output of this industry which uses the factor whose supply has increased relatively intensively and to a decline in output of the other industry. In our variable returns to scale model, let us change the stock of labor ($L$) and hold constant land endowment ($T$) and prices of final commodities. Again we use (5′) to (8′), substitute (15), and solve for:

$$\hat{M} = \frac{|\theta|\lambda''_{TF}}{\beta}\hat{L} \tag{19}$$

$$\hat{F} = \frac{-|\theta|\lambda''_{TM}}{\beta}\hat{L}\,. \tag{20}$$ [10]

Clearly, the Rybczynski Theorem extends to the variable returns to scale case in and only if $\beta$ is positive, since $\lambda''_{ij}$ is always positive by Assumption 3. Together with our results for the Stolper-Samuelson Theorem it confirms Jones, statement that: "The signs of the $\alpha$ and $\beta$ coefficients thus indicate whether two established propositions arising in the theory of international trade retain their validity in the presence of externalities," [**4**, (269)].

Finally, we refer to the relation between changes in output and relative prices of final commodities at fixed endowments.[11] Again we utilize (5′) to (8′), set $\hat{L} = \hat{T} = 0$, and solve for:

$$\hat{M} = \frac{\mu_M}{\beta}(\hat{p}_M - \hat{p}_F) \tag{21}$$

$$\hat{F} = -\frac{\mu_F}{\beta}(\hat{p}_M - \hat{p}_F) \tag{22}$$

which shows that output changes of a given commodity are directly related to changes in relative prices if and only if $\beta$ is positive, since $\mu_j > 0$.

## 3. STABILITY AND THE SIGN OF $\beta$

From the above results we conclude that it is not possible to extend the Rybczynski and Stolper-Samuelson Theorems and the relation between output and relative prices from the constant to the variable returns to scale case in a straightforward manner. The main obstacle lies in the inability of pure comparative statics analysis to provide us with determinate signs of $\beta$ and $\alpha$, as defined in Section 2. It is at this point that stability analysis comes to our assistance. We can show that, under quite reasonable assumptions concerning the dynamic adjustment mechanism of the system, a necessary condition for stability

[10] Similarly,

$$\hat{M} = -\frac{|\theta|\lambda''_{LF}}{\beta}\hat{T}\,, \qquad \hat{F} = \frac{|\theta|\lambda''_{LM}}{\beta}\hat{T}\,.$$

[11] This question is dealt with in Kemp [**5**, (166)], and Herberg and Kemp [**3**, (409–413)].

of our system is that $\beta$ is positive. This implies that for stable systems the Rybczynski Theorem and the direct relation between equilibrium output and final commodity prices always hold in the presence of external economies; and that the same is true for the Stolper-Samuelson Theorem provided average and marginal factor intensities are the same; i.e., $|\lambda'|$ and $|\lambda|$ have the same sign.[12]

In the Jones model of Section 2 we deal with four goods: two final commodities ($M$, $F$) and two primary factors ($L$, $T$). For the primary factors total supply is fixed and returns are variable, for the final commodities quantities supplied are variable and prices are exogenously given. The assumptions of fixed factor endowments, constant commodity prices, and perfect competition virtually prescribe how the dynamic adjustment mechanism of the system should be specified. In the commodity market, if under perfect competition the price of a final commodity exceeds average costs there exists an incentive for existing firms to produce more and for new firms to enter the industry. Equilibrium is established at output levels where average costs equal the exogenously given price and profits are zero. Hence, the dynamic adjustment in the commodity market is described by

$$\dot{M} = d_1(p_M - a_{LM}w - a_{TM}r) \tag{23}$$

$$\dot{F} = d_2(p_F - a_{LF}w - a_{TF}r)\,, \tag{24}$$

where "$\cdot$" denotes differentiation with respect to time and $d_1, d_2$ are positive coefficients measuring the speed of adjustment. A Marshallian adjustment process[13] is assumed with quantities adjusting as the demand price differs from the supply price. The demand price is identical with the exogenously given (world) price whereas the supply price is measured by the average costs of producing a given commodity. In the factor market, where total endowment quantities are exogenously given, factor returns will adjust. If aggregate demand originating in industries $M$ and $F$ for a given factor should exceed (fall short of) total endowment with this factor, its return will tend to rise (decline):

$$\dot{w} = d_3(L_M + L_T - L) = d_3(a_{LM}M + a_{LF}F - L) \tag{25}$$

$$\dot{r} = d_4(T_M + T_F - T) = d_4(a_{TM}M + a_{TF}F - T)\,, \tag{26}$$

where '$d$' is again a positive adjustment coefficient and $L_j$ and $T_j$ stand for the aggregate amounts of labor and land demanded by industry $j$. We are facing a Walrasian adjustment mechanism with the fixed endowment assumption implying that returns will have to adjust. Finally,we assume that each firm instantaneously chooses its optimal input coefficients for a given level of industry output and input price ratios.

As we denote the equilibrium values of the four endogenous variables by $M^*$, $F^*$, $w^*$, and $r^*$' the system is locally stable if given any initial position $M^0$, $F^0$,

[12] $\beta = |\lambda'||\theta|\alpha$; if $|\lambda'|$ and $|\lambda|$ have the same sign, then $\alpha$ will be positive if $\beta$ is positive, since $|\lambda|$ and $|\theta|$ have the same sign.

[13] For an analysis of Marshallian adjustment under increasing returns to scale in a closed economy see Aoki [**1**].

$w^0$, and $r^0$ in the small neighborhood of $M^*$, $F^*$, $w^*$, and $r^*$, the system generates time paths $M(t)$, $F(t)$, $w(t)$ and $r(t)$ such that $\lim_{t\to\infty} F = F^*$, $\lim_{t\to\infty} M = M^*$, $\lim_{t\to\infty} w = w^*$, and $\lim_{t\to\infty} r = r^*$, where $t$ stands for time. A necessary and sufficient condition for local stability is provided by the Routh-Hurwicz conditions [7, (165)] for which, in turn, we have to derive the Jacobian matrix $J = DA$ of the system of simultaneous equations (23) to (26):

$$(27)\quad J = DA = \begin{bmatrix} \dfrac{d_1 p_M R_M}{M} & 0 & -d_1 a_{LM} & -d_1 a_{TM} \\ 0 & \dfrac{d_2 p_F R_F}{F} & -d_2 a_{LF} & -d_2 a_{TF} \\ d_3 a_{LM}(1 - R_{LM}) & d_3 a_{LF}(1 - R_{LF}) & \dfrac{-d_3 \gamma_L}{w} & \dfrac{d_3 \gamma_L}{r} \\ d_4 a_{TM}(1 - R_{TM}) & d_4 a_{TF}(1 - R_{TF}) & \dfrac{d_4 \gamma_T}{w} & \dfrac{-d_4 \gamma_T}{r} \end{bmatrix}.$$

In deriving the elements of $J$ we utilized the previously stated expressions for $\hat{a}_{ij}$, being dependent on $(w/r)$ and industry output of commodity $j$, and we also set $\gamma_L = M a_{LM} \theta_{TM} \sigma_M + F a_{LF} \theta_{TF} \sigma_F$ and $\gamma_T = M a_{TM} \theta_{LM} \sigma_M + F a_{TF} \theta_{LF} \sigma_F$. According to the Routh-Hurwicz Theorem a necessary condition for local stability of the system is that $|J|$ is positive.

For the derivation of fruitful comparative statics theorems, such as the Rybczynski and Stolper-Samuelson Theorems, it is essential that we assume stability of the equilibrium under consideration. Unless equilibrium is stable, a change in endowment or commodity prices may not lead to a new equilibrium position, and the comparative statics results become vacuous. So we assume that our equilibrium is stable which implies that $|J|$ is positive. But once we know the sign of $|J|$ we also can determine the sign of $\beta$, which proved so important in extending the above mentioned theorems from the constant to the variable returns to scale case. As we recall that multiplication of any row (or column) by a scalar $k$ changes the value of the determinant $k$-fold, we can see that

$$(28)\quad |J| = \frac{d_1 d_2 d_3 d_4 p_M p_F L T}{M F w r} \begin{vmatrix} -R_M & 0 & \theta_{LM} & \theta_{TM} \\ 0 & -R_F & \theta_{LF} & \theta_{TF} \\ \lambda'_{LM} & \lambda'_{LF} & -\delta_L & \delta_L \\ \lambda'_{TM} & \lambda'_{TF} & \delta_T & -\delta_T \end{vmatrix} = \Phi\beta .$$

Since $\Phi$ is always positive and $|J|$ is positive by the stability condition, $\beta$ must be positive as well. Hence, the assumption of stability allows us to draw the following conclusions concerning the Rybczynski Theorem, the Stolper-Samuelson Theorem, and the relation ship between final commodity ontput and prices:

(a) *The Rybczynski Theorem as developed for constant returns to scale carries over to the variable returns to scale case.* This can be seen from (19) and (20); since $\beta$ and $\lambda''_{Tj}$ are positive, an increase in $L$ will raise (lower) production of $M$ and lower (raise) production of $F$ if $|\theta|$ is positive (negative). The theorem holds for homothetic and non-homothetic production functions.

(b) *An increase in relative price of commodity j leads to a positive change in output of the same commodity under variable as well as under constant returns to scale.* This can be seen from (21) and (22); since $\beta$ and $\mu_j$ are positive, $M(F)$ is directly (inversely) related to $p_M/p_F$. Again the conclusion holds for homothetic and non-homothetic production functions.

(c) *The Stolper-Samuelson Theorem, as known for constant returns to scale, is valid in the case of variable returns to scale if and only if the industry which uses a given factor relatively intensively in an average sense uses the same factor relatively intensively also in a marginal sense*; i.e., $|\lambda'|$ and $|\lambda|$ have the same sign. From (16) and (17) we recall that the theorem is valid if and only if $\alpha$ is positive. But $\alpha = \beta|\lambda'||\theta|$, which implies that $\alpha$ will have the same sign as $\beta$ if and only if $|\lambda'|$ and $|\lambda|$ have the same sign. If production functions are homothetic, as in the Kemp analysis **[5]**, the Stolper-Samuelson always holds in the presence of variable returns to scale. For non-homothetic functions, as used in Jones **[4]**, $|\lambda'|$ and $|\lambda|$ may have a different sign and the theorem as stated in its average factor intensity form may break down. However, the Stolper-Samuelson Theorem definitely will hold in its marginal form: a small rise in the price of a given commodity will raise returns on this factor which is used intensively in a marginal sense in the production of this good and lower returns on the other, marginally less intensively used, factor.

The procedure used in extending the Rybczynski and Stolper-Samuelson Theorems to variable returns to scale models raises the important question as to whether it actually is possible that the system is stable under increasing or decreasing returns to scale. There is no meaning to the results stated in (a) to (c) if the stability hypothesis is vacuous. Hence, we must be able to prove that there exists some class of variable returns to scale production functions under which the system will be stable, at least for some set of adjustment speeds.

Fisher and Fuller **[2]** have developed a proof that under some very general conditions there exists a set of adjustment speeds such that the characteristic equation under concern is stable. Given that all speeds of adjustment are positive, as in our model, and writing $J = DA$ where $D$ is a positive diagonal and $A$ a real $n \times n$ matrix, the Fisher-Fuller Theorem (or rather its corollary) states that:[14] "if $A$ has a sequence of nested principal minors of order 1 through $n$, with the sign of the $i$-th minor being $(-1)^i$, then there exists a positive diagonal matrix $D$ such that the characteristic equation of $DA$ is stable"; where nested sequence of principal minors means that "rows and columns included in a principal minor of order $s + 1 \ldots$ can be chosen so that $s$ of these appear in a principal minor of order $s \ldots$ for $s = 1, \ldots, n - 1$." **[6]**. Concerning our problem the stability hypothesis is non-vacuous if we can show that $A$ in (27) has at least

[14] Strictly speaking the Fisher-Fuller Theorem [**2**, (418)] is more general than stated in the text. But since all our adjustment speeds are positive we use a corollary of the theorem as stated by Quirk and Ruppert [**6**, (320)].

one such nested sequence of principal minors with signs $(-1)^i$, $i = 1, 2, 3, 4$.

Jones, while allowing for increasing and decreasing returns to scale, has restricted the classes of production functions by making Assumptions 1 to 3. If $\beta > 0$, — which, as we will demonstrate, is not *a priori* excluded by the existence of decreasing or increasing returns to scale, — then these assumptions imply that there exist at least two such nested sequences of principal minors with sign $(-1)^i$. First, let us denote a first order principal minor of $A$ obtained by deleting all but the $i$-th row and column by $M_i$, a second order principal minor of $A$ obtained by deleting all but the $i$-th and $j$-th rows and columns by $M_{ij}$ $(i, j = 1, \ldots, 4;\ i \neq j)$, etc. Then the nested sequences of principle minors of $A$ whose sign patterns we are going to check are:

(a) $M_3, M_{13}, M_{134}, M_{1234}$ (b) $M_3, M_{23}, M_{234}, M_{1234}$

(c) $M_4, M_{14}, M_{134}, M_{1234}$ (d) $M_4, M_{24}, M_{234}, M_{1234}$.

From (27) we immediately can see that the signs of $M_3, M_4, M_{134}$, and $M_{234}$ are negative. While the signs of the second order principal minors are not so obvious, we can, with the help of Assumptions 1 and 3, determine that at least two of the second order pricipal minors are positive; their values are:

$$
\begin{aligned}
M_{13} &= a_{LM}^2(1 - R_{LM}) - \frac{p_M R_M \gamma_L}{wM} = \frac{L_M}{M}\left[a_{LM}(1 - R_{LM}) - \frac{R_M \gamma_L}{\theta_{LM} M}\right] \\
M_{23} &= a_{LF}^2(1 - R_{LF}) - \frac{p_F R_F \gamma_L}{wF} = \frac{L_F}{F}\left[a_{LF}(1 - R_{LF}) - \frac{R_F \gamma_L}{\theta_{LF} F}\right] \\
M_{14} &= a_{TM}^2(1 - R_{TM}) - \frac{p_M R_M \gamma_T}{rM} = \frac{T_M}{M}\left[a_{TM}(1 - R_{TM}) - \frac{R_M \gamma_T}{\theta_{TM} M}\right] \\
M_{24} &= a_{TF}^2(1 - R_{TF}) - \frac{p_F R_F \gamma_T}{rF} = \frac{T_F}{F}\left[a_{TF}(1 - R_{TF}) - \frac{R_F \gamma_T}{\theta_{TF} F}\right].
\end{aligned} \tag{29}
$$

Next we go back to equation (15) which states Assumption 3. After we substitute $\delta_L L = \gamma_L$, $\delta_T T = \gamma_T$, $|\theta| = (\theta_{LM} - \theta_{LF}) = -(\theta_{TM} - \theta_{TF})$, and $\lambda'_{ij} = \lambda_{ij}(1 - R_{ij})$, we can write Assumption 3 as:

$$
\begin{aligned}
\lambda'_{LM} - \frac{R_M \delta_L}{|\theta|} &= \frac{M}{L}\left[a_{LM}(1 - R_{LM}) - \frac{R_M \gamma_L}{(\theta_{LM} - \theta_{LF})M}\right] > 0 \\
\lambda'_{LF} + \frac{R_F \delta_L}{|\theta|} &= \frac{F}{L}\left[a_{LF}(1 - R_{LF}) - \frac{R_F \gamma_L}{(\theta_{LF} - \theta_{LM})F}\right] > 0 \\
\lambda'_{TM} + \frac{R_M \delta_T}{|\theta|} &= \frac{M}{T}\left[a_{TM}(1 - R_{TM}) - \frac{R_M \gamma_T}{(\theta_{TM} - \theta_{TF})M}\right] > 0 \\
\lambda'_{TF} - \frac{R_F \delta_T}{|\theta|} &= \frac{F}{T}\left[a_{TF}(1 - R_{TF}) - \frac{R_F \gamma_T}{(\theta_{TF} - \theta_{TM})F}\right] > 0 .
\end{aligned} \tag{15'}
$$

As we compare (29) with (15′) we conclude that: if $|\theta|$ is positive, then Assumptions 1 and 3 imply that $M_{13}$ and $M_{24}$ are positive, since $1/(\theta_{LM} - \theta_{LF}) > 1/\theta_{LM}$ and $1/(\theta_{TF} - \theta_{TM}) > 1/\theta_{TF}$; if $|\theta|$ is negative, then the two assumptions imply that $M_{23}$ and $M_{14}$ are positive since $1/(\theta_{LF} - \theta_{LM}) > 1/\theta_{LF}$ and $1/(\theta_{TM} - \theta_{TF}) > 1/\theta_{TM}$. Hence, at least two of the second order principal minors of the nested sequences (a) to (d) must be positive given the rather general assumptions made by Jones. Finally, we illustrate that $M_{1234} = \beta = |\theta|\,|\lambda'| - R_M\mu_M - R_F\mu_F$ can be positive at least for some classes of increasing and decreasing returns to scale production functions. For example, as we impose the simplifying assumption that $|\lambda'|$ and $|\lambda|$ have the same sign (and are non-zero) then $|\theta||\lambda'|$ must be positive. This, in turn, implies that $M_{1234}$ is positive if and only if $|\theta||\lambda'| > R_M\mu_M + R_F\mu_F$. Clearly this condition is satisfied under decreasing ($R_j < 0$) and constant ($R_j = 0$) returns to scale, since $\mu_j > 0$. But $M_{1234}$ also will be positive for sufficiently small increasing returns to scale; i.e., for sufficiently small, though positive, values of $R_j$. A specific example can be found in Kemp [5] who shows that, for Cobb-Douglas production functions with returns to scale being the same in both industries ($R_M = R_F = R$), $M_{1234}$ is positive if $|\theta||\lambda| > R$.

From the last paragraph we conclude that if $M_{1234} > 0$, which in itself is not inconsistent with the assumption of increasing or decreasing returns to scale, the Fisher-Fuller conditions are satisfied since there exist at least two nested sequences of principle minors with sign $(-1)^i$ for the minor of the $i$-th order. Hence, at least for some variable returns to scale production functions there exist speeds of adjustment under which the Jones model will be stable. However, what the relative magnitudes of adjustment speeds in the goods and factor markets must be to assure stability of the system is quite difficult to determine. For increasing returns to scale we can see, however, that *ceteris paribus* the slower the speeds of adjustment in the two factor markets the less likely it is that the system is stable. This follows from the Routh-Hurwicz Theorem which states that the sum of the first order principle minors must be negative. And since in the presence of increasing returns to scale only the factor market first order principle minors ($M_3$, $M_4$) are negative, small values of $d_3$ and $d_4$ are detrimental to stability of the system. Furthermore, the Fisher-Fuller Theorem and its proof [2] point in this direction since the speeds of adjustment have to be relatively large in markets where the nested sequence of minors starts, namely in one of the factor markets.

*University of Cincinnati, U.S.A.*

## REFERENCES

[1] Aoki, Masahiko, "A Note on Marshallian Process under Increasing Returns," *Quarterly Journal of Economics*, LXXXIV (February, 1970), 100–112.

[2] Fisher, Michael E. and A. T. Fuller, "On the Stabilization of Matrices and the Convergence of Linear Iterative Processes," *Proceeding of the Cambridge Philosophical Society*, LIV (October, 1958), 417–425.

[3] Herberg, Horst and Murray C. Kemp, "Some Implications on Variable Returns to Scale," *Canadian Journal of Economics*, II (August, 1969), 403–415.

[4] Jones, Ronald M., "Variable Returns to Scale in General Equilibrium Theory," *International Economic Review*, X (October, 1968), 261–272.

[5] KEMP, MURRAY C., *The Pure Theory of Internationol Trade and Investment* (Englewood Cliffs, N. J.: Prentice Hall, 1969).
[6] QUIRK, JAMES AND RICHARD RUPPERT, "Qualitative Economics and the Stability of Equilibrium," *Review of Economic Studies*, XXXII (October, 1965), 311-326.
[7] ——— AND RUBIN SAPOSNIK, *Introduction to General Equilibrium Theory and Welfare Economics* (New York, N. Y.; McGraw-Hill, 1968).

# The Rybczynski, Stolper-Samuelson, and Factor-Price Equalization Theorems Under Price Uncertainty

By WOLFGANG MAYER*

Until quite recently the pure theory of international trade largely disregarded the role of uncertainty in determining production and trade patterns. Virtually all theorems had been based on the assumption that decision makers operate in an environment of perfect certainty. William Brainard and Richard Cooper in a seminal contribution finally abandoned this assumption and introduced uncertainty with the objective of explaining the diversification of trade. Since then a rapidly expanding literature has adopted the uncertainty assumption for the study of various trade topics, such as production and trade patterns in Ricardian models[1] and the allocation of resources among industries in neoclassical general equilibrium production models.[2] The common theme of all those writings is the question whether the theorems known for certainty models maintain their validity when some form of uncertainty is introduced.

The primary objective of this paper is to examine whether the content of the Rybczynski, Stolper-Samuelson, and Factor-Price Equalization theorems, as well as of Samuelson's Reciprocity relation, and the direct relationship between industry output of a given commodity and its own (expected) price can be generalized to the uncertainty model. Uncertainty is introduced by assuming that final commodity prices are random variables and that individual firms facing these prices exhibit risk-averse behavior. The basic description of the firm's behavioral relations is adopted from Agnar Sandmo. All other assumptions employed are those of the traditional two-factor, two-commodity model.

My findings are very straightforward and extremely comforting. Subject to one small modification, the introduction of price uncertainty does not destroy the validity of any of the above-stated theorems and relations. The modification consists of replacing the words "change in price" in the certainty model with the words "change in expected price, with higher central moments constant" in the uncertainty model. The claim that these theorems can conveniently be extended to the uncertainty case is quite surprising since we explicitly introduced risk-averse behavior on the part of firms. This outcome, however, is not accidental. It will be shown that for perfectly competitive industries, with firms freely entering and leaving, the risk attitudes of individual firms have little influence on industry-wide resource allocations.

Since my findings are at odds with those of the current literature,[3] a second objective of this paper is to relate the model to

* Associate professor of economics, University of Cincinnati. I am indebted to an anonymous referee for comments on an earlier version of this paper.

[1] See, for example, the papers by Murray Kemp and Nissan Liviatan, Roy Ruffin, and Stephen Turnovsky.

[2] Thomas Rothenberg and Kenneth Smith, initially, and later Raveendra Batra (1974, 1975a,b) focused on those issues.

[3] More precisely, my results differ from those derived by Batra.

those developed by Batra, on the one hand, and Rothenberg and Smith, on the other hand. There exist some quite visible differences between their respective models and ours. In particular, the choice of the random variable is different. However, a less obvious but much more important difference concerns the setup of our model. Neither Batra nor Rothenberg and Smith make a clear distinction between the behavior of the individual firm, where the decision process under uncertainty takes place, and of the entire industry, from which resource allocation patterns are derived. This lack of distinction between firm and industry behavior does not lead to any serious problems in the analysis of Rothenberg and Smith since they assume not only that production functions are homogeneous of degree one[4] but also that firms are risk indifferent. Batra, on the other hand, allows for risk-averse firms and in this case the distinction is crucial. I will show that Batra's models are really not long-run equilibrium models, but they are intermediate-run models in which factors of production are freely mobile between industries, while the number of firms in a given industry is fixed. Provided firms are not risk indifferent, the assumption of uncertainty will affect the validity of most trade theorems as derived from intermediate-run models; the Factor-Price Equalization theorem breaks down completely, whereas the Rybczynski and Stolper-Samuelson theorems are critically impaired.

Section I, which emphasizes the distinction between output variables of the representative firm and of the entire industry, states the model from which I derive the above-mentioned trade theorems in Section II. Section III sheds some light on the specification adopted by Batra and its implications for the trade theorems under consideration.

[4] If individual firms produce subject to decreasing returns to scale, then a situation arises which is similar to that of the risk-averse firm which produces subject to constant returns to scale. In both cases, output of the firm is an increasing function of (expected) price. And it is not legitimate to relate the industry production function directly to that of the representative firm unless the number of firms in the industry is fixed.

## I. Production Equilibrium of the Firm, Industry, and Economy

This model deals with a small, open economy in which there are two industries producing two final commodities, $X_1$ and $X_2$. The economy is endowed with two primary factors of production, labor ($L$) and capital ($K$), which are fully employed and perfectly mobile between industries, but fixed in aggregate endowment. The production processes of firms in the two respective industries are such that relative factor intensities are different everywhere. Perfect competition prevails in both factor and commodity markets, and there do not exist any economies or diseconomies of scale in either industry. Unlike the standard models of this type, I introduce uncertainty by assuming that individual firms, although they are price takers, must make their production decisions before the internationally determined price of their commodity becomes known to them.

As far as the actual presentation of the model is concerned, I start with specifying production behavior at the firm level, then move on to the industry, and finally state the equilibrium production conditions for the whole economy.[5]

An individual firm in industry $j$ is assumed to perceive the price of commodity $j$, $p_j$, subjectively as a random variable with density function $h_j(p_j)$ and expected value $\mu_j$, $j=1,2$. The firm's objective is to

[5] For more detailed analyses of the competitive firm under price uncertainty the reader is referred to Sandmo (whose approach and notation I have adopted), to David Baron, or to Hayne Leland.

maximize expected utility, $U_j$, from profits, $\pi_j$; i.e.,

$$\max_{X_j} E_j[U_j(\pi_j)] \tag{1}$$

where $E_j$ is an expectations operator. The utility function is assumed to be bounded from above and twice differentiable, with the derivative signs $U_j'>0$ and $U_j''<0$. The latter sign condition introduces risk-averse behavior to which we add the further assumption that the firm's absolute risk aversion, as measured by $-U_j''(\pi_j)/U_j'(\pi_j)$,[6] is a decreasing function of profits. Finally, it is postulated that $U(0)=a$, where $a$ is an arbitrarily chosen real number which the representative entrepreneur assigns to a situation of zero profits.[7] The firm's profit function is

$$\pi_j = p_jX_j - wL_j - rK_j \tag{2}$$

where $L_j$ and $K_j$ denote the amount of labor and capital employed by a given firm in industry $j$. The symbols $w$ and $r$ stand for the corresponding factor returns. The production function of a firm in industry $j$ is represented by

$$X_j = X_j(L_j,K_j) \tag{3}$$

which is assumed to be twice differentiable, strictly quasi concave, and homogeneous of degree one, with the marginal products of both factors being positive. Considering these properties of the production function, the firm's profit function can be rewritten in the form

$$\pi_j = X_j(p_j - a_{Lj}w - a_{Kj}r) \tag{2'}$$

where $a_{Lj}=L_j/X_j$ and $a_{Kj}=K_j/X_j$ are a function of the factor returns ratio, $w/r$, only.[8] Substituting (2′) into (1), the first- and second-order conditions for maximum expected utility from profits are:

$$E_j[U_j' (p_j - a_{Lj}w - a_{Kj}r)] = 0 \tag{4}$$

$$E_j[U_j'' (p_j - a_{Lj}w - a_{Kj}r)^2] < 0 \tag{5}$$

Based on these conditions, one can derive the firm's supply curve as a function of expected price assuming that the degree of riskiness remains unaltered.[9] As Sandmo (p. 69) has demonstrated, the assumptions of our model imply that the firm's supply curve is upward sloping. The firm, of course, also has the option of not producing at all. The entrepreneur will in fact not engage in production at all unless he is going to be at least as well off as when he is not producing. Before we assumed that $U_j(0)=a$. A necessary condition for long-run equilibrium of a competitive firm is that expected utility from profits when production is positive is at least as large as when production, and therefore profits, are zero; or stated differently:[10]

$$X_j > 0 \text{ only if } E_j[U_j(\pi_j)] \geqq a \tag{6}$$

Hence, we need equations (4)–(6) in order to determine the equilibrium output of a competitive firm under price uncertainty.

In order to determine the production equilibrium of the whole economy, we now must specify the long-run equilibrium conditions for both competitive industries in addition to those for the individual firms. This requires the further assumption that all firms in a given industry have identical production functions, utility functions,

[6] This, of course, is the Arrow-Pratt measure of absolute risk aversion.

[7] Since zero production activity yields zero long-run profits, $U(0) = a$ represents for the entrepreneur the alternative to producing.

[8] Given that both inputs must be chosen before the final commodity price becomes known to the producer, the optimal input combination of the competitive firm is not affected by the introduction of price uncertainty; see Batra and Aman Ullah. For the case where capital inputs must be chosen before, but labor after the final commodity price becomes known, see Duncan Holthausen.

[9] More precisely, all higher central moments are held constant.

[10] This condition was initially stated by Baron (p. 473, equation (30)).

and probability assessments. In particular, $U_j(0)=a$ is assumed to be the same for every firm. Consequently, from now on we will talk about the production behavior of a given industry's representative firm.

Long-run equilibrium of the $j$th industry requires that for all firms the condition

$$E_j[U_j(\pi_j)] = a \tag{7}$$

is satisfied. The assumption of identical firms and the absence of barriers to entering or leaving a competitive industry imply that any difference in $E_j[U_j(\pi_j)]$ from $U_j(0)=a$ leads to long-run adjustments of the industry's number of firms until the equality of (7) is reestablished. This enables us to conclude that, at constant factor returns, the industry supply curve is a horizontal line, although the individual firm's supply curve is upward sloping.[11]

A few comments on the nature of the firm's and industry's long-run equilibrium position appear to be appropriate. First of all, the risk-averse entrepreneur's expected profits are positive,[12] whereby the value of the expected profits equals the risk premium. Second, the existence of positive expected profits is not inconsistent with the assumption of constant returns to scale production functions.[13] Total product will be exhausted by ordinary factor payments plus the risk premium. Finally, one can summarize the condition for long-run equilibrium by the following relationships: expected price = average cost + average risk premium = marginal cost + marginal risk premium.[14]

The whole economy is in production equilibrium if the above-stated minimum expected utility condition is satisfied for all firms in both industries and if both factors are fully employed:

$$E_1[U_1(\pi_1)] = a \tag{8}$$

$$E_2[U_2(\pi_2)] = a \tag{9}$$

$$a_{L1}X_1^* + a_{L2}X_2^* = L \tag{10}$$

$$a_{K1}X_1^* + a_{K2}X_2^* = K \tag{11}$$

The specification of (8) and (9) is based on the fact that any decision maker is a potential entrepreneur for either industry and to him $U_1(0)=a=U_2(0)$. This, however, should not be interpreted as implying that the risk premiums and, therefore, expected profits must be the same in both industries. They may be and usually will be different, whereby their impact on resource allocations is similar to that of a tax imposed on output of the respective industries. Proceeding to equations (10) and (11), the asterisks attached to $X_j$ indicate that they refer to industry output variables. The distinction between output of the whole industry $X_j^*$, and of the representative firm in that industry $X_j$, is necessary since the output variables contained in (8) and (9) refer to the representative firm, whereas those contained in (10) and (11) refer to the whole industry. Considering the properties of $a_{ij}$ and of $\pi_j$, we can see that the system of four equations (8)–(11) contains six endogenous variables: $w$, $r$, $X_1$, $X_2$, $X_1^*$, and $X_2^*$. In spite of the inequality of the number of equations and variables, we can find unique solutions for $w$, $r$, $X_1^*$, and $X_2^*$, since $E_j[U_j'(p_j-a_{Lj}w-a_{Kj}r)]=0$ from (4) and, therefore, the solution values of the four mentioned variables are independent of $X_j$.

## II. Revisiting Some Trade Theorems Under Price Uncertainty

In this section we are going to explore whether the introduction of price uncer-

[11] If firms of a given industry had either different probability beliefs or different utility functions, then the industry supply curve may be upward sloping. For some remarks on this point, see Sandmo, p. 72.

[12] Proofs of this proposition can be found in Sandmo, p. 71, and Baron, p. 476.

[13] This can easily be seen after realizing that under uncertainty $w \leqq \mu_j X_{Lj}$ and $r \leqq \mu_j X_{Kj}$, which has been demonstrated by Batra and Ullah.

[14] This, of course, is just a verbal restatement of Baron's equation (34).

tainty forces us to revise or modify some of the classic theorems which are known for the conventional two-commodity, two-factor, constant returns to scale trade models with price uncertainty. In particular, we are going to check whether the validity of the Rybczynski, Stolper-Samuelson, and Factor-Price Equalization theorems, as well as of the positive relation between production of a given commodity and its own price, carries over to the uncertainty model. We also will deal with the impact of a change in the degree of price uncertainty on factor returns and factor allocations.

All my comparative statics results are based on the system spelled out in (8)–(11). Before I differentiate these equations totally, I would like to make a few comments on some technical matters involved in the differentiation procedure. First, I should repeat that the input coefficients $a_{ij}$ are functions of the factor returns ratio $w/r$, only. Their cost-minimizing value changes along the unit isoquant, as described by (12) and (13) where[15] $\sigma_j>0$ is the elasticity of substitution in production and

$$(12) \quad da_{Lj} = -a_{Lj}\sigma_j\Phi_{Kj}[(dw/w) - (dr/r)] \qquad j = 1,2$$

$$(13) \quad da_{Kj} = a_{Kj}\sigma_j\Phi_{Lj}[(dw/w) - (dr/r)]$$

$$\Phi_{Kj} = a_{Kj}r/(a_{Lj}w + a_{Kj}r)$$

and

$$\Phi_{Lj} = a_{Lj}w/(a_{Lj}w + a_{Kj}r)$$

are the cost shares of capital and labor, respectively, in the production of commodity $j$.[16] Second, when we consider exogenous changes on the part of final commodity prices, we are going to distinguish two forms of changes. One refers to a small change in a commodity's expected price, with all higher central moments held constant; this is equivalent to a change in final commodity price in the certainty model. The other is a small change in the degree of price uncertainty, with expected price held constant. For a more detailed discussion on that point, the reader is referred to Sandmo, pp. 67–69.

Total differentiation of (8)–(11), substitution of (12) and (13), and use of Sandmo's technique with respect to changes in expected price and the degree of uncertainty yield

$$(14) \quad a_{L1}E_1[U_1']dw + a_{K1}E_1[U_1']dr = E_1[U_1']d\theta_1 + E_1[U_1'(p_1 - \mu_1)]d\gamma_1$$

$$(15) \quad a_{L2}E_2[U_2']dw + a_{K2}E_2[U_2']dr = E_2[U_2']d\theta_2 + E_2[U_2'(p_2 - \mu_2)]d\gamma_2$$

$$(16) \quad a_{L1}dX_1^* + a_{L2}dX_2^* - \delta_L(dw/w) + \delta_L(dr/r) = dL$$

$$(17) \quad a_{K1}dX_1^* + a_{K2}dX_2^* + \delta_K(dw/w) - \delta_K(dr/r) = dK$$

where

$$\delta_L = \sum_{j=1}^{2} X_j^* a_{Lj}\sigma_j\Phi_{Kj}$$

and

$$\delta_K = \sum_{j=1}^{2} X_j^* a_{Kj}\sigma_j\Phi_{Lj}$$

are positive terms. In deriving (14) and (15) advantage is taken of the cost-minimization condition $(w\,da_{Lj}+r\,da_{Kj})=0$, which follows immediately from (12) and (13), and of the first-order condition for maximum expected utility

$$E_j[U_j'(p_j - a_{Lj}w - a_{Kj}r)] = 0$$

which must always be satisfied in equilibrium. Changes in the exogenous variables of (14) and (15) refer to an increase in expected price $d\theta_j>0$, and to an increase

[15] In order to derive (12), and similarly (13), we define $a_{Lj}=L_j/X_j=1/f_j(k_j)$, where $k_j=K_j/L_j$. Total differentiation of $a_{Lj}$ and substitution of the definition of the elasticity of substitution $\sigma_j=(dk_j/k_j)/[(dw/w)-(dr/r)]$ yields $da_{Lj}=-(f_j'/f_j)a_{Lj}k_j\sigma_j[(dw/w)-(dr/r)]$. Equation (12) is then obtained by substituting $[(w/r)+k_j]$ for $f_j/f_j'$ and equating $(f_j'/f_j)k_j$ with $rK_j/(wL_j+rK_j)$.

[16] In the certainty model, the equivalent expressions are $\Phi_{Kj}=(rK_j)/(p_jX_j)$ and $\Phi_{Lj}=(wL_j)/(p_jX_j)$. With price a random variable, it is no longer possible to give $\Phi_{Lj}$ and $\Phi_{Kj}$ this interpretation since in equilibrium it may not hold that $p_j=a_{Lj}w+a_{Kj}r$.

in the degree of price uncertainty $d\gamma_j > 0$, whereas changes in the exogenous variables of (16) and (17) refer to an increase in the endowment of labor and capital, respectively.

Our first task is to examine the impact of endowment changes on the country's production pattern and to compare the obtained results with those known for the certainty model. Provided that final commodity prices are looked upon by firms with certainty and that the other assumptions of our model are satisfied, the Rybczynski theorem states that an increase in the economy's endowment with a given factor leads to a rise in output of the industry which uses that factor relatively more intensively and to a decline in the other industry's output.[17] The corresponding relation under price uncertainty is derived by solving (14) to (17) for:

$$\partial X_j^*/\partial L = (-1)^h a_{Kh}/A \tag{18}$$

$$\partial X_j^*/\partial K = (-1)^j a_{Lh}/A \tag{19}$$

where $A = a_{L1}a_{K2} - a_{K1}a_{L2}$ and where here, as well as in the remaining parts of the paper, $j = 1,2$ and $h = j+1$ if $j = 1$ and $h = 1$ if $j = 2$. Clearly, the Rybczynski theorem holds without modification for the case of price uncertainty since $A$ is positive or negative depending on the first or the second commodity being relatively labor intensive. In fact, the expressions stated in (18) and (19), although derived from a model with random prices, are exactly the same as in the price-certainty model.[18]

Under the assumption of price certainty, the Stolper-Samuelson theorem states that an increase in a given final commodity's price leads to a rise in real returns on the factor which is used relatively more intensively in the production of that commodity and to a decline in real returns on the other factor. In the model under consideration, final commodity prices are random variables. Consequnetly, the interpretation of the corresponding relations must be modified. First, we relate changes in factor returns to a change in expected price, with all higher central moments held constant. Second, when we talk about real returns we must replace this notion with the concept of expected real returns; for example, expected real returns on labor in terms of the $j$th commodity are given by $w/\mu_j$. After this clarification, we solve for changes in nominal returns:

$$\partial w/\partial \theta_j = (-1)^h a_{Kh}/A \tag{20}$$

$$\partial r/\partial \theta_j = (-1)^j a_{Lh}/A \tag{21}$$

which shows that nominal returns on labor (capital) rise if the $j$th commodity is labor (capital) intensive. The Stolper-Samuelson theorem, which is expressed in terms of real returns, holds as well. If expected real returns are expressed in terms of commodity $h$, then equations (20) and (21) give us that result. If the expected real returns are expressed in terms of commodity $j$, then the Stolper-Samuelson theorem is satisfied if the absolute values of

$$[(\mu_j)/w]/[(\partial w)/(\partial \theta_j)]$$

and

$$[(\mu_j)/r]/[(\partial r)/(\partial \theta_j)]$$

exceed one. Realizing that in equilibrium $\mu_j \geqq a_{Lj}w + a_{Kj}r$, it is easy to see that equations (20) and (21) imply this condition.

From the results presented in (18) to (21) it follows immediately that Paul Samuelson's Reciprocity theorem (1953,

[17] See T. M. Rybczynski, p. 338.

[18] This, however, is not saying that the quantitative values of $\partial X_j^*/\partial L$ and $\partial X_j^*/\partial K$ are identical for certainty and uncertainty models as long as endowments and (expected) final commodity prices are the same. The value of $a_{ij}$ in the uncertainty model may not be the same as in the certainty model, since the degree of uncertainty affects the equilibrium values of $(w/r)$ to which $a_{ij}$ is related.

p. 10) carries over to the model with price uncertainty as well; i.e.,

(22) $$\partial X_j^*/\partial L = \partial w/\partial \theta_j$$

and $$\partial X_j^*/\partial K = \partial r/\partial \theta_j$$

In the uncertainty model we also must explain how a change in the degree of riskiness affects factor returns as expected commodity prices are held constant. Recalling again that an increase in price uncertainty is expressed by $d\gamma_j$, we obtain:

(23) $$\partial w/\partial \gamma_j = (-1)^h a_{Kh} E_j[U_j'(p_j - \mu_j)]/E_j[U_j']A$$

(24) $$\partial r/\partial \gamma_j = (-1)^j a_{Lh} E_j[U_j'(p_j - \mu_j)]/E_j[U_j']A$$

Since $E_j[U_j'(p_j-\mu_j)]/E_j[U_j']$ is negative under the assumptions of our model,[19] rising uncertainty about the value of $p_j$ leads to a reduction in returns on the factor which is used relatively more intensively in the production of commodity $j$ and to an increase in the other factor's returns. In interpreting these results, it must be emphasized, we do not require that the initial position is one of certainty.

Next we turn to the Factor-Price Equalization theorem. Unimpeded trade of final commodities between two countries will lead to the equalization of factor returns in both countries, provided final commodity prices are nonrandom, production functions of firms in a given industry are the same in both countries, and all the other general assumptions as spelled out in Section I apply to both countries.[20] As can easily be seen, a straightforward extension of the Factor-Price Equalization theorem to the case of price uncertainty is not possible, unless some additional rather restrictive conditions are satisfied. Of course, as is true in the certainty model, factor returns are still independent of factor endowments. However, factor returns are crucially dependent on the utility functions and probability assessments of firms. In order to assure equalization of factor returns, we must add the further restrictions that firms in a given industry have identical utility functions *and* probability beliefs in both countries. If these restrictions are not satisfied—for example, if we assume that utility functions and expected prices are the same in both countries, but uncertainty beliefs differ—then the equilibrium factor returns will differ between the two countries.

Finally, we establish the relation between changes in output of a given commodity and its own expected price, with higher central moments held constant,

(25) $$\partial X_j^*/\partial \theta_j = [(\delta_K a_{Lh} + \delta_L a_{Kh})\cdot(a_{Kh} r + a_{Lh} w)]/[wrA^2]$$

and the degree of price uncertainty, with expected price held constant:

(26) $$\partial X_j^*/\partial \gamma_j = \{E_j[U_j'(p_j - \mu_j)]/E_j[U_j']\}\cdot\{\partial X_j^*/\partial \theta_j\}$$

Output of a given commodity responds positively to an increase in its own expected price; again, the expression of (25) is exactly the same as in the certainty case. And output responds negatively to a rise in the degree of price uncertainty, since the term $E_j[U_j'(p_j-\mu_j)]/E_j[U_j']$ is negative. Again, this result is independent of the assumption that the initial position is one of certainty.

A brief summary of my main findings and a few remarks on the nature of the model yielding them conclude this section. I have shown that the Rybczynski effect, the Stolper-Samuelson theorem, and the

[19] We can write $E_j[U_j'(p_j-\mu_j)]/E_j[U_j']$ as $cov(U_j', p_j)/E_j[U_j']$ which must be negative if firms are risk averse.

[20] For a listing of the assumptions and a simple proof of the theorem see Samuelson (1949, p. 182).

positive relation between output and its own (expected) price extend without major modification to models where final commodity prices are random variables. And the Factor-Price Equalization theorem carries over provided we add the assumptions that utility functions and probability assessments of a given industry's firms are identical in both countries. The reason why random prices do not introduce any serious complications is due to the fact that the risk-averse behavior of the individual firms is not reflected in the shape of the long-run industry supply curve, which is the supply curve relevant for the study of economy-wide resource allocations. The assumption that all existing and potential firms of an industry have identical production functions, utility functions, and probability assessments, combined with the condition that in the long run firms are free to enter or leave an industry, implies that the industry's long-run supply curve at constant factor returns is perfectly elastic with respect to expected price. Stated differently, the shape of individual firms' supply curves has no impact on the shape of the industry's long-run supply curve. However, I should add that the utility function and probability beliefs of the representative firm are not completely without influence on the industry supply curve. The minimum expected price at which the industry will produce some positive amount of output depends on the firm's production function, utility function, and probability beliefs, as well as on the prevailing factor returns.

### III. Alternative Models

As was mentioned in the introduction, Rothenberg and Smith (R-S), on the one hand, and Batra (B), on the other hand, have analyzed the question of resource allocation under uncertainty in models which differ from mine in some substantive ways. The distinctive feature of the R-S model is their assumption that firms maximize expected profits rather than expected utility from profits. The distinctive feature of the B models is that resource-allocation changes are derived from the first-order conditions for maximum expected utility on the part of individual firms. The main purpose of this section is to find out how the adoption of these two respective features affects the above-stated trade theorems.[21] Since the introduction of the R-S assumption does not create any serious difficulties, I will concentrate mainly on the Batra paper. In particular, I shall demonstrate that the B-feature can be justified only if the number of firms in a given industry is assumed to be constant. Then I argue that this assumption runs counter to the nature of a long-run competitive equilibrium situation. And finally I prove that the Batra specification implies the partial breakdown of the Rybczynski and Stolper-Samuelson theorems and the complete breakdown of the Factor-Price Equalization theorem.

The assumption that firms are maximizing expected profits,[22] as made by R-S, and not expected utility from profits as in my model, implies that firms are risk indifferent. When combined with the assumption that production functions are homogeneous of degree one, the first-order conditions for maximum expected profits of a representative firm are

$$a_{Lj}w + a_{Kj}r = \mu_j \qquad j = 1, 2 \tag{27}$$

[21] Unfortunately, I cannot just reproduce the results obtained by R-S and B, respectively, and compare them with mine. Their choice of random parameters is different from mine. In order to allow for meaningful comparisons I adopt their respective approaches and introduce the same random parameter, namely final commodity prices, as in my model.

[22] All other assumptions spelled out in Section I are maintained; in particular, it still is assumed that all firms in a given industry have identical production functions and probability beliefs.

In addition to being the first-order conditions for the firm's maximum expected profits, (27) is also the long-run equilibrium condition for the $j$th industry; firms will enter or leave the industry until average cost of production equals expected commodity price for each of them.[23] Consequently, production equilibrium of the whole economy can be described by (27) in combination with the resource constraints stated in (10) and (11) of Section I. Obviously, the only difference between the certainty and uncertainty model is that in the latter expected price of commodity $j$, ($\mu_j$) replaces price ($p_j$). Allowing for this modification, the Rybczynski, Stolper-Samuelson, and Factor Price Equalization theorems carry over to uncertainty models in a straightforward manner. And as we compare these results with those from our model, we can draw the important conclusion that these trade theorems hold for uncertainty models, irrespective of whether firms are risk averse or risk indifferent.

Batra bases his studies of resource allocation under uncertainty on the first-order conditions from the maximization of expected utility and on the economy's full-employment constraints (see, for example, Batra, 1974, p. 53, or 1975a, pp. 260–61). Hence, in our notation and framework, his economy's production equilibrium is stated as:

$$E_1[U_1'(p_1 - a_{L1}w - a_{K1}r)] = 0 \quad (28)$$

$$E_2[U_2'(p_2 - a_{L2}w - a_{K2}r)] = 0 \quad (29)$$

$$a_{L1}X_1^* + a_{L2}X_2^* = L \quad (30)$$

$$a_{K1}X_1^* + a_{K2}X_2^* = K \quad (31)$$

Again we must recall that the output variables of (28) and (29) refer to the representative firm ($X_j$), whereas the output variables of (30) and (31) refer to the whole industry ($X_j^*$). As was the case with my model of Section I, the system of four equations (28)–(31) contains six endogenous variables: $w$, $r$, $X_1$, $X_2$, $X_1^*$, and $X_2^*$. The main difference, however, is that (28)–(31) will in general not yield unique solution values of $w$, $r$, $X_1^*$, and $X_2^*$ in terms of the exogenous variables. The crucial implication of the Batra specification is that the solution values of $w$, $r$, $X_1^*$, $X_2^*$ are not independent of the values of $X_1$ and $X_2$, since $E_j[U_j''(p_j - a_{Lj}w - a_{Kj}r)^2] \neq 0$.[24] Stated differently, the solution values of the above-stated variables are not independent of the number of firms in a given industry.

The B procedure can be justified if one adds the further assumption that the number of firms in a given industry, $n_j$, is predetermined and does not change as industry output varies. Holding $n_j$ constant, we can substitute

$$X_j = X_j^*/n_j \quad (32)$$

into (28) and (29) and solve for $w$, $r$, $X_1^*$, and $X_2^*$ uniquely. While the addition of such an assumption solves one problem, it raises a second, more fundamental one. Holding the number of firms in a given industry constant conflicts with the long-run behavioral description of a perfectly competitive industry. A basic characteristic of perfect competition is that in the long run there is freedom to enter or leave the industry.

Then what do the Batra models describe? Since both factors are mobile between industries, but the number of firms in a given industry is fixed, one could call them "intermediate-run" analyses of resource allocation in a competitive environment. This implies that, at constant factor returns, the industry's intermediate-run supply curve is simply the sum of the in-

[23] This implies that equations (8) and (9) of Section I are replaced by the two equations $E_j(\pi_j)=0$, $j=1,2$.

[24] See the second-order conditions for a maximum, equation (5).

dividual firms' supply curves. The shape of the industry's supply curve, therefore, is directly linked to the shape of the firms' supply curves which, in turn, reflect risk-averse behavior. This stands in sharp contrast to my model, in which the shape of the industry's supply curve does not in any way reflect the degree of risk aversion of firms.

I now proceed with a brief examination of the trade theorems, discussed in Section II, for the intermediate-run model.. After substitution of (32), total differentiation of (28)–(31) yields

$$(33)\quad C_1dX_1^* + D_1a_{L1}dw + D_1a_{K1}dr = D_1d\theta_1 + F_1d\gamma_1$$

$$(34)\quad C_2dX_2^* + D_2a_{L2}dw + D_2a_{K2}dr = D_2d\theta_2 + F_2d\gamma_2$$

$$(35)\quad a_{L1}dX_1^* + a_{L2}dX_2^* - \delta_L(dw/w) + \delta_L(dr/r) = dL$$

$$(36)\quad a_{K1}dX_1^* + a_{K2}dX_2^* + \delta_K(dw/w) - \delta_K(dr/r) = dK$$

where I have used the following abbreviating symbols:

$$C_j = -E_j[U_j''(p_j - a_{Lj}w - a_{Kj}r)^2/]n_j > 0$$

$$D_j = E_j[U_j' + U_j''X_j \cdot (p_j - a_{Lj}w - a_{Kj}r)] > 0$$

$$F_j = E_j\{[U_j' + U_j''X_j(p_j - a_{Lj}w - a_{Kj}r)] \cdot [p_j - \mu_j]\}$$

whose sign is generally indeterminate. But $F_j$ is negative if the initial position is one of certainty, in which case $a_{Lj}w + a_{Kj}r = \mu_j$. The rest of the notation used in (33)–(36) is the same as in Sections I and II, and we again utilize the relation $wda_{Lj} + rda_{Kj} = 0$.

Let us take (33)–(36) and derive expressions for the impact of changing endowments on final commodity production:

$$(37)\quad \partial X_j^*/\partial L = (-1)^h a_{Kh}AD_1D_2/\Delta + C_hD_j\delta_K(a_{Lj}w + a_{Kj}r)/(\Delta wr)$$

$$(38)\quad \partial X_j^*/\partial K = (-1)^j a_{Lh}AD_1D_2/\Delta + C_hD_j\delta_L(a_{Lj}w + a_{Kj}r)/(\Delta wr)$$

where

$$\Delta = [D_1D_2A^2 + D_2C_1(a_{L2}w + a_{K2}r) \cdot (\delta_K a_{L2} + \delta_L a_{K2})/(wr) + C_2D_1(a_{L1}w + a_{K1}r) \cdot (\delta_K a_{L1} + \delta_L a_{K1})/(wr)$$

The sign of $\Delta$ must always be positive. As we proceed with the interpretation of (37) and (38), we can see that in both equations the second term on the right-hand side is positive, whereas the first term's sign depends on relative factor intensities. The first term is positive in (37) if and only if the $j$th commodity is labor intensive, whereas the first term in (38) is positive if and only if the $j$th commodity is capital intensive. As we combine the two terms in each equation we can draw the conclusion that an increase in a given factor's endowment always leads to a rise in output of the commodity which is relatively more intensive in that factor. However, the factor increase does not necessarily lead to a decline in output of the commodity which is relatively less intensive in that factor. Hence, the validity of the Rybczynski theorem is partially impaired.

Next, we look at the responses of factor returns to a change in the expected price of commodity $j$, with higher central moments held constant:

$$(39)\quad \partial w/\partial\theta_j = (-1)^h a_{Kh}AD_1D_2/\Delta + C_hD_j(a_{Lj}\delta_K + a_{Kj}\delta_L)/(\Delta r)$$

$$(40)\quad \partial r/\partial\theta_j = (-1)^j a_{Lh}AD_1D_2/\Delta + C_hD_j(a_{Lj}\delta_K + a_{Kj}\delta_L)/(\Delta w)$$

As was the case for (37)–(38), the second term on the right-hand side of both (39) and (40) is always positive, while the first term's sign depends on relative factor intensities; it is positive in (39) if and only if the *j*th commodity is labor intensive and it is positive in (40) if and only if the *j*th commodity is capital intensive. Consequently, an increase in the expected price of a given commodity always leads to a rise in nominal returns on the factor which is used relatively more intensively in its production. But the expected price increase does not necessarily lead to a decline in nominal returns on the factor which is used relatively less intensively in its production. This implies that the validity of the Stolper-Samuelson theorem is also partially impaired, since in terms of the *h*th commodity—whose expected price has been held constant—expected real returns on a factor may rise even though it is used relatively less intensively in the commodity whose expected price has risen.[25, 26]

A comparison of (37)–(38) with (39)–(40) and the realization that the definitions of $\delta_L$ and $\delta_K$ as stated in Section II imply that $\delta_L w = \delta_K r$ yields

$$\text{(41)} \qquad \partial X_j^*/\partial L = \partial w/\partial \theta_j$$

$$\text{and} \qquad \partial X_j^*/\partial K = \partial r/\partial \theta_j$$

Hence, Samuelson's Reciprocity relation remains valid.

In the intermediate-run model factor returns are no longer independent of endowments. An increase in a given factor's endowment leads to a decline in its own returns, as can be seen from:[27]

$$\text{(42)} \quad \partial w/\partial L = -[C_1C_2\delta_K/r + C_1D_2a_{K2}^2 + C_2D_1a_{K1}^2]/\Delta$$

$$\text{(43)} \quad \partial r/\partial K = -[C_1C_2\delta_L/w + C_1D_2a_{L2}^2 + C_2D_1a_{L1}^2]/\Delta$$

Since factor returns depend on endowments, unimpeded trade between two countries will in general not lead to the equalization of factor returns even if the firms of a given industry have identical production functions, utility functions, and probability assessments. Hence, in the intermediate-run model the Factor-Price Equalization theorem breaks down completely.

The positive relation between output of a given commodity and its own price remains unaffected in the intermediate-run model. This can be seen from

$$\text{(44)} \quad \partial X_j^*/\partial \theta_j = D_1D_2[(a_{Lh}\delta_K + a_{Kh}\delta_L) \cdot (a_{Lh}w + a_{Kh}r)]/[wr\Delta]$$

where both the denominator and numerator are always positive.[28]

I conclude this section with the observation that the introduction of a constraint on the number of firms in a given industry leads to results which differ significantly from those obtained when the number of firms is variable. The differences are a consequence of different industry behavior patterns. In the intermediate-run model there is a direct link between the risk-averse behavior of the individual firm and

[25] It is still true, however, that the wage-rental ratio, $(w/r)$, rises if the *j*th commodity is labor intensive and declines if it is capital intensive. This can easily be derived from (39) and (40).

[26] The response of nominal factor returns to a change in the degree of price uncertainty, holding expected price constant, is $\partial w/\partial \gamma_j = [F_j/D_j]/[(\partial w)/(\partial \theta_j)]$ and $\partial r/\partial \gamma_j = [F_j/D_j]/[(\partial r/\partial \theta_j)]$, where the sign of $D_j$ is positive and that of $F_j$ is indeterminate. If, however, it is assumed that the initial position is one of certainty, then $F_j < 0$ and a rise in price uncertainty always has the opposite impact on factor returns of what the impact of an expected price rise is.

[27] The signs of $\partial w/\partial K$ and $\partial r/\partial L$, on the other hand, are indeterminate. However, it also can be shown that $\partial(w/r)/\partial K > 0$ and $\partial(w/r)/\partial L < 0$.

[28] A change in the degree of uncertainty affects output negatively if the initial position is one of certainty, as can be seen from $[\partial X_j/\partial \gamma_j] = [F_j/D_j][\partial X_j^*/\partial \theta_j]$.

the whole industry. In the long-run models, this link is much weaker, especially if all firms of an industry are identical in every respect. In this case only the minimum expected price at which the industry is going to produce anything at all is dependent on the degree of risk aversion. The shape of the industry supply curve, at constant factor returns, is independent of the firm's risk-averse behavior. However, this result is based on rather strong assumptions. If we relax some of those assumptions, then it is quite possible that even in long-run models the industry supply curve's shape depends on the degree of risk aversion of firms. This, for example, will be the case if we assume that firms of a given industry are identical in every respect except that they exhibit different degrees of risk aversion. In this example, the number of firms in the industry will be a function of expected price and the industry supply curve would be upward sloping. As a result of this modification, the simple extensions of the trade theorems, presented in Section II, to the uncertainty case would no longer be possible.

## REFERENCES

**D. Baron,** "Price Uncertainty, Utility, and Industry Equilibrium in Pure Competition," *Int. Econ. Rev.*, Oct. 1970, *11*, 463–80.

**R. N. Batra,** "Resource Allocation in a General Equilibrium Model of Production under Uncertainty," *J. Econ. Theory*, May 1974, *8*, 50–63.

———, "Production Uncertainty and the Heckscher-Ohlin Theorem," *Rev. Econ. Stud.*, Apr. 1975, *42*, 259–68.

———, *The Pure Theory of International Trade under Uncertainty*, New York 1975.

——— **and A. Ullah,** "Competitive Firm and the Theory of Input Demand under Price Uncertainty," *J. Polit. Econ.*, May/June 1974, *82*, 537–48.

**W. C. Brainard and R. N. Cooper,** "Uncertainty and Diversification of International Trade," in *Food Res. Inst. Stud. in Agr. Econ., Trade and Develop.*, 1968, *8*, 257–85.

**D. M. Holthausen,** "Input Choices and Uncertain Demand," *Amer. Econ. Rev.*, Mar. 1976, *66*, 94–103.

**M. C. Kemp and N. Liviatan,** "Production and Trade Patterns under Uncertainty," *Econ. Rec.*, June 1973, *49*, 215–27.

**H. E. Leland,** "The Theory of the Firm Facing Uncertain Demand," *Amer. Econ. Rev.*, June 1972, *62*, 278–91.

**T. J. Rothenberg and K. R. Smith,** "The Effect of Uncertainty on Resource Allocation in a General Equilibrium Model," *Quart. J. Econ.*, Aug. 1971, *85*, 440–59.

**R. J. Ruffin,** "Comparative Advantage under Uncertainty," *J. Int. Econ.*, Aug. 1974, *4*, 261–73.

**T. N. Rybczynski,** "Factor Endowments and Relative Commodity Prices," *Economica*, Nov. 1955, *22*, 336–41.

**P. A. Samuelson,** "International Factor Price Equalization Once Again," *Econ. J.*, June 1949, *59*, 181–97.

———, "Prices of Factors and Goods in General Equilibrium," *Rev. Econ. Stud.*, Oct. 1953, *21*, 1–20.

**A. Sandmo,** "On the Theory of the Competitive Firm under Price Uncertainty," *Amer. Econ. Rev.*, Mar. 1971, *61*, 65–73.

**S. J. Turnovsky,** "Technological and Price Uncertainty in a Ricardian Model of International Trade," *Rev. Econ. Stud.*, Apr. 1974, *41*, 201–17.

Journal of International Economics 30 (1991) 105–120. North-Holland

# Endogenous labor supply in international trade theory

## Two Alternative Models

Wolfgang Mayer*

*University of Cincinnati, Cincinnati, OH 45221, USA*

Received February 1989, revised version received April 1990

This paper presents two models of endogenous labor supply adjustment. In the first, traditional setup, work hours are flexible and the number of workers is fixed. In the second, work hours are fixed and labor force participation is endogenous. For both models, the impacts of world price, capital endowment, tariff, and technology changes on labor supply, output, and national income are examined, and various 'perverse' responses are highlighted.

## 1. Introduction

The literature on variable labor supply in international trade models is rather short. A seminal paper by Kemp and Jones (1962) has been modified and elaborated by Frenkel and Razin (1975), Martin (1976), Neary (1978), and Martin and Neary (1980). Furthermore, Dixit and Norman (1980) specify a model with endogenous labor, and Woodland (1982) adds to their specification the derivation of some comparative statics results.

A notable feature of the literature is that the findings of Kemp and Jones, and Martin and Neary, on the one hand, do not coincide with the findings in Woodland.[1] Our first task, therefore, is to clarify that the former keep unearned income, from capital ownership and tariff revenues, constant, while the latter endogenizes it. Since income from labor, capital, and tariff revenues adjusts simultaneously in a general equilibrium framework, endogenization of unearned income is important to understand the impact of exogenous shocks to the economy. We, therefore, base our discussion on the assumption of endogenous unearned income.

The first part of the paper employs the usual labor supply model, in which the number of workers is fixed, but work hours can be adjusted. In the labor literature, as surveyed by Johnson and Layard (1986), this assumption is

*Suggestions for revisions by three anonymous referees are gratefully appreciated.

[1]Although Woodland refers to the relevant literature, he neither points these differences out nor explains why they exist.

0022-1996/91/$03.50 

associated with the long run. After confirming and interpreting the results obtained by Woodland on the relationship between commodity price changes, labor supply, and commodity output, we present some new results, namely that: (a) technological progress can lead to a decline in national income even for a small country without distortions; (b) the Rybczynski effect of capital growth becomes magnified; and (c) the income effect of a tariff change differs from that of a world price change. Also, we show that with variable labor supply it no longer is necessary that, in a two-country, two-commodity world, a country with better technology to produce a certain good will export this good and a country with higher propensity to consume a certain good will import this good.

The second part of the paper examines labor supply in a trade model when the number of work hours is fixed but labor force participation is variable. The labor literature associates this model with the short run, and bases the participation decision on differences in peoples' preferences for work. Since the introduction of differences in tastes causes problems of aggregation in trade models, we base the participation decision on differences in peoples' capital ownership and other sources of unearned income. At issue is whether the conclusions from the variable work hours model carry over unscathed. It is found that, while the overall thrust of the arguments is similar, the detailed results are quite different. In particular, the income effect of a world price increase in the labor supply relation depends now on the degree of substitutability between income and leisure; capital growth may result in a decline in national income; and the distribution of tariff revenues alone has a crucial influence on total labor supply adjustments.

Section 2 sets up the variable work hours model, examines the impact of world price, capital endowment, technology and tariff changes on the supply of labor, output, and national income, and sheds light on possible trade patterns under variable labor supply. Section 3 introduces the model with fixed work hours and endogenous labor force participation. It looks at the same type of exogenous shocks and draws comparisons about effects on employment and income.

## 2. Labor supply with variable work hours

### 2.1. The model

Consider a small, open economy with a fixed capital stock, $K$, and a constant number of identical people, $N$, whose work hours are variable. There are two industries, producing $X_1$ and $X_2$, production functions are homogeneous of degree one in labor and capital, markets are perfectly competitive, and factors are fully mobile between industries.

A person's utility depends on consumption of two commodities, $c_1$ and $c_2$, and leisure, $H$, all of which are normal goods. Given the usual properties of the utility function, the aggregate expenditure function of all individuals is:[2]

$$e = e(p, L, U), \tag{1}$$

where $p = \pi(1+t)$ is the domestic price of the second in terms of the first good, $\pi$ is the corresponding world price, $t$ is an ad valorem tariff rate on the second good, $L$ denotes the economy's total labor supply, and $U$ is a social welfare indicator. The expenditure function has the properties:[3] $e_p = C_2$ is the total demand for good two; $e_L = \tilde{w}$ is a person's reservation wage; $e_{LL} > 0$; $1/e_u$ is the marginal utility of income; and $e_{pp} = \partial C_2/\partial p < 0$ is the compensated demand effect of a price change of good 2.

The economy's total value of output produced is:

$$R = X_1 + pX_2 = R(p, L, K), \tag{2}$$

where $R_p = X_2$, $R_L = w$ and $R_K = r$, with $w$ and $r$ denoting returns on labor and capital, respectively. Furthermore, under incomplete specialization, $R_{LL} = R_{KL} = R_{KK} = 0$, and $R_{Lp} = R_{pL} = \partial w/\partial p = \partial X_2/\partial L$ and $R_{Kp} = R_{pK} = \partial r/\partial p = \partial X_2/\partial K$, with signs according to the Stolper–Samuelson theorem.

The small, open economy is in equilibrium when expenditure equals the value of output plus any tariff revenues, $T$, and the reservation wage of workers equals the wage offered by firms:

$$e[\pi(1+t), L, U] = R[\pi(1+t), L, K] + T, \tag{3}$$

$$e_L[\pi(1+t), L, U] = R_L[\pi(1+t), L, K], \tag{4}$$

where tariff revenues, $T$, from imports, $M_2$, are:

$$T = \pi t(e_p - R_p) = \pi t M_2. \tag{5}$$

Substituting (5) in (3), one can solve (3) and (4) for the economy's labor supply, $L$, and welfare, $U$, in terms of world price, $\pi$, capital endowment, $K$, and tariff rate, $t$. This specification relates the supply of labor not just to the wage rate, but also to unearned income from capital ownership and the distribution of tariffs. It follows Dixit and Norman (1980) and is similar to

[2] The aggregate expenditure function, $e = e(p, L, U)$, is derived from the expenditure functions of the $N$ identical individuals. For a representative individual the function is $E = E(p, l, u)$, where $l$ and $u$ are the person's labor supply and utility, respectively. Summing over all $N$ people, one obtains $e = NE(p, L/N, U/N) = e(p, L, U)$, where $L = lN$ and $U = uN$, and $N$ is suppressed since it is constant throughout the analysis.

[3] See Dixit and Norman (1980) for properties of expenditure and revenue functions.

Woodland's, but differs from Kemp and Jones (1962), as well as Martin and Neary (1980) who did not endogenize unearned income.

### 2.2. Labor supply responses to exogenous shocks

#### 2.2.1. Changes in the world price of imports

The relationship between the import good's world price, on the one hand, and labor supply and industry output, on the other hand, has received much attention in the relevant literature. To obtain this relationship, we differentiate (3) and (4) with respect to $\pi$, set $t=0$, hold $K$ constant, and solve for

$$dL/d\pi = [e_{LU}(e_p - R_p) - e_u(e_{Lp} - R_{Lp})]/[e_u e_{LL}]$$

$$= -(m_L/w)M_2 + [L/p][\eta_{Lp} + \eta_{Lw}(\partial w/\partial p)(p/w)], \qquad (6)$$

where $-1 < m_L = w(\partial L/\partial e) < 0$ is the marginal propensity to supply labor (with leisure assumed to be a normal good), and $\eta_{Lp}$, positive (negative) when *leisure* and good 2 are complements (substitutes), and $\eta_{Lw} > 0$ are compensated elasticities of supply of labor with respect to price and wage rate, respectively.[4] The labor supply response to a world price change consists of an *income effect*, denoted by $-(m_L/w)M_2$, and a *substitution effect*, as stated by the second term on the RHS. The income effect of an import price rise is positive as the higher price lowers people's real income which, in turn, reduces demand for leisure and raises the supply of labor. The substitution effect, on the other hand, results from the commodity price increase's direct effect, $\eta_{Lp}$, as well as from the indirect effect, through the wage change, on the supply of labor. The sign of this substitution effect depends on both relative factor intensities in production and whether the import good and leisure are substitutes or complements. Specifically, if the first, the export good is capital intensive in production, $(\partial w/\partial p)(p/w) > 1$, and a substitute for leisure in consumption, which implies that $(\eta_{Lp} + \eta_{Lw}) > 0$, the substitution effect must be positive.[5] Combining income and substitution effects, one can conclude:

*A price rise of the import good definitely raises the country's labor supply if the export good is capital intensive in production and a substitute for leisure in consumption.*

The expression stated in (6) agrees with Woodland (1980, p. 244), but differs from what Kemp and Jones (1962) and Martin and Neary (1980) had

[4]Households supply labor such that $w = e_L(p, L, U)$. At a constant wage rate, $\partial L/\partial e = -(e_{LU}/e_{LL}e_U)$; at constant utility, $\eta_{Lw} = (\partial L/\partial w)(w/L) = w/(e_{LL}L)$ and $\eta_{Lp} = (\partial L/\partial p)(p/L) = -(pe_{Lp})/(Le_{LL})$.

[5]This property is always satisfied for homothetic utility functions.

obtained. The reason is that the latter hold unearned income constant, such that the economy's budget constraint, as given in (3), becomes:[6]

$$e(p, L, U) = LR_L(p, L, K). \tag{3'}$$

Differentiating (3′) and (4) with respect to $\pi$ yields:

$$\mathrm{d}L/\mathrm{d}\pi = [L/\pi]\{[\eta_{Lp} + \eta_{Lw}(\partial w/\partial p)(p/w)] - m_L[(pC_2)/(wL) - (\partial w/\partial p)(p/w)]\}. \tag{6'}$$

The labor supply response to a world price change is indeterminate, as $m_L < 0$ and $\eta_{Lw} > 0$ have opposite signs. Even if the export good is capital intensive in production and a substitute for leisure, rising import prices do not necessarily raise the supply of labor, as in the specification with endogenized unearned income.

The import industry's output response to a world price change is derived by differentiating $X_2 = R_p(p, L, K)$ with respect to $\pi$, accounting for the dependence of $L$ on $\pi$:

$$\mathrm{d}X_2/\mathrm{d}\pi = R_{pp} + R_{pL}(\mathrm{d}L/\mathrm{d}\pi) = (\partial X_2/\partial p) + (\partial X_2/\partial L)(\mathrm{d}L/\mathrm{d}\pi). \tag{7}$$

Although $(\partial X_2/\partial p) > 0$ always, $(\partial X_2/\partial L)(\mathrm{d}L/\mathrm{d}\pi)$ is not necessarily positive, as we know from (6), and therefore perverse output effects can occur. However, under our specification of endogenized unearned income, such a perverse output effect cannot occur if the export good is capital intensive in production and a substitute for leisure in consumption. In the model with fixed unearned income, on the other hand, more detailed restrictions must be imposed to eliminate perverse output effects.

### *2.2.2. Changes in capital endowments*

With fixed unearned income, capital endowment changes have no impact on labor supply. In our model, however, there are clear-cut labor supply

[6]An alternative interpretation of the Kemp–Jones and Martin–Neary setup is that consumers are not identical, but there are two groups, i.e. unearned income recipients and workers. The drawback of this interpretation is that it implies the restriction that the former never work no matter how low their income and the latter always work no matter how high their income.

effects, as can be seen from differentiating (3) and (4) with respect to $K$, with $\pi$ constant and $t=0$:

$$dL/dK = -(e_{LU}R_K)/(e_{LL}e_U) = (r/w)m_L < 0. \tag{8}$$

Since capital growth is accompanied by reduced labor supply, any capital endowment change has a magnified Rybczynski effect when the labor supply is variable. As $R_{pL}$ and $R_{pK}$ have opposite signs, one can see this from

$$dX_2/dK = \partial X_2/\partial K + (\partial X_2/\partial L)(dL/dK) = R_{pK} + R_{pL}(r/w)m_L. \tag{9}$$

Although capital growth is accompanied by a decline in labor supply, immiserizing capital growth will not occur. Recalling that $R$ measures the value of the economy's output, one can see that

$$dR/dK = R_K + R_L(dL/dK) = r(1+m_L) > 0. \tag{10}$$

*Capital growth brings about a decline in labor supply and an enlarged Rybczynski effect. National income responds positively even though labor supply shrinks.*

*2.2.3. Technological advances*

While capital growth always leads to a higher value of output of the economy, the same is not necessarily true for technology advances when the labor supply is variable, as shown next.

Neutral technological advances in a given industry is equivalent to a price increase of its commodity, such that the revenue function of eq. (2) is stated as:[7]

$$R = R(\theta p, L, K), \tag{2'}$$

where $\theta$, initially equal to one, is a technology shift parameter in the second industry's production function. Substituting (2′) into (3) and correspondingly in the $R_L$ function (4), differentiating with respect to $\theta$, while holding $\pi$ and $K$ constant, and solving the system, yields:

$$dL/d\theta = -[pR_pe_{LU} - pR_{Lp}e_U]/[e_Ue_{LL}] = m_LpX_2/w + \eta_{Lw}L(\partial w/\partial p)(p/w), \tag{11}$$

[7]See Jones (1970, p. 76) and Dixit and Norman (1980, p. 138).

which must be negative if the industry that experiences a technology improvement is capital intensive in production. In such a situation:

*A technology advance may reduce the economy's value of output.*

This can be seen from:

$$\mathrm{d}R/\mathrm{d}\theta = pR_p + R_L(\mathrm{d}L/\mathrm{d}\theta) = pX_2(1+m_L) + wL\eta_{Lw}(\partial w/\partial p)(w/p). \tag{12}$$

The technology advance must raise national income if the advancing second industry is labor intensive. However, if the second industry is capital intensive, the industry ($X_2$) is small, or people's propensity to consume leisure is high, national income could decline.[8] The first two of these conditions are likely to be found in less developed countries.

*2.2.4. Tariff changes*

A tariff raises the domestic price of the import good, like a world price increase, but it also generates revenues. As a result, the income effect of the labor supply function becomes different from what it was for a world price change. To show this we substitute (5) into (3), and differentiate (3) and (4) with respect to $t$, while holding $\pi$, $L$, and $K$ constant. Provided there was free trade initially, one can solve for

$$\mathrm{d}L/\mathrm{d}t = L[\eta_{Lp} + \eta_{Lw}(\partial w/\partial p)(p/w)]. \tag{13}$$

Only the substitution effect of the relationship between labor supply and world price changes remains. The income effect disappears for small departures from free trade because the loss in consumer surplus is just equal to the gain in revenues and producer surplus. If, however, there is a tariff already in place, then there will be a positive income effect.[9] However, the magnitude of the income effect does not depend on the level of imports, but on the responsiveness of compensated import demand to the price change. Hence,

*As in the case of a world price increase, a tariff raises the supply of labor if the*

[8]Note that only national income but not welfare declines, since the latter accounts for the gain in leisure too.

[9]The general expression for the labor supply effect of a tariff is:

$$\mathrm{d}L/\mathrm{d}t = \{\pi/\Omega\}\{[L/p][1 - m_2t/(1+t)][\eta_{Lp} + \eta_{Lw}(\partial w/\partial p)(p/w)] + [(m_L/w)\pi t][(\partial C_2/\partial p)|_U - (\partial X_2/\partial p)]\},$$

where

$$\Omega = \{[1 - m_2t(1+t)] - [m_Lt/(1+t)][(\eta_{Lp}/\eta_{Lw}) + (\partial w/\partial p)(p/w)]\} > 0$$

if the system is stable.

*export good is capital intensive in production and a substitute for leisure in consumption. However, if the export good is labor intensive, the directions of labor supply response may differ for tariff and world price changes.*

### 2.3. Trade patterns

A country's trade pattern depends on its production technologies, consumption preferences, and factor endowments relative to the rest of the world. With fixed factor endowments, a country will import a good if, ceteris paribus, it has inferior technology in producing the good, a higher propensity to consume the good, or less of the factor which the good employs relatively intensively. These determinants of trade patterns, however, do not remain unscathed by the introduction of variable labor supply. While it still is true that a capital-abundant country will import the labor-intensive good, a country with an inferior technology to produce or higher propensity to consume a certain good will not necessarily become an importer of this good once trade opens.

Let us describe the autarky equilibria of two countries that differ from each other only with respect to one feature, namely either the level of technology in the second industry or the propensity to consume the second good. We will assess the impact of such a difference on the second good's autarky price, whereby the country with the higher autarky price imports the good once trade starts.

Autarky equilibrium requires that a country's expenditure equals its income, all goods markets clear, and factor markets are in equilibrium:

$$e(p, L, U; \beta) = R(p, L, K; \theta), \tag{14}$$

$$e_p(p, L, U; \beta) = R_p(p, L, K, \theta), \tag{15}$$

$$e_L(p, L, U; \beta) = R_L(p, L, K, \theta), \tag{16}$$

where $\beta$ and $\theta$ are shift parameters, which initially are equal to one for both countries. By increasing one of the parameters for the home country, we can assess how the home country's autarky price will differ and what kind of trade pattern will emerge after the opening of trade.

#### 2.3.1. Differences in production technologies

First, we look at two countries that are completely identical except for the home country having a technologically more advanced second industry. As shown in (2′), the technology parameter enters the revenue function as $R=R(p\theta, L, K)$. Substituting in and differentiating (14)–(16), with $\theta=1$ initially, yields:

$$dp/d\theta=\{e_{LL}[R_p(m_2-1)-R_{pp}]-[(R_{pL}-e_{pL})(R_{Lp}-R_p e_{LU}/e_U)p]\}/\Delta, \tag{17}$$

where $\Delta=-[e_{LL}(e_{pp}-R_{pp})-(e_{pL}-R_{pL})^2]>0$. Although the first term in (17) is negative, biasing the home country towards exporting the second good, the second term is not necessarily positive, as $(R_{pL}-e_{pL})$ and $(R_{Lp}-R_p e_{Lu}/e_u)$ may have opposite signs. Considering both terms, the direct effect of the second industry's technology improvement on excess demand may be more than offset by an indirect effect as the supply of labor adjusts to technological change. As a result:

*It is possible that the country with a technology advantage in the second industry becomes an importer of the second good.*

*2.3.2. Differences in consumption preferences*

In order to describe two countries that are identical except for differences in their preferences for commodity consumption, we write the expenditure function as:

$$e=\varepsilon(p,\beta)g(L,U), \tag{18}$$

where $\beta$ is a taste parameter whose increase raises the country's propensity to consume the second good. It is assumed that $\beta$ is larger than one in the home country, which implies that $m_2$ is larger in the home country since $dm_2/d\beta>0$. No restrictions are imposed on the sign of $\varepsilon_\beta$.

Substitution of (18) into (14) and differentiation of (14)–(16) with respect to $\beta$ yields:

$$dp/d\beta=\{(e_{LL}e_U e)(dm_2/d\beta)$$

$$+[we_\beta][m_2-(\partial w/\partial p)(p/w)][e_{LU}-e_U e_L/e]\}/\Delta p, \tag{19}$$

where $\Delta=-e_U[(e_{pp}-R_{pp})e_{LL}-(e_{pL}-R_{PL})^2>0$, we used $(e_{pU}/e_U)=(e_p/e)=m_2/p=e_{pL}/e_L$, as well as $e_{LL}(e_\beta e_{pU}-e_{p\beta}e_U)=e_{LL}e_U(e_p e_\beta \quad -e_{p\beta}e)/e=-e_{LL}e_U e(dm_2/d\beta)/p$. Although the first term on the RHS of (19) is positive and tends to raise the autarky price of the second good, the second term's sign is indeterminate. The source for a possibly perverse trade pattern is again the labor supply adjustment whose effect on excess demand may more than offset the direct effect from the higher propensity to consume.[10,11]

## 3. Variable labor force participation

### 3.1. The model

In the short run, many workers have limited options for adjusting their work hours. Instead, they can choose whether or not to participate in the labor force. This section describes the economy's labor supply adjustments when labor force participation is endogenized, whereby all workers are assumed to have identical homothetic preferences, but different ownership of capital.

The $i$th person's income, $y^i$, which equals expenditure, $e^i$, is given by:

$$y^i = wL^i + \phi^i(rK + T), \tag{20}$$

where $L^i = L$, the standard work hours, if the person works, $L^i = 0$ if the person does not work, and $\phi^i = (rK^i + \tau^i)/(rK + T)$ is the $i$th person's share of unearned income.

The decision to work is based on comparing utility yielded in the absence of work, $U_0^i$, with what it would be in the presence of work, $U_\omega^i$, where

$$U_0^i = U^i[p, \phi^i(rK + T), 0], \qquad U_\omega^i = U[p, wL + \phi^i(rK + T), L] \tag{21}$$

are indirect utility functions, with price, income, and labor as arguments. The $i$th person will work if $U_\omega^i > U_0^i$, whereby it is assumed that this is always the case when $\phi^i = 0$, and will not work if $U_\omega^i < U_0^i$. For the marginally participating worker, $\tilde{U}_\omega = \tilde{U}_0$. Assuming that the marginal utility of income rises with leisure and falls with income, it follows that $\partial U_0^i/\partial e^i > \partial U_\omega^i/\partial e^i$ at a given value of $\phi^i$; that is, for a person with a given share of the economy's unearned income, the marginal utility of income is greater when he does not work than when he works.

Given that there are $I$ people in the economy, total labor supply, $N$, is:

$$N = IL \int_0^{\tilde{\phi}} f(\phi)\, \mathrm{d}\phi, \tag{22}$$

[10] We can show that $\mathrm{d}p/\mathrm{d}\theta < 0$ and $\mathrm{d}p/\mathrm{d}\beta > 0$ always if the two countries had identical labor supplies rather than just identical population sizes. It is the endogenous adjustment in labor supplies that creates the possibility of perverse trade patterns.

[11] When two countries differ with respect to willingness to work, we can show that the country with the higher willingness to work will export the labor-intensive commodity. No paradoxical trade pattern arises.

where $f(\phi)$ measures the proportion of the population with unearned income share $\phi$, and $\tilde{\phi}$ is determined by:

$$U_0\{p, \tilde{\phi}[rK+T], 0\} = U_\omega\{p, [wL+\tilde{\phi}(rK+T)], L\}. \tag{23}$$

For given values of $K$, $\pi$, and $t$, one can solve for $\tilde{\phi}$ and, thereby, identify the marginally participating worker.

The economy is in equilibrium if, for every person $i$, expenditure equals income, such that

$$e^i[p, L^i, U^i] = wL^i + \phi^i(rK+T), \tag{24}$$

where $e^i = e^i_0$ and $U^i = U^i_0$ when $L^i = 0$, and $e^i = e^i_\omega$ and $U^i = U^i_\omega$ when $L^i = L$. For the marginally participating worker, for whom $\tilde{U}_0 = \tilde{U}_\omega$, one can write (24) as:

$$\tilde{e}_\omega\{p, L, \tilde{U}_0[p, \tilde{\phi}(rK+T), 0]\} = wL + \tilde{\phi}(rK+T). \tag{25}$$

As exogenous changes occur, (24) reveals how they affect the utility of the person who keeps the same work status, either $L^i = 0$ or $L^i = L$, before and after the change. From (25), one can derive how such shocks alter the identity of the marginally participating worker. When initially marginal workers switch their work status, the economy's labor supply changes as $\mathrm{d}N/\mathrm{d}\tilde{\phi} > 0$ from (22).

### *3.2. Labor force participation and supply changes*

#### *3.2.1. Changes in world prices*

Again we first examine the impact of a world price change on the supply of labor. We take (25), set $t = T = 0$, and differentiate with respect to $\pi$, while holding $L$ and $K$ constant. Recalling that $w = R_N$ and $r = R_K$, we obtain:

$$[A-1]rK[\mathrm{d}\tilde{\phi}/\mathrm{d}\pi] = -[(\partial\tilde{e}_\omega/\partial p) + (\partial\tilde{e}_\omega/\partial\tilde{U})(\partial\tilde{U}_0/\partial p)]$$

$$-A[\tilde{\phi}KR_{Kp}] + [LR_{Np} + \tilde{\phi}KR_{Kp}],$$

where $A = (\partial\tilde{e}_\omega/\partial\tilde{U})(\partial\tilde{U}_0/\partial\tilde{e}_0) > 1$ as $\partial U_\omega/\partial e_\omega < \partial U_0/\partial e_0$. To simplify the above expression, we note that $p(\partial\tilde{e}_\omega/\partial p) = p\tilde{C}_{2\omega} = \tilde{\alpha}_\omega C_2$ and $(\partial\tilde{U}_0/\partial p) = -\tilde{C}_{20}(\partial\tilde{e}_0/\partial\tilde{U}_0) = -\tilde{\alpha}_0 C_2(\partial\tilde{e}_0/\partial\tilde{U}_0)$, where $\tilde{C}_{2\omega}$ and $\tilde{C}_{20}$ are the marginal worker's demand for the second good under the alternative states of working and not working, $C_2$ is the economy's aggregate demand for good 2, and $\tilde{\alpha}_0 = (r\tilde{\phi}K)/R$ and $\tilde{\alpha}_\omega = (wL + r\tilde{\phi}K)/R$ are the income shares of the marginal worker when not working and when working, respectively. Furthermore, we insert $[\tilde{\alpha}_0 R_p - \tilde{\alpha}_0(R_{pN}N + R_{pK}K)] = 0$ in the second bracketed term on the RHS and $[\tilde{\alpha}_\omega R_p - \tilde{\alpha}_\omega(R_{pN}N + R_{pK}K)] = 0$ in the third bracketed term on the RHS.[12] This allows us to solve for

$$d\tilde{\phi}/d\pi = \frac{\{[\tilde{\alpha}_0 A - \tilde{\alpha}_\omega] M_2 - wN\tilde{\alpha}_0[A - 1 + L/(N\tilde{\phi})][(R_{Kp}/R_K) - (R_{Np}/R_N)]\}}{(A-1)rK}. \quad (26)$$

As was the case in the variable work hours model, there are again two effects. The first effect, expressed by $[\tilde{\alpha}_0 A - \tilde{\alpha}_\omega]M_2$, however, has now an indeterminate sign, as $A > 1$ but $\tilde{\alpha}_0/\tilde{\alpha}_\omega < 1$. A rise in the import price lowers the real income of the marginal worker in both the working and nonworking situation, and if the income reduction in the latter situation exceeds that in the former, the supply of labor tends to rise.[13] The second effect, on the other hand, again depends on relative factor intensities in production, as $R_{pN}$ and $R_{pK}$ have opposite signs as expressed by the Stolper–Samuelson theorem. As was the case in the variable work hours model, the second effect is positive if the import industry is labor intensive. We can conclude that:

*The labor supply response to a world price increase of the import good is positive if leisure and income are poorly substitutable in consumption and the import good is labor intensive in production.*

### *3.2.2. Changes in capital endowments*

Next, we consider a change in the economy's capital endowment, with constant world prices and no tariffs. Such a change has an impact on the economy's labor supply only if it alters the unearned income of the marginal worker. If, on the other hand, overall capital grows because nonworkers add to their capital endowment, then labor supply will remain unchanged. In this subsection we assume that overall capital endowment changes, but the distribution of capital ownership remains the same. With this in mind, we differentiate (25) with respect to $K$ and find that a person with a smaller unearned income share now becomes the marginal worker; that is:

$$d\tilde{\phi}/dK = -(\phi/K) < 0. \quad (27)$$

Using (22), the total labor supply response to a capital endowment change is:

[12]Note that $R_p$ is homogeneous of degree one in factor supplies.

[13]We can show that this would be the case for utility functions that are homothetic in income and leisure if the elasticity of substitution between income and leisure is less than one everywhere.

$$\mathrm{d}N/\mathrm{d}K = -[N/K][f(\tilde{\Phi})\tilde{\Phi}] \Big/ \left[\int_0^{\tilde{\Phi}} f(\phi)\,\mathrm{d}\phi\right]. \tag{28}$$

This expresses that:

*The labor supply decreases as the economy's capital endowment rises, when the distribution of capital ownership remains unchanged.*

Next, we examine the change in total output, $R$, as the labor supply falls in response to capital growth. From $R = R(p, N, K)$ and (28), we obtain:

$$\mathrm{d}R/\mathrm{d}K = r + w(\mathrm{d}N/\mathrm{d}K) = r\left\{1 - [(wN)/(rK)][f(\tilde{\Phi})\tilde{\Phi}] \Big/ \left[\int_0^{\tilde{\Phi}} f(\phi)\,\mathrm{d}\phi\right]\right\}, \tag{29}$$

and conclude that:

*Different from the variable work hours case, it now is possible that national income declines as the capital stock rises. This outcome is more likely when the group of marginal workers is very large.*

Although capital growth may reduce the value of national income produced, it will not reduce welfare for anybody. Those whose work status does not change as they accumulate more capital will definitely be better off as their income rises, while other things remain unchanged. The marginal worker will be better off too since he also would gain from the rise in income if he did not switch his work status. But since the switch itself is made to improve welfare, he becomes even better off.

### *3.2.3. Changes in the standard work hours*

People are subject to longer standard work hours in some countries than others. We therefore ask the question: Do longer standard work hours affect the rate of labor force participation and total labor supply? Differentiation of (25) with respect to $L$, holding $p$, $r$, $K$, and $w$ constant, yields:

$$\mathrm{d}\tilde{\Phi}/\mathrm{d}L = [w - (\partial\tilde{e}_{\omega}/\partial L)]/[(A-1)rK], \tag{30}$$

where $\partial\tilde{e}_{\omega}/\partial L$ is the flexible work-hours reservation wage of the marginal worker when employed $L$ hours. Since for the marginally participating worker $\partial\tilde{e}/\partial L > w$ at $L$, labor force participation must decline when the standard work hours are raised. However, this does not mean that labor supply necessarily decreases too, as the remaining workers are now employed for longer hours. Without specific information one cannot draw any definite conclusions about the direction of total labor supply change when labor force participation falls in response to a rise in the length of the standard work hour.

*3.2.4. Changes in tariffs*

Labor force participation is crucially linked to the distribution of unearned income. Hence, redistribution of income alone can affect the country's overall supply of labor. For example, one could take income from all the idle, such that some of them have an incentive to become workers, and give it to workers other than the marginal ones, so all current workers continue to participate in the labor force. An increase in labor supply would result.

A tariff raises the issue of distribution of tariff revenues. As in the variable work hours model, we again assume that initially there are no tariffs. However, we do not impose any prior restrictions on how much of tariff revenues goes to a certain person. With this in mind, we return to (25) and rewrite it as:

$$\tilde{e}_\omega\{\pi(1+t), L, U_0[\pi(1+t), \tilde{\phi}rK+\tilde{\lambda}_0\pi M_2 t, 0]\} = wL + r\tilde{\phi}K + \tilde{\lambda}_\omega \pi M_2 t, \qquad (25')$$

where $\tilde{\lambda}_\omega$ and $\tilde{\lambda}_0$ are the shares of tariff revenues marginal workers would receive when working and not working, respectively. Going through the same steps as in the derivation of (26), differentiation of (25′) with respect to $t$ yields:

$$\frac{\mathrm{d}\tilde{\phi}}{\mathrm{d}t} = \frac{\{[A(\tilde{\alpha}_0-\tilde{\lambda}_0)-(\tilde{\alpha}_\omega-\tilde{\lambda}_\omega)]\pi M_2 - wN\tilde{\alpha}_0[A-1+L/(N\tilde{\phi})][R_{Kp}/R_K - R_{Np}/R_N]}{(A-1)rK}. \qquad (31)$$

The substitution effect, reflected in the second bracketed term of (31), is the same as in case of a world price change. The fact that the distribution of tariff revenues is relevant for labor force participation effects is reflected by the terms $(\tilde{\alpha}_0-\tilde{\lambda}_0)$ and $(\tilde{\alpha}_\omega-\tilde{\lambda}_\omega)$ in the income effect. The term $(\tilde{\alpha}_0-\tilde{\lambda}_0)$ expresses the difference between the marginal worker's income share before tariffs and his share of tariff revenues when not working, while $(\tilde{\alpha}_\omega-\tilde{\lambda}_\omega)$ measures the same difference when working. Eq. (31), therefore, reveals that:

*If the marginal worker's shares of tariff revenues are exactly the same as his income shares before tariffs, the income effect is zero and labor supply must rise (fall) if the import good is relatively labor (capital) intensive. However, even if the import good were capital intensive, the government could still raise the labor supply through a tariff if it distributed tariff revenues primarily to workers rather than nonworkers.*[14]

## 4. Concluding remarks

We presented two alternative specifications of labor supply and incorporated them into the standard two-commodity, two-factor trade model of a small country. All results are highlighted in the text and will not be repeated here. However, we like to make some general observations about the role of endogenous labor supply in trade models.

(1) In both models presented, it is important to endogenize unearned income, as its adjustments cause income effects that drastically affect the direction of labor supply and output changes.

(2) In the traditional model with variable work hours, several 'perverse' results other than the relationship between own price and output are possible. In particular, technological progress can lead to a decline in national income, and trade patterns, based on technology or consumption preference differences, may be reversed.

(3) The labor force participation model introduces some new features due to the indivisibility of labor. Most important, redistributions of income can change labor supply and output, even if consumers have identical, homothetic preferences. This implies that trade patterns too can be influenced by the distribution, and not just the total endowment, of capital.

(4) Although we have uncovered several possibilities that 'economic growth' may lead to a decline in national income, this growth is not truly immiserizing. If we considered the impact of growth on the utility of individuals, one could see that people become better off.

[14]This means that $\lambda_0$ becomes small and $\lambda_\omega$ becomes large.

## References

Dixit, A. and V. Norman, 1980, Theory of international trade (Cambridge University Press, Cambridge).

Frenkel, J.A. and A. Razin, 1975, Variable factor supplies and the production possibility frontier, Southern Economic Journal 41, 410–419.

Johnson, G.E. and P.R. Layard, 1986, The natural rate of unemployment: Explanation and policy, in: O. Ashenfelter and R. Layard, eds., Handbook of labor economics II (North-Holland, Amsterdam).

Jones, R.W., 1970, The role of technology in the theory of international trade, in: R. Vernon, ed., The technology factor in international trade (Columbia University Press, New York).

Kemp, M.C. and R.W. Jones, 1962, Variable labor supply and the theory of international trade, Journal of Political Economy 70, 30–36.

Martin, J.P., 1976, Variable factor supplies and the Heckscher–Ohlin–Samuelson model, Economic Journal 86, 820–831.
Martin, J.P. and J.P. Neary, 1980, Variable labor supply and the pure theory of international trade: An empirical note, Journal of International Economics 10, 549–559.
Neary, J.P., 1978, Capital subsidies and employment in an open economy, Oxford Economic Papers 30, 334–356.
Woodland, A.D., 1982, International trade and resource allocation (North-Holland, Amsterdam).

# PART II
# International Trade Policy

# THEORETICAL CONSIDERATIONS ON NEGOTIATED TARIFF ADJUSTMENTS

*By* WOLFGANG MAYER*

## I. Introduction

TRADE liberalization does not come about automatically, but requires full cooperation of all interested countries.[1] Accordingly, the General Agreement on Tariffs and Trade emphasizes the importance of tariff negotiations as a means to expand international trade and to raise economic welfare of the participating parties.[2] After some early small-scale attempts at negotiated tariff reductions within GATT, the Kennedy Round of 1963–67 and the Tokyo Round of 1973–79 represent two major recent efforts at substantial multilateral tariff reductions and a general lessening of quantitative restrictions. These recent negotiating rounds differed from earlier tariff negotiations with respect to both magnitude of tariff cuts[3] and procedure of cutting. Concerning procedures in the Kennedy and Tokyo Rounds, tariff reductions were no longer negotiated on an item-by-item basis, but comprehensive tariff-cutting formulae were adopted.[4] Once agreed upon, such formulae constrain negotiators in their further quest for cutting tariffs.

Although tariff negotiations have played an important role in the actual conduct of international trade relations, trade theory has paid scant attention to the topic of negotiated tariff adjustments. Only H. G. Johnson (1965) discusses tariff bargaining explicitly. His paper's emphasis, however, lies on the role of noneconomic objectives in the formulation of optimal tariff policy. Other writings, on preferential trading by Kemp (1969) and bilateral trading agreements with monopolistic discrimination by Caves (1974), are related to our topic but do not explore the main issue of this paper, namely what outcomes are possible in negotiated tariff settlements.

The purpose of this paper is to develop a theoretical framework within which the possible outcomes of tariff negotiations can be described. These collusive equilibria are then compared with the tariff retaliation equilibrium,[5] on the one hand, and the free trade point, on the other hand. Comparison with the former reveals to what extent countries benefit from tariff negotiations instead of engaging in tariff warfare. Comparison with the

*An anonymous referee's suggestions were most helpful in preparing the final draft of this paper.

[1] On the importance of full cooperation, see Meier (1973), p. 3.

[2] GATT Article XXVIII.

[3] In the Kennedy Round tariffs were to be cut by 50% and in the Tokyo Round by 60%. In addition, nuisance tariffs were to be eliminated completely.

[4] Tariff-cutting formulae define the paths along which tariff cuts are to be negotiated.

[5] Properties of tariff retaliation equilibria are fully discussed in H. G. Johnson (1953–4).

latter serves the purpose of clarifying whether trade negotiations actually can lead to a free trade situation. As will be demonstrated, the paradox may arise that adopting the process of negotiations may prevent attainment of this goal.

Outcomes of tariff negotiations crucially depend on the *relative strengths* of the negotiating parties and the *negotiation rules.* Concerning relative strengths, it is instructive to employ the usual distinction between small and large countries and to contrast the possible negotiated outcomes between more or less equal strengths (large versus large) countries with the negotiated outcomes between very unequal strengths (large versus small) countries. While in both equal and unequal strengths settings all countries can achieve welfare gains through negotiations, the attainment of free trade is not possible in the unequal strengths situation.

With respect to negotiation rules, two situations are distinguished. First, the rule is adopted that the negotiating parties only agree on such tariffs or subsidies which make each country at least as well off as in a retaliation equilibrium and from which no further improvements are possible without reducing welfare of at least one country. This rule may be called an *unconstrained collusive behavior rule.* Second, account is taken of the fact that prior commitments on the part of the negotiating countries may impose further restrictions on their behavior during the negotiations, leading to different forms of *constrained collusive behavior rules.* Historically important is the case that, before the magnitude of the tariff cut is negotiated, countries first decide on a tariff-cutting formula. Since both Kennedy and Tokyo Rounds were marked by fundamental disagreement between the U.S. and the E.E.C. over the kind of tariff-cutting formula to be adopted—the U.S. pushing for linear cuts and the E.E.C. for tariff harmonization[6]—it seems appropriate to illustrate the type of tariff settlements which can come about under these alternative tariff-cutting formulae.

Finally, the paper points out that the outcome of tariff negotiations may depend on a country's ability to redistribute income within the country. First, it is assumed that complete redistribution of income is possible and that, therefore, no distinct interest groups must be accounted for. The country's preferences are described by a standard community utility function. Later, however, account is taken of the case that complete redistribution of income is generally not possible, that distinct interest groups exist, and that the political process enables these groups to have their interests reflected in the policy-maker's preferences. Hence, possible tariff settlements are investigated when a welfare function is introduced which accounts for group interests.

[6] These and other tariff-cutting formulae and their expected impact on economic welfare are examined in Cline *et. al.* (1977).

Section II develops a simple two-country, two-commodity model, in which tariffs and subsidies are the only negotiation instruments.[7] Both countries are assumed to be large, no separate interest groups exist, and the collusive behavior rules are unconstrained. Section III introduces the scenario of one large and one small country engaged in tariff negotiations. Section IV imposes the constraint that negotiations have to proceed according to a given tariff-cutting formula. The general issue of how collusive equilibria may be altered by the existence of such constraints is discussed and differences between linear, U.S.-favored, and harmonizing, E.E.C.-favored, formulae are highlighted. Finally, Section V introduces distinct interest groups within a country and links possible outcomes of tariff settlements to the existence of such interest groups.

## II. Tariff agreements between large countries

### A. *Structure of the model*

A two-commodity, two-country world is postulated in which both home country and rest of the world are large enough to affect the terms of trade and in which import tariffs or subsidies are the only form of trade restrictions. In our analysis, variables referring to the rest of the world are marked by an asterisk whereas no such special symbol is attached to the home country's variables. Assuming that there are no special interest groups, the two countries' respective preferences are represented by strictly quasiconcave community utility functions,

$$U = U(D_1, D_2) \quad \text{and} \quad U^* = U^*(D_1^*, D_2^*), \tag{1}$$

where $D_j(D_j^*)$ denotes consumption of commodity $j$ in the home (foreign) country. Neither commodity is allowed to be inferior in consumption. The two countries' production possibility loci,

$$X_1 = T(X_2) \quad \text{and} \quad X_1^* = T^*(X_2^*), \tag{2}$$

are strictly concave to the origin, with $X_j(X_j^*)$ standing for output of commodity $j$ by the home (foreign) country. Perfect competition and no transport costs are assumed, with the home country importing the second commodity, $M_2 > 0$, and the rest of the world importing the first commodity, $M_1^* > 0$. Finally, the restriction is imposed that all trading equilibria are unique in the relevant range.

Tariff negotiation models are best presented in the tariff rather than commodity space, as the relations between economic welfare and tariff rates are of primary interest. Consequently, the utility functions of equation (1)

[7] The general approach of this paper can also be applied to the case of quotas as negotiation instruments.

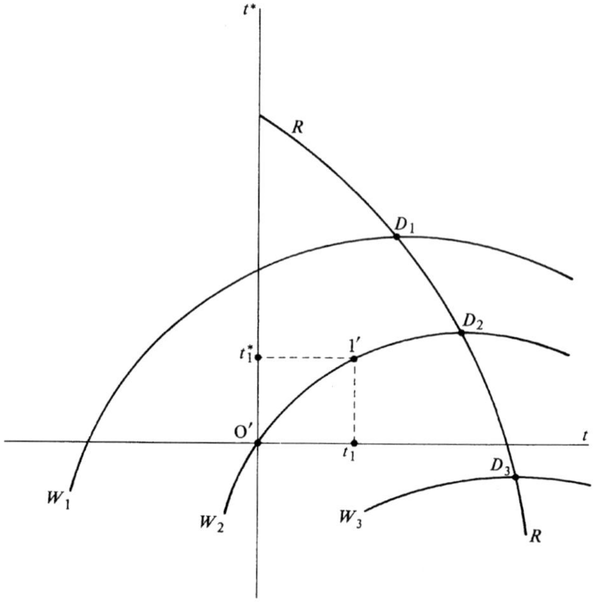


FIG. 1.

are transformed into:[8]

$$W = W(t, t^*) \quad \text{and} \quad W^* = W^*(t, t^*), \tag{3}$$

where $W(W^*)$ stands for the home (foreign) country's maximum utility obtainable given the home country's ($t$) and rest of the world's ($t^*$) tariff rates.

Figure 1 portrays the home country's indifference map in the tariff plane. Each indifference curve is described by the combinations of domestic ($t$) and foreign ($t^*$) tariffs among which the home country is indifferent. These tariff indifference curves are denoted by $W_g$, with the home country becoming better off as subscript g rises in value. An expression for the slope of the tariff indifference curves is derived in Appendix I and stated in (A.7). In general, nothing can be said about the curvature of these curves.

The tariff indifference map of Fig. 1 is derived from the offer curve diagram of Fig. 2. In the latter, each country's offer curve, denoted by $F$ and $F^*$, is shown in three alternative positions corresponding to three different own tariff rates. The subscripts attached to $F$ and $F^*$ are positive for tariffs,

[8] This transformation is possible only if trading equilibria are unique. Throughout the paper the uniqueness assumption is made.

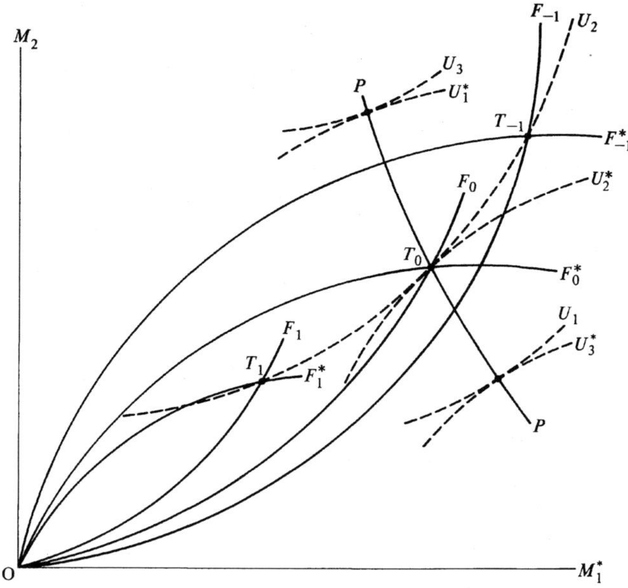


FIG. 2.

negative for subsidies, and zero for unrestricted trade. Trade indifference curves, in turn, are marked with $U_g$ and $U_g^*$ for home country and rest of the world respectively, where again a country is better off the higher the value of subscript g.

Under free trade, the equilibrium trading point in Fig. 2, $T_0$, lies on trade indifference curve $U_2$. As both countries' tariffs are zero, the corresponding point in the tariff plane of Fig. 1 is $0'$. Returning to Fig. 2, it can be seen that point $T_1$ on $U_2$ becomes a trading equilibrium if appropriate tariff rates are imposed, let us say $t_1$ and $t_1^*$. Since the $(t_1, t_1^*)$ combination yields the same utility to the home country as free trade, in Fig. 1 another point on the tariff indifference curve $W_2$, namely point $1'$, can be drawn in. As this procedure is repeated for each combination of $(t, t^*)$ which makes the two countries' offer curves intersect along $U_2$ of Fig. 2, all other points on $W_2$ of Fig. 1 can be derived.

Step-by-step construction of tariff indifference curves reveals that, for nonnegative values of $t$, their slopes are positive, zero, or negative depending on the home country's actual tariff being less than, equal to, or larger than its *optimal* tariff.[9] Of particular interest are the zero-slope points on the

[9] This conclusion also follows from the slope expression of (A. 7).

various tariff indifference curves, as they indicate the home country's optimal tariff rates corresponding to all possible tariff rates prevailing in the rest of the world. These zero-slope points of the tariff indifference curves, marked by $D_g$, are connected in Fig. 1 to trace out the *RR* locus. This locus is drawn in as it provides essential information in determining the tariff war equilibrium between the two countries, the worst possible alternative to a negotiated settlement.[10]

B. *Outcomes of negotiated tariff settlements*

The two countries' tariff negotiators meet with the objective of adjusting tariffs or granting subsidies such that both countries become at least as well off as they would be in a conflict or tariff war equilibrium and that no further welfare gains can be made by either country without the other one losing. Hence, an *unconstrained collusive behavior rule* is postulated. Tariff (subsidy) combinations which satisfy these rules are generally not unique, but determine the core of the tariff agreement.[11]

Formally stated, each country strives for a tariff (subsidy) combination $(t, t^*)$ which maximizes its utility, given the utility level of the other country and given that each country's newly attained utility level is at least as high as that prevailing at the conflict equilibrium, also called threatpoint. Hence, we

$$\begin{aligned} &\max\ W(t, t^*) && \text{and} \quad \max\ W^*(t, t^*) \\ &\quad \text{s.t.}\ W^*(t, t^*) = \bar{W}^* && \quad\quad \text{s.t.}\ W(t, t^*) = \bar{W} \\ &\quad\quad W \geqq \underline{W} && \quad\quad\quad W \geqq \underline{W} \\ &\quad\quad W^* \geqq \underline{W}^* && \quad\quad\quad W^* \geqq \underline{W}^*, \end{aligned} \tag{4}$$

where $\bar{W}$ and $\bar{W}^*$ are predetermined constants, and $\underline{W}$ and $\underline{W}^*$ are the two countries' respective threatpoint utility levels.

The core of the tariff agreement is most conveniently determined by employing the tariff indifference curve apparatus of the previous subsection. Figure 3 portrays the tariff indifference map of both home country and rest of the world, whereby the latter's tariff indifference curves are derived from the offer curve diagram of Fig. 2 analogous to the previously discussed derivation of the home country's tariff indifference curves.[12] Figure 3 also depicts both countries' optimal tariff curves, *RR* and $R^*R^*$, and the locus of points along which the two countries' tariff indifference curves are tangent to each other, *CC*.

[10] The properties of *RR* and its positioning relative to the corresponding locus of the other country are discussed in H. G. Johnson (1953).

[11] Here and elsewhere in the paper the term 'core' is used to define the set of final settlements which result in no further recontracting.

[12] A slope expression for the rest of the world's tariff indifference curve is stated in (A.8) of Appendix I.

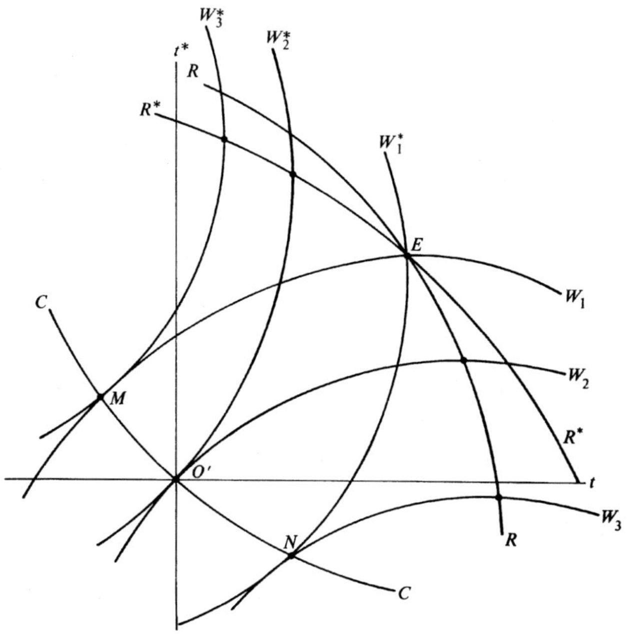


FIG. 3.

The condition that no further tariff (subsidy) changes can raise one country's welfare without lowering the other country's welfare implies that only tariff (subsidy) combinations along the *CC* locus represent possible outcomes of the tariff negotiations. The second collusive behavior rule is that the tariff agreement makes each country at least as well off as at the conflict equilibrium. The conflict equilibrium[13] represents the threatpoint, as tariff warfare is the worst alternative to a cooperative solution. In Fig. 3, this threatpoint is marked by *E*, where the two countries' optimal tariff curves intersect.[14] Combining the two collusive behavior rules, the tariff settlement must consist of tariff (subsidy) combinations which lie on the *MN* segment of the *CC* locus.

[13] It is assumed that the conflict equilibrium is unique. As H. G. Johnson (1953–4) points out, however, multiple equilibria and tariff cycles cannot be excluded.

[14] Point *E* represents, of course, a non-cooperative Nash equilibrium. A Nash-cooperative solution could be obtained at a determinate point on the *CC* locus between *M* and *N* by maximizing $[W(t, t^*) - \underline{W}][W^*(t, t^*) - \underline{W}^*]$ with respect to $t$ and $t^*$.

Several features of the possible outcomes of tariff negotiations are noteworthy:

1. The agreement must yield a tariff-subsidy combination which satisfies the relation

$$t + t^* + tt^* = 0. \tag{5}$$

This relation of equation (5) must hold since along the Pareto-optimal *CC* locus of Fig. 3, just as along the Pareto-optimal *PP* locus of Fig. 2, the domestic prices of the second in terms of the first commodities in the two countries must be the same. But since $p = \pi(1+t)$ and $p^* = \pi/(1+t^*)$, where $\pi$ denotes the international terms of trade, equating $p$ with $p^*$ yields equation (5). Condition (5) states that there exists an infinite number of tariff-subsidy combinations of the two countries which lead to Pareto optimality. If one country imposes a tariff the other country must offer a subsidy, and raising of the tariff requires that the subsidy is increased at a decreasing rate in order to maintain Pareto optimality.

2. Tariffs by both countries cannot be the outcome of the negotiations. As is clear from equation (5), as well as from the position of the *MN* segment in Fig. 3, the agreement must stipulate either free trade for both or a tariff by one and a subsidy by the other country.

3. Free trade may not be attainable through negotiations. Although the free trade point must be situated on the *CC* locus of Fig. 3, it is not necessarily a point on the crucial *MN* segment of the *CC* locus. Depending on the position of the threatpoint, it is possible that one, but not both countries, are better off at the threatpoint than in free trade.[15]

4. Negotiated tariff settlements are superior to the outcome of a tariff war. The conflict equilibrium (*E*) results from a situation where the two countries' tariff indifference curves are locally perpendicular to each other, whereas they must be tangent to each other along the *CC* locus. Hence, there must be a point on *CC* which dominates point *E*.

## III. Tariff agreements between a large and a small country

So far it has been assumed that both negotiating parties are sufficiently large to affect the international terms of trade. The present section deals with an alternative setting, namely where only one country is large whereas the other country is too small to have any control over the international terms of trade. This represents the situation of very unequal strengths negotiating parties.

It is assumed here that the rest of the world is still large whereas the home country is small. Figure 4 illustrates the resulting bargaining situation in the

[15] H. G. Johnson (1953–4) emphasizes that one country may be better off under trade warfare than free trade.

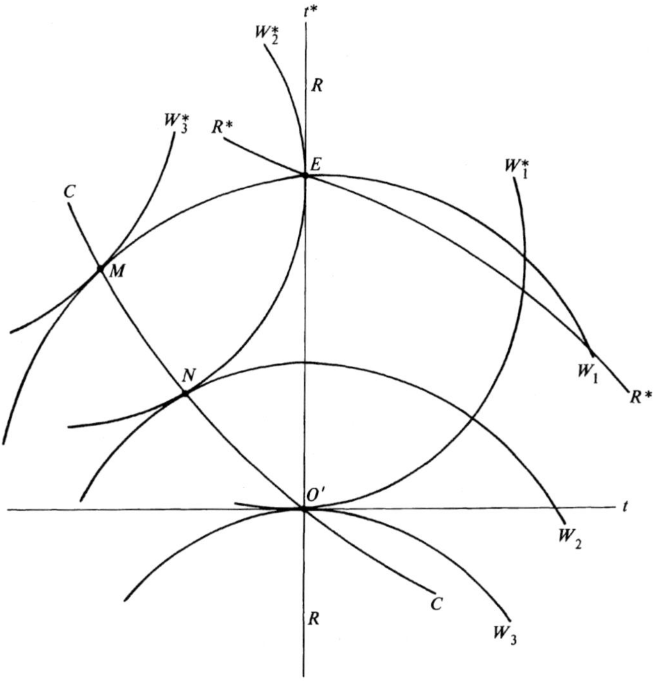


FIG. 4.

tariff plane. For the rest of the world, which faces the home country's less than perfectly elastic offer curve, shapes and positioning of tariff indifference curves ($W_g^*$) and optimal tariff locus ($R^*R^*$) are similar, although not exactly the same, as in Fig. 3.[16] For the home country, which faces the rest of the world's perfectly elastic offer curve, the optimal tariff locus ($RR$) now runs along the $t^*$ axis, as free trade is optimal for a small country no matter what the tariff level of the opposing large country is. The resulting threatpoint, therefore, is determined by the rest of the world's optimal tariff rate when there is no tariff in the home country, namely at point $E$.

Even though one country is small, tariff negotiations still offer the opportunity for increased economic wellbeing to both countries. Given the unconstrained collusive behavior rules that both countries become at least as well off as at the threatpoint and that neither country can make further gains without losses to the other, the possible outcomes of the tariff negotiations

[16] Note, however, that at $t = t^* = 0$ the slope of the rest of the world's tariff indifference curve is zero.

are again described by the tariff-subsidy combinations along *MN*. Considering these possible tariff settlements between a small and a large country, two points are particularly noteworthy:

1. A small country is not best off if it unilaterally adopts a free trade policy. The small country can gain from tariff negotiations if it grants an import subsidy. The frequently made statement that free trade is best for a small country only applies to noncollusive situations.

2. The tariff settlement cannot lead to a free trade policy by either country. Compared to the noncollusive warfare equilibrium, the small country will grant import subsidies rather than maintain a free trade regime and the large country will agree to a lower, but always positive, tariff.

## IV. Negotiations under collusive behavior constraints

The Kennedy Round's approach to tariff negotiations differed from earlier attempts at reducing tariffs in that it tried to substitute a simple tariff-cutting formula for the traditional item-by-item bargaining over tariffs. As Evans (1971) points out, these negotiating rules implied a two-stage negotiation procedure. First, a tariff-cutting formula had to be agreed upon, which would automatically apply to all commodities for which no explicit exception was allowed. Second, the magnitude of tariff reductions according to this formula had to be negotiated, as well as the precise nature of the exceptions. This two-step procedure, again adopted in the Tokyo Round,[17] was preferred to the item-by-item approach, as it allowed for a far more comprehensive tariff agreement.

In both Kennedy and Tokyo Rounds, fundamental disagreement about the specific form of the tariff-cutting formula developed between the U.S. and the E.E.C. countries. The U.S. favored linear cuts of tariffs implying that, regardless of the initial tariff level, all tariffs should be cut by the same percentage. The E.E.C., on the other hand, favored harmonizing cuts, implying that tariffs whose initial values are higher should be reduced by a larger percentage.[18]

Acceptance of the principle of tariff-cutting formulae means that the path of tariff adjustments is to be agreed upon first and a specific point on the path is to be negotiated later. In this second stage of negotiations, deciding on the magnitude of the tariff adjustments, the agreed-upon formula represents a further constraint on possible negotiated settlements. Consequently, the previously stated collusive behavior rules are further constrained by the existence of a tariff-cutting formula.

The purpose of this section is to contrast the previously established

[17] See Cline *et. al.* (1977).

[18] See Meier (1973) for the Kennedy Round and Cline *et. al.* for the Tokyo Round.

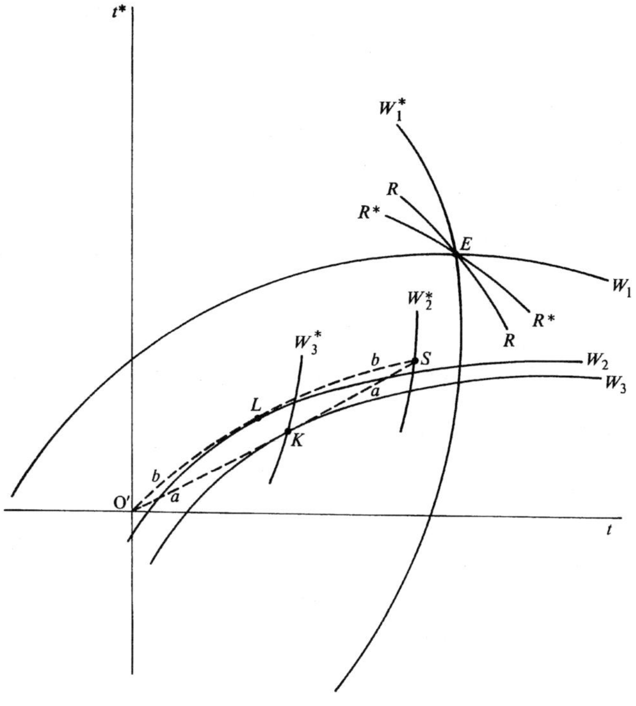


FIG. 5.

conclusions about negotiated tariffs cuts with the possible outcomes when both parties agree on the principle of working with tariff-cutting formulae. In particular, the implications of linear and harmonizing formulae are highlighted.

Possible outcomes of tariff negotiations are illustrated in Fig. 5. As in Section II, it again is assumed that two large countries negotiate, and therefore tariff indifference curves ($W_g$, $W_g^*$), optimal tariff loci ($RR$, $R^*R^*$), and threatpoint ($E$) are drawn just as in Fig. 3. In addition, the initial tariff combination is indicated by point $S$.

The U.S. proposal of linear tariff cuts required that both countries' tariffs be cut at the same rate, whereby the magnitude of the reduction was subject to further negotiations; i.e.

$$\mathrm{d}t/t = \mathrm{d}t^*/t^* = \alpha, \tag{6}$$

where $\alpha < 0$ refers to the rate at which tariffs are to be adjusted. Given the linear rule and the initial tariff or starting point $S$, the final agreement must lie somewhere on the *aa* ray of Fig. 5. That each country is at least as well off as at the threatpoint ($E$) is clearly satisfied at all points between $S$ and $0'$. Furthermore, the condition must be satisfied that neither country can make further gains without the other country losing. Applying this rule to the *aa* locus, it is revealed that moving from $S$ to $K$ improves the welfare of both countries. At $K$, the *aa* locus is just tangent to the home country's tariff indifference curve. Hence, moving beyond $K$ towards $0'$ raises only the rest of the world's welfare, whereas it lowers the home country's welfare. Consequently, under the linear-constraint collusive behavior rule, the tariff settlement is reached at some point along the $K0'$ segment of *aa*.

The E.E.C. proposal of harmonizing tariff cuts implied that higher tariffs are to be cut at a faster rate than lower tariffs. Among different possible specifications, we adopt a formula used in Cline *et. al.* (1977) which at one point was actually proposed by the E.E.C.:

$$dt/t = -t \quad \text{and} \quad dt^*/t^* = -t^*, \tag{7}$$

where this formula may be applied a number of times in iterative fashion, with the exact number of iterations subject to negotiations. Assuming that the home country's initial tariff is higher than that of the rest of the world, as indicated by point $S$, the path of possible settlements which satisfy equation (7) is traced out by the *bb* locus. Again moving from the initial tariff position $S$ towards the origin, welfare increases for both countries from $S$ to $L$, but rises for the rest of the world only and declines for the home country from $L$ to $0'$. Hence, the harmonization constraint on collusive behavior puts the tariff settlement somewhere on the $L0'$ segment of the *bb* locus.

Concerning tariff negotiations under the above-stated constraints, two features should be emphasized:

1. Under both linear and harmonizing constraints, the eventual tariff agreement must be one of free trade or tariffs by both countries. This differs drastically from the model with unconstrained collusive behavior rules for which tariffs by both countries was not a possible solution.

2. The U.S. position of linear and the E.E.C. position of harmonizing tariff cuts were strong reflections of their respective economic interests. As U.S. tariffs were on the average higher than E.E.C. tariffs—in 1973, the average tariff rate on all imports was 7.1% for the U.S. and 4.2% for the E.E.C.—point $S$ in the diagram quite accurately reflects the initial position before the Tokyo Round, if the U.S. is called the home country and the E.E.C. is the rest of the world. Looking at the two tariff adjustment paths from the U.S. (E.E.C.) point of view, for every point on the harmonization (linear) path there exists at least one point on the linear (harmonization) path which yields at least as high a level of utility. Hence, the U.S. and E.E.C. choices of tariff-cutting formulae were strong reflections of their respective economic preferences.

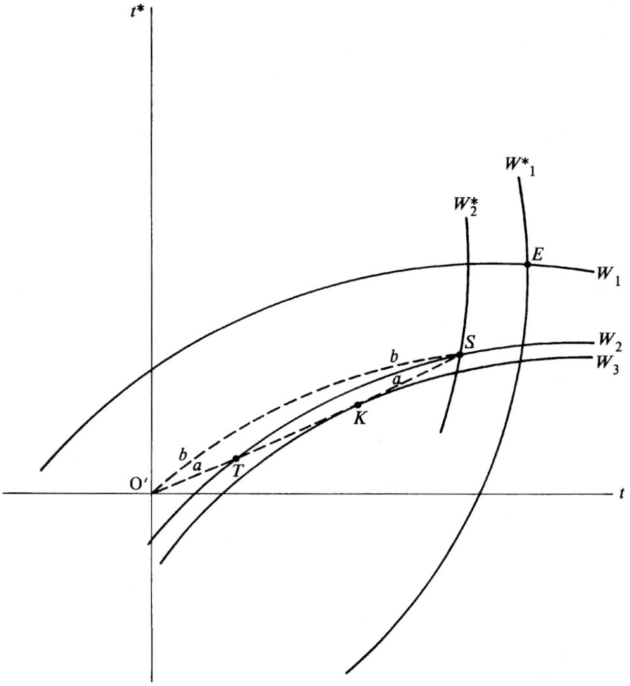


FIG. 6.

Both linear and harmonizing formulae, as defined in equations (6) and (7), are tariff-cutting formulae. Once accepted, tariffs can not be raised any more. This, in effect, implies that the prevailing tariff levels, indicated by point $S$, rather than point $E$, represent the actual threatpoint when the magnitude of tariff adjustments is negotiated. In this situation, neither country will agree to a new tariff combination which makes it worse off than it was at the initial point $S$.

The explicit acceptance of the constraint that no tariffs will be raised has important implications for the possible outcomes of negotiations. First of all, the set of possible outcomes may be considerably smaller than in the case where $E$ is the threatpoint. As illustrated in Fig. 6, it is quite possible that free trade is not anymore attainable although it was with $E$ as threatpoint. Hence, one country may prefer the *status quo*, with the constraint that no tariffs are to be raised, to free trade. Second, one or all tariff-cutting formulae may be unacceptable to a given country. For example, Fig. 6 illustrates that the harmonization formula is totally unacceptable to the home country. The *status quo* point $S$ is superior to every other point on the harmonization locus $bb$. On the other hand, along the linear adjustment locus, $aa$, all points between $S$ and $T$ are superior to point $S$. Hence, the home country will negotiate tariff reductions only if the linear (or a less harmonizing) formula is adopted.[19] For the linear formula, the outcome must lie on segment $KT$, as neither country can make further gains without the other one losing along this segment.

## V. Tariff agreements in the presence of interest groups

In many countries there exist interest groups whose incomes are diversely affected by tariff adjustments and who, therefore, try to influence the negotiation process. Given this scenario, the issue arises as to how their presence affects the general properties of the tariff agreement.

The current section introduces interest groups in the most elementary fashion. Only the home country is assumed to have distinct interest groups, whereby the number of groups is limited to two. Compensating income transfers are not possible between groups and their respective utility functions and the aggregate welfare function are assumed to be of such forms that only total economic welfare, but not aggregate demand and trade patterns, are affected by the redistribution of income in the home country. For the rest of the world, on the other hand, preferences are, as in equation (1), still represented by a community utility function. Finally, it again is assumed that both countries are large and that only unconstrained collusive behavior rules exist.

For the home country, the community utility function of equation (1) is now replaced by the social welfare function

$$Z = Z(U^1, U^2), \tag{8}$$

where $Z$ is a welfare index for the home country which depends on the two groups' utilities as denoted by $U^k$, $k = 1, 2$. The underlying utility function of group $k$,

$$U^k = U^k(D_1^k, D_2^k) \tag{9}$$

is not just strictly quasiconcave but also homothetic, with one group's function being a monotonic increasing transformation of the other group's function. Consequently, both groups have identical linear income-consumption paths, and aggregate demand for a given commodity is independent of the distribution of income. From these properties it follows that

$$D_j^1 = \gamma D_j \quad \text{and} \quad D_j^2 = (1-\gamma) D_j, \tag{10}$$

[19] This situation is likely to occur when countries try to lower tariffs in successive tariff rounds. The outcome of a given tariff round may put one country in a position where it cannot gain anymore as tariffs are cut according to a given formula.

where $D_j$ is aggregate demand for commodity $j$ in the home country, $D_j^k$ is group $k$'s demand for commodity $j$, and $\gamma$ is the first group's income share. Concerning the income share, it most generally is assumed that it depends on the two respective tariff rates; i.e.

$$\gamma = \gamma(t, t^*) \tag{11}$$

where at least one of $\partial\gamma/\partial t = \gamma_t$ and $\partial\gamma/\partial t^* = \gamma_{t^*}$ is assumed to be nonzero.

The home country, where two distinct interest groups exist, and the rest of the world, where no such interest groups exist, again aim at finding tariff (subsidy) combinations which allow no further improvements of one country's welfare without hurting the other and which are superior to the threatpoint. The first of these conditions, Pareto optimality, is satisfied provided

$$t + t^* + tt^* = S\Phi,^{20} \tag{12}$$

where $S$, the marginal rate of substitution between group one's income share and overall income, is nonzero and $\Phi$, an expression further elaborated in Appendix II, is generally also nonzero. Hence, in general $S\Phi \neq 0$ and therefore the positioning of the Pareto-optimal tariff (subsidy) locus with interest groups, as described by equation (12), considerably differs from that of the case without interest groups, as stated in equation (5). Most importantly, as shown in Appendix II, $S\Phi \neq 0$ implies that free trade can no longer be an outcome to tariff negotiations.

Figure 7 portrays three alternative positions of the Pareto-optimal tariff-subsidy combinations under different assumptions about the impact of tariffs on the distribution of income and overall welfare. If, in the relevant range of tariffs and subsidies, $S\Phi$ is either positive or negative everwhere, free trade cannot be an outcome to tariff negotiations. On the other hand, tariffs by both countries or subsidies by both countries may very well be negotiated. Hence, in the presence of interest groups the possible negotiation solutions are quite different from what they were in the case of no interest groups. This latter case is also shown in Fig. 7, namely in form of the $CC$ locus when $S\Phi = 0$.

The alternative $CC$ loci of Fig. 7 only describe Pareto optimality. Which segment of a given locus contains the range of possible tariff (subsidy) outcomes also depends on the location of the threatpoint. Since this point's position crucially depends on the detailed assumptions about the rate of substitution between the distribution of income and overall income, etc., it and the corresponding tariff indifference curves are not explicitly drawn to

[20] Equation (12) is derived in Appendix II, where it is stated as (A.14). It may be worth noting that in the special case where the distribution of income depends on the *domestic terms of trade only*, $S\Phi \gtrless 0$ depending on whether a rise in the domestic price of the import commodity leads to a welfare-increasing or decreasing redistribution of income.

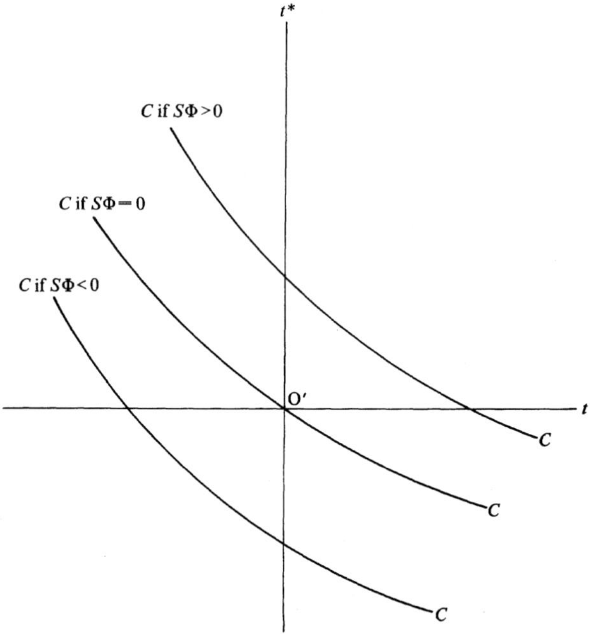


FIG. 7.

avoid unnecessary cluttering of the diagram. Our assertion, that free trade will generally be unattainable in the presence of interest groups, is independent of the position of the threatpoint

## VI. Conclusions

The paper developed a simple theoretical framework for examining the outcomes of tariff negotiations and emphasized the importance of country size, negotiation rules, and domestic interest groups in determining the general nature of possible tariff agreements. The main findings are summarized under the following four points:

1. For large countries, with no separate interest groups, and with no special constraints on negotiation procedures, negotiations must lead to a Pareto-optimal outcome. However, the outcome is not necessarily free trade. In fact, free trade may be unattainable. Whatever the negotiated agreement may be, it will be superior to a tariff configuration which results from confrontations.

2. When large and small countries negotiate tariff reductions, free trade

cannot be the outcome. The commonly suggested strategies for small countries to opt for free trade and for large countries to impose 'optimal tariffs' is equivalent to a tariff-war outcome. This outcome is inferior to a collusive agreement with subsidies of the small and lower than 'optimal' tariffs by the large country.

3. Tariff-cutting formulae, once accepted by all parties, impose severe constraints on the possible outcomes and free trade is unlikely to be attained. The paper also sheds light on why the U.S. favored linear and the E.E.C. favored harmonizing tariff cuts in both Kennedy and Tokyo Rounds.

4. In the presence of interest groups negotiations generally will not lead to free trade.

*University of Cincinnati,*
*Cincinnati, Ohio* 45213

## APPENDIX I

Here an expression for the slope of the home country's tariff indifference curve is derived, the corresponding expression for the rest of the world is stated, and the condition for Pareto-optimal tariff (subsidy) combinations is developed.

First, it is convenient to restate the home country's utility function of equation (1) in its indirect form:

$$V = V(p, Y), \tag{A.1}$$

where $V$ is the home country's maximum attainable utility, given $p$, the home country's price of the second in terms of the first commodity, and $Y$, its income in terms of the first commodity. Recalling the meaning of the symbols $\pi$, $t$, $X_i$, and $M_2$, as stated in the main text, $p$ and $Y$ are described by:

$$p = \pi(1+t)$$
$$Y = X_1 + pX_2 + \pi t M_2. \tag{A.2}$$

Substitution of (A.2) in (A.1), total differentiation of (A.1), use of Roy's identity $V_p = -D_2 V_Y$ and of the relation $dX_1 + p\,dX_2 = 0$ along the production transformation curve, and some simplifying manipulations yield:

$$dV = V_y(-M_2\,d\pi + \pi t\,dM_2). \tag{A.3}$$

Following Jones (1969), the import functions are specified as

$$M_2 = M_2(\pi, t)$$
$$M_1^* = M_1^*(\pi, t^*), \tag{A.4}$$

where $\partial M_2/\partial\pi < 0$, $\partial M_1^*/\partial\pi > 0$, $\partial M_2/\partial t < 0$, and $\partial M_1^*/\partial t^* < 0$. The balance of payments equation is

$$M_1^* = \pi M_2. \tag{A.5}$$

Differentiating (A.4) and (A.5) allows us to solve for

$$dM_2 = \{[(\partial M_2/\partial t)(\epsilon^* - 1)]\,dt + [\epsilon(\partial M_1^*/\partial t^*)/\pi]\,dt^*\}/\Delta$$
$$d\pi = \{[\pi(\partial M_2/\partial t)/M_2]\,dt - [\pi(\partial M_1^*/\partial t^*)/M_1^*]\,dt^*\}/\Delta,$$

where $\epsilon = -(\pi/M_2)(\partial M_2/\partial\pi) > 0$, $\epsilon^* = (\pi/M_1^*)(\partial M_1^*/\partial\pi) > 0$, and $\Delta = \epsilon + \epsilon^* - 1 > 0$ if the Marshall-Lerner conditions are satisfied. Substitution of the $dM_2$ and $d\pi$ expressions in (A.3) yields:

$$dV = \frac{V_Y M_1^*}{\Delta}\left[\frac{\beta(1+t-t\epsilon^*)}{(1+t)}dt - \frac{\beta^*(1+\epsilon t)}{(1+t^*)}dt^*\right], \tag{A.6}$$

where $\beta = -[(1+t)/M_2][\partial M_2/\partial t] > 0$ and $\beta^* = -[(1+t^*)/M_1^*][\partial M_1^*/\partial t^*] > 0$.

The slope of the home country's tariff indifference curve is obtained from (A.6) by setting $dV = 0$ and solving for:

$$\left.\frac{dt^*}{dt}\right| = \frac{\beta(1+t-t\epsilon^*)/(1+t)}{\beta^*(1+t\epsilon)/(1+t^*)}. \tag{A.7}$$

The slope of the rest of the world's tariff indifference curve can be derived analogously. Here it is simply stated as

$$\left.\frac{dt^*}{dt}\right|^* = \frac{\beta(1+t^*\epsilon^*)/(1+t)}{\beta^*(1+t^*-t^*\epsilon)/(1+t^*)}. \tag{A.8}$$

Pareto-optimal tariff (subsidy) combinations require that the two countries' tariff indifference curves are tangent to each other. Equating (A.7) with (A.8) yields

$$(t + t^* + tt^*)\Delta = 0, \tag{A.9}$$

which reduces to equation (5) of the main text, as $\Delta > 0$.

## APPENDIX II

Here we derive equation (12) of the main text, which describes the Pareto-optimal tariff (subsidy) combinations when there are two distinct interest groups in the home country.

The home country's welfare function is now

$$Z = Z\{V^1[p, \gamma Y], V^2[p, (1-\gamma)Y]\}, \tag{A.10}$$

where the group utility functions, $V^1$ and $V^2$, are written in their indirect form and where

$$\gamma Y = Y^1 \quad \text{and} \quad (1-\gamma)Y = Y^2 \tag{A.11}$$

are the two groups' respective incomes. Substitution of (A.2) in (A.10), total differentiation of the same equation, use of Roy's identities $V_p^1 = -D_2^1 V_Y^1$ and $V_p^2 = -D_2^2 V_y^2$ for indirect utility functions, and considering that for homothetic group utility functions as assumed $D_2^1 = \gamma D_2$ and $D_2^2 = (1-\gamma)D_2$, yields

$$dZ = G_Y(-M_2 d\pi + \pi t\, dM_2) + G_\gamma\, d\gamma, \tag{A.12}$$

where $G_Y = Z_{V^1} V_Y^1 \gamma + Z_{V^2} V_Y^2 (1-\gamma) > 0$ and $G_\gamma = (Z_{V^1} V_Y^1 - Z_{V^2} V_Y^2)Y$ which is greater than, equal to, or less than zero depending on whether an increase in group one's income share raises, leaves unchanged, or lowers overall welfare.

As we substitute the expressions for $dM_2$ and $d\pi$, as derived in Appendix I, and differentiate $\gamma$, as defined in equation (11), with respect to $t$ and $t^*$, we obtain:

$$dZ = \left\{\frac{G_Y M_1^*}{\Delta}\left[\frac{\beta(1+t-t\epsilon^*)}{(1+t)}\right] + G_\gamma \gamma_t\right\} dt - \left\{\frac{G_Y M_1^*}{\Delta}\left[\frac{\beta^*(1+t\epsilon)}{(1+t^*)}\right] - G_\gamma \gamma_{t^*}\right\} dt^*.$$

Setting $dZ = 0$, one can solve for the slope of the home country's tariff indifference curve

$$\left.\frac{dt^*}{dt}\right| = \frac{[G_Y M_1^* \beta(1+t-t\epsilon^*)]/[\Delta(1+t)] + G_\gamma \gamma_t}{[G_Y M_1^* \beta^*(1+t\epsilon)]/[\Delta(1+t^*)] - G_\gamma \gamma_{t^*}}. \tag{A.13}$$

Comparing the slope expressions of the tariff indifference curves with interest groups, (A.13), and without interest groups, (A.7), it is clear that they differ only if a change in the distribution of income affects overall welfare; i.e. if $G_\gamma \neq 0$.

Pareto-optimal tariff (subsidy) combinations in the presence of interest groups in the home country, but not in the rest of the world, are obtained by equating (A.13) with (A.8). After some simplifying manipulations one obtains:

$$t + t^* + tt^* = S\Phi, \qquad \text{(A.14)}$$

where $S = G_\gamma / G_Y$ and $\Phi = [\gamma_t(1+t)(1+t^* - t^*\epsilon)/(\beta M_1^*)] + [\gamma_{t^*}(1+t^*)(1+\epsilon^* t^*)/(\beta^* M_1^*)]$. Provided there is a trade-off between the distribution of income and aggregate income, i.e. $G_\gamma / G_Y \neq 0$, it is generally not true any more that Pareto-optimal tariff (subsidy) combinations satisfy the previously established relation $(t + t^* + tt^*) = 0$.

That free trade is generally not on the Pareto-optimal locus can be seen by setting $t = t^* = 0$ in (A.14) and solving for

$$0 = (G_\gamma / G_Y M_1^*)(\gamma_t/\beta + \gamma_{t^*}/\beta^*), \qquad \text{(A.15)}$$

which can be satisfied only if either the income distribution does not matter ($G_\gamma = 0$) or the second bracket of (A.15) is accidentally zero. Recall that it was assumed that at least one of $\gamma_t$ or $\gamma_{t^*}$ is nonzero.

## REFERENCES

CAVES, R. E. (1974), "The Economics of Reciprocity: Theory and Evidence of Bilateral Trading Arrangements," in *International Trade and Finance, Essays in Honor of Jan Tinbergen*, ed. by Willy Sellekaerts, White Plains, N.Y., 17–54.

CLINE, W. R., KAWANABE, N., KRONSJO, T. O. M. and WILLIAMS, T. (1977), *Trade Negotiations in the Tokyo Round*, Washington, D.C., Brookings.

EVANS, J. W. (1971), *The Kennedy Round in American Trade Policy: The Twilight of the GATT?*, Cambridge, Mass., Harvard Press.

JOHNSON, H. G. (1953–4), "Optimum Tariffs and Retaliation," *Review of Economic Studies*, vol. 21 (2), 142–153.

JOHNSON, H. G. (1965), "An Economic Theory of Protectionism, Tariff Bargaining, and the Formation of Customs Unions," *Journal of Political Economy*, vol. 73, 256–283.

JONES, R. W. (1969), "Tariffs and Trade in General Equilibrium: Comment," *American Economic Review*, vol 59, 418–424.

KEMP, M. C. (1969), *A Contribution to the General Equilibrium Theory of Preferential Trading*, Amsterdam, North Holland.

MEIER, G. M. (1973), *Problems of Trade Policy*, Oxford, Oxford University Press.

Journal of International Economics 7 (1977) 363–377. © North-Holland Publishing Company

# THE NATIONAL DEFENSE TARIFF ARGUMENT RECONSIDERED

Wolfgang MAYER*

*University of Cincinnati, Cincinnati, OH 45221, U.S.A.*

Received August 1975, revised version received November 1976

What is a country's optimal trade policy when embargoes and other trade interruptions are threatening? In addressing this issue, the paper emphasizes the nature of adjustment impediments when an effective embargo forces the economy to alter its production pattern abruptly. A production subsidy on the imported good represents the optimal policy choice, a tariff being a second-best instrument. The tariff's superiority to free trade implies, in turn, that the conventional classification of the national defense tariff as a noneconomic argument is inappropriate since economic efficiency criteria alone can justify the tariff.

## 1. Introduction

The national defense tariff argument has been an integral part of the tariff literature since Adam Smith (1776, pp. 429–431) who already had presented a well-reasoned justification for the adoption of a national defense tariff, thereby recognizing it as an important exception to the principle of free trade. That the argument has survived to the present day with undiminished vigor is evidenced in the writings of Haberler (1936), Black (1959), Kindleberger (1973), Samuelson (1976) and many others. The essence of the argument is that in some instances noneconomic ends, such as political and military security, rather than economic ends dictate the course of trade policy. Consequently, a tariff may be called for even though it seems to violate economic efficiency criteria. Although this reasoning implies that the tariff's ultimate objective is the attainment of some form of maximum welfare for society, the literature has relied much more on general descriptive argumentations rather than on a rigorous optimization approach.

The primary objective of this paper is to adopt the basic assumptions behind the existing national defense tariff writings, to develop a simple optimization

*I wish to express my appreciation to Jagdish Bhagwati and an anonymous referee for their comments on an earlier draft of this paper. The current, revised version also reflects some additional insights I gained from reading two manuscripts which deal with the same general topic area, one by Bhagwati and Srinivasan (1976) and the other by Tolley and Wilman (1977). In some respects, my paper represents a special case of the more general theory expounded by Bhagwati and Srinivasan.

model on the basis of this set of assumptions, and to determine the resulting optimal trade policy. In particular, we want to demonstrate that the national defense tariff can be justified on economic efficiency grounds only. The main assumptions of the model are that: (a) precipitous trade interruptions, such as import embargoes, are possible; (b) if such interruptions occur and a change in the production pattern is necessitated, there are costs to production adjustments; and (c), individual producers and consumers have imperfect foresight believing that prices they are facing at a given point in time are going to continue forever.[1] Given these assumptions, the policymaker's goal is to select a tariff, tax, or subsidy which maximizes society's expected welfare.

The main conclusions of this paper can be summarized under the following four points, provided trade interruptions take the form of an import embargo. First, if a tariff is the only policy instrument available, the optimal pre-embargo tariff rate on imports is positive. Second, if the probability of an embargo, as perceived by the policymaker, rises the optimal tariff rate rises as well. Third, a tariff on imports is only a second-best policy. When adjustment costs arise only on the production side and producers and consumers can be taxed (subsidized) at different rates, a production subsidy alone is superior to a tariff.[2] Fourth, optimal trade policies are generally not independent of the initial production pattern and the time period the policymaker allows for implementing the optimal trade policy. The value of the optimal production subsidy rises with the length of the planned policy implementation period, up to a well-defined maximum value.

Our findings are derived from a very simple model which has been stripped to its minimally necessary features. Section 2 spells this model out in detail, whereby the emphasis is put on the role of adjustment costs. While the main text treats adjustment costs in the most general form, a specific case is explored in the appendix. Section 3 concentrates on the optimal defense tariff issue, while section 4 shows that a production subsidy is superior to a tariff.

## 2. The model

Assumed is a two-commodity, small open economy whose trade flows with other economies may be subjected to exogenous interruptions, such as import embargoes.[3] The main impact of an embargo on the economy is the need for

[1]Assumption (a) is at the core of all the writings on defense tariff. Assumption (b) has been explicitly stated by Black (1959, p. 201). More recently, Cheh (1974) concludes from an empirical study that a country's willingness to lower its tariffs is greatly dependent on the magnitude of labor adjustment costs. The literature says relatively little about assumption (c). However, some explicit or implicit behavioral assumptions with respect to consumers and producers must be made, since they are quite crucial in determining the optimal policy prescriptions.

[2]This conclusion is quite in line with Bhagwati's (1971) listing of appropriate trade policies in the presence of domestic production distortions. In this case, a production tax-cum-subsidy is superior to a tariff which, in turn, is superior to free trade.

immediate changes in the production and consumption patterns. In general, these forced adjustments are not costless to the economy, as significant adjustment impediments may exist on both the production and consumption side. Since adjustment impediments on the production side are likely to be particularly important, we introduce the simplifying assumption that impediments occur only on the production and not at all on the consumption side.[4]

The notion of adjustment costs on the production side requires theoretical elaborations.[5,6] As a starting point, we define the economy's *potential* production possibility locus, $PPL^p$, as the locus of maximum attainable combinations of outputs if changes in the production patterns do not result in any adjustment costs.[7] The functional form of the $PPL^p$ is given by:

$$X_2 = H(X_1), \tag{1}$$

where $X_j$ denotes industry output of commodity $j$, and it is assumed that $-\infty < H_1 < 0$ and $-\infty < H_{11} \leqq 0$. This locus must be distinguished from the *actual* production possibility locus, $PPL^a$, which describes the economy's actual ability to transform $X_1$ into $X_2$ during a predetermined period of time. The shorter the period prescribed for the transformation process, the more significant are the adjustment impediments and the larger are the adjustment costs in terms of lost output. Consequently, the existence of adjustment costs implies that in general the economy's production pattern cannot be changed along the $PPL^p$, if there is a time constraint to transforming $X_1$ into $X_2$. Stated differently, the $PPL^a$ depends not only on the economy's endowments and state of technology, as the $PPL^p$ does, but also on the initial production pattern $(\bar{X}_1, \bar{X}_2)$ and on the specified length of the adjustment period, $A$; that is,

$$X_2 = F(X_1; \bar{X}_1, \bar{X}_2, A). \tag{2}$$

[3]For the entire analysis of this paper it is assumed that a complete embargo on imports is the only possible form of trade interruption. A more general formulation, namely that foreign trade may be interrupted at different degrees of severity, could be introduced by allowing for a random world price ratio which has the free-trade price as an upper and the long-run autarky price as a lower bound. It should be added that we make no attempts to explore the country's reasons for expecting an embargo. In general, the reasons must be sought in political tensions rather than pure economic warfare, since the rest of the world would not be affected by the economic policies of a small country. On the question of economic warfare, see Wan (1961).

[4]Tolley and Wilman (1976), in a partial equilibrium framework, introduce adjustment impediments on the consumption side as well.

[5]The main text examines the theory of adjustment costs in the most general form. The appendix supplements this exposition with a specific example, namely the case of a two-factor economy where one factor is temporarily immobile as changes in the production pattern are called for.

[6]Our general approach of adjustment costs for the economy as a whole is an extension of Alchian's (1959) theory of adjustment costs at the firm level.

[7]In the special case of a two-factor, two-commodity economy, the locus is defined by the conditions that both factors are fully employed and that the marginal rate of substitution in production is the same in both industries.

Before we examine the impact of the various arguments in $F$ on $X_2$, we state the general principle that adjustment costs are directly related to the magnitude of the adjustment and inversely to the length of the time period during which the adjustment is to take place. If $A$ is sufficiently long – let us say $\bar{A}$ – the adjustment costs become negligible. In this case, the $PPL^a$ and $PPL^p$ coincide, and the maximum value of $X_2$ which can be produced (at a given $X_1$) becomes independent of the initial production pattern.[8] If, one the other hand, $A < \bar{A}$, then the $PPL^a$ is situated inside the $PPL^p$, with the possible exception of point $(\bar{X}_1, \bar{X}_2)$, which may be a point on the $PPL^p$. It is this situation of $A < \bar{A}$ which underlies the following discussion of the derivative signs of eq. (2). First, we assume, as usual, that $-\infty < F_1 = \partial X_2/\partial X_1 < 0$ and $-\infty < F_{11} = \partial^2 X_2/\partial X_1^2 < 0$. Next, we use the above-mentioned principle that adjustment costs are directly related to the magnitude of the adjustment in determining the signs of $F_2 = \partial X_2/\partial \bar{X}_1$ and $F_3 = \partial X_2/\partial \bar{X}_2$. Let us assume that we are evaluating these derivatives at a point where $X_1 > \bar{X}_1$ and $X_2 < \bar{X}_2$.[9] If we raise $\bar{X}_1$, holding $X_1, \bar{X}_2$ and $A$ constant, then the magnitude of the required adjustment becomes smaller, adjustment costs are less, and ceteris paribus more of $X_2$ can be produced; i.e. $F_2 > 0$ if $X_1 > \bar{X}_1$. On the other hand, if $\bar{X}_2$ is raised, holding $X_1, \bar{X}_1$ and $A$ constant, the difference between $X_2$ and $\bar{X}_2$ and, therefore, adjustment costs rise, implying that ceteris paribus less of $X_2$ can be produced, i.e. $F_3 < 0$ if $X_2 < \bar{X}_2$. Correspondingly, one can show that $F_2 < 0$ and $F_3 > 0$ if, at the point where the derivatives are evaluated, $X_1 < \bar{X}_1$ and $X_2 > \bar{X}_2$. Finally, we deduce from the principle that adjustment costs decline with rising length of the adjustment period, that $F_4 = \partial X_2/\partial A > 0$ and $F_{14} = \partial^2 X_2/(\partial X_1\, \partial A) > 0$. The longer the adjustment period, the more of $X_2$ can be produced and the easier it is to transform $X_1$ into $X_2$ for given values of $X_1$, $\bar{X}_1$, and $\bar{X}_2$.[10]

The concept of the economy's $PPL^a$ has been introduced since it is this production possibility locus which the policymaker must take into consideration. First of all, the policymaker must realize that, once the embargo has been imposed, the post-embargo $PPL^a$ is relevant for production adjustments during this period. The post-embargo ability to transform $X_1$ into $X_2$ crucially depends on the pre-embargo production pattern. Denoting post-embargo variables with asterisks and pre-embargo variables without asterisks, the post-embargo $PPL^a$ can be stated as:

$$X_2^* = F^*(X_1^*; X_1, X_2, A^*), \tag{2'}$$

where $A^*$ can be interpreted as the adjustment period from the announcement

[8]More precisely, if $A \geqq \bar{A}$, then $\partial X_2/\partial \bar{X}_1 = F_2 = 0$ and $\partial X_2/\partial \bar{X}_2 = F_3 = 0$.

[9]The fact that $(\bar{X}_1, \bar{X}_2)$ represents one point on the $PPL^a$ implies that for all other points on the $PPL^a$ either $X_1 > \bar{X}_1$ and $X_2 < \bar{X}_2$ or $X_1 < \bar{X}_1$ and $X_2 > \bar{X}_2$.

[10]These sign postulates correspond to propositions 7 and 8 in Alchian (1959).

to the complete enforcement of the embargo. Usually, $A^*$ will be very short. In addition to (2′), the policymaker must also consider the economy's pre-embargo $PPL^a$. The implementation of trade policies which counter embargo threats generally call for adjustments of both the existing production and consumption pattern. In order to change the production pattern, it is quite essential what the production point at the time of the decision is and during which time period the adjustment to the desired new production point is to be completed.[11] Consequently, the pre-embargo $PPL^a$ is

$$X_2 = F(X_1; \bar{X}_1, \bar{X}_2, A), \tag{2''}$$

where $A$ is the time period set aside for implementing the new trade policy and $(\bar{X}_1, \bar{X}_2)$ is the production pattern at the beginning of the implementation period.

On the consumption side, it is assumed that the preference rankings of consumers can be represented by a community utility function which possesses the conventional properties of continuous second-order derivatives, strict quasi-concavity, and no bliss point. Furthermore, both commodities are assumed to be normal goods in consumption. And as was indicated before, no adjustment difficulties are assumed to exist on the part of consumers.

Finally, we must make some assumptions about the invididual agents, consumers and producers, that operate in our economy. A framework of perfect competition with no externalities is assumed. Both consumers and producers look upon existing prices as constant and certain over their entire decision horizon. In particular, they disregard the implications of an embargo threat.[12] These assumptions imply that at a given point in time the economy is in equilibrium if the marginal rate of transformation equals the producer price ratio and the marginal rate of substitution in consumption equals the consumer price ratio.

The role of the policymaker is to select policy measures – and indirectly a pre-embargo production and consumption pattern – which maximizes society's expected welfare, given the embargo threat, adjustment impediments on the production side, and zero foresight on the part of individual consumers and producers.

[11]A country which decides on altering its production pattern for national defense reasons typically sets itself a time table during which all resource allocations must be completed. The time table itself may be affected by the imminence of the embargo threat. In this paper, however, $A$ is assumed to be exogenously given.

[12]Optimal policy choice crucially depends on the behavior of individual consumers and producers. If all embargo costs were internalized, then no government interference in the form of tariffs, taxes, or subsidies would be necessary since social and private optimum would coincide. For a partial equilibrium model with internalized embargo costs, see Tolley and Wilman (1977).

## 3. Selecting an optimal tariff

In this section we want to determine the optimal tariff rate under the assumptions that an import tariff, $t$, is the only policy instrument and that the economy operates as described in the preceding section. It also is assumed that the second commodity is imported as long as some trade with the rest of the world exists. The policymaker's objective is to maximize the country's expected community utility, as expressed by:[13]

$$\max_t E(U) = \pi U(D_1^*, D_2^*)+(1-\pi)U(D_1, D_2), \tag{3}$$

where $0 \leqq \pi \leqq 1$ is the probability of an embargo as perceived by the policymaker, and $D_j^*$ and $D_j$ denote post- and pre-embargo demand[14] for commodity $j$ respectively.

The values of $D_j^*$ and $D_j$ in (3) are not just any demand values, but those which satisfy the consumer and producer equilibrium conditions. The post-embargo equilibrium conditions, describing a position of autarky, are:

$$D_1^* = X_1^*, \tag{4}$$

$$D_2^* = X_2^*, \tag{5}$$

$$U_1^*/U_2^* = -F_1^*, \tag{6}$$

where $U_j^* = \partial U/\partial D_j^*$, $F_1^* = \partial X_2^*/\partial X_1^*$, and $X_2^*$ has been defined in (2′). For any given pre-embargo production pattern, $(X_1, X_2)$, and value of $A^*$, one can solve (2′), (4), (5) and (6) for the equilibrium post-embargo production and consumption values, $X_1^*$, $X_2^*$, $D_1^*$ and $D_2^*$. The pre-embargo equilibrium conditions, on the other hand, are:

$$D_1+pD_2 = X_1+pX_2, \tag{7}$$

$$-F_1 = 1/p(1+t), \tag{8}$$

$$U_2/U_1 = p(1+t), \tag{9}$$

[13]The policymaker projects a future date with respect to which the probability of an embargo is assessed and society's expected welfare is maximized. The approach represents a one-period analysis as society's welfare at earlier or later dates, even if affected by the policymaker's actions, is disregarded. The one-period approach has been chosen over the more realistic multiperiod model for reasons of simplicity and clearer exposition. Our conjecture is that the qualitative conclusions of the one-period model will generally extend to the multiperiod model. For an attempt to determine optimal trade policies in such a dynamic framework, the reader is referred to Lapan (1976).

[14]Both post- and pre-embargo variables refer to the same date in the future. Once the projected date has been reached, the country is (post-embargo situation) or is not (pre-embargo situation) embargoed by the rest of the world.

where $U_j = \partial U/\partial D_j$, $F_1 = \partial X_2/\partial X_1$, $p$ is the world price of the second in terms of the first commodity, and $X_2$ has already been described in (2″). In addition to consumer and producer equilibrium, as stated by eqs. (8)–(9), the balance of payments must be in equilibrium, eq. (7). From (2″), (7), (8) and (9) solution values for the pre-embargo variables $X_1$, $X_2$, $D_1$ and $D_2$ can be obtained. These solution values depend not only on the world price, $p$, and tariff rate, $t$, but also on the production pattern at the time of the policy choice, $(\bar{X}_1, \bar{X}_2)$, and on the policy implementation period as long as $A < \bar{A}$. Summarizing this discussion, both $D_j^*$ and $D_j$ in (3) depend on $p$, $t$, $(\bar{X}_1, \bar{X}_2)$ and $A$.

Given that $t$ is the only choice variable, the first- and second-order conditions for a maximum of (3) are:

$$\mathrm{d}E(U)/\mathrm{d}t = \pi[U_1^*(\partial D_1^*/\partial t)+U_2^*(\partial D_2^*/\partial t)]+(1-\pi)[U_1(\partial D_1/\partial t) + U_2(\partial D_2/\partial t)] = 0, \tag{10}$$

$$\mathrm{d}^2E(U)/\mathrm{d}t^2 < 0. \tag{11}$$

While eq. (11) does not require any further explanation for our purposes, we want to derive a more explicit expression for (10) so that we can conveniently determine the sign of the optimal tariff rate, denoted by $\hat{t}$. Of course, eqs. (2′), (2″) and (4)–(9) are the basis for this deriva tion.

First, we note that $\partial X_j^*/\partial t = \partial D_j^*/\partial t$, and that

$$\partial X_2^*/\partial t = F_1^*(\partial X_1^*/\partial t)+(F_2^*+F_3^*F_1)(\partial X_1/\partial t), \tag{12}$$

where $F_2^* = \partial X_2^*/\partial X_1$, $F_3^* = \partial X_2^*/\partial X_2$, and $F_1 = \partial X_2/\partial X_1$, from (2′) and (2″). We can rewrite the first bracketed term on the right-hand side of (10) as:

$$U_2^*(F_2^*+F_3^*F_1)(\partial X_1/\partial t), \tag{13}$$

after substitution of (12) and realizing that $U_1^*+U_2^*F_1^* = 0$. The second bracketed term on the right-hand side of (10) can be simplified by factoring $U_1$ out and substituting (9), which yields:

$$U_1[(\partial D_1/\partial t)+p(\partial D_2/\partial t)]+U_1pt(\partial D_2/\partial t). \tag{14}$$

From (2″), (7) and (8) we derive:

$$[(\partial D_1/\partial t)+p(\partial D_2/\partial t)] = (1+pF_1)(dX_1/\partial t) = -pt(\partial X_2/\partial t), \tag{15}$$

and after substitution of (15) into (14) and (14) into the second bracketed term on the right-hand side of (10), we obtain:

$$[U_1(\partial D_1/\partial t)+U_2(\partial D_2/\partial t)] = U_1pt(\partial M_2/\partial t), \tag{16}$$

where $M_2 = (D_2 - X_2)$ are the pre-embargo imports of the second commodity.[15]

Our basic conclusions concerning the optimal defense tariff are based on the equation

$$\pi U_2^*(F_2^*+F_3^*F_1)(\partial X_1/\partial t)+(1-\pi)U_1pt(\partial M_2/\partial t) = 0, \tag{10'}$$

which has been obtained by substituting (13) and (16) into (10). In order to determine the sign of the optimal tariff rate, $\bar{t}$, we first note that $U_2^* > 0$, $U_1 > 0$, $(\partial X_1/\partial t) < 0$ and $(\partial M_2/\partial t) < 0$.[16] That leaves us with the term $(F_2^*+F_3^*F_1)$, whose sign is much less obvious. One can show, however, that under the assumptions made in section 2 – in particular, that the second commodity is imported – the following sign must prevail:

$$(F_2^*+F_3^*F_1) < 0 \quad \text{if} \quad M_2 > 0. \tag{17}$$

This relationship will hold because, if commodity two is imported during the pre-embargo period, more of the second and less of the first commodity will be produced after the imposition of the embargo as compared with the pre-embargo production pattern; i.e. $X_2^* > X_2$ and $X_1^* < X_1$. From the discussion of the signs of $F_2$ and $F_3$ in the second section, we know that these inequalities imply that $F_2^* < 0$ and $F_3^* > 0$.[17] Combined with the assumption that $-\infty < F_1 < 0$, (17) is determined.

With this information in mind, we can draw the following conclusions from (10'):

*Conclusion 1. With positive probability of a trade embargo,* $0 < \pi < 1$, *the optimal tariff rate,* $\bar{t}$, *is positive.*

Free trade is suboptimal if sudden and unexpected embargoes can occur and there are adjustment impediments to the necessitated change in the production pattern. A positive import tariff should be imposed during the pre-embargo period, given that a tariff is the only policy instrument. The optimal degree of protection depends on the subjective assessment of $\pi$, the relative importance of the two commodities to society as expressed by $U$, and the properties of the

[15] $M_2$ is positive by assumption.

[16] The signs of $(\partial X_1/\partial t)$ and $(\partial M_2/\partial t)$ are obtained from (2″), (7), (8) and (9) after substitution of $M_2 = D_2 - X_2$.

[17] Obviously, if the assumption were made that $M_2$ is negative, then $(F_2{}^* + F_3{}^*F_1)$ would be positive.

economy's actual production possibility loci in the pre- and post-embargo situation. In particular, it should be pointed out that the optimal tariff value, $\bar{t}$, depends on the production pattern at the time of the policy choice, $(\bar{X}_1, \bar{X}_2)$, and on the planned policy implementation period, $A$.

*Conclusion 2. With zero probability of a trade embargo, $\pi = 0$, the optimal tariff rate, $\bar{t}$, is zero.*

Free trade is still the optimal trade policy, if there are no dangers of trade interruptions, even though there exist adjustment impediments.

*Conclusion 3. Given absolute certainty of a trade embargo, $\pi = 1$, the country's optimal trade policy is one of long-run autarky.*

The assumption that $\pi = 1$ reduces (10′) to the condition that $(F_2^* + F_3^* F_1) = 0$, since $U_1^*$ and $\partial X_1/\partial t$ are nonzero. The condition that $(F_2^* + F_3^* F_1) = 0$, in turn, implies that $X_2^*$ is independent of $X_1$ and $X_2$. As we mentioned in footnote 8, this is always the case if $A^* \geqq \bar{A}$, i.e. there are no adjustment costs and the pre- and post-embargo production possibility loci coincide. But since it is explicitly assumed that $A^* < \bar{A}$, the condition can be satisfied only at one point, namely where $X_1^* = X_1$ and $X_2^* = X_2$. Since there is no distinction between pre- and post-embargo production pattern, long-run autarky is implied.

*Conclusion 4. As the probability of a trade embargo rises, the optimal tariff rate, $\bar{t}$, will rise as well.*

This result is derived from differentiation of (10′) with respect to $\pi$:

$$\frac{\partial \bar{t}}{\partial \pi} = -\frac{U_2^*(F_2^* + F_3^* F_1)(\partial X_1/\partial t) - ptU_1(\partial M_2/\partial t)}{\mathrm{d}^2 E(U)/\mathrm{d}t^2} > 0, \tag{18}$$

where we utilized the second-order condition for a maximum, eq. (11), in the sign interpretation of (18).

*Conclusion 5. With positive probability of a trade embargo, $0 < \pi < 1$, but no adjustment costs, the optimal tariff rate, $\bar{t}$, is zero.*

Conclusions 1–4 were based on the assumption that any changes in the production pattern will result in adjustment costs. In conclusion 5 we assume that there exists a positive embargo threat but no adjustment impediments. As was pointed out in section 2, in this case the actual and potential production possibility loci are identical which, when applied to our specific problem, implies that

$(F_2^* + F_3^* F_1) = 0$. This result, of course, emphasizes the importance of adjustment impediments in justifying tariffs for national defense reasons, as was originally done by Black (1959, p. 201).

## 4. A production subsidy is superior

In the third section it has been assumed that a tariff is the only available policy instrument, implying that prices facing domestic consumers and producers are identical. In this section the assumptions are changed by allowing the policymaker to affect consumer and producer price ratios separately by imposing consumption taxes (subsidies) and production taxes (subsidies) respectively.

A production subsidy on the second commodity is denoted by $t_p$ and a consumption tax by $t_c$. The policymaker's objective is now to select those values of $t_p$ and $t_c$ which maximize expected utility, as stated in (3), given that $D_j^*$ and $D_j$ in (3) are the optimal demand values at the post- and pre-embargo equilibrium respectively. The post-embargo equilibrium conditions are still stated by (4)–(6), since they are not directly affected by the introduction of different choice variables. The pre-embargo equilibrium conditions, on the other hand, must be altered to:

$$D_1 + pD_2 = X_1 + pX_2, \tag{7'}$$

$$-F_1 = 1/p(1+t_p), \tag{8'}$$

$$U_2/U_1 = p(1+t_c). \tag{9'}$$

The first-order conditions for a maximum of (3), given that $t_p$ and $t_c$ are the choice variables, are:

$$\begin{aligned} \partial E(U)/\partial t_p &= \pi U_2^*(F_2^* + F_3^* F_1)(\partial X_1/\partial t_p) \\ &\quad + (1-\pi)U_1[(\partial X_1/\partial t_p)t_p/(1+t_p) + (\partial D_2/\partial t_p)pt_c] \\ &= 0, \end{aligned} \tag{19}$$

$$\partial E(U)/\partial t_c = U_1(1-\pi)pt_c = 0, \tag{20}$$

where we utilized (2′), (2″), (4)–(6) and (7′)–(9′), and employed similar manipuations as in the derivation of (10′).[18] Provided the second order conditions for a maximum of (3) are satisfied, one can solve (19) and (20) for the optimal values

[18]Essential for obtaining the expression in (20) is the fact that $\partial X_1/\partial t_c = 0$. Also recall that $F_2^* + F_3^* F_1)$ is negative under our assumptions.

of $t_c$ and $t_p$:

$$\bar{t}_c = 0, \tag{21}$$

$$\bar{t}_p = [\pi U_2^*(F_2^* + F_3^* F_1)]/[(1-\pi)U_1 p F_1 > 0, \tag{22}$$

leading us to the following conclusion.

*Conclusion 6. With positive probability of a trade embargo, $0 < \pi < 1$, and adjustment impediments on the production side, a country is better off by imposing an optimal production subsidy on the imported good rather than a tariff.*

A comparison of conclusion 6 with conclusion 1 must be interpreted in light of the known theory of optimal trade policy in the presence of distortions. As has been demonstrated by Bhagwati and Ramaswami (1963), Bhagwati, Ramaswami and Srinivasan (1969) and Bhagwati (1971), the existence of domestic production distortions calls for a production tax-cum-subsidy as the country's first-best trade policy. More specifically, a production tax-cum-subsidy is superior to a tariff which, in turn, is superior to free trade. The model of our paper introduces adjustment costs only on the production side but not on the consumption side. That amounts to a case of domestic production distortions, and therefore our conclusions represent a special case of Bhagwati's (1971) ranking of trade policies in the presence of distortions.

The value of the optimal production subsidy, $\bar{t}_p$, depends among other factors on the production pattern at the time of the trade-policy choice, $(\bar{X}_1, \bar{X}_2)$, and on the planned policy implementation period. $A$.[19] As an example of this dependence, we are now going to show how a change in $A$ affects $\bar{t}_p$. This analysis emphasizes the importance of time in the decision process of the policymaker.

In order to determine the sign of $\partial \bar{t}_p/\partial A$, we first rewrite (19), setting $t_c$ equal to zero:

$$\pi U_2^*(F_2^* + F_3^* F_1) - (1-\pi)U_1 p F_1 t_p = 0, \tag{19'}$$

which is further modified after substitution of $G_2 = U_1 F_1 < 0$ and $G_1 = U_2^*(F_2^* + F_3^* F_1) < 0$.

$$\pi G_1(X_1) - (1-\pi) p t_p G_2(X_1) = 0. \tag{19''}$$

[19]The optimal tariff rate, $\bar{t}$, in section 3 was also dependent on the initial production pattern and the value of $A$.

The procedure of expressing (19) as (19″) can be employed because every variable in the various terms of (19′) can be expressed as a function of $X_1$.[20]

Differentiation of the first-order condition, as stated in (19″), with respect to $A$ yields:

$$\frac{\partial \bar{t}_p}{\partial A} = \frac{-[\pi G_1' - (1-\pi)pt_p G_2'][\partial X_1/\partial A]}{[\pi G_1' - (1-\pi)pt_p G_2'][\partial X_1/\partial t_p] - (1-\pi)pG_2}\,. \tag{23}$$

For the sign interpretation of (23) we utilize the second-order conditions for a maximum of $E(U)$, which imply that

$$\partial^2 E(U)/\partial t_p^2 = [\pi G_1' - (1-\pi)pt_p G_2'][\partial X_1/\partial t_p] - (1-\pi)pG_2 < 0.$$

And since $G_2 < 0$ and $\partial X_1/\partial t_p < 0$, the second-order conditions further imply that

$$\pi G_1' - (1-\pi)pt_p G_2' > 0.$$

Consequently, the denominator of (23) is negative and the first bracketed term in the numerator of (23) is positive. This leaves us with the term $-[\partial X_1/\partial A]$, which can be written as $F_{14}/F_{11}$.[21] Returning to section 2, where we had assumed that $F_{14} > 0$ and $F_{11} < 0$, we can conclude that:

$$\partial \bar{t}_p/\partial A > 0. \tag{24}$$

*Conclusion 7. Provided $\bar{A} > A$, the optimal value of the production subsidy rises with the length of the adjustment period.*

This last of our conclusions can be interpreted as follows. If the policy implementation period is so long that there are no adjustment costs caused by implementing the optimal trade policy, then $A \geqq \bar{A}$ and the corresponding optimal production subsidy takes on a certain, well-defined value. If, on the other hand, the adjustment period is shortened such that $A < \bar{A}$ and the adjustment costs of implementation are positive, then the policymaker has to consider not only the potential welfare losses from an embargo, but also the welfare losses due to adjustment of the production pattern during the pre-embargo period. As a result, less of a pre-embargo adjustment is called for, implying that the production subsidy is smaller when $A < \bar{A}$ than when $A \geqq \bar{A}$.

[20]The values of $D_1^*$, $D_2^*$, $X_1^*$ and $X_2^*$ can be uniquely solved for in terms of $X_2$ and $X_1$ from (2′) and (4)–(6); $D_1$, $D_2$ and $X_2$ can be uniquely solved for in terms of $X_1$ from (2″), (7′) and (9′).

[21]$F_{14}/F_{11}$ is derived from (7′)–(9′) and (2″).

**Appendix**

In section 2 we discussed the role of adjustment impediments in restricting the economy's $PPL^a$ in a general way. Now we want to provide a more specific example, namely the case of a two-commodity, two-factor economy where one factor is temporarily immobile while the other factor is perfectly mobile between sectors.[22] The purpose of the example is to obtain some more explicit expressions for the various derivative signs which characterize the $PPL^a$.

The industry production functions are assumed to be strictly quasiconcave and homogeneous of degree one; they are stated as

$$X_j = X_j(V_{1j}, V_{2j}), \qquad j = 1, 2, \tag{A.1}$$

where $V_{ij}$ is the amount of input $i$ used in the production of commodity $j$. Perfect competition is assumed and full employment is prevailing such that

$$V_{i1}+V_{i2} = V_i, \qquad i = 1, 2, \tag{A.2}$$

where $V_i$ is the total endowment with factor $i$.

We now take the two equations of (A.1), substitute the full employment restrictions of (A.2), differentiate the obtained expressions totally, and perform a few manipulations. This yields:

$$\mathrm{d}X_2 = -(X_{12}/X_{11})\mathrm{d}X_1+X_{21}[(X_{12}/X_{11})-(X_{22}/X_{21})]\mathrm{d}V_{21}, \tag{A.3}$$

where $X_{ij} = \partial X_j/\partial V_{ij}$. Next, we assume that it is the second factor which is temporarily immobile between industries. This implies that $\mathrm{d}V_{21} = \mathrm{d}V_{22} = 0$. The first factor, on the other hand, is perfectly mobile. Given these assumptions, we obtain the slope expression for the $PPL^a$ from (A.3) by setting $\mathrm{d}V_{21} = 0$.

$$F_1 = \partial X_2/\partial X_1 = -(X_{12}/X_{11}) < 0. \tag{A.4}$$

The curvature of this locus is described by:

$$\begin{aligned} F_{11} &= \partial^2 X_2/\partial X_1^2 = [-1/X_{11}^2][X_{11}X_{12,12}(\mathrm{d}V_{12}/\mathrm{d}V_{11}) \\ &\quad -X_{12}X_{11,11}][\mathrm{d}V_{11}/\mathrm{d}X_1] \\ &= (1/X_{11})^3[X_{11}X_{12,12}+X_{12}X_{11,11}], \end{aligned} \tag{A.5}$$

[22]For a more complete analysis of a general equilibrium production model of this type, see Mayer (1974).

where $X_{ij,ij} = \partial^2 X_i/\partial V_{ij}^2$ and $\mathrm{d}V_{12}/\mathrm{d}V_{11} = -1$. As can easily be shown, strict quasiconcavity and homogeneity of degree one of the production function imply that $X_{ij,ij} < 0$ and, therefore, that $F_{11} < 0$.

A change in the initial production pattern affects $X_2$ by altering the value of $V_{21}$ in (A.3). If $\bar{X}_1$ and $\bar{X}_2$ are situated on the *PPL*ᵖ, such that $\bar{X}_2 = H(\bar{X}_1)$, and a change in $\bar{X}_1$ is accompanied by a corresponding change in $\bar{X}_2$, then we differentiate eq. (2) to obtain:

$$\mathrm{d}X_2 = F_1 \mathrm{d}X_1 + (F_2 + F_3 H_1)\mathrm{d}\bar{X}_1. \tag{A.6}$$

Substitution of (A.4) into (A.3), and a comparison of (A.3) with (A.6), shows that

$$(F_2+F_3H_1)\mathrm{d}\bar{X}_1 = X_{21}[(X_{12}/X_{11})-(X_{22}/X_{21})]\mathrm{d}V_{21}, \tag{A.7}$$

where $\mathrm{d}\bar{X}_1$ represents a change in $\bar{X}_1$ along the $PPL^{\mathrm{p}}$ and $\mathrm{d}V_{21}$ is the resulting change in employment of the second factor in the first industry. Since $\bar{X}_1$ and $V_{21}$ always change in the same direction along the $PPL^{\mathrm{p}}$ and $X_{21} > 0$, it follows that

$$(F_2+F_3H_1) \gtreqless 0 \quad \text{as} \quad (X_{21}/X_{11}) \gtreqless (X_{22}/X_{12}), \tag{A.8}$$

where $(X_{2j}/X_{1j})$ is the marginal rate of substitution in production in industry $j$. As long as production takes place on the $PPL^{\mathrm{p}}$, the marginal rate of substitution must be the same in both industries and $(F_2+F_3H_1) = 0$. If, on the other hand, production takes place on the $PPL^{\mathrm{a}}$, but not on the $PPL^{\mathrm{p}}$, then the two marginal rates of substitution will differ and $(F_2+F_3H_1) \neq 0$. Under the assumption that $X_1 > \bar{X}_1$ and $X_2 < \bar{X}_2$, it must be that $X_{21}/X_{11} > X_{22}/X_{12}$. This condition must hold, since $(X_1, X_2)$ differs from $(\bar{X}_1, \bar{X}_2)$ because $V_{11}$ has been raised and $V_{12}$ has been lowered while holding $V_{21}$ and $V_{22}$ constant. This implies that $X_{21}/X_{11}$ rises and $X_{22}/X_{12}$ falls relative to the values which were prevailing at $(\bar{X}_1, \bar{X}_2)$. Correspondingly, one can show that if $X_1 < \bar{X}_1$ and $X_2 > \bar{X}_2$, then $X_{21}/X_{11} < X_{22}/X_{12}$.

Our main text operates with the assumption that the second commodity is imported. Since this implies that $X_1^* < X_1$ and $X_2^* > X_2$, it is obvious that $(F_2^*+F_3^*F_1) < 0$, as stated in eq. (17).

## References

Alchian, A.A., 1959, Costs and outputs, in: Abramovitz et al., eds., The allocation of economic resources: Essays in honor of Bernard F. Haley (Stanford University Press, Stanford, CA) 23–40.

Bhagwati, Jagdish and V.K. Ramaswami, 1963, Domestic distortion, tariffs, and the theory of optimum subsidy, Journal of Political Economy 71, 44–50.

Bhagwati, Jagdish, V.K. Ramaswami and T.N. Srinivasan, 1969, Domestic distortions, tariffs, and the theory of optimum subsidy: Some further results, Journal of Political Economy 77, 1005–1010.

Bhagwati, Jagdish, 1971, The generalized theory of distortions and welfare, in Bhagwati et al., eds., Trade, balance of payments and growth: Essays in honor of Charles P. Kindleberger (North-Holland, Amsterdam) 69–90.

Bhagwati, Jagdish and T.N. Srinivasan, 1976, Optimal trade policy and compensation under endogenous uncertainty: The phenomenon of market disruptions, Journal of International Economics 6, 317–336.

Black, J., 1959, Arguments for tariffs, Oxford Economic Papers, N.S. XI, 191–208.

Cheh, J., 1974, United States concessions in the Kennedy Round and short-run labor adjustment costs, Journal of International Economics 4, 323–340.

Haberler, G., 1936, The theory of international trade with its applications to commercial policy, Transl. by A. Stonier and F. Benham (Hodge, London).

Kindleberger, Charles P., 1973, International economics, 5th ed., (Irwin, Homewood, IL).

Lapan, H.E., 1976, International trade, factor market distortions and the optimal dynamic subsidy, American Economic Review 66, 335–346.

Mayer, W., 1974, Short-run and long-run equilibrium for a small open economy, Journal of Political Economy 82, 955–967.

Samuelson, P.A., 1976, Economics, 10th ed. (McGraw-Hill, New York).

Smith, A., 1776, An inquiry into the nature and causes of the wealth of nations, ed. by E. Cannan, 1937, New York.

Tolley, G.S. and T.D. Wilman, 1977, The foreign dependence question, mimeo, Journal of Political Economy, forthcoming.

Wan, H.Y., 1961, A contribution to the theory of trade warfare, Unpublished doctoral thesis, M.I.T.

**INTERNATIONAL ECONOMIC REVIEW**
Vol. 23, No. 3, October, 1982

# THE TARIFF EQUIVALENCE OF IMPORT STANDARDS*

BY WOLFGANG MAYER[1]

## 1. INTRODUCTION

Most countries' trade authorities attempt to control the quality of imported commodities. Generally, commodities have to meet well-defined standards on ingredients, features, packaging, etc., before they are approved for marketing in a given country. The publicly stated justification for these import standards is consumer protection. Actual and potential foreign competitors, however, frequently assert that protection of domestic producers is the real reason for import standards. It is claimed that import standards result in significant impediments to the free flow of internationally traded goods. Indeed, a study by the United States Tariff Commission [1974, Ch. X] provides ample evidence that import standards already are in wide use, result in protection for many industries in different countries, and possess the potential of becoming a major trade barrier in the future.[2]

The international trade literature mentions import standards in various discussions of nontariff trade barriers, e.g. Baldwin [1970], Caves and Jones [1981], or Stern [1973]. While the protective nature of import standards is recognized in general, there is little rigorous analytical work on the effectiveness of such measures as instruments of industry protection. In particular, no attempt has been made to evaluate the magnitude of the protective effects of import standards and to compare them with the protective impact of tariffs. The purpose of this paper is to formulate a model which allows evaluation of the tariff equivalence of import standards.[3] It is demonstrated that there exist different combinations of tariffs and import standards which grant a constant level of protection to a given industry. From this trade-off relation a measure of the tariff equivalence of import standards is obtained. The measure's value is shown to depend on the foreign producers' ability to adjust output quality and on the domestic consumers' willingness to switch between commodities of different qualities. Based on this

* Manuscript received July 7, 1981; revised February 22, 1982.

[1] Research on this topic was supported by NSF Grant SES-7905703. Helpful comments by a referee are gratefully acknowledged.

[2] That they represent not just a potential, but an actual trade barrier was confirmed by Robert S. Strauss in the Congressional Hearings of the Subcommittee on Transportation and Commerce [1979]. Strauss testified that "standards and certification activities affected 69 percent of our international trade in 1977." In recognition of this problem, negotiations in the Tokyo Round involved a major attempt at agreeing on a multilateral standards code.

[3] This study focuses on the protective effects of import standards only and ignores those which result from inspection costs. The latter could be treated like transport costs.

theoretical framework, it finally is indicated how actual tariff equivalence values can be calculated.

The analysis is developed in a general equilibrium framework which embodies some recent developments in consumer and producer theory with differentiated products.[4] Section 2 starts with the model's assumptions and describes consumer and producer equilibria when commodities have a quality dimension. Section 3 portrays a small open economy whose consumers buy differentiated products from both domestic and foreign firms and whose policymakers employ tariffs and import standards as possible protective measures. Finally, Section 4 formulates an explicit tariff equivalence measure of import standards.

## 2. THE MODEL

2.1. Definitions and Assumptions. The objects of market transactions are called *commodities*. Each commodity possesses objectively measurable characteristics which, as in Fisher and Shell [1971], Muellbauer [1974], and Willig [1978], are summarized by an index which reflects overall quality. Commodity quality is not exogenously given, but endogenously selected by producers. As is the case for most actual production processes, it is assumed that there exist quality controls. Consequently, production technologies allow for variations in inputs, as well as choices between quality and quantity of output at given input levels.

An *industry* consists of all firms that employ the same production technology, whether or not they produce identical commodities. Since firms can control output quality and not all firms of the industry necessarily set the same controls, an industry's output is not necessarily homogeneous. However, it is assumed that all commodities produced by a given industry are similar, as they serve the same basic consumption purpose from the buyers' point of view. Commodities that serve the same basic consumption purpose are said to belong to the same *commodity group*, whereby commodities of a given group are of either domestic or foreign origin.

We are dealing with a two-country, two-factor, two-commodity-group world in which the home country is small and the rest of the world is large. Each country's endowments of labor and capital are fixed, factors are perfectly mobile within each country, there are no externalities, and both producers and consumers have perfect information. The home country imports commodities that are heterogeneous, as consumers acquire both domestically and foreign produced commodities of the same group. Tariffs and import standards are the only instruments for controlling import flows of heterogeneous products.

2.2. Production Equilibrium. The production technology of a representative firm in industry $j$ is described by

[4] The model's structure is particularly influenced by Rosen [1974], Leland [1977], and Willig [1978].

$$x_j = F_j(L_j, K_j, q_j), \tag{1}$$

where $L_j$ and $K_j$ denote labor and capital used in the production of $x_j$, the firm's physical quantity of output. The symbol $q_j$ indicates both the firm's quality control and the commodity's quality associated with a given setting of the control.[5,6] Production functions are strictly quasiconcave and homogeneous of degree one in inputs, and possess continuous second-order derivatives and positive marginal products. Provided quality choice has a Hicks-neutral impact on input use, the production function can be rewritten as

$$x_j = b_j(q_j)f_j(L_j, K_j). \tag{2}$$

Concerning changes in commodity quality, it is assumed that raising quality reduces output at an increasing rate, such that

$$\partial b_j/\partial q_j < 0 \quad \text{and} \quad \partial b_j^2/\partial^2 q_j < 0. \tag{3}$$

Firms are assumed to be price takers, as they cannot affect the price of a given-quality commodity, and there is free entry to the industry. But the (maximum) price at which an individual firm can sell its commodity, $p_j$, does vary with the quality of the commodity produced, i.e.

$$p_j = h_j(q_j).^7 \tag{4}$$

Industry $j$'s representative firm can adjust both inputs and commodity quality. Profit maximization by the firm results in the choice of commodity quality such that

$$b_j(\partial h_j/\partial q_j) = -h_j(\partial b_j/\partial q_j). \tag{5}$$

Commodity quality is increased until additional revenues from higher-priced quality is just offset by reduced revenues from declining physical output, which must be foregone for extra quality. While output quality is determinate, the firm's optimal quantity of output is indeterminate as production functions are homogeneous of degree one in inputs.

The competitive industry is in equilibrium when profits are zero, i.e.

[5] Strictly speaking, a commodity's quality depends on the firm's choice of its quality control and certain country-specific factors over which it has no control. Assuming a constant relation between quality produced and choice of quality control, as well as no change in the country-specific factors, the units of measurement for quality control and commodity quality can be chosen in such a way that they take on the same value of $q_j$.

[6] Production functions which contain quality controls as an argument were introduced by Leland [1977].

[7] Equation (4) describes the maximum price which either domestic or foreign buyers are willing to pay for a given quality product. In the small, open economy model of the next section it is assumed that domestic firms only sell in the home market and do not export the qualitatively differentiated commodity. Accordingly, the $h_j$-function faced by domestic firms, which is portrayed later as the $h$-locus of Figure 1, indicates the prices at which domestic producers can sell different qualities to domestic consumers. As will become clear later, the price faced by domestic firms for given quality depends on both foreign production and domestic demand conditions.

$$p_j = c_j, \tag{6}$$

where $c_j$ is the average cost of production for the representative firm in industry $j$. Given the model's assumptions, the firm's average cost can be evaluated from the slope of the economy's production possibility locus. Considering the specification of production functions in equation (2), the production possibility locus of a two-factor, two-industry economy can be expressed as

$$X_1 = b_1(q_1)T[X_2/b_2(q_2)], \tag{7}$$

where $-\infty < T' < 0$, $-\infty < T'' \leqq 0$, and $X_j$ is industry $j$'s quantity of output, provided all its firms produce the same quality. The average cost of producing the first commodity, measured in terms of the second commodity, is then:

$$c_1 = -\partial X_2/\partial X_1 = -b_2(q_2)/[b_1(q_1)T']. \tag{8}$$

Equation (8) reveals that the firm's average cost depends on the allocation of resources between industries, as expressed by $T'$, as well as on the qualities of commodities produced, as indicated by the values of $b_1$ and $b_2$. In order to simplify the remaining analysis, the paper proceeds under the assumption that only firms of the first industry have control over commodity quality, whereas commodities of the second industry are of predetermined quality. Accordingly, we set $b_2 = 1$ for convenience from now on.

2.3. Consumption Equilibrium. Consumers of a given country are assumed to be identical and to have continuous preference orderings over commodity groups one and two. As assumed in the preceding subsection, group one commodities are qualitatively differentiated, while group two commodities are homogeneous. When commodities have a quality dimension, it is convenient to assume that consumer preferences are represented by a repackaging utility function,

$$U = U[D_1/\Psi_1(q_1), D_2], \tag{9}$$

where $U$ is a utility index, $D_j$ is the quantity, $q_j$ is the quality, and $D_j/\Psi_j$ is the service flow which commodity $j$ yields to the consumer. For given quantities of the first good, service flows are assumed to rise with quality at a decreasing rate, i.e. $\partial\Psi_1/\partial q_1 < 0$ and $[(\partial^2\Psi_1/\partial q_1^2)/\Psi_1] - 2[(\partial\Psi_1/\partial q_1)/\Psi_1]^2 > 0$.

The individual consumer cannot affect the price of a given-quality commodity, but faces different prices for different quality commodities. Furthermore, the relationships between price and quality faced by the consumer may be different for domestically and foreign produced commodities.[8] Accordingly, we write

$$\tilde{p}_1 = g_1(q_1) \quad \text{and} \quad p_1^* = g_1^*(q_1), \tag{10}$$

[8] As will be explained later, the prices at which consumers can obtain different qualities are the competitive firms' reservation price loci. We assume that there are sufficient differences in production conditions between the domestic and foreign country to lead to different loci of (minimum) prices at which domestic and foreign firms respectively are willing to sell qualitatively differentiated commodities.

where $\tilde{p}_1$ and $p_1^*$ respectively are the domestic and foreign price of the first commodity of quality $q_1$ in terms of the homogeneous second commodity as faced by the consumer. If consumers consider the purchase of foreign-produced commodities they also may be constrained by the existence of import standards, such that

$$q_1 \geqq \bar{q}_1, \tag{11}$$

where $\bar{q}_1$ is an import standard on group one commodities.[9] Utility-maximizing choice by domestic consumers, who buy the qualitatively differentiated commodities from both domestic and foreign producers, implies that

$$[U_1/U_2]/\Psi_1(\tilde{q}_1) = g_1(\tilde{q}_1) \tag{12}$$

$$[U_1/U_2]/\Psi_1(q_1^*) = g_1^*(q_1^*) \tag{13}$$

$$g_1(q_1)[\partial\Psi_1/\partial\tilde{q}_1]/\Psi_1(\tilde{q}_1) + \partial g_1/\partial\tilde{q}_1 = 0 \tag{14}$$

$$g_1^*(q_1^*)[\partial\Psi_1/\partial q_1^*]/\Psi_1(q_1^*) + \partial g_1^*/\partial q_1^* \geqq 0, \tag{15}$$

provided the quality choice of domestic consumers is neither the maximum nor minimum quality producible by domestic producers.[10] The symbols $\tilde{q}_1$ and $q_1^*$ indicate the quality of the domestically and foreign produced commodities *chosen* at prices $\tilde{p}_1$ and $p_1^*$ respectively. Equations (12) and (13) state that prices consumers are willing to pay equal the prices they face in the market for both the domestically and foreign produced commodity. With equalities holding for both equations, consumers are indifferent between chosen domestic quality $\tilde{q}_1$ at price $\tilde{p}_1$ and chosen foreign quality $q_1^*$ at price $p_1^*$.[11] Although one cannot determine how much of the *individual* consumer's first commodity choice comes from domestic or foreign producers, it will be possible to determine these magnitudes at the aggregate level, as will become clear later. Equations (14) and (15), on the other hand, state that the additional price consumers are willing to pay for added quality is no larger than the increase in market price for higher quality. Should the inequality hold in equation (15), consumers face import standards that force them into buying foreign quality which exceeds the quality they would buy in the absence of these standards. In contrast to commodity quantity, the consumer's quality choice is uniquely determined, given appropriate properties of the $g_1$ and $g_1^*$ functions.

[9] Although the same standards may apply to domestically produced commodities as well, it is implicitly assumed that they are not binding on domestic firms.

[10] These conditions are equivalent to Rosen's [1974] conditions on optimal choice in the presence of commodity characteristics.

[11] The individual consumer buys either domestic or foreign or some domestic and some foreign quality. The individual is indifferent between these choices. Although some domestic and some foreign qualities may be chosen, it is assumed, as in Rosen [1974, p. 37], that mixing of produced qualities to create a new weighted-average quality is not possible. For example, the consumer may be indifferent between a given bottle of Californian Zinfandel at $5 and a given bottle of Italian Chianti at $6, but cannot create an intermediate quality by mixing the two.

## 3. OPEN ECONOMY EQUILIBRIUM

This section describes the equilibrium conditions for a small, open economy whose consumers purchase from both domestic and foreign producers of group one commodities. The smallness assumption implies that the home country is a price taker of imported commodities; prices at which the rest of the world supplies different-quality commodities are independent of the home country's demand for them. The assumption that domestic consumers in equilibrium buy both domestic and foreign group-one commodities is made to illustrate the trade-off between tariffs and import standards.[12] Tariffs and import standards are the only policy instruments for affecting the flow of border-crossing commodities.

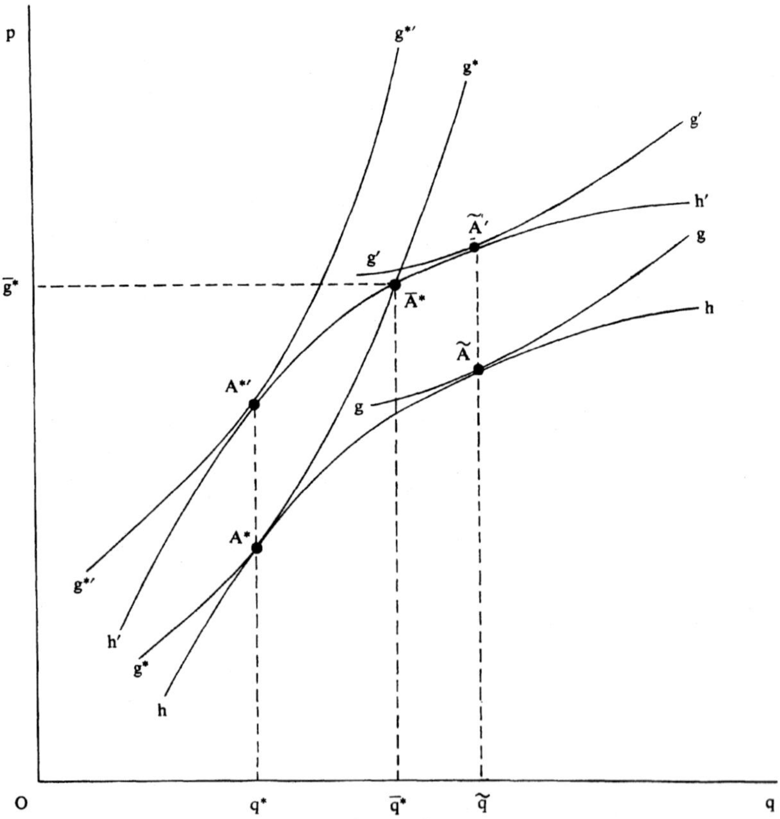


FIGURE 1

[12] For other types of trade patterns see Mayer [1980].

We stated in Subsection 2.2 that prices faced by domestic producers of the first industry vary with the quality of their product, i.e. $p_1 = h_1(q_1)$. The price at which the firm can sell a product in a given market is, in turn, the maximum price consumers are willing to pay for this quality, possibly adjusted for taxes. Hence, the prices faced by domestic and foreign producers of group one commodities in the home country are expressed by the reservation price function of domestic consumers, as described by $[U_1/U_2]/\Psi_1(q_1)$. This reservation price locus, which is denoted by $h$ in Figure 1, states the maximum prices consumers are willing to pay for different qualities at a given level of utility. In Subsection 2.3 we stated that prices faced by domestic consumers vary with product quality, i.e. $\tilde{p}_1 = g_1(q_1)$ and $p_1^* = g_1^*(q_1)$ depending on the domestic or foreign origin of the commodity. These prices are, in turn, the minimum prices domestic and foreign producers have to receive, possibly adjusted for taxes, in order to produce given quality commodities. In our model of zero-profit equilibria and tariffs, this means that

(16) $$g_1 = c_1(q_1) \quad \text{and} \quad g_1^* = c_1^*(q_1)(1+t),$$

where $c_1^*$ is the rest of the world's average cost of producing group one commodity of quality $q_1$, and $t$ is an *ad valorem* import tariff rate. Since the home country is small, $c_1^*$ only depends on quality, but not on the home country's volume of import demand. The average cost for domestic producers, $c_1$, on the other hand, depends on the volume of sales as well.[13] Using equation (8), we can restate equation (16) as

(16.1) $$g_1 = -1/[b_1(q_1)T'] \quad \text{and} \quad g_1^* = c_1^*(q_1)(1+t).$$

Based on the above expressions for prices faced by producers and consumers respectively, as well as on the previously developed producer and consumer equilibrium conditions, we now state the equilibrium conditions for the home country which produces and imports group-one commodities:

(17) $$[U_1/U_2]/\Psi_1(\tilde{q}_1) = -1/[b_1(\tilde{q}_1)T']$$

(18) $$[U_1/U_2]/\Psi_1(q_1^*) = c_1^*(q_1^*)(1+t)$$

(19) $$[\partial\Psi_1/\partial\tilde{q}_1]/\Psi_1(\tilde{q}_1) - [\partial b_1/\partial\tilde{q}_1]/b_1(\tilde{q}_1) = 0$$

(20) $$[\partial\Psi_1/\partial q_1^*]/\Psi_1(q_1^*) + [\partial c_1^*/\partial q_1^*]/c_1^*(q_1^*) \geqq 0$$

(21) $$p_1^* D_1^* + \tilde{D}_2 - \tilde{X}_2 = 0,$$

where $D_j^*$ and $\tilde{D}_j$ respectively denote the equilibrium quantities of domestic demand for foreign and domestically produced commodity $j$ and $\tilde{X}_j$ is domestic production of commodity $j$ in equilibrium. Equation (21) represents the country's balance of payments constraint. The equilibrium quality of the domestically produced and consumed group one commodity, $\tilde{q}_1$, can be solved for from

[13] All domestic output of group-one commodities is domestically consumed.

equation (19) above. Similarly, equation (20) can be solved for the quality of imported group-one commodities, $q_1^*$, provided import standards are not binding. If import standards are binding, then $q_1^*=\bar{q}_1^*$. Finally, the home country's equilibrium demand for the imported good, $D_1^*$, the exportable, $\tilde{D}_2$, and the domestically produced group one commodity, for which $\tilde{D}_1=\tilde{X}_1$, can be solved from equations (17), (18), and (21), with the help of (7).

The basic properties of the small, open economy equilibrium are portrayed in Figure 1. The $gg$ and $g^*g^*$ loci indicate the prices of domestic and foreign group-one commodities of different quality faced by domestic consumers, when there are no tariffs. As stated before, they are identical to the domestic and foreign firms' respective average cost curves for producing different qualities. In accordance with equation (3), these curves rise at an increasing rate. In the diagram it is implicitly assumed that differences in climates, soil, or other country-specific factors result in different positionings of the two countries' average cost curves. With the state of technology and all resource endowments fixed, a given country's average cost curve shifts when resources are reallocated between industries. Accordingly, an expansion of the home country's first industry is associated with an upward shift of the $gg$ locus, say, to $g'g'$. The small country assumption, on the other hand, implies that changes in domestic demand for foreign-produced group-one commodities have no effect on the positioning of the $g^*g^*$ locus. The $hh$ locus, finally, shows the prices of different qualities which domestic and foreign producers face in the small home country's market. It reflects the domestic consumers' willingness to pay for one unit of the first commodity as quality is varied, but utility is held constant.

Figure 1 is designed to portray equilibria under three alternative assumptions about trade policies. First, *free trade* is postulated. This implies that $t=0$ in equation (18) and equality holds in equation (20). At point $\tilde{A}$ of Figure 1, equations (17) and (19) are satisfied, whereas equations (18) and (20) hold at point $A^*$. The corresponding equilibrium qualities of imported and domestically produced goods are indicated by $q^*$ and $\tilde{q}$ respectively. Second, *tariffs* on the imported first-group commodity are imposed. Now domestic consumers face foreign prices as indicated by the $g^{*\prime}g^{*\prime}$ locus. While $g^*=c^*$ in the diagram, $g^{*\prime}=c^*(1+t)$. Provided importing continues after the tariff imposition, the $hh$ locus must shift to $h'h'$ and the $gg$ locus to $g'g'$ in order to satisfy the tangency conditions contained in equations (17)–(21) at points $\tilde{A}'$ and $A^{*\prime}$. Accordingly, the home producers' average cost curve shifts upward, resulting in a reallocation of resources from the second to the first industry. Consequently, firms in the first industry enjoy protection[14]. Under our third equilibrium, an *import*

[14] The diagram shows that the quality of imports and domestically produced goods remains unaffected by tariffs. This result immediately follows from equations (19) and (20). More specifically this result is contingent on our assumptions of Hicks-neutral quality adjustments in production, repackaging utility functions in consumption, and tariff rates which are independent of product quality. These restrictions also imply certain limitations on the general applicability of the next section's tariff equivalence formulae.

***quality standard*** of $\bar{q}_1^*$ is imposed while there are no tariffs. Domestic consumers no longer can import the previously acquired quality of $q^*$ as it falls short of the standard set at $\bar{q}^*$. The minimum price at which foreign firms are willing to sell group-one commodities of quality $\bar{q}^*$ is now $\bar{g}^*$. Provided imports continue after import standards are imposed, equations (17)–(21), with inequality in equation (20), will continue to hold only if $hh$ and $gg$ shift up until the former cuts $g^*g^*$ at $\bar{A}^*$. In our diagram this happens to be the case when $gg$ and $hh$ reach the same positions they took in the preceding tariff example, indicated by $g'g'$ and $h'h'$. Consequently, the chosen import standard results in the same allocation of resources as the chosen tariff before. Identical protective effects, as measured by the reallocation of resources to the first industry, can be achieved through either tariffs or import standards for firms of the first industry.

## 4. TARIFF EQUIVALENCE OF IMPORT STANDARDS

We finally are in a position to examine rigorously the possible tradeoffs between tariffs and import standards in assuring a constant level of protection to the home country's first industry. The degree of protection to the first industry is measured by the magnitude of resource reallocation caused by departure from free trade. If prevailing values of tariffs and import standards lead to more resources allocated to the first industry than under free trade, then the first industry is protected. From the specification of the economy's production side one can see that there exists a unique relationship between the industry allocation of factors and prices faced by producers, provided the first commodity's quality remains unchanged. Consequently, as long as tariffs and import standards have no effect on *domestic* commodity quality, $\tilde{q}_1$, any combination of tariffs and import standards which results in the same price faced by producers implies identical degrees of protection to the first industry.

In Section 3 it was argued that the price faced by domestic producers of the first commodity, $p_1$, is the maximum price domestic consumers are willing to pay for a given-quality commodity. Evaluated at the equilibrium solution for domestic quality, $\tilde{q}_1$, we have:

$$\tilde{p}_1 = [U_1/U_2]/\Psi_1(\tilde{q}_1). \tag{22}$$

Furthermore, it follows from equation (18) that in equilibrium

$$\tilde{p}_1 = [c_1^*(q_1^*)\Psi_1(q_1^*)/\Psi_1(\tilde{q}_1)]\,[1 + t]. \tag{23}$$

Equation (23) reveals that the price of the home-produced, first commodity depends on both domestic and imported qualities, as well as the tariff rate. Import standards are one possible policy instrument for protection provided the standards are binding; i.e. $q_1^* = \bar{q}_1^*$. The tariff rate, $t$, is the other policy instrument. And the third influence on $\tilde{p}_1$, namely domestic quality, $\tilde{q}_1$, although endogenous, is independent of both $t$ and $\bar{q}_1^*$, as can be seen from equation (19).

The possibility of substituting import standards for tariffs in providing industry one with a constant level of protection can be evaluated by differentiating equation (23) with respect to $t$ and $\bar{q}_1^*$, while holding $\tilde{p}_1$ fixed; this yields

$$(24) \qquad \hat{t} = -(\sigma_1^* - \eta_1^*)\hat{\bar{q}}_1^*,$$

where $\hat{t}=dt/(1+t)$ and $\hat{\bar{q}}_1^*=d\bar{q}_1^*/\bar{q}_1^*$. The term $\sigma_1=(\bar{q}_1^*/c_1^*)(\partial c_1^*/\partial \bar{q}_1^*)>0$ indicates the rest of the world's average cost response to quality changes, and $\eta_1^*=-[\bar{q}_1^*/\Psi_1(\bar{q}_1^*)][\partial \Psi_1/\partial \bar{q}_1^*]>0$ represents a measure of the consumers' reservation price response to quality changes.[15] Although both $\sigma_1^*$ and $\eta_1^*$ are positive, one can immediately see from equation (20) that $(\sigma_1^*-\eta_1^*)>0$ as long as import standards exceed the consumers' free trade import quality choice. Hence, equation (24) expresses that a one percent increase in quality standards is equivalent to a $(\sigma_1^*-\eta_1^*)$ percent rise in tariffs in protecting the first industry. From the definition of $\sigma_1^*$ and $\eta_1^*$ one can further see that as the value of $(\sigma_1^*-\eta_1^*)$ rises the more difficult it is for foreign producers and the easier it is for domestic consumers to adjust to the enforced import quality standards.

For the effective conduct of trade policies it is important that the tariff equivalence value of import standards can be calculated. Our final task is to show that such tariff equivalence measures can be calculated, provided valid quality indices or characteristics measures exist for the commodity in question and estimates of cost and demand responses to quality changes can be obtained.

The value of $\sigma_1^*$ in equation (24) can be obtained from empirical studies of foreign producers' average cost functions, $c_1^*=c_1^*(w^*, r^*, q_1^*)$ where $w^*$ and $r^*$ represent the foreign country's returns on labor and capital respectively. The value of $\eta_1^*$, on the other hand, cannot be obtained directly from estimates of demand parameters as the $\Psi_1$ function is not revealed through directly observable consumer behavior. However, $\eta_1^*$ can be measured in a roundabout manner. For the utility function of equation (9), the corresponding demand function for the imported good, $D_1^*$, is:[16]

$$(25) \qquad D_1^* = B_1[p_1^*\Psi_1(q_1^*), Y]\Psi_1(q_1^*) = D_1^*(p_1^*, q_1^*, Y),$$

where $Y$ is the domestic consumers' income. Based on equation (25), estimates of both the price elasticity of demand, $\varepsilon_1^*$, and the quality elasticity of demand, $\rho_1^*$, can be obtained for the imported commodity. And since

$$\varepsilon_1^* = -[p_1^*/D_1^*][\partial D_1^*/\partial p_1^*] = -[\Psi_1(q_1^*)p_1^*/B_1^*][\partial B_1^*/\partial(p_1^*\Psi_1)],$$

$$\rho_1^*=[q_1^*/D_1^*][\partial D_1^*/\partial q_1^*]=\{[q_1^*/\Psi_1(q_1^*)][\partial\Psi_1/\partial q_1^*]\}\cdot$$
$$\{1+[\Psi_1(q_1^*)p_1^*/B_1^*][\partial B_1^*/\partial(p_1^*\Psi_1)]\},$$

it follows from the definition of $\eta_1^*$ that

$$(26) \qquad \eta_1^* = \rho_1^*/(\varepsilon_1^* - 1).$$

[15] More precisely, it is the percentage change in the maximum price the consumer is willing to pay as quality is raised by a given percentage such that utility remains constant.

[16] See Willig [1978].

Hence, the tariff equivalence of import standards, as expressed in equation (24), can be calculated from estimates on foreign cost responses to quality change, as well as on domestic price and quality elasticities of demand.

The preceding discussion of tariff equivalence of import standards was based on the assumption that a commodity's quality is measured by an index and that import standards are stated in terms of that index. In fact, such general quality indices exist for some agricultural products, such as wheat or rice,[17] where general or special grades are assigned to describe the product's quality. For many commodities, however, import standards are specified in terms of one or more specific commodity features rather than overall quality. Accordingly, we wish to show how our analysis can be modified to accommodate the case of import standards with respect to individual characteristics.

The suggested modification requires two changes in assumptions. First, firms now have control over specific commodity features in the production process; and, second, consumers' service flows from commodities now depend on these separate features rather than overall quality. Accordingly, we assume that

$$c_1 = c_1(Z_{11}, Z_{12},\dots, Z_{1n}) \tag{27}$$

$$\Psi_1 = \Psi_1(Z_{11}, Z_{12},\dots, Z_{1n}), \tag{28}$$

where $Z_{1j}$ is the $j$-th feature or characteristic of commodity one. With the remaining specifications of the model unchanged, the trade-off relation between tariffs and import standards on characteristics is:

$$\hat{t} = -\sum_{j=1}^{n} (\sigma^*_{1j} - \eta^*_{1j})\,\hat{\bar{Z}}^*_{1j}, \tag{29}$$

where $\bar{Z}^*_{1j}$ is the import standard imposed on the $j$-th feature of the imported first commodity, $\sigma^*_{1j}=(\bar{Z}^*_{1j}/c^*_1)(\partial c^*_1/\partial \bar{Z}^*_{1j})$, and $\eta^*_{1j}=-(\bar{Z}^*_{1j}/\Psi_1)(\partial \Psi_1/\partial \bar{Z}^*_{1j})$. Using estimates of cost and demand function parameters to obtain values for $\sigma^*_{1j}$ and $\eta^*_{1j}$, it is again possible to calculate the tariff equivalence of one or more import standards on commodity features.

In public discussions importing countries generally claim that import standards are adopted to protect domestic consumers. Exporters, on the other hand, generally assert that import standards represent a hidden form of industry protection. Concerning the industry protection effect, our tariff equivalence expressions of equations (24) and (29) clarify two points. First, domestic producers always enjoy protective effects, as long as imported quality under import standards exceeds what it would be in the absence of standards. Whenever fully-informed domestic consumers cannot import the quality they would choose without restrictions, industry protection effects are present. Second, the tariff equivalence of an import standard is generally less than the standards-attributed increase in unit cost to foreign producers. As long as $\eta^*_{1j}>0$, i.e. consumers benefit from

[17] These grades are discussed in the U.S. Department of Agriculture reports on the wheat industry [1979] and rice industry [1979].

improved quality, a given percentage increase in unit cost required to meet the import standards overstates the true protective effects of these standards.

*University of Cincinnati*

REFERENCES


BALDWIN, R. E., *Nontariff Distortions of International Trade* (Washington, D.C.: The Brookings Institution, 1970).

CAVES, R. E. AND R. W. JONES, *World Trade and Payments*, 3rd edition (Boston: Little, Brown, and Co., 1981).

FISHER, F. M. AND K. SHELL, "Taste and Quality Change in the Pure Theory of the True Cost of Living Index," in Z. Griliches, ed., *Price Indexes and Quality Change: Studies in New Methods of Measurement* (Cambridge, Mass.: Harvard University Press, 1971).

LELAND, H., "Quality Choice and Competition," *American Economic Review*, 67 (March, 1977), 127–47.

MAYER, W., "International Trade in Qualitatively Differentiated Commodities," presented at the 1980 Econometric Society Meeting in Denver (mimeo, 1980).

MUELLBAUER, J., "Household Production Theory, Quality, and the Hedonic Technique," *American Economic Review*, 64 (December, 1974), 977–94.

ROSEN, S., "Hedonic Prices and Implicit Markets: Product Differentiation in Pure Competition," *Journal of Political Economy* 82, (January/February, 1974), 34–55.

STERN, R., "Tariffs and Other Measures of Trade Control: A Survey of Recent Developments," *Journal of Economic Literature*, 11 (September 1973), 857–88.

SUBCOMMITTEE ON TRANSPORTATION AND COMMERCE, *Standards Code of the Trade Agreements Act of* 1979. Hearings, 96th Congress (June 28, 1979), Serial 96–58.

U.S. DEPARTMENT OF AGRICULTURE, *U.S. Wheat Industry*, Agricultural Economic Report No. 432 (1979).

U.S. DEPARTMENT OF AGRICULTURE, *U.S. Rice Industry*, Agricultural Economic Report No. 433 (1979).

U.S. TARIFF COMMISSION, *Nontariff Trade Barriers*, Report to the Committee on Finance of the U.S. Senate and its Subcommittee on International Trade, Part 2, TC Publication 665 (Washington, D.C.: 1974).

WILLIG, R. D., "Incremental Consumer's Surplus and Hedonic Price Adjustments," *Journal of Economic Theory*, 17 (April, 1978), 227–253.

# The infant-export industry argument

WOLFGANG MAYER / University of Cincinnati

*Abstract.* When actual consumption experiences are required to learn about a commodity's qualities, subsidization of infant-exporters can be justified as a first-best policy measure. This paper develops a dynamic model of optimal foreign market cultivation and examines the type and magnitude of trade intervention that is warranted and how this intervention adjusts over time. It also focuses on changing production, consumption, and trade patterns, as well as on welfare implications for individuals and society as the subsidization process unfolds. International borrowing is allowed and is shown to cushion against severe welfare losses in the early phases of export subsidization.

*L'argument en faveur de la protection d'une industrie d'exportation dans la phase initiale de son développement.* Quand on ne peut apprécier les qualités d'un bien qu'en le consommant effectivement, on peut défendre comme politique optimale les subventions aux exportateurs dans la phase initiale de production de leur bien. Ce mémoire développe un modèle dynamique de mise en valeur optimale des marchés étrangers et examine quel type d'intervention est justifiée, quelle intensité de support est nécessaire, et à quel moment cette aide doit être modifiée à mesure que le temps passe. L'auteur examine aussi les implications pour la structure de la production, de la consommation et du commerce de ce type d'intervention ainsi que ses effets sur le niveau de bien-être des individus et de la collectivité. L'emprunt international permet d'amortir le choc de pertes de bien-être importantes dans les phases initiales de la subvention des exportations.

## INTRODUCTION

The infant-export industry argument attempts to justify subsidization of exports as a first-best policy measure. Bhagwati (1968) has pointed out that the entering of new foreign markets may require considerable market-cultivating expenditures on the part of exporting firms. However, each firm's efforts at overcoming foreign-buyer resistance benefit not only itself but also all other firms that try to sell the same product in the same new market. Accordingly, the social returns on investments in foreign

I greatly appreciate the constructive comments of two anonymous referees as well as suggestions and assistance by Boualem Bendjilali.

Canadian Journal of Economics / Revue canadienne d'Economique XVII, No. 2
May / mai 1984. Printed in Canada / Imprimé au Canada

market cultivation exceed the private returns, and intervention in the form of export subsidization is justified to raise society's welfare.

There are at least three distinct areas of economic writings where discussions of or allusions to the infant-export industry argument can be found: the areas of international trade theory, international trade policy, and economic development. Somewhat surprisingly, the trade-theoretic literature is least informative on export subsidization arguments. A notable exception, as mentioned already, is Bhagwati (1968), who emphasizes that not all arguments in support of export subsidies are invalid, as seems to be implied by the non-treatment of export subsidization in the remaining trade literature.[1] He argues in particular that externalities in cultivating new foreign markets may justify export subsidies as first-best policy measures. The international trade-policy literature, on the other hand, contains far more frequent allusions to the infant-export industry argument. The recent debate over the effectiveness and appropriateness of current GATT provisions on export subsidization is a case in point (e.g., Pestieau, 1978 and Malmgren, 1978). It is widely accepted that certain well-defined exceptions to the general principle of prohibiting export subsidies should be granted in the case of infant-export industries. The third area of economics in which export subsidization is frequently discussed is the area of economic development (e.g., Little, Scitovsky, and Scott, 1970). Disappointment with past import substitution experiences was the initial force behind advocating export promotions.[2] Empirical evidence of strong, positive relations between export performance and economic growth has added impetus to the adoption of such policies (e.g., Michaely, 1977; Balassa, 1978; and Heller and Porter, 1978). To the extent that export promotion policies are supported by some form of theoretical argument, the infant-export industry idea usually stands in the forefront.[3]

Although the notion of an infant-export industry has been firmly accepted in the economic literature, the underlying theory remains quite sketchy. Bhagwati has provided a basic rationale for subsidizing infant-exporters, but his treatment of the topic is quite brief and, at least to our knowledge, there has not been any significant follow-up on his work. Therefore, it seems important to develop a more complete understanding of the underlying theory. This paper represents a step towards this goal. We construct a relatively simple dynamic model of foreign-market cultivation in which subsidies to infant-exporters indeed represent a first-best policy.[4] First, we examine the general nature of optimal trade policies, determining what type of intervention is appropriate, what the optimal degree of intervention is at a given point in time, and how optimal intervention changes over time as foreign-market cultivation progresses. Second, we analyse adjustments in domestic consumption and production patterns as well as in exports and the balance of trade, which arise during

1 Bhagwati (1968) explains the lack of attention by trade theorists with the remark: 'catch hold of any trade theorist and he is certain to rule them [export subsidies] out as first-best policies.'
2 The switch from import substitution to export subsidization policies started in the early 1960s.
3 An important exception is Savasini (1978), whose analysis is based on Bhagwati (1968).
4 In the literature on the much better known 'infant-industry argument' a fully specified dynamic model has been constructed by Clemhout and Wan (1970).

the initial intervention and ensuing market cultivation period. And finally, we study the welfare implications of these adjustments for the nation as a whole, as perceived by a social planner, and for each individual household. Among the latter, factor ownership is allowed to vary. In particular, the distinction between short-run losses and long-run gains from export subsidization is highlighted.

Foreign-market cultivation activities tend to have a lasting impact. A one-time market-cultivating expenditure results in a flow of benefits that extends far into the future. Consequently, the export-subsidizing country's welfare gains tend to become more pronounced in the long run only, after significant welfare losses may have been incurred in the short run. One way of alleviating these short-run welfare losses is to borrow in the international market and temporarily run a balance of trade deficit. This paper allows for international borrowing. The balance of trade constraint is not binding at each instant of time, but only over the entire period of foreign market cultivation. Accordingly, making adjustments in the balance of trade over time is one of the issues considered.

The infant-exporter may not face perfectly elastic demand for its product in the foreign market. Once the foreign market is penetrated, the exporter may have some control over foreign prices. Hence, the optimal trade policy will have to reflect both the country's market cultivation goals and its monopoly power. In our paper we define a 'net' optimal tariff or subsidy and demonstrate how market cultivation and monopoly elements shape it.

The second section states the model's basic assumptions about the markets in which the infant-export industry tries to sell. In particular, it is argued that consumers may be unfamiliar with the quality of some commodities they consider for purchase. For some commodities complete product familiarity can be gained through inspection before purchase, but for others actual consumption experiences are required.[5] It is assumed that product familiarization through consumption experience is described by an Arrow-type learning-by-doing (consuming) formulation. In addition, this section states the decision problem faced by an economic planner given the ability to run balance of trade surpluses or deficits. The third section deals with optimal trade intervention at a given point in time. Specifically, it shows to what extent optimal policy is guided by market cultivation and monopoly considerations. The fourth section focuses on the dynamics of tariffs and subsidies, as well as on adjustments of consumption and production, exports and the balance of trade, and the ensuing welfare ramifications. The analysis is based on the assumption that the economic planner's time preference is zero. As Ramsey (1928) has argued, social planners who allocate goods over different generations of people should not have a positive time preference. We finally allude to required adjustments in our conclusions if the time preference were positive and some other restricting assumptions of our model were relaxed.

5 The significance of consumption experience as an information process on commodity quality has been pointed out by, among others, Nelson (1970). It also plays an important role in the habit formation literature of, for example, Pollak (1970), Von Weizsäcker (1971) or Yaari (1977).

## THE MODEL

*Assumptions*

Consider a two-industry economy whose production possibilities are described by

$$X_2 = F(X_1), \tag{1}$$

where $-\infty < F_{x_1} < 0$, $-\infty < F_{x_1x_1} < 0$, and $X_j$ denotes industry output of commodity $j$, $j = 1, 2$. Producers of the first commodity make up the infant-export industry while producers of the second commodity form a rest-of-the-economy industry. The first commodity is of such nature that buyers cannot discern its true quality through inspection prior to purchase; actual consumption experience is required to gain complete information on the commodity. Accordingly, the need to cultivate new markets may arise for the first commodity. The second commodity's quality, on the other hand, can be determined through inspection alone and no market cultivation is needed.

Domestic consumers know all about the quality of the home-produced commodities, since they have consumed them and learned about their quality ever since production started. The community's preferences, as perceived by the social planner, are assumed to be described by

$$U = f_1(D_1) + f_2(D_2), \tag{2}$$

where $U$ is an index of society's welfare, $D_j$ denotes the domestically consumed quantity of commodity $j$, $j = 1, 2$, $f_{D_j} > 0$, $f_{D_jD_j} < 0$, and the utility function is bounded from above.

Foreigners, in contrast to domestic consumers, are not fully familiar with the infant-export industry's product. Product familiarity is measured by $V$, $0 \leqq V \leqq 1$, which expresses the fraction of full information a representative consumer in the new foreign market actually holds. While some product familiarity, $\bar{V} < 1$, can be gained through inspection alone, full product familiarity, $V = 1$, necessitates actual consumption experience. Similar to other learning-by-doing processes, the rate of product familiarization, $\dot{V} = dV/dt$, is assumed to depend on the prevailing level of foreign consumption, $D_1{}^*$, and the extent to which the product's quality is yet unknown, $(1 - V)$. Specifically, we assume the foreign consumer's learning function to be

$$\dot{V} = \alpha(1 - V)D_1{}^*, \tag{3}$$

where $\alpha$ represents a positive learning coefficient, and the assumption is made that consumers do not forget previously acquired product knowledge. Implicit is the belief that once-acquired product knowledge is instantly refreshable and verifiable through inspection before purchase. The form of equation (3) also implies that a given consumption flow adds less to product knowledge the more familiar consumers are with the product.

The price foreign consumers are willing to pay for the infant-exporter's product,

$p^*$, is, ceteris paribus, directly related to the degree of product familiarity.[6] Measured in terms of the homogeneous second commodity, the foreign demand price is given by

$$p^* = p^*(V, D_1^*), \tag{4}$$

where $p_V^* > 0$ and $p_{VV}^* < 0$ for $V < 1$, $\lim_{V \to 1} p_V^* = 0, p_{D_1^*}^* \leqq 0$ and $p_{D_1^*V}^* = 0$.

Hence, we allow for the possibility of a downward sloping foreign demand curve but assume that its slope is independent of $V$.

Individual consumers and producers are assumed to operate in perfectly competitive markets. Furthermore, there is a social planner whose sole task is to implement economic policies that maximize society's welfare. Since the benefits of a given act of product familiarization extend far into the future, maximization of society's welfare requires that the (discounted) stream of utility,

$$\int_0^\infty e^{-rt}[f_1(D_1) + f_2(D_2)]dt, \tag{5}$$

be maximized over time, where $r$ is a constant discount rate expressing the social planner's time preference.

The home country's consumption set is constrained by its production possibilities, equation (1), and relevant balance of payments restrictions. This paper allows for borrowing and lending at the constant international interest rate $\rho$.[7] The only constraints imposed are that properly discounted export receipts equal import payments over the entire decision horizon and that there are no further borrowing or lending in long-run equilibrium as the market cultivation process has been completed; that is,

$$\int_0^\infty e^{-\rho t}[p^*(V, D_1^*)D_1^* + (X_2 - D_2)]dt = 0 \tag{6}$$

$$\lim_{t \to \infty} [p^*(V, D_1^*)D_1^* + (X_2 - D_2)] = 0. \tag{7}$$

*General statement of the decision problem*

Firms of the infant-export industry consider selling in both domestic and foreign markets. If, in the absence of government intervention, the domestic autarky price, $p^A$, exceeds the price foreigners are willing to pay after inspecting the product, $p^*(\bar{V},$

6 Such a relationship between demand price and product familiarity coefficient can easily be derived from a repackaging-type utility function in which gaining product familiarity is equivalent to getting more of the commodity. Such repackaging utility functions, with a quality index rather than product familiarity coefficient as argument, are discussed in Fisher and Shell (1971), Willig (1978), and Deaton and Muellbauer (1980). The relationship between demand price and product quality is derived in Rosen (1974).

7 Although the country may have some control over the price of its export good in a specific foreign market, it is too small to affect the interest rate that prevails in all international markets.

0), firms have no immediate incentive to export. On the other hand, if $p^A < p^*(\bar{V}, 0)$, firms of the infant export industry will export even without government intervention. In this case the initial situation is characterized by domestic ($D_1$) and foreign ($D_1{}^*$) sales levels such that $p(D_1) = p^*(V, D_1{}^*)$.

Individual firms' exporting decisions are based on short-run profit considerations. Firms know that foreign consumption breeds product familiarity and raises prices attainable on future sales, but this initiates no special efforts by an individual firm to cultivate export markets. Each firm's sales are too small to have a more than negligible impact on product familiarity and foreign demand price.

Foreign consumers who are fully familiar with the infant exporter's product have the inverse demand function $p^*(1, D_1{}^*)$. It is quite possible that $p(\bar{V}, 0) < p^A < p^*(1, 0)$, implying that firms have no immediate or short-run incentive to export, although such an incentive would exist if foreigners had gained full product familiarity. Since firms are guided by short-run prospects only, international trade may never open up. It is here that the social planner comes in. What is optimal for individual firms may not be optimal for society as a whole. The social planner must decide whether society will benefit from international trade, in spite of initial losses from exporting, and what the optimal path of cultivating the foreign market is. Even if trade comes about without government intervention, as $p^A < p^*(\bar{V}, 0)$, the social planner must determine whether the resulting trade pattern coincides with what is best for society and what kind of corrective interventions are called for.

*Specific formulation of the decision problem*

Society's welfare, as perceived by the social planner, is maximized if domestic and foreign consumption of domestically produced goods are such that they

$$\max_{D_1, D_2, D_1{}^*} \int_0^\infty e^{-rt}[f_1(D_1) + f_2(D_2)]dt$$

$$\text{s.t.} \int_0^\infty e^{-\rho t}[p^*(V, D_1{}^*)D_1{}^* + F(D_1 + D_1{}^*) - D_2]dt = 0,$$

$$\dot{V} = \alpha(1 - V)D_1{}^*, \tag{8}$$

with equation (7) holding and equation (1) substituted in the isoperimetric balance of payments constraint. An infinite time horizon is chosen, since there is no natural stopping time for this type of problem. The maximand integral of equation (8) is convergent, since the utility function is bounded from above and the rate of time preference, $r$, is positive.

Domestic consumption of each commodity is assumed to be positive in the relevant range. And although international borrowing is possible, the social planner imposes the restriction that at no time actual domestic consumption can exceed what it will be (in long-run equilibrium) when foreigners have gained full product familiarity, $\bar{D}_j$; that is,

$$0 < D_j \leqq \bar{D}_j,\ j = 1, 2.^{8} \tag{9}$$

Finally, there is a non-negativity constraint on exports, $D_1{}^*$; that is,

$$0 \leqq D_1{}^*. \tag{10}$$

The current-value Hamiltonian, $H$, corresponding to equation (8), is written as

$$H = [f_1(D_1) + f_2(D_2)] + \mu_1 e^{-(\rho-r)t}[p^*(V, D_1{}^*)D_1{}^* + F(D_1 + D_1{}^*) - D_2] + \mu_2 e^{rt}\alpha(1 - V)D_1{}^*, \tag{11}$$

where the multipliers $\mu_1$ and $\mu_2$ express the marginal contributions of accumulated national wealth and foreign product familiarity prevailing at time $t$, respectively, to domestic welfare when discounted back to the initial period. For the analysis to come, we redefine

$$m_1 = \mu_1 e^{-(\rho-r)t} \text{ and } m_2 = \mu_2 e^{rt}. \tag{12}$$

Considering the constraints of equations (9) and (10), the current value Lagrangian is written as

$$L = [f_1(D_1) + f_2(D_2)] + m_1[p^*(V, D_1{}^*)D_1{}^* + F(D_1 + D_1{}^*) - D_2] + m_2\alpha(1 - V)D_1{}^* + \lambda_1(\bar{D}_1 - D_1) + \lambda_2(\bar{D}_2 - D_2) - \lambda_3 D_1{}^*, \tag{13}$$

where $\lambda_i$, $i = 1, 2, 3$, are multipliers associated with constraints on the control variables.

## OPTIMAL EXPORT SUBSIDIES

In this section we shall determine whether and how the government should intervene in the competitive markets to assure maximum welfare to society. Only the need for intervention at a given point in time is examined, while the study of adjustments in optimal intervention over time is delayed until the next section.

Among the necessary conditions for maximizing society's welfare are the 'optimality conditions':

$$f_{D_1} + m_1 F_{x_1} - \lambda_1 = 0, \tag{14}$$

$$f_{D_2} - m_1 - \lambda_2 = 0, \tag{15}$$

$$m_1(\text{MR}^* + F_{x_1}) + m_2\alpha(1 - V) - \lambda_3 = 0, \tag{16}$$

where $\lambda_1 \geqq 0$ and $\lambda_1(\bar{D}_1 - D_1) = 0$, $\lambda_2 \geqq 0$ and $\lambda_2(\bar{D}_2 - D_2) = 0$, and $\lambda_3 \geqq 0$ and $\lambda_3 D_1{}^* = 0$. The term $\text{MR}^* = (p^* + p_{D_1{}^*}{}^* D_1{}^*)$ indicates marginal revenues from selling in the foreign market, which are assumed to decline with increased sales.

8 This restriction is imposed to avoid possible complications from indefinitely postponing the paying-back of earlier loans.

First, we consider possible justification for intervention in domestic consumption or production activities. Two situations are distinguished: one, where domestic consumption falls short of the long-run ceiling, $D_j < \bar{D}_j$; and the other, where consumption of at least one commodity has reached the long-run ceiling. In the first case, $\lambda_1 = \lambda_2 = 0$ and equations (14) and (15) imply that

$$(f_{D_1}/f_{D_2}) = -F_{x_1}. \tag{17}$$

Optimality requires that the marginal rate of substitution in consumption equals the marginal rate of transformation in production. Since this condition will be satisfied in a competitive economy, intervention in production or consumption is not warranted. In the second case, however, when consumption has reached its long-run level for at least one commodity, some form of intervention is required. For example, if $D_2 = \bar{D}_2$ but $D_1 < \bar{D}_1$, then $[f_{D_1}/(f_{D_2} - \lambda_2)] = -F_{x_1}$ from equations (14) and (15). Defining the producers' supply price by $p = -F_{x_1}$, the domestic consumers' demand price by $p_c = (f_{D_1}/f_{D_2})$, and an ad valorem consumption subsidy on the first commodity by $s_c$, then

$$s_c = (p - p_c)/p = (\lambda_2/f_{D_2}) > 0. \tag{18}$$

Consumption of the first commodity must be subsidized relative to the second commodity to ensure that the former grows to its long-run ceiling without the latter expanding any further.

Justification for export subsidization is the central issue of this paper. In order to study the question more closely we have to examine equation (16). This relation states that if exporting is optimal at all, the level chosen should equate society's marginal loss from selling the first commodity abroad, $m_1(p - \text{MR}^*)$, with the marginal gain from raising the foreigners' information level, $m_2\alpha(1 - V)$. The working of the competitive market alone, however, will not assure this socially optimal export level. Government intervention is called for on two accounts: the existence of externalities in market cultivation through exporting and the ability to affect the foreign demand price at a given level of foreign product familiarity.

Let us first concentrate on the market cultivation aspect only and assume away any monopoly power in the foreign market such that $\text{MR}^* = p^*$ in equation (16).[9] The export subsidy rate, $s$, is defined as

$$s = (p - p^*)/p. \tag{19}$$

In the absence of monopoly power, the export subsidy rate for market cultivation is optimal if

$$s = [m_2\alpha(1 - V)]/[m_1 p], \tag{20}$$

using equations (16) and (19). As long as product familiarity is not complete, $V < 1$, and more product familiarity enhances society's welfare, $m_2 > 0$, the optimal export subsidy is positive. Export subsidization, rather than other forms of intervention, is

9 This can be interpreted as the small-country case of foreign market cultivation.

called for, since product familiarization occurs through consumption of the export good. If foreign consumers gained information on product quality through advertising or other forms of signalling, these activities rather than exporting should be subsidized.

Next, we abstract from the market cultivation aspect and concentrate on the more familiar intervention due to monopoly power. Hence, we assume that $V = 1$ and that $\text{MR}^* = p^*(1 - 1/\epsilon^*)$, where $\epsilon^* < \infty$ expresses the foreign country's import elasticity of demand for the infant-exporter's product. From equation (16), the optimal tariff rate in the absence of market cultivation, $\tau$, is then

$$\tau = (p^* - p)/p = 1/(\epsilon^* - 1), \tag{21}$$

which is the usual formula for an optimal tariff under monopoly power.

We define a 'net' optimal tariff rate, $T = (p^* - p)/p$, for the case when both market cultivation and monopoly power elements are present. Substitution of equations (20) and (21) in (16), noting that $p^* = p(1 + T)$, yields

$$T = \tau - s - s\tau. \tag{22}$$

The 'net' optimal tariff on exports (approximately) equals the difference between the optimal export tariff rate in the monopoly case and the optimal export subsidy rate in the market cultivation case, since the last term on the RHS of equation (22) tends to be very small. In the early stages of market penetration, where $D_1{}^*$ is very small and $\epsilon^*$ tends to be quite large, the export subsidy will be the dominating component in equation (22). However, once foreign consumers have become fully informed, $T = \tau > 0$.

## THE DYNAMICS OF TAXES, TRADE, AND WELFARE

After justifying the existence of export subsidies for market cultivation purposes, we want to examine changes in the optimal export subsidy rate over time. Also, we shall discuss the dynamic adjustments in domestic consumption and production, exports and the balance of trade, as well as the nation's[10] and each individual's welfare.

The dynamic analysis is conducted under the assumption that the social planner's time preference rate, $r$, is zero. In this assumption we follow Ramsey (1928), who argued that social planners who are concerned with the intergenerational allocation of goods should not have a positive rate of time preference.[11] In addition to introducing intergenerational unbiasedness the assumption improves the tractability of the model's dynamic analysis.

As one would expect, setting $r = 0$ implies that the maximand of equation (8) is no

10 'The nation's welfare' refers to welfare as perceived by the social planner. It would coincide with each individual's welfare if losers could be fully compensated by gainers.

11 This assumption plays a very important role in the growth literature; see Burmeister and Dobell (1970). It also should be noted that under the expectation of growing income due to the opening of trade the international interest rate would be positive, even if consumers in all countries had a zero time preference; see Böhm-Bawerk (1959, 259–89).

longer convergent. One can replace equation (8), however, with

$$\int_0^{\infty} [f_1(D_1) + f_2(D_2) - f_1(\bar{D}_1) - f_2(\bar{D}_2)]dt, \tag{8'}$$

whose absolute value states the accumulated shortfall of society's actual from long-run welfare.[12] In addition to the optimality conditions of equations (14)–(16), the necessary conditions for an optimal solution to the problem specifically formulated above, as amended by equation (8′), contain the state and co-state equations:

$$\dot{V} = \alpha(1 - V)D_1^*, \tag{23}$$

$$\dot{m}_1 = -m_1\rho, \tag{24}$$

$$\dot{m}_2 = -D_1^*[m_1 p_V^* - \alpha m_2], \tag{25}$$

where $r$ has been set equal to zero. Equation (24) reveals that $m_1$ declines monotonically over time and that it is independent of $V$ and $m_2$. Adjustments in $V$ and $m_2$, on the other hand, are more complex, since they depend on $V$, $m_1$, and $m_2$. In particular, it must be noted that $D_1^*$ in equations (23) and (25) depends on $V$, $m_1$, and $m_2$, as can be seen from equations (14) and (16). If domestic consumption of the first good has not yet reached the long-term ceiling, $D_1 < \bar{D}_1$, one can show that

$$\begin{aligned} dD_1^* = \{[(p - \text{MR}^*)f_{D_1D_1} - m_1\text{MR}^*F_{x_1x_1}]dm_1 \\ - [f_{D_1D_1} + m_1F_{x_1x_1}]\,[\alpha(1 - V)dm_2 + (p_V^*m_1 - \alpha m_2)dV]\}/\Delta, \end{aligned} \tag{26a}$$

where

$$\Delta = f_{D_1D_1}m_1(\text{MR}_{D_1}{}^{**} + F_{x_1x_1}) + m_1{}^2\text{MR}_{D_1}{}^{**}F_{x_1x_1} > 0.$$

If, on the other hand, domestic consumption of the first commodity has reached the long-run level, $D_1 = \bar{D}_1$, then

$$\begin{aligned} dD_1^* = [(p - \text{MR}^*)dm_1 - \alpha(1 - V)dm_2 \\ - (p_V^*m_1 - \alpha m_2)dV]/[m_1(\text{MR}_{d_1}{}^{**} + F_{x_1x_1})]. \end{aligned} \tag{26b}$$

Returning to equations (23)–(25), we are interested in finding a steady-state solution, where $\dot{V} = \dot{m}_1 = \dot{m}_2 = 0$. Starting with the condition that $\dot{V} = 0$, it is apparent from equation (23) that it is satisfied if $V = 1$. In other words, product familiarity keeps adjusting until it has become complete. And since $\alpha D_1^* > 0$ for an exporting country, product familiarity continues to rise monotonically as long as foreigners remain incompletely informed. Second, one can easily see from equation (24) that $\dot{m}_1 = 0$ only if $m_1 = 0$; and as mentioned already $m_1$ declines monotonically over time. Finally, there is the $\dot{m}_2 = 0$ condition, which, according to equation (25), is satisfied if

$$m_1 p_V^* = \alpha m_2. \tag{27}$$

First, it is noted that in steady state, where $m_1$ is zero and $p_V^*$ is finite, $m_2$ must be

12 For a discussion of this formulation, see Takayama (1974, 444–68).

zero. But if we are not in steady state and $m_1 > 0$ and $p_V^* > 0$, equation (27) reveals that $m_2$ must be positive. In particular, this is the case at $V = \bar{V}$ and $m_1 = \mu_1 > 0$, when the optimal intervention policy is first adopted. One can portray the $\dot{m}_2 = 0$ locus in the $V - m_2$ plane of figure 1, keeping in mind that $m_1$ also adjusts along the line. The heavy-line $\dot{m}_2 = 0$ locus is constructed by first obtaining alternative loci of $V - m_2$ combinations along which $\dot{m}_2 = 0$ given different constant values of $m_1$. These loci are marked by $Vm_2^0$, $Vm_2^1$, $Vm_2^2$, corresponding to $m_1^0 > m_1^1 > m_1^2$, and their slopes are negative as $(dm_2/dV)|\bar{m}_1 = (m_1 p_{VV}^*/\alpha) < 0$ from equation (27). Then we recall that $V$ is monotonically increasing while $m_1$ is monotonically decreasing over time. Hence, the higher the value of $V$ in figure 1 the lower the value of $m_1$ and corresponding position of the $Vm_2$ locus. At $V^0$ the relevant point on the $\dot{m}_2 = 0$ locus is $A^0$, at $V^1$ the corresponding point is $A^1$, and so on, until the entire $\dot{m}_2 = 0$ locus is traced out.

Figure 1 portrays the $\dot{m}_2 = 0$ and $\dot{V} = 0$ loci and indicates that steady state is attained at point $S$. For other points in the $(V - m_2)$ plane the relevant adjustment forces are indicated by arrows. Finally, the optimal adjustment path to steady state is indicated by the $RS$ trajectory, implying that $m_2$ decreases over time as $V$ rises.

*Consumption production and export paths*

The adoption of optimal trade policies results in two types of adjustments by the economy. First, there is a one-time shock to the economy as the previous suboptimal policy is replaced by the newly adopted optimal policy. Typically, this involves discrete jumps in production and consumption. Second, there is the gradual, time-consuming adjustment towards the economy's long-run equilibrium as the optimal policy measures themselves are adjusted.

The one-time shock to the economy is best illustrated by a diagram. In figure 2 we draw the country's production possibility locus, $FF$, and assume that initially there is no trade. The autarky consumption and production point is at $A$ and the price line prevailing in the foreign market is $p^*(\bar{V}, 0)$. In order to avoid cluttering the diagram we draw the remaining parts of the diagram under the assumption that the country has no monopoly power and that the balance of trade constraint is binding.[13] The newly imposed optimal export subsidy instantly raises domestic prices, with new production at point $B$ and consumption at $C$, while international trade first takes place at the terms of trade of $p^*(\bar{V})$. Consequently, the initial, one-time adjustment in consumption is from $A$ to $C$, in production from $A$ to $B$, in exports from $D_1^* = 0$ to $D_1^* = \tilde{D}_1^*$, and in national welfare, as perceived by the social planner, from $U^2$ to $U^0$.

The second type of adjustment continues until steady state is attained. Again allowing for monopoly power and borrowing, we start with domestic consumption of the second commodity; differentiation of equation (15) with respect to time yields

$$\dot{D}_2 = \dot{m}_1/f_{D_2D_2} = -m_1\rho/f_{D_2D_2} > 0, \qquad (28)$$

as long as $D_2 < \bar{D}_2$.[14] Domestic consumption of the home country's import good

13 The monopoly power element would require a Baldwin envelope construction.

14 This result corresponds to Yaari's (1964) optimal consumption path over an individual's lifetime.

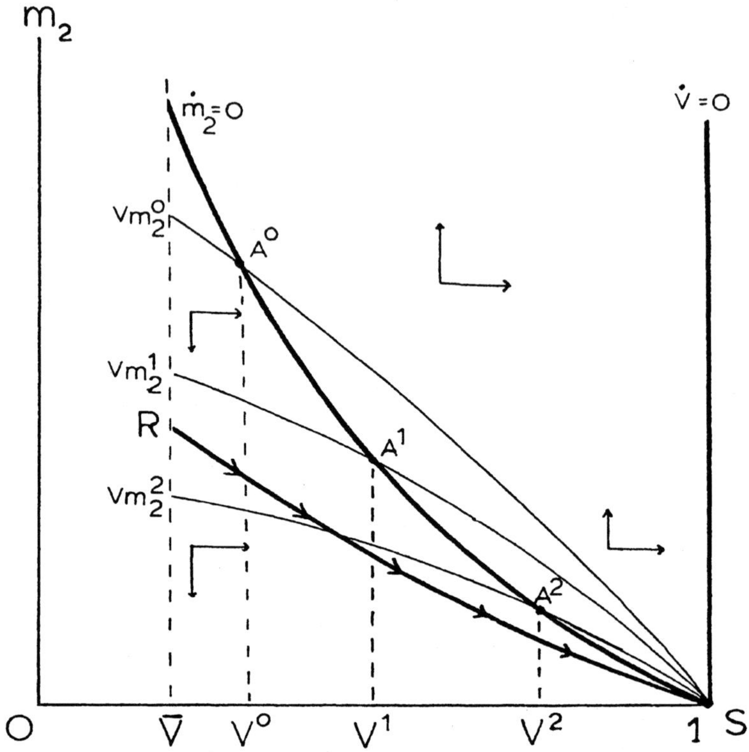


FIGURE 1

rises monotonically until the long-run consumption level is reached. The adjustment path is independent of the rest of the economic system, in particular of the product familiarization and export subsidization process.

Consumption of the first commodity, $D_1$, on the other hand, depends on $V$ and $m_2$, as well as on $m_1$. Differentiating equations (14) and (16) with respect to time, substituting equations (23)–(25), and solving for $\dot{D}_1$ yields

$$\dot{D}_1 = -\rho m_1{}^2[p\text{MR}_{D_1*}{}^* + \text{MR}^* F_{x_1x_1}]/\Delta > 0, \tag{29}$$

where $\Delta$ has been defined in the context of equation (26a). Consequently, domestic consumption of the exportable also rises monotonically as long as $D_1 < \bar{D}_1$.

From figure 2 one also can see that society's welfare declines initially as the government imposes an optimal trade policy. After this one-time loss, however, there will be a gradual improvement in welfare as time passes, since

$$\dot{U} = f_{D_1}\dot{D}_1 + f_{D_2}\dot{D}_2 > 0, \tag{30}$$

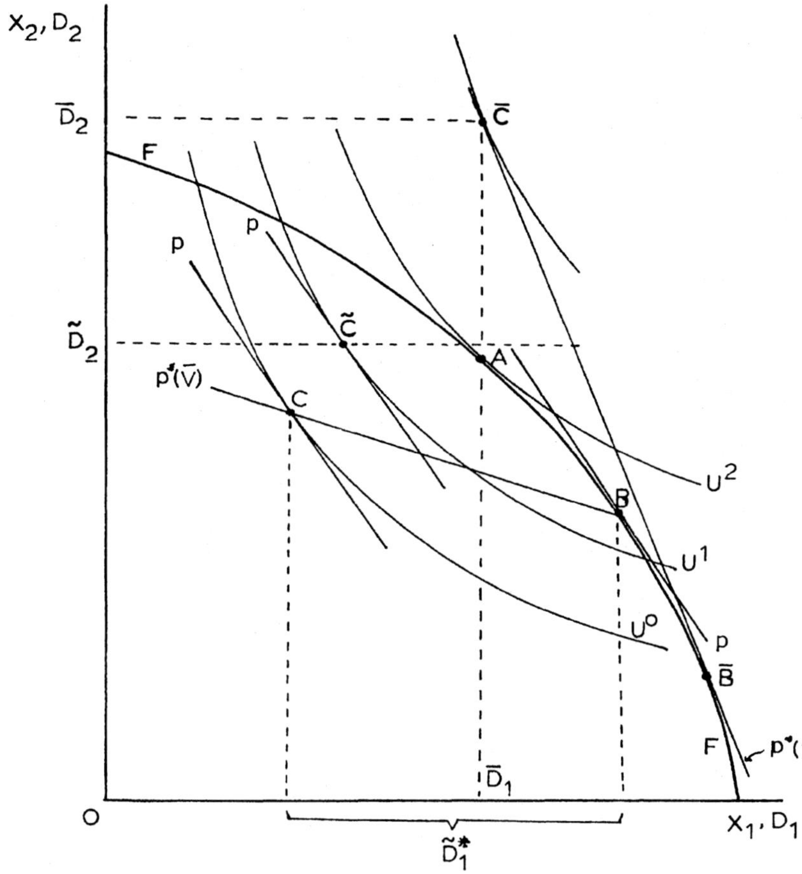


FIGURE 2

as long as $D_j < \bar{D}_j$ for at least one $j = 1, 2$. As will be pointed out later in more detail, these gains in society's welfare are not necessarily shared by everyone in society. Although equation (30) implies that everybody could become better off if losers were compensated by gainers, these compensations are generally not possible, and the benefits from this 'optimal' policy may be quite unevenly spread among households.[15]

15 More precisely, one can show that each person has a different optimal export subsidy rate that depends on his ownership of factors of production. Those who gain most from export promotion would favour a higher rate than is optimal for society as a whole. For a discussion of individually optimal tariff rates see Mayer (1983).

In contrast to domestic consumption, the dynamic adjustment of exports is much less clear-cut. Using equations (26a) and (23)–(25), one can see that

$$\dot{D}_1{}^* = m_1\rho[-(p - \text{MR}^*)f_{D_1D_1} + m_1F_{x_1x_1}\text{MR}^*]/\Delta, \tag{31a}$$

when $D_1 < \bar{D}_1$. The first term in the bracket is positive, while the second is negative. The initial opening of trade, of course, raises exports to $\tilde{D}_1{}^*$ in figure 2, but thereafter there may be periods when exports fail to grow. However, once domestic consumption of the first commodity has reached the long-run ceiling, $D_1 = \bar{D}_1$, exports definitely will grow until the product familiarization process is completed. This can be seen from equations (26b) in conjunction with equations (23)–(25):

$$\dot{D}_1{}^* = -\rho(p - \text{MR}^*)/(\text{MR}_{D_1{}^*}{}^* + F_{x_1x_1}) > 0. \tag{31b}$$

Domestic production changes are also easily derived. The initial switch in production from point $A$ to $B$ in figure 2 is followed by a gradual expansion of the infant-export industry and a corresponding contraction of the rest-of-the-economy industry. Since $X_1 = D_1 + D_1{}^*$, one can easily see that

$$\dot{X}_1 = \dot{D}_1 + \dot{D}_1{}^* = -m_1\rho[m_1p\text{MR}_{D_1{}^*}{}^* + (p - \text{MR}^*)f_{D_1D_1}]/\Delta > 0, \tag{32}$$

when $D_1 < \bar{D}_1$; and $\dot{X}_1 = \dot{D}_1{}^*$, as stated in equation (31b), when $D_1 = \bar{D}_1$. It follows immediately that

$$\dot{X}_2 = F_{x_1}\dot{X}_1 < 0 \text{ and } \dot{p} = -F_{x_1x_1}\dot{X}_1 > 0. \tag{33}$$

While the second industry contracts, the domestic price of the infant-export industry's good continues to rise.

*The dynamics of export subsidies and tariffs*

The aim of this subsection is to show that the export subsidy component of the optimal tariff rate, $s$, does not necessarily decline during the entire adjustment process to long-run equilibrium. Although the export subsidy element will eventually disappear, there may be times when it temporarily rises. However, one also can determine a certain upper limit on $s$ beyond which the export subsidy definitely should not go; and this upper limit tends to decline over time.

The optimal export subsidy rate for market cultivation had been defined in equation (20) for the case of no monopoly power. Differentiating it with respect to time and substituting equations (23)–(25) yields

$$\dot{s} = -s[(D_1{}^*p_V{}^*m_1/m_2) + (\dot{p}/p) - \rho]. \tag{34}$$

The sign of $\dot{s}$ is not determinate, since the first two terms on the RHS contribute towards lowering $s$, while the last term tends to raise it. Only if the international interest rate is very small will there be a tendency for the pure export subsidization rate to decline over time.

The expression for the optimal export subsidy in the absence of monopoly power, $s = [m_2\alpha(1 - V)]/[m_1p]$, makes it difficult to calculate the actual numerical value of $s$ at a given point in time, since neither $m_1$ nor $m_2$ is directly observable. Accordingly, it seems desirable to approximate the value of the optimal export subsidy. In practice, the main problem is to impose a certain upper limit on the rate, since lobbying groups for export subsidies, once the case has been favoured in general, will press for the highest possible rates. Society, of course, does not gain from any degree of export subsidization, but only from subsidization at or close to the optimal rate. One way of determining such an upper limit on $s$ is to recall that $\dot{m}_2 < 0$ during the entire adjustment process. Hence, equation (25) implies that $p_V^* > (\alpha m_2/m_1)$, and after substitution in equation (20) we obtain

$$s < p_V^*(1 - V)/p. \qquad (35)$$

At least under ideal conditions, the terms forming the expression on the RHS of equation (35) can be observed. The expression on the RHS forms the upper limit. In contrast to the optimal subsidy value itself, this upper limit can be shown to decline monotonically over time.[16]

The monopoly component of the optimal net tariff rate also adjusts over time. Here it is noted only that in general the direction of its adjustment is not determinate. Accordingly, a priori one also cannot say anything about changes in the optimal net tariff rates over time.

*The balance of trade*

The country in question is allowed to borrow and lend in the international market at interest rate ρ. The only constraints are that the properly discounted balance of trade equals zero over the entire adjustment period and that the balance of trade constraint becomes binding for each period after the process of market cultivation is completed. But balance of trade surpluses or deficits are possible at different times during the adjustment period.

Again we must distinguish between the initial, instantaneous impact of the newly adopted trade policy and the gradual adjustments thereafter. In figure 2, where for the sake of convenience we had assumed that the balance of trade constraint is binding, the new consumption point was given by $C$. If, however, international borrowing is possible, the new consumption point could very well lie beyond the balance of trade constraint, say at $\tilde{C}$. But how can we determine the precise position of $\tilde{C}$? First, we return to equation (15), which says that in the initial period $f_{D_2} = \mu_1$, where $\mu_1$ has been defined as the marginal contribution of national wealth (or accumulated income) to society's welfare in the initial period. Hence, $\mu_1$, which is constant in value over time, crucially depends on how much income the economy generates along the optimal production adjustment path. Knowing $\mu_1$, one can then solve for $D_2$, which may be larger, smaller, or the same as it was in autarky. Say in figure 2 the optimal initial $D_2$ is $\tilde{D}_2$. Second, equation (17) must be satisfied, implying that the domestic

16 The change in the upper limit over time is $\{[p^*_{VV}(1 - V) - p^*_V]p\dot{V} - p^*_V(1 - V)\dot{p}\}/p^2 < 0$.

price line is tangent to an indifference curve. This condition is satisfied at point $\tilde{C}$ along the $\tilde{D}_2$ line. In our specific example, borrowing softens the short-run welfare loss that would occur if optimal market cultivating policies were adopted under a binding balance of trade constraint.

A priori one cannot conclude that there always will be borrowing in the early phases of the adjustment process. However, the less foreign consumers are familiar with the new product and the less they are initially willing to pay, the more likely it is that the country runs an initial balance of trade deficit.

The balance of trade at time $t$, $B(t)$, is defined as

$$B(t) = p^*(V, D_1{}^*)D_1{}^* - (D_2 - X_2). \quad (36)$$

Its gradual adjustment towards long-run equilibrium can be evaluated by differentiating equation (36) with respect to time:

$$\dot{B} = D_1{}^*p_V{}^*\dot{V} - [(p - \text{MR}^*)\dot{X}_1 + \text{MR}^*\dot{D}_1 + \dot{D}_2]. \quad (37)$$

In deriving equation (37) we utilized equation (1), added and subtracted $\text{MR}^*\dot{D}_1$, and set $\dot{D}_1 + \dot{D}_1{}^* = \dot{X}_1$. Two opposing forces affect the balance of trade during the adjustment process. Rising product familiarity raises the price foreigners are willing to pay and tends to improve the balance of trade. On the other hand, adjustments in domestic consumption and production, the second part of the RHS of equation (37), are such that the balance of trade tends to deteriorate when evaluated at constant terms of trade. As a result, the balance of trade may go through different phases before it approaches long-run equilibrium.

*The impact on individual households*

An inevitable by-product of the implementation of new trade policies is that the welfare effects vary greatly among households. The 'optimal' export subsidization program, as outlined above, would indeed be best for all if unlimited redistribution of gains were possible. In reality, however, this is not the case, and some individuals' welfare may actually decline as many others benefit from the new program. In order to shed more light on the distribution of gains and losses, we now assume that individuals possess different amounts of factors of production and, therefore, income. Furthermore, each persons utility function is homothetic, such that a redistribution of income does not alter aggregate demand.[17]

The $i$th individual's utility function is

$$U^i = f_1{}^i(d_1{}^i) + f_2{}^i(d_2{}^i), \quad (38)$$

where $d_j{}^i$ denotes consumption of commodity $j$ by individual $i$, and $f_j{}^i$ has the same derivative properties as $f_j$ of equation (2). Since the utility function is homothetic, one can rewrite equation (38) as

$$U^i = h^i[g_1(d_1{}^i) + g_2(d_2{}^i)] = h^i[G^i], \quad (38')$$

17 The following approach is based on Mayer (1983).

where $G^i$ is homogeneous of degree one in the two commodities and $(\partial h^i/\partial G^i) > 0$. Homotheticity also implies that at given prices each person's and therefore the entire nation's expenditure share on a given commodity is the same; that is, $(d_j^i/y^i) = (D_j/Y)$, where $y^i$ and $Y$ denote the $i$th individual's and whole nation's total income. It is convenient now to define the $i$th individual's share of national income by $\theta^i = (y^i/Y)$ and to substitute $d_j^i = \theta^i D_j$ in equation (38′). Considering the homogeneity of degree one property of $G^i$, this yields

$$U^i = h^i\{\theta^i[g_1(D_1) + g_2(D_2)]\}. \tag{38''}$$

The welfare implications of the export subsidization program on individuals' welfare can be evaluated by differentiating equation (38″) with respect to time:

$$\dot{U}^i = (\partial h^i/\partial G^i)\{[g_1(D_1) + g_2(D_2)]\dot{\theta}^i + \theta^i[g_{D_1}\dot{D}_1 + g_{D_2}\dot{D}_2]\}. \tag{39}$$

Clearly, there are two ways through which a person's welfare is affected: changes in the distribution of income, as indicated by $\dot{\theta}^i$, and changes in overall consumption levels, as indicated by $\dot{D}^j$. After the initial imposition of the optimal export policy both $\dot{D}_1$ and $\dot{D}_2$ are positive, and therefore the second effect always contributes to more individual welfare. The first effect, on the other hand, differs among people, since the export subsidization program alters individuals' shares of national income.

At a given point in time the nation's as well as each person's income consists of factor income, receipts from net tariffs, and international borrowings. Concerning factors of production, it is assumed that the country's endowments are fixed, but ownership of factors varies among people. For example, in a two-by-two model with labour and capital, the $i$th individual owns $L^i$ units of labour and $K^i$ units of capital, and the corresponding income from factor ownership alone is $(wL^i + rK^i)$, where $w$ and $r$ denote returns on labour and capital respectively. The $i$th person's share of total factor income, $\bar{\theta}^i$, is then

$$\bar{\theta}^i = (wL^i + rK^i)/(wL + rK), \tag{40}$$

where $L$ and $K$ are the nation's endowments of labour and capital, respectively. Concerning net tariff revenues and net borowings, we assume here that they are unbiased with respect to the distribution of income; that is, they do not affect a person's income share as based on his or her factor income. Accordingly, each person's share of total income, $\theta^i$, is assumed to be the same as each person's share of factor income, $\bar{\theta}^i$.

Given a country's factor endowments and ownership distribution, changes in $\bar{\theta}^i$ over time depend on the specific nature of the underlying production structure. For example, we may consider a Heckscher-Ohlin framework, with its standard assumptions, in which $X_1$ and $X_2$ are produced. For such a model we first differentiate equation (40) with respect to time:

$$\dot{\bar{\theta}}^i = \{\theta^i(k - k^i)wr]/(w + rk)\}\,\{[(\dot{w}/w) - (\dot{r}/r)]/(\dot{p}/p)\}\,(\dot{p}/p) \tag{41}$$

where $k = K/L$ and $k^i = K^i/L^i$ denote the country's and $i$th individual's capital-labour ratios, respectively. In the Heckscher-Ohlin model $[(\dot{w}/w) - (\dot{r}/r)]/(\dot{p}/p) \gtreqless 0$ as the infant-export industry's good is relatively labour- or capital-intensive. Also we know that during the entire adjustment process $\dot{p} > 0$. Consequently, a person's income share rises (falls) over time if that person compared with the nation as a whole is relatively well (poorly) endowed with the infant-export industry's relatively intensively used factor. For example, if the export industry were relatively capital-intensive, then $[(\dot{w}/w) - (\dot{r}/r)]/(\dot{p}/p) < 0$ and $\dot{\theta}^i > 0$ if $k^i > k$.

Now we can return to equation (39) and evaluate the welfare ramifications of the export subsidization policies on individuals. People that are relatively well endowed with the infant-export industry's intensive factor gradually improve their well-being during the adjustment to long-run equilibrium, since both $\dot{\theta}$ and $\dot{D}_j$, $j = 1, 2$, are positive in equation (39). Even those whose income shares decline may raise their overall utility, because the positive overall effect on aggregate consumption levels more than outweighs the negative income redistribution effect. However, it also is quite possible that some people experience a gradual erosion of their well-being, the decline in their income share being the prevalent force. Such losers will be found among people whose ownership ratio of the infant-export industry's intensively used factor is extremely low.

## QUALIFICATIONS AND CONCLUSIONS

This paper justified the subsidization of exports for market cultivation as a first-best policy measure and described the optimal time paths for domestic consumption and production, exports and the balance of trade, as well as national and individual welfare that result from these policies. Since the model contains a number of specific assumptions, we want to indicate briefly to what extent our conclusions hinge on them.

The basic principle that the need for foreign-market cultivation justifies the subsidization of exports, as discussed in the third section, is rather insensitive to the specific assumptions made. As long as the product familiarization process works through consumption of the export good, exports should be subsidized. On the other hand, the dynamics of the system, as portrayed in the fourth section, is quite sensitive to the specific assumptions made. In particular, it hinges on the magnitude of the social planner's time preference, the specific nature of the learning-by-consuming process, and the form of the utility function.

With respect to time preferences, we followed Ramsey's suggestion that a zero rate of time preference is most appropriate when intergenerational equity considerations are involved. If, however, one allowed for a positive time preference and assumed that the international market interest rate exceeds the rate of time preference, $\rho > r$, one no longer could conclude that consumption of the first commodity, $D_1$, and national welfare, $U$, monotonically rise over time. On the other hand, it still would be true that production of the export good, $X_1$, and consumption of the import good, $D_2$, monotonically rise. Adjustments in the balance of trade and the optimal rate of export subsidization will become slightly more intractable.

The principle feature of the specified learning-by-consuming process was that once-acquired information can be instantly refreshed through inspection. Hence, there is no forgetting. If this assumption were relaxed and forgetting allowed, then it would be possible that steady state is attained at less than full product familiarity. Of course, the dynamics of the system would be significantly affected as well.

Our utility function's form implies that the marginal utility of one commodity is independent of the quantity of the other commodity consumed. If a more general form with non-zero cross-partials were adopted, the complexity of the analysis would increase considerably. The main change in substance would be that the time path of $D_2$, which in our model is independent of the learning-by-consuming process, would become a more integral part of the total system.

It also must be pointed out that the optimal export subsidy analysis of this paper rested on necessary conditions for the optimal choice of controls. In our model with zero rate of time preferences, these necessary conditions can also be shown to be sufficient for optimality. The long-run gains from export subsidization always must outweigh the short-run losses, since the former are permanent and the latter are temporary, and neither gains nor losses are discounted. If, however, the discount rate were positive, it is quite conceivable that export subsidization does not represent an optimal policy in spite of long-run welfare gains.[18] If the short-run losses are extensive and much time passes before small and heavily discounted long-run gains materialize, it may be best to refrain from subsidizing an infant-exporter.

With these qualifications in mind, this paper allows us to draw the following conclusions:

1. Export subsidization is justified when externalities arise in the act of exporting. If foreign markets had to be cultivated through other activities, such as advertising, then subsidization of these activities rather than of exporting would represent the first-best policy.
2. If the country in question is large, the optimal trade policy consists of a mix of market cultivation subsidies and monopoly tariff. The net optimal tariff rate may be positive, therefore, even though the process of foreign market cultivation has not been completed.
3. Although the reason for export subsidization, namely, lack of product familiarity, will gradually decline, one cannot conclude that the optimal subsidy rate (in the absence of monopoly power) has to decline monotonically as well. Temporary phases of rising optimal subsidy rates are possible.
4. In general, export subsidization results in significant short-run welfare losses to society as a whole and to many individuals in this society. Borrowing in international markets may cushion these welfare effects.

18 In terms of notions known from the infant-industry argument literature, this means that the 'Mill test' is satisfied, but the 'Bastable test' is not; see Kemp (1960).

5. The promise of long-run gains from selling to a cultivated foreign market justifies export subsidization if society has no positive rate of time preference. With a positive discount rate, the prospect of long-run gains may not be enough to offset earlier short-run losses.
6. An individual's interest in subsidizing the infant-export industry is strongest if the person is relatively well endowed with that industry's intensively used factor. But even people with the 'wrong' factor ownership may end up better off with export subsidization than without.
7. There is no definite pattern of balance of trade and export volume changes as the foreign market is cultivated.

## REFERENCES


Balassa, B. (1978) 'Exports and economic growth: further evidence.' *Journal of Development Economics* 5, 181–9

Baldwin, R.E. (1979) *The Multilateral Trade Negotiations: Towards Greater Liberalization?*, (Washington, DC: American Enterprise Institute)

Bhagwati, J. (1968) *The Theory and Practice of Commercial Policy: Departures from Unified Exchange Rates.* Special Papers in International Economics (Princeton, NJ: Princeton University Press)

Böhm-Bawerk, E. (1959) *Capital and Interest*, vol. 2, translated by G.D. Huncke (South Holland, IL: Libertarian Press)

Burmeister, E. and A.R. Dobell (1970) *Mathematical Theories of Economic Growth* (New York: Macmillan)

Clemhout S. and H.Y. Wan (1970) 'Learning-by-doing and infant industry protection.' *Review of Economic Studies* 37, 33–56

Deaton, A. and J. Muellbauer (1980) *Economics and Consumer Behaviour*, (Cambridge: Cambridge University Press)

Fisher, F.M. and K. Shell (1971) 'Taste and quality change in the pure theory of the true cost of living index.' In Z. Griliches, ed., *Price Indexes and Quality Change: Studies in New Methods of Measurement* (Cambridge, MA: Harvard University Press)

Heller, P.S. and R.C. Porter (1978) 'Exports and growth: an empirical reinvestigation.' *Journal of Development Economics* 5, 181–93

Kemp, M.C. (1960) 'The Mill-Bastable infant industry dogma.' *Journal of Political Economy* 68, 65–7

Little, I., T. Scitovsky, and M. Scott (1970) *Industry and Trade in Some Developing Countries: A Comparative Study* (New York: Oxford University Press)

Malmgren, H.B. (1978) 'Negotiation of rules on subsidies in a world of economic interventionism.' In S.J. Warnecke, ed., *International Trade and Industrial Policies* (New York: Holmes and Meier)

Mayer, W. (1983) 'Endogenous tariff formation.' Mimeo, University of Cincinnati

Michaely, M. (1977) 'Exports and growth: an empirical investigation.' *Journal of Development Economics* 4, 49–53

Nelson, P. (1970) 'Information and consumer behavior.' *Journal of Political Economy* 78, 311–29

Pestieau, C. (1978) 'Revising the GATT approach to subsidies: a Canadian view.' In S.J. Warnecke, ed., *International Trade and Industrial Policies* (New York: Holmes and Meier)

Pollak, R.A. (1970) 'Habit formation and dynamic demand functions.' *Journal of Political Economy* 78, 745–63

Ramsey, F.P. (1928) 'A mathematical theory of savings.' *Economic Journal* 38, 543–59

Rosen, S. (1974) 'Hedonic prices and implicit markets: product differentiation in pure competition.' *Journal of Political Economy* 82, 34–55

Takayama, A. (1974) *Mathematical Economics* (Hinsdale, IL: Dryden Press)

Von Weizsäcker, C.C. (1971) 'Notes on endogenous change in tastes.' *Journal of Economic Theory* 3, 345–72

Willig, R.D. (1978) 'Incremental consumer's surplus and hedonic price adjustments.' *Journal of Economic Theory* 17, 227–53

Yaari, M.E. (1964) 'On the consumer's lifetime allocation process.' *International Economic Review* 5, 304–17

— (1977) 'How to eat an appetite-arousing cake.' Research Memorandum No. 26, Center Res. Math. Econ. and Game Theory, Hebrew University of Jerusalem

# PART III

# Political Economy of Trade-Policy Formation

# Endogenous Tariff Formation

By WOLFGANG MAYER*

Interest in the process of tariff formation has grown considerably during the last decade. Robert Baldwin (1976, 1982), William Brock and Stephen Magee (1978, 1980), as well as Ronald Findlay and Stanislaw Wellisz (1982) have suggested alternative models for studying the economic and political forces that interact in determining a country's actual tariff structure.[1] The underlying premise of these studies is that political decisions on tariff rates are reflections of the selfish economic interests of voters, lobbying groups, politicians, or other decision makers in trade policy matters.[2,3]

Brock and Magee, as well as Findlay and Wellisz, treat tariff formation as a noncooperative game among competing economic interest groups.[4] In Brock and Magee's papers, the tariff positions of opposing political parties are explained, where each party maximizes its chances of being elected, and the probability of reelection hinges on contributions from tariff-sensitive lobbying groups. In Findlay and Wellisz, the economic interests of land and capital owners are opposed, with labor standing on the sidelines. Baldwin, on the other hand, postulates majority voting by owners of productive factors. Hence, Baldwin introduces a collective decision rule to tariff determination which plays a major role in the public choice literature.[5] Specifically, he argues that accepted optimal trade policy prescriptions, such as free trade for a small country, would be voted in by factor owners if voters' tastes were homothetic and there were no restrictions on income redistributions, no voting and information costs, and no possibilities for logrolling. However, when these ideal assumptions are gradually removed, Baldwin (1976, p. 71) suggests that actual tariff rates are decisively affected by economic groups which are large in size and whose potential gains or losses are substantial.

Baldwin's discussion is rich in detail and offers many valuable insights. Most important, it breaks new ground in suggesting determinants of actual tariffs, such as the distribution of factors of production, the existence of voting costs, and the specific nature of the underlying economic and political system. The purpose of this paper is to study some of these alternative determinants of tariff rates in a rigorously formulated general equilibrium model. In particular, the paper attempts to evaluate the dependence of actual tariff rates on factor-ownership distribution, voter eligibility and participation rules, and the degrees of factor mobility and industry diversification in the economy.

The standard assumption on factor ownership, which also is adopted by Baldwin (1982, p. 268), states that each person owns one factor of production only. This implies that all owners of a given factor form a

*Department of Economics, University of Cincinnati, Cincinnati, OH 45221. Comments by John Pomery, Raymond Riezman, and Ronald Jones are greatly appreciated.

[1] In addition to the literature on endogenous tariff formation, there are a number of authors (for example, Jagdish Bhagwati, 1982; Arye Hillman, 1982; and Elias Dinopoulos, 1983), who discuss endogenous tariff adjustments in response to exogenous changes in the international terms of trade. How the initial tariff rate was selected is, however, not part of their decision problem. Also there is a growing empirical literature on changing tariff structures of various countries, such as the works by Jonathan Pincus (1975), Richard Caves (1976), G. K. Helleiner (1977), as well as Howard Marvel and Edward Ray (1983).

[2] The relationship between public policymaking and economic interests is widely discussed in the public choice literature, such as in Anthony Downs (1957), James Buchanan and Gordon Tullock (1962), and Dennis Mueller (1979).

[3] A quite different approach at explaining tariff structures has been used by Edward Ray (1974).

[4] For extensions of these modes, see Leslie Young and Magee (1983), Wellisz-Findlay (1983), and Wellisz and John Wilson (1983).

[5] For a thorough discussion of majority voting rules, see Duncan Black (1948a,b) and Mueller.

well-defined interest group whose membership is independent of the prevailing tariff rate. Accordingly, voter allegiances are exogenously imposed rather than endogenously determined. Baldwin's correct observation, that majority voting could eliminate all trade of a capital-abundant country if there were more workers than capitalists, suggests that this standard assumption on factor ownership has limited appeal in explaining actual tariff structures under majority voting. This paper changes the standard assumption by allowing a person to own more than one factor of production. Also, factor-ownership shares may differ among people. As a result, the number of factor owners voting for or against a given tariff change will no longer be fixed, but will depend on the prevailing tariff rate. Under shifting voter allegiances, a tariff equilibrium is attained when no majority can be found to push for either an increase or a reduction in the existing tariff rate. Whether such an equilibrium tariff is positive, zero, or negative crucially hinges on the underlying factor-ownership distribution. I demonstrate that each factor owner has an optimal tariff rate whose value is uniquely related to the individual's factor ownership. In the special case of majority voting with no voting costs, it is the median factor owner's optimal tariff rate that will be chosen to become the actual tariff rate.

Given a country's distribution of factor ownership, tariff equilibria are affected by voter eligibility rules and participation costs. Some factor owners may not be eligible to participate in the voting process. Others are eligible but have no incentive to participate as voting costs are high relative to benefits from enacting or preventing a proposed tariff change.[6] Over the last century, most countries have undergone drastic liberalizations with respect to voter eligibility rules. But even today there are many factor owners, such as young people or foreign workers, who are not permitted to vote. This paper also relates actual tariff structures to voter eligibility rules and, more importantly, to the existence of significant voting costs on the part of factor owners.

Tariff formation is discussed under two alternative assumptions about the underlying production structure. First, I employ the common two-by-two Heckscher-Ohlin model, later a multisectoral factor-specific model is introduced. The advantage of the former is that it is sufficiently simple to illustrate the tariff formation process and it offers a plausible explanation for long-run tariff adjustments as factor-ownership distribution, voting costs, or voter eligibility rules change. Its main shortcoming is its failure to explain the frequently observed phenomenon that a relatively small industry, that does not have support from the majority of eligible voters, succeeds in gaining tariff protection. The factor-specific multisector model is more appropriate for studying such industry-specific efforts to raise a given tariff. In such a model, higher tariffs on a given import good lead to significant welfare gains for the average specific-factor owner in the protected industry but to rather small welfare losses for average specific-factor owners in all other industries. The small number of big potential gainers, therefore, has much greater incentives to participate in the political process than the large number of small potential losers, whenever there exist significant voting costs. Hence, I am proving rigorously what Baldwin (1976, p. 71) hypothesizes and Anthony Downs suggested, namely that small important producer groups can be quite successful in securing import protection.

In addition to studying the determinants of actual tariff rates, I will ask whether there exist factor-ownership distributions under which the majority of voters would support a free-trade policy for a small country. Stated differently, I am in search of those factor-ownership distributions that, given the assumed production structure, result in Pareto-efficient resource allocations.

Section I states general assumptions about consumer preferences, factor distributions, and tariff revenue redistributions in a Heck-

[6] In the tariff formation literature, voting costs have been emphasized by Baldwin. More generally, they play an important role in discussions of the voter's calculus; for example, Downs, William Riker and Peter Ordeshook (1968), or Mueller (pp. 121–24). Sam Peltzman (1976) incorporates voting costs into his general theory of regulation.

scher-Ohlin model, and describes what tariff rate is optimal for a given person with predetermined factor ownership. Section II deals with the impact of tariff changes on the individual's economic interests, as measured by real income changes, and demonstrates how the actual tariff rate is chosen under majority voting. The relationship between the chosen tariff rate and changing voting costs is emphasized in this context. Section III introduces a multisector, factor-specific production model, as discussed in Ronald Jones (1975) and expanded in Roy Ruffin and Jones (1977). My aim is to demonstrate that, under rather neutral assumptions, there is a very strong presumption that a small industry will succeed in gaining import protection even though all other industries are hurt.

## I. Optimal Tariff Rates in a Heckscher-Ohlin Model

### A. *Assumptions*

Consider a small open economy in which capital and labor are employed to produce two commodities, $X_1$ and $X_2$. Each inhabitant of this country possesses one unit of labor and no or some positive amount of capital; that is, $L^i = 1$ and $K^i \geqq 0$, where $L^i\,(K^i)$ denotes labor (capital) owned by individual $i$, $i = 1,\ldots, I$. Both factors are perfectly mobile between the two industries, all markets are competitive, and the firms' production functions are homogeneous of degree one.

Preferences of the country's inhabitants are assumed to be homothetic and identical,[7] such that a redistribution of income will affect neither the country's aggregate demand nor imports, as long as total income remains unchanged. Preferences of individual $i$ are described by an indirect utility function,

$$(1)\qquad U^i = U^i(p, y^i), \qquad i = 1,\ldots, I,$$

where $U^i$ denotes maximum utility attainable by individual $i$, given the price of the first in terms of the second commodity, $p$, and income of individual $i$, $y^i$, measured in terms of the second commodity. There are three potential sources of income: ownership of labor, ownership of capital, and redistributions from tariff revenues. Total income of individual $i$ is

$$(2)\qquad y^i = w + rK^i + T^i,$$

where $w$ and $r$ denote the returns on labor and capital, respectively, $T^i$ represents tariff revenues received by individual $i$, and $L^i = 1$. Concerning the redistribution of tariff revenues, it is assumed that there are predetermined rules that are not voted on in conjunction with the tariff issue, and that are neutral with respect to the overall distribution of income. Neutrality means that the $i$th individual's share of total tariff revenues is identical to the $i$th person's income share from factor ownership, $\phi^i$; that is,

$$(3)\qquad T^i = \phi^i T,$$

where $T$ represents total tariff revenues and

$$(4)\qquad \phi^i = (w + rK^i)/(wL + rK).$$

In equation (4), $L$ is the total labor supply or number of inhabitants and $K = \Sigma_i^I K^i$. Also, it should be noted that $\Sigma_i^I \phi^i = 1$. Substituting (3) and (4) in (2) yields

$$(2')\qquad y^i = \phi^i(wL + rK + T) = \phi^i Y,$$

where $Y$ denotes the economy's total income in terms of the second commodity.

Finally, it is assumed that, for all relevant tariff rates, incomplete specialization in production prevails and the first commodity is imported. Total tariff revenues are expressed as

$$(5)\qquad T = t\pi M,$$

where $t$ is the tariff rate, $\pi$ the world price, and $M$ the imported quantity of the first commodity.

[7] Furthermore, the $i$th individual's direct utility function is assumed to be homogeneous of degree one in the two commodities.

B. *Optimal Tariff Rates for Individuals*

When factor ownership differs among a country's people, their welfare is not affected uniformly by a tariff increase, as can be seen by substituting (2′) in (1):

$$(1') \qquad U^i = U^i(p, \phi^i Y), \qquad i = 1, \ldots, I.$$

The $i$th person's maximum attainable utility depends on its own income share, in addition to domestic prices and aggregate income as faced by all individuals. If a tariff rate is changed, all people are confronted with identical price and aggregate income changes, but in general with different effects on their income share. Consequently, a given tariff change benefits some and hurts others, whereby the magnitude of welfare changes may vary greatly among gainers and losers. Inequality in the factor-ownership distribution is responsible for this differentiation in welfare effects.

To see the impact of a tariff increase on a given individual's welfare, let us substitute $p = \pi(1+t)$ in (1′) and differentiate (1′) with respect to $t$:

$$(6) \quad (\partial U^i/\partial t) = (\partial U^i/\partial y^i) \times \left[-\phi^i \pi D_1 + \phi^i(\partial Y/\partial t) + Y(\partial \phi^i/\partial t)\right],$$

where $D_1$ denotes aggregate demand for the first commodity. In deriving (6), use is made of Roy's Identity and of the property of homothetic utility functions that the $i$th person's demand for a commodity equals the product of its income share and aggregate demand for the same commodity.

The economy's aggregate income is given by

$$(7) \qquad Y = wL + rK + T = pX_1 + X_2 + t\pi M,$$

where $X_j$ indicates industry output of commodity $j$, $j = 1, 2$. Differentiating (7) with respect to $t$ yields

$$(8) \qquad (\partial Y/\partial t) = \pi D_1 + t\pi(\partial M/\partial t),$$

where $\partial M/\partial t < 0$. After substitution of (8), equation (6) can be rewritten as

$$(6') \quad (\partial U^i/\partial t) = (\partial U^i/\partial y^i) \times \left[\phi^i t\pi(\partial M/\partial t) + Y(\partial \phi^i/\partial t)\right].$$

There are two channels through which individual welfare is altered by a tariff increase: changes in the tariff-weighted value of imports, $t\pi(\partial M/\partial t)$, and changes in the individual's income share, $(\partial \phi^i/\partial t)$. While imports always decline as import tariffs rise,[8] the direction of change of a person's income share depends on individual factor endowments relative to the nation as a whole, on the one hand, and on the relative factor intensity of the import industry, on the other hand. More will be said on this point shortly.

A tariff rate is optimal for individual $i$ if $(\partial U^i/\partial t) = 0$ in (6′) and $U^i$ is strictly concave in $t$.[9] Assuming the concavity property is satisfied, the optimal tariff rate for individual $i$, $\tilde{t}^i$, is given by

$$(9) \quad \tilde{t}^i = -\left[Y/(\pi \partial M/\partial t)\right]\left[(\partial \phi^i/\partial t)/\phi^i\right].$$

Since $-(\partial M/\partial t) > 0$, a person's optimal tariff rate is positive, zero, or negative as a higher tariff raises, keeps constant, or lowers the person's income share.

The relationship between a tariff and a given person's income share, in turn, depends on that person's endowments, as well as on the production structure through which factor returns and commodity prices are linked. For example, in the present section, the economy's production side is described by a Heckscher-Ohlin model. Differentiating the income-share expression of (4) with respect to $t$, we obtain

$$(10) \quad (\partial \phi^i/\partial t) = \left\{[wL]/\left[(wL + rK)^2(1+t)\right]\right\} \times \left\{r(k - k^i)(\hat{w} - \hat{r})/\hat{p}\right\},$$

[8] For a precise expression, see Jones (1969).

[9] Implicitly it is assumed that the import tariff is the only instrument to alter a person's welfare. Hence, the question of what the first-best instrument would be to redistribute income is not addressed in this paper.

where $k = K/L$ and $k^i = K^i/L^i = K^i$. The "hat" indicates percentage changes and $(\hat{w} - \hat{r})/\hat{p}$ is positive (negative) as the first or import commodity is relatively labor- (capital) intensive in production. Equation (10) reveals that a tariff increase results in a higher (lower) income share for the $i$th individual if the individual, compared to the nation as a whole, is relatively well (poorly) endowed with the import good's intensively used factor of production; that is, $\partial\phi^i/\partial t > 0$ if either $k^i < k$ and $k_1 < k_2$ or $k^i > k$ and $k_1 > k_2$, where $k_j$ is the capital-labor ratio in industry $j$ and good one is imported.

In light of this relationship between income shares and tariffs, the following conclusions can now be drawn about individually optimal tariff rates, as stated in (9):

1) The optimal import tariff is positive (negative) for people who are relatively well (poorly) endowed with the import good's intensively used factor.

2) The greater the difference between individual and national endowment ratios, the greater the deviation of individually optimal tariff or subsidy rates from free-trade policy.[10]

3) The optimal tariff rate is zero for each person whose personal capital-labor ownership ratio equals the national capital-labor endowment ratio.

## II. Tariff Determination Under Majority Voting

Actual tariffs are assumed to be the result of majority voting, where votes reflect the economic interests of those that are eligible and willing to participate in the tariff formation process. This section starts with a description of the relationship between a person's economic interests, on one side, and actual tariff rates, as well as personal factor endowments, on the other side. It is followed by an analysis of tariff equilibria under alternative majority voting rules.

[10]If each person owned only labor or only capital, as usually assumed, there would be just one optimal trade policy for the "worker" and another one for the "capitalist," irrespective of individual persons' factor-ownership shares.

### A. *Real Income Effects of Tariff Changes*

Changes in real income indicate to what extent a person's economic interests are affected. Measured in units of the second commodity, the real income change of individual $i$ brought about by a tariff increase can be expressed as

$$(11)\quad B^i(k^i, t) = (\partial U^i/\partial t)/(\partial U^i/\partial y^i),$$

where $\partial B^i/\partial k^i > 0$ $(<0)$ if the imported good is relatively capital (labor) intensive and $\partial B^i/\partial t < 0$ always.

In order to show that $\partial B^i/\partial k^i > 0$ for a capital-intensive import good, let us first determine the value of the individual endowment ratio, $\tilde{k}^j$, at which the prevailing tariff rate $t$ would be optimal. Using (9) and (10), the value of $\tilde{k}^j$ must be such that

$$(9')\quad t = -\left[\frac{Y}{\pi(\partial M/\partial t)}\right] \times \left[\frac{wL(\hat{w} - \hat{r})}{(wL + rK)\hat{p}(1+t)}\right]\left[\frac{r(k - \tilde{k}^j)}{(w + r\tilde{k}^j)}\right].$$

Next, we return to the definition of $B^i$ and employ (6′) to obtain

$$(11')\quad B^i(k^i, t) = \phi^i\left[t\pi(\partial M/\partial t) + Y(\partial\phi^i/\partial t)/\phi^i\right].$$

Substitution of (9′) for $t$ and of (10) for $(\partial\phi^i/\partial t)$, as well as some manipulations, yield

$$(11'')\quad B^i = -\left[\frac{(\hat{w} - \hat{r})}{\hat{p}(1+t)}\right] \times \left[\frac{Ywr}{(w + r\tilde{k}^j)(wL + rK)}\right][k^i - \tilde{k}^j],$$

where $-[(\hat{w} - \hat{r})/\hat{p}] > 0$ for a capital-intensive import good. Equation (11″) expresses that a given tariff increase raises (lowers) the $i$th person's real income if the $i$th person's capital-labor endowment ratio, $k^i$, exceeds

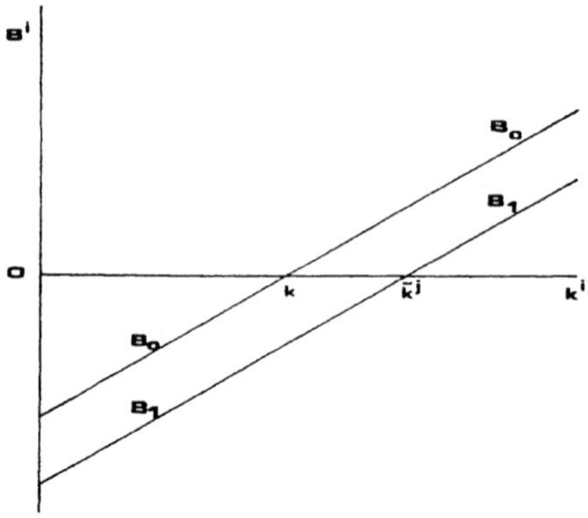


FIGURE 1

(falls short of) the capital-labor endowment ratio, $\bar{k}^j$, of the person for whom the prevailing tariff rate is optimal. Furthermore, $(\partial B^i/\partial k^i)$ must be positive since, at a given tariff rate, no term inside the first two brackets of (11″) will change as $k^i$ varies.

The negative sign of $(\partial B^i/\partial t)$, on the other hand, immediately follows from the utility function's properties of strict concavity in tariff rates and homogeneity of degree one in commodities.

The relationship between $B^i$, on the one hand, and $k^i$ and $t$, on the other hand, is depicted in Figure 1 for an economy whose import industry is relatively capital intensive. The $B_0B_0$ locus is drawn under the assumption that there is free trade. Since $t=0$ when $\bar{k}^j=k$, it follows from (11′) that $B^i \gtreqless 0$ as $k^i \gtreqless k$. The $B_0B_0$ locus is upward sloping as real income gains from tariff increases rise with the magnitude of a person's capital ownership. The $B_1B_1$ locus, on the other hand, is drawn under the assumption that the actual tariff rate is positive, that is, $t>0$. This tariff rate would be optimal for a person with endowment ratio $\bar{k}^j$. Only those individuals gain from further tariff increases for whom $k^i>\bar{k}^j$, while all others lose. Consequently, if the level of tariffs is raised, the number of people who gain from further tariff increases becomes smaller, while the number of people who lose becomes larger.

## B. *Majority Voting without Restrictions*

A tariff rate is called an equilibrium tariff rate when no majority of voters can be formed to alter that rate. Duncan Black (1948a) demonstrated that, in the absence of voting costs, such an equilibrium exists if voters possess "single-peaked" preferences and that the adopted policy is determined by the median voter's peak preference. Black's equilibrium condition is indeed satisfied in my tariff choice model, as each factor owner has a unique optimal tariff rate. Accordingly, the median voter's optimal tariff rate, denoted by $\bar{t}^m$, becomes the equilibrium tariff rate under majority voting.

Who the median voter is depends on voter eligibility rules and the distribution of factor ownership. Concerning eligibility, assume at this point that there are no restrictions; each factor owner has one vote and participates in voting. Concerning factor ownership, it is assumed that capital is unevenly distributed, ranging from no capital ownership, $k^i=0$, to maximum capital ownership, $k^i=k^{\max}$. It is convenient to describe capital-labor ownership ratios by $k(e)$, where $e$ is an index such that $0\leq e\leq 1$. All people with no capital ownership are indexed with $e=0$, and $e$ rises as the capital-labor ownership ratio rises; that is, $k(0)=0$, $\partial k/\partial e>0$, and $k(1)=k^{\max}$. The proportion of factor owners with the same factor ownership is defined as $f[k(e)]\geqq 0$, where $\int_0^1 f[k(e)]\,de=1$. As

$$(12)\qquad \int_0^1 k(e)f[k(e)]\,de=K/L=k,$$

the economy's capital-labor endowment ratio is the mean of the factor-ownership distribution. Equations (9) and (10) revealed that a given person's optimal tariff rate hinges on the relation between its own and the whole economy's capital-labor ratio. Applied to the median voter whose preferences are crucial for the actual choice of tariff rates, one can evaluate the *sign* of the economy's equilibrium tariff rate, $t^*$, by comparing the *median* with the *mean* of the factor-ownership distribution. Provided the distribution is unimodal,

$$(13)\qquad t^*=\bar{t}^m \gtreqless 0,$$

as the distribution is skewed to the left, symmetric, or skewed to the right. A tariff (subsidy) on capital-intensive imports will be voted in if the majority of people has capital-labor ownership ratios that exceed (fall short of) the capital-labor endowment ratio of the country. And a small country will choose free trade as its policy in the special case of a symmetric distribution.[11,12]

For most nonsocialist countries there is strong evidence that capital-labor ownership distributions are not symmetric, but skewed to the right. Accordingly, one would expect a built-in tendency towards protection of labor's interests, through subsidies on capital-intensive imports or tariffs on labor-intensive imports. However, this intrinsic bias in favor of labor may not translate into prolabor tariff legislation if it is negated by voter eligibility and participation restrictions, as discussed next.

### C. *Majority Voting under Restrictions*

Downs, Buchanan and Tullock, Baldwin, Peltzman, and many others have emphasized that there are considerable costs to participants in the voting process.[13] Voter participation costs imply that some eligible voters may choose not to exercise their voting rights. If participation costs exceed the gains from a proposed tariff change, an individual is best off not to vote at all. But even if gains from proposed tariff actions exceed voting costs, voter participation is not certain. Following Peltzman, this paper assumes that the probability of a person voting (or the fraction of people with identical factor ownership which will participate) is directly related to the magnitude of "net" gains.[14]

A person with capital-labor ownership index $e$ will enjoy a net gain from a tariff increase if, for a given $t$,

$$B[k(e),t]-c(e)>0, \tag{14}$$

where $c(e)$ denotes the real income loss from voting, or simply voter participation costs, for people with factor-ownership ratio $k(e)$. The fraction of people with $k(e)$ that will vote for a tariff increase, $\rho(e)$, is

$$\rho(e)=\rho\{B[k(e),t]-c(e)]\}, \tag{15}$$

where $0 \leq \rho < 1$ and $\rho' \geqq 0$. Since the total number of people with factor ownership $k(e)$ equals $f[k(e)]L$, the total number of votes for a *tariff increase*, $E$, is

$$E=L\int_{\tilde{e}}^{1}\rho(e)f[k(e)]\,de, \tag{16}$$

where $\tilde{e}$ is the factor-ownership index for persons with zero net gains from the tariff rise; that is, for those with $B[k(\tilde{e}),t]=c(\tilde{e})$.

Similarly, a person will enjoy a net gain from a tariff *decrease*, if

$$D[k(e),t]-c(e) = -B[k(e),t]-c(e)>0, \tag{17}$$

where $D$ is the real income gain from a tariff decrease. The fraction of people with factor-ownership ratio $k(e)$ that vote for the tariff

[11] Hence, if the capital-labor ownership distribution is symmetric and there are no voting restrictions, majority voting results in a Pareto-efficient allocation of resources.

[12] Under the assumptions of this model—one issue, all individuals vote, symmetric, unimodal factor distribution—free trade would also be chosen in a two-party representative democracy.

[13] The terms "voting" and "voter participation costs" have a broader meaning than marking a ballot and incurring costs in going to the voting booth. Voting can be interpreted as any form of communicating a person's response to a given policy proposal whether through the ballot, letters to political representatives, participation in political meetings, or public demonstrations. Since a politician in a two-party representative democracy will also choose the median-voter's optimal tariff, informing politicians of one's attitudes is a form of voting. Voting costs include all expenses incurred in transmitting this information. In parts of the public choice literature, voting costs also include information-gathering costs. Strictly speaking, this is legitimate only if $B^i$ is independent of such information-gathering costs.

[14] Peltzman's formulation of voting probabilities as related to net income changes is a convenient way of accounting for the free-rider problem associated with voting on tariff policies. On the problem of free riding and political participation, see Mancur Olson (1965).

decrease is denoted by $0 \leq \sigma(e) < 1$, where $\sigma$ is positively related to the left-hand expression in (17). The total number of votes cast for a tariff decrease, $A$, is

$$A = L\int_0^{\bar{\tilde{e}}} \sigma(e) f[k(e)]\, de, \tag{18}$$

where $\bar{\tilde{e}}$ is the factor-ownership index for persons with zero net gains from the tariff decline; that is, for those with $D[k(\bar{\tilde{e}}), t] = c(\bar{\tilde{e}})$.

If, at a given tariff rate, $E > A$, a majority will vote for higher tariffs. As the tariff is raised, the voting strength of proponents ($E$) for a tariff increase will decline while opponents ($A$) increase their votes. This follows from (16) and (18), as $\sigma$, $\tilde{e}$, and $\bar{\tilde{e}}$ are directly and $\rho$ is inversely related to $t$. An equilibrium tariff finally is established, when $E = A$, or[15]

$$\int_{\tilde{e}}^1 \rho(e) f[k(e)]\, de = \int_0^{\bar{\tilde{e}}} \sigma(e) f[k(e)]\, de. \tag{19}$$

It is clear that the equilibrium tariff depends on the factor distribution at both tails, that is, for people with indexes $e \geq \tilde{e}$ and $e \leq \bar{\tilde{e}}$, as well as on voting probabilities on the part of winners, $\rho(e)$, and losers, $\sigma(e)$. Whether a person is going to vote at all and with what probability, in turn, depends on the person's factor-ownership ratio, voting costs, and actual tariff rate.

It is relatively easy to see that the equilibrium tariff rate with voting costs, $t^*$, is less than the optimal tariff rate of the marginal gainer from a tariff increase, $\tilde{t}(\tilde{e})$, and larger than the optimal tariff rate of the marginal gainer from a tariff decrease, $\tilde{t}(\bar{\tilde{e}})$.[16]

Hence, the equilibrium tariff will be the optimal tariff of a nonvoting factor owner.

Depending on the specifically made assumptions on factor-ownership distributions and voting probabilities, different hypotheses on tariff determination can be developed. Here, it only should be noted that free trade would be adopted if factor-ownership distribution, voting costs, and voting probabilities were symmetric.[17]

Earlier I mentioned the role of voter eligibility restrictions as a possible determinant of actual tariff rates. Even today, every country excludes some factor owners from voting. Major restrictions result from age, residency, and citizenship criteria. Young factor owners, as well as migrant and alien workers, are generally not eligible to vote. In the past, women and poor people, including small property owners and small taxpayers, were excluded as well. Such eligibility restrictions are really a special form of prohibitive voter participation costs. Their major effect is that the factor-ownership distribution of voters is no longer identical to that of the population. In most instances these restrictions tend to cut off, or at least flatten, the left tail of the factor-owner distribution. With the exclusion of many "capital poor" people, eligible voters are more likely to protect the interests of capital owners; if the factor-ownership distribution of all people is symmetric, a tariff on the capital-intensive import good will be voted in as the factor-ownership ratio of the median voter exceeds the endowment ratio; and even if there is positive skewness, as suggested before, it still is possible that the median voter's optimal tariff is positive.

Changing voting rules affects the identity of the median voter and thereby tariff policy. If it is accepted that past voting restrictions were directed against workers and small capital owners, one should observe that the gradual dismantling of voting restrictions has been associated with or followed by declining tariffs on capital-intensive imports and rising tariffs on labor-intensive imports. Em-

[15]Adjustment to such an equilibrium implies the possibility of repeated voting on the same tariff issue. While repeated voting in the sense of going again and again to the voting booth is quite unrealistic, repeated voting through other forms of communications from the public to the politician is far more realistic.

[16]At the equilibrium tariff, $t^*$, there exists a marginal voter among net gainers from a tariff increase for whom $B[k(\tilde{e}), t^*] = c(\tilde{e})$. Without voting costs, the marginal gainer's optimal tariff $\tilde{t}(\tilde{e})$ is such that $B[k(\tilde{e}), t] = 0$. Since $(\partial B/\partial t) < 0$ and $c(\tilde{e}) > 0$, it must be that $t^* < \tilde{t}(\tilde{e})$. Similarly, one can show that $t^* > \tilde{t}(\bar{\tilde{e}})$.

[17]Symmetric voting probabilities mean that, for all $(B - c) > 0$, $\rho = \sigma$ if $(B - c) = (D - c)$.

pirical support for this hypothesis, as presented by Bennett Baak and Edward Ray (1982) for the United States, is not fully conclusive.

## III. Protection of Industry-Specific Interests[18]

The discussion of tariff formation in a Heckscher-Ohlin type economy emphasized the role of factor-ownership distributions, voting costs, and voter eligibility in determining tariffs. Where a given factor is employed (i.e., its association with a given industry) was irrelevant. This framework seems most suitable in explaining long-run tariff trends, especially in relationship to changes in voter eligibility rules, voting costs, or overall factor-ownership distributions. It is much less suitable, however, in explaining more short-term attempts by individual industries to gain tariff protection. In particular, it sheds no light on the frequently observed phenomenon that a single industry succeeds in raising tariffs on its product, even though the vast majority of eligible voters does not benefit from such a policy. In the following, I introduce a many-industries model with specific factors to show how majority voting can result in tariff protection of a small industry. First, I lay out the model and discuss the impact of a tariff increase on a person's income share. Later, I demonstrate how a small minority of gaining factor owners can become a majority of actual voters for a tariff increase on a given commodity.

### A. *The Model*

The production structure of this section is described by Jones' (1975) multicommodity model with specific factors. There are $n>2$ industries, each of which employs a fixed amount of a factor specific to that industry, $V_j$, $j=1,\dots,n$, and a variable amount of a mobile factor, $V_N$. The mobile factor is employed in all industries. Since we are again concerned with the implications of tariffs for income shares of different individuals, the main interest lies in the relationships between commodity and factor prices in such a model. When needed, I will take these relationships from the Jones paper, using the same notation where appropriate.

With many commodities, the $i$th individual's indirect utility function is stated as

$$U^i=U^i(p_1,1,p_3,\dots,p_N;\phi^iY), \tag{20}$$

where $p_j$ is the domestic price of commodity $j$ in terms of the second commodity. The $i$th person's income share in the presence of $n$ specific factors is

$$\phi^i=\left[R_NV_N^i+\sum_{j=1}^{n}R_jV_j^i\right]\Bigg/\left[R_NV_N+\sum_{j=1}^{n}R_jV_j\right], \tag{21}$$

where $R_j$, $j=1,\dots,n$, and $R_N$ denote returns on the $j$th specific and the mobile factor, respectively, $V_j^i$ and $V_N^i$ are the $i$th person's ownership of the $j$th specific and mobile factor, and $V_j$ and $V_N$ are the corresponding factor endowments of the country. Let us consider the mobile factor to be labor and assume, as before, that each individual owns one unit; that is, $V_N^i=1$.

Total income, $Y$, consists again of domestic factor income and tariff revenues. It is assumed that the first $m$ commodities are imported and the other $(n-m)$ commodities are exported in the relevant range of tariff rates. Denoting imports (exports) of the $j$th commodity by $M_j$ $(E_j)$ and the corresponding import (export) tariff by $t_j$ $(\tau_j)$, the economy's income is

$$Y=\sum_{j=1}^{n}p_jX_j+\sum_{j=1}^{m}t_j\pi_jM_j+\sum_{j=m+1}^{n}\tau_jp_jE_j. \tag{22}$$

[18] The association of tariffs with the economic interest of sector-specific groups is one of three models tested by Caves.

As was the case in the two-by-two Heckscher-Ohlin model, it is again asked how the $i$th individual's welfare is affected by a given tariff change, say on the $g$th commodity. Differentiation of (20) with respect to $t_g$ and some manipulations yield:

$$(23)\quad (\partial U^i/\partial t_g) = (\partial U^i/\partial y^i)\Bigg\{ Y(\partial\phi^i/\partial t_g) + \phi^i\Bigg[\sum_{j=1}^{m} t_j\pi_j(\partial M_j/\partial t_g) + \sum_{m+1}^{n} \tau_j p_j(\partial E_j/\partial t_g)\Bigg]\Bigg\},$$

indicating that personal welfare effects depend on how a given tariff change affects a person's income share, on the one hand, and the tariff-weighted value of imports plus exports, on the other hand. Note that the direction of the change in the tariff-weighted value of imports and exports is generally not known without further restrictions; but it will be zero under the restriction that initially there is free trade. Corresponding to the analysis in Section II, it would be possible to utilize (23) for all $g=1,\dots n$ and derive an optimal tariff vector for individual $i$. As shown by Murray Kemp (1969, p. 298) for multicommodity optimal tariff structures of a country, such an optimal tariff vector is one-dimensionally indeterminate. And, without imposing severe restrictions, relatively little can be said about the precise structure of the tariff vector. Fortunately, for the issue under consideration, namely how a single industry can succeed in gaining tariff protection, knowledge of the optimal tariff vector is not crucial.

### B. *Tariff-Induced Changes in Income Shares*

An individual associates with the interests of a given industry if his or her specific factor ownership is concentrated in that industry. In order to emphasize this association between an individual's and a given industry's interests in describing voting behavior, assume now that each person possesses at most one *type* of specific factor in addition to one unit of the mobile factor. The income share of individual $i$ with specific factor ownership in industry $h$, $h=1,\dots,n$, therefore, is defined as

$$(21')\quad \phi_h^i = (R_N + R_h V_h^i)\Bigg/\left(R_N V_N + \sum_{j=1}^{n} R_j V_j\right).$$

Differentiation of (21′) with respect to $t_g$ indicates how a tariff increase on commodity $g$ affects the $i$th individual's income share:

$$(24)\quad (1+t_g)\,\partial\phi_h^i/\partial t_g = \left[\frac{R_h V_h^i}{\left(R_N V_N + \sum_{j=1}^{n} R_j V_j\right)}\right]\left[\frac{(\hat{R}_h - \hat{R}_N)}{\hat{p}_g}\right] - \phi_h^i\left\{\sum_{j=1}^{n}\alpha^j\left[\frac{(\hat{R}_j - \hat{R}_N)}{\hat{p}_g}\right]\right\},$$

where $\alpha^j = R_j V_j/(R_N V_N + \sum_{j=1}^{n} R_j V_j)$ is the $j$th specific factor's distributive share in national factor income,

$$\sum_{j=1}^{n}\alpha^j = 1-\alpha^N,$$

and $$\alpha^N = R_N V_N\Bigg/\left(R_N V_N + \sum_{j=1}^{n} R_j V_j\right).$$

The term in braces on the right-hand side of (24) can be interpreted as the "$g$th commodity's bias with respect to the mobile factor." Ruffin and Jones (calling the mobile factor labor and denoting its return by $w_L$ instead of our $R_N$) define "commodity $j$ to be unbiased with respect to labor if the relative change in the wage rate ($w_L$) brought about by an increase in $p_j$ is precisely the average for the changes in all factor prices" (p. 339). And the average of all factor price changes is obtained by weighting each factor's relative price change by the factor's share in national income. Hence, one can define commodity $g$ to be biased against, unbiased, or biased towards the mobile factor as

$$(25)\quad b_g = \sum_{j=1}^{n} \alpha^j\left[(\hat{R}_j - \hat{R}_N)/\hat{p}_g\right]$$

$$= \left[\sum_{j=1}^{n} \alpha^j \hat{R}_j + \alpha_N \hat{R}_N - \hat{R}_N\right]/\hat{p}_g \gtreqless 0.$$

The sign of the first term on the right-hand side of (24) crucially depends on the $i$th individual's association with a given industry. If an individual's specific factor ownership is in the industry whose tariff rate is raised (i.e., $g = h$), one can show that

$$(26)\quad (\hat{R}_g - \hat{R}_N)/\hat{p}_g = \sum_{\substack{h=1\\ h\neq g}}^{n} \beta_h/\theta_{gg} > 0,$$

where I utilized equations (13) and (14) of the Jones (1975) paper, $\beta_g > 0$ indicates the relative change in the mobile factor's return as the $g$th commodity's price rises by 1 percent and $\theta_{gg} = (R_g V_g)/(p_g X_g)$ denotes the cost share of the specific factor in the production of commodity $g$. Substitution of (26) in (24) reveals that an individual's income share will definitely rise if commodity $g$ is biased towards labor or not biased at all. If, on the other hand, an individual's specific ownership is in an industry whose tariff rate is not changed (i.e., $g \neq h$), then one can show that

$$(27)\quad (\hat{R}_h - \hat{R}_N)/\hat{p}_g = -\beta_g/\theta_{hh} < 0.$$

Consequently, the individual's income share will definitely decline, if commodity $g$ is biased against labor or not biased at all. Finally, it should be noted that the first term on the right-hand side of (24) is zero for people with only labor but no specific factor ownership. Their income shares rise, remain unchanged, or fall, as commodity $g$ is biased towards, unbiased, or biased against labor.

In the special case where the above-stated bias is zero (i.e., $b_g = 0$ in (25)), Ruffin and Jones (pp. 339–40) prove that $\beta_g$ also represents the fraction of total factor income generated in industry $g$; that is, if $b_g = 0$, then

$$(28)\quad \beta_g = p_g X_g \bigg/ \left(R_N V_N + \sum_{j=1}^{n} R_j V_j\right).$$

Furthermore, it should be noted that under all circumstances—whether commodity $g$ is labor biased or not, it must hold that $\sum_{h=1}^{n} \beta_h = 1$.

In the next subsection, the assumption that the commodity on which the tariff is imposed is unbiased towards labor is used. Under this assumption, only the income shares of specific factor owners in the "protected" industry will rise. Specific factor owners in all other industries will suffer a decline in their income shares, and income shares of people who are workers only will not be affected.

### C. *Industry Protection under Majority Voting*

Factor owners are assumed to vote their economic interests. Equation (23) above revealed that a given tariff increase affects a person's welfare through two forces: changes in the person's income share and changes in the tariff-weighted value of exports and imports. One could easily construct a scenario such that the latter change is positive and one could conclude that it is, at least, conceivable that a majority of voters gain from a given tariff increase, even though owners of the specific factor in the protected industry are a minority. While this possibility has to be recognized, the intent here is not to adopt a set of unusual assumptions for demonstrating that a small industry can gain tariff protection under majority voting. Instead, the objective is to postulate a rather neutral set of plausible assumptions to substantiate my contention. These assumptions are

1) Initially, free trade is prevailing and only one industry, namely industry $g$, tries to gain tariff protection;[19]

[19] If several industries try to obtain tariff protection more or less at the same time, the possibility of logrolling must be allowed for. In this case, a unique equilibrium generally will not exist.

2) Commodity $g$ is unbiased with respect to the mobile factor (i.e., $b_g = 0$);

3) There are voter participation costs and these costs are the same for every voter, whether voting for a tariff or a subsidy.

In the presence of voting costs, the decision to participate in voting is based on an individual's assessment of tariff-induced real income changes relative to voting costs. The real income change from leaving free trade and imposing a tariff on commodity $g$, as experienced by the $i$th individual with specific factor ownership in industry $h$, is given by

$$(29)\quad B^i_{hg} = Y(\partial\phi^i_h/\partial t_g) = Y\left[(R_h V^i_h)\Big/\left(R_N V_N + \sum_{j=1}^{n} R_j V_j\right)\right] \times\left[(\hat{R}_h - \hat{R}_N)/\hat{p}_g\right],$$

where the assumptions above and equations (23) and (24) were employed. If individual $i$ owns a specific factor in the industry where the tariff increase takes place, then

$$(30)\quad B^i_{gg} = Y(1-\beta_g)\beta_g\lambda^i_g > 0,$$

where $\lambda^i_g = (V^i_g/V_g)$ denotes the $i$th individual's ownership share of specific factor $g$, and where we used (26) and (28), the property $\Sigma^n_{h=1;\, h\neq g}\beta_h = (1-\beta_g)$, and the definition of $\theta_{gg}$ in reducing (29) to (30). Alternatively, if individual $i$ owns a specific factor employed in any other, not protected industry $h$, then

$$(31)\quad B^i_{hg} = -Y\beta_h\beta_g\lambda^i_h < 0,$$

using (27). Finally, for all those people who do not own any specific factor, as $V^i_g = V^i_h = 0$, there is no real income change in the small neighborhood of the initial free-trade equilibrium.[20]

An assessment of real income changes of people owning specific factors in either the protected or one of the many other industries reveals that the former will gain while the latter will lose. Accordingly, only a small fraction of all factor owners would favor such a tariff increase and it would not be voted in by a majority if all factor owners participated in voting. In fact, the majority of people would gain from a subsidy on importing commodity $g$. In the presence of voting costs, however, the *magnitude of gains or losses* relative to voting costs must be considered as well. Equations (30) and (31) state that the magnitude of real income changes depends on the value of national income, $Y$, and a person's specific factor-ownership share, $\lambda^i_h$. But, most important, it depends on the relative sizes of the protected industry and of the industry whose specific factor is owned, as $\beta_g$ and $\beta_h$ measure the respective industries' shares in national income. The industry-size element in affecting real income is most significant since it introduces an asymmetry between the magnitude of gains and losses for people with identical specific factor-ownership shares held in the protected and nonprotected sectors, respectively. More precisely, for all $\lambda^i_g = \lambda^i_h$, where $h = 1,\ldots, n$ and $h \neq g$,

$$(32)\quad B^i_{gg} > -B^i_{hg},$$

as $(1-\beta_g) > \beta_h$ always, if there are more than two industries. As shown next, this asymmetry between the size of gains and losses implies that, with voting costs, a minority of factor owners may become a majority of participating voters.[21]

Per capita voting costs $c$ were assumed to be the same for both supporters and opponents of the tariff increase. A factor owner definitely will refrain from voting if real income gains from a tariff or subsidy increase do not exceed voting costs. Hence, a person will not participate in voting for a tariff

[20] This is the same conclusion as the one obtained by Ruffin and Jones for the case when tariff proceeds are redistributed (see their p. 344).

[21] One can show that, in the small neighborhood of the initial free-trade point, the sum of total real income gains is exactly equal to the sum of real income losses when all factor owners are accounted for.

increase if

$$B^i_{gg} = Y\beta_g(1-\beta_g)\lambda^i_g \leqq c. \quad (33a)$$

And a person will not participate in voting for a tariff decrease or subsidy if

$$D^i_{hg} = -B^i_{hg} = Y\beta_g\beta_h\lambda^i_h \leqq c, \quad (33b)$$

where $D^i_{hg}$ is the subsidy-induced real income gain to person $i$ owning some of specific factor $h$. People with factor ownership shares $\lambda^i_g \leqq \tilde{\lambda}^i_g$ and $\lambda^i_h \leqq \tilde{\tilde{\lambda}}^i_h$ definitely will not participate in voting, where

$$\tilde{\lambda}^i_g = c/[Y\beta_g(1-\beta_g)] \quad (34)$$

$$\text{and} \quad \tilde{\tilde{\lambda}}^i_h = c/[Y\beta_g\beta_h], \quad h \neq g;\ h = 1,\ldots,n,$$

can be called the specific factor-ownership share of the marginal voter for a tariff and subsidy, respectively. Comparing these ownership shares of marginal nonparticipants in voting, one can see that

$$\tilde{\tilde{\lambda}}^i_h > \tilde{\lambda}^i_g \quad (35)$$

as $[(1-\beta_g)/\beta_h] > 1$ always. The separation between definite nonvoters and potential voters occurs at a much higher endowment share in the many nonprotected industries than in the single protected industry. Hence, it is quite possible that only a few large specific factor owners in each losing industry remain potential resisters to the tariff increase, while a large number of factor owners in the gaining industry tend to support it. In fact, it is quite possible that losers will pose no active resistance at all to the proposed departure from free trade.

A simple example will illustrate the magnitudes by which the marginal nonparticipants' factor-ownership ratios may differ between gainers and losers. First, assume there are 10 industries: for each industry $\beta_h = .1$, and voting costs and income are such that $\tilde{\lambda}^i_g = 1/10{,}000$. Then $(1-\beta_g)/\beta_h = 9$ and $\tilde{\tilde{\lambda}}^i_h = 9/10{,}000$. Second, assume there are 100 industries $\beta_h = .01$ for each industry, and again $\tilde{\lambda}^i_g = 1/10{,}000$. In this case, $\tilde{\tilde{\lambda}}^i_h = 99/10{,}000$. The examples illustrate that the marginal nonparticipant's factor-ownership share is far greater among losers than gainers, and that it tends to rise the more diversified the economy is (i.e., the more sectors it has).

So far, I have only tried to describe the separation line between definite nonvoters and potential voters among factor owners in both protected and nonprotected industries. The number of potential voters in the two opposing camps crucially depends on the height of voting costs, the distribution of specific factor ownerships in the various sectors, and the degree of diversification of the economy. As mentioned above, it is quite possible that a minority of factor owners gaining from a tariff increase becomes a majority of potential voters. However, even if losing factor owners maintain a majority of potential voters, it still is quite possible that the gaining industry's factor owners will succeed in obtaining tariff protection. What matters for tariff policy formation are actual votes rather than potential votes, and the minority of potential votes among gainers could easily become a majority of actual votes as will be shown next.

The probabilities of potential voters' participation in voting depend, as mentioned in Section II, on the magnitude of net gains from a certain outcome. Denoting the probability of a specific factor owner in industry $g$ to vote for the tariff increase by $\rho_g$ and the probability of a specific factor owner in industry $h$ to vote for a subsidy or tariff decrease by $\sigma_h$, we have

$$\rho_g = \rho[B_{gg} - c] \quad \text{and} \quad \sigma_h = \sigma[D_{hg} - c], \quad (36)$$

where $\rho_g = 0$ for $(B_{gg} - c) \leqq 0$, $\sigma_h = 0$ for $(D_{hg} - c) \leqq 0$ and $\rho'_g > 0$, $\sigma'_h > 0$ in the range of positive net gains. Unrestricted comparisons of $\rho_g$ with $\sigma_h$ are, of course, not possible. If, however, it is assumed that the voting probabilities for given values of net gains are the same, then we can compare the voting probabilities of factor owners in different industries with the same specific factor ownership shares. Assuming that $\lambda_g = \lambda_h$, one can see that

$$\rho_g = \rho[B_{gg} - c] > \sigma_h = \sigma[(B_{gg} - c) - (B_{gg} - D_{hg})], \quad (37)$$

since $B_{gg} > D_{hg}$, using (32) and (33b). Potential voters with identical factor ownership shares are more likely to vote if they are gainers than if they are losers from a tariff increase. Hence, it is quite possible that a majority of potential voters against a tariff increase becomes a minority of actual voters once voting probabilities are accounted for.

I have demonstrated that the existence of voting costs can be most instrumental in helping a small industry gain tariff protection. The push for protection is, however, not unlimited since resistance to tariff increases will rise and the forces for tariff increases will weaken as the tariff rate, $t_g$, further departs from zero. This can be seen from (23) which for $t_g > 0$ and all other $t_j = \tau_j = 0$, becomes

$$(23') \quad \left(\partial U^i/\partial t_g\right) = \left(\partial U^i/\partial y^i\right)\left\{Y\left(\partial \phi^i/\partial t_g\right) + \phi^i t_g \pi_g\left(\partial M_g/\partial t_g\right)\right\}.$$

Since $(\partial M_g/\partial t_g) < 0$, each person's real income change is affected by a negative force in addition to the income share change. The higher $t_g$, the less the gainers will gain and the more the losers will lose. Hence, the drive for a further increase in $t_g$ will eventually stall as no majority can be formed to keep raising the tariff rate.

My findings support Baldwin's conjecture that a small group of big gainers may succeed in obtaining tariff protection. Crucial for this occurrence is that each person's specific factor ownership is relatively concentrated in one industry and that there are voting costs. In this case, a large number of losers from a tariff increase becomes a much smaller number of potential voters which, in turn, becomes an even smaller number of actual voters. Among gaining factor owners, there also will not be full voter participation, but the shrinkage tends to be much less. In the end, the gainers may be successful in gaining tariff protection through a majority vote.

## V. Concluding Remarks

This paper argues that a country's actual tariff policy is the result of its underlying factor-ownership distribution. There are two links in the chain of causality between factor-ownership distribution and tariff policy. The first link describes how the economic interests of people in a given tariff policy are related to the factor-ownership distribution. One may call it the "economic link" since the economy's production structure is the main determinant of the process through which a person's real income is affected. I deal with two alternative production structures. The two-by-two Heckscher-Ohlin model, that is highly aggregated and frequently associated with long-run portrayals of production structures, seems most useful in explaining long-run changes in the overall tariff structure. The many-commodity model, with specific factors, on the other hand, seems more appropriate in explaining day-to-day attempts by individual industries or interest groups in gaining tariff protection. Irrespective of the production structure, each person is shown to have an optimal tariff policy that generally differs from the actual policy. The second link between factor-ownership distribution and tariff policy may be called the "political link" as it refers to the political process through which economic interests are translated into actual tariff policy. My analysis emphasizes the sensitivity of tariff policies to changing voter eligibility rules and voter participation costs under majority voting. In particular, it is demonstrated how a small minority of factor owners can succeed in gaining tariff protection for its industry under majority voting provided voting costs are significant.

This paper's assumptions concerning both the economic structure and political process were deliberately chosen to allow tracing of the path from factor-ownership distributions to tariff policies. Although the assumptions are quite standard in the trade-theoretic and public choice literature, it would be most desirable to relax some of the restrictions. Concerning the economic link, future research should explore more general descriptions of factor-ownership distributions, imperfect information of factor owners on real income effects of tariff changes, and nonhomothetic tastes. Concerning the political link, one should try to account for multiple-issue voting and logrolling, policy formation in a representative democracy, and the working of a multiparty system.

## REFERENCES

**Baak, Bennett D. and Ray, Edward John,** "The Political Economy of Tariff Policy: A Case Study of the United States," mimeo., Ohio State University, February 1982.

**Baldwin, Robert E.,** "The Political Economy of Postwar U.S. Trade Policy," *The Bulletin*, Graduate School of Business Administration, New York University, 1976.

______, "The Political Economy of Protection," in J. N. Bhagwati and T. N. Srinivasan, eds., *Import Competition and Response*, Chicago: University of Chicago Press, 1982, 263–86.

**Bhagwati, Jagdish N.,** "Shifting Comparative Advantage, Protectionist Demands, and Policy Response," in his and T. N. Srinivasan, eds., *Import Competition and Response*, Chicago: University of Chicago Press, 1982, 153–84.

**Black, Duncan,** (1948a) "On the Rationale of Group Decision Making," *Journal of Political Economy*, February 1948, *56*, 23–34.

______, (1948b) "The Decision of a Committee Using a Special Majority," *Econometrica*, July 1948, *16*, 245–61.

**Brock, William A. and Magee, Stephen P.,** "The Economics of Special Interest Politics: The Case of the Tariff," *American Economic Review Proceedings*, May 1978, *68*, 246–50.

______ **and** ______, "Tariff Formation in a Democracy," in J. Black and B. Hindley, eds., *Current Issues in International Commercial Policy and Diplomacy*, London: Macmillan, 1980, 1–9.

**Buchanan, James M. and Tullock, Gordon,** *The Calculus of Consent*, Ann Arbor: University of Michigan Press, 1962.

**Caves, Richard E.,** "Economic Models of Political Choice: Canada's Tariff Structure," *Canadian Journal of Economics*, May 1976, *9*, 278–300.

**Dinopoulos, Elias,** "Import Competition, International Factor Mobility and Lobbying Response: The Schumpeterian Industry Case," *Journal of International Economics*, May 1983, *14*, 395–410.

**Downs, Anthony,** *An Economic Theory of Democracy*, New York: Harper and Row, 1957.

**Findlay, Ronald and Wellisz, Stanislaw,** "Endogenous Tariffs, The Political Economy of Trade Restrictions, and Welfare," in J. N. Bhagwati and T. N. Srinivasan, eds., *Import Competition and Response*, Chicago: University of Chicago Press, 1982, 223–34.

**Helleiner, G. K.,** "The Political Economy of Canada's Tariff Structure: An Alternative Model," *Canadian Journal of Economics*, May 1977, *10*, 318–26.

**Hillman, Arye L.,** "Declining Industries and Political-Support Protectionist Motives," *American Economic Review*, December 1982, *72*, 1180–87.

**Jones, Ronald W.,** "Tariffs and Trade in General Equilibrium: Comment," *American Economic Review*, June 1969, *59*, 418–24.

______, "Income Distribution and Effective Protection in a Multicommodity Trade Model," *Journal of Economic Theory*, August 1975, *11*, 1–15.

**Kemp, Murray C.,** *The Pure Theory of International Trade and Investment*, Englewood Cliffs: Prentice Hall, 1969.

**Marvel, Howard P. and Ray, Edward J.,** "The Kennedy Round: Evidence on the Regulation of International Trade in the United States," *American Economic Review*, March 1983, *73*, 190–97.

**Mueller, Dennis C.,** *Public Choice*, Cambridge: Cambridge University Press, 1979.

**Olson, Mancur,** *The Logic of Collective Action*, Cambridge: Harvard University Press, 1965.

**Peltzman, Sam,** "Toward a More General Theory of Regulations," *Journal of Law and Economics*, August 1976, *19*, 211–40.

**Pincus, Jonathan J.,** "Pressure Groups and the Pattern of Tariffs," *Journal of Political Economy*, August 1975, *83*, 757–78.

**Ray, Edward J.,** "The Optimum Commodity Tariff Rates in Developed and Less Developed Countries," *Review of Economics and Statistics*, August 1974, *56*, 369–77.

**Riker, William H. and Ordeshook, Peter C.,** "A Theory of the Calculus of Voting," *American Political Science Review*, March 1968, *62*, 25–42.

**Ruffin, Roy and Jones, Ronald W.,** "Protection and Real Wages: The Neoclassical Ambiguity," *Journal of Economic Theory*, April 1977, *14*, 337–48.

**Wellisz, Stanislaw and Findlay, Ronald,** "Some Thoughts on Protection and Rent-Seeking in Developing Countries," International Economics Research Center Paper No. 30, Columbia University, June 1983.

______ **and Wilson, John D.,** "A Theory of Tariff Formation," mimeo., Columbia University, August 1983.

**Young, Leslie and Magee, Stephen P.,** "Factor Returns and Resource Allocation in the Political Economy of Trade Distortions," presented at the North American Summer Meeting of the Econometric Society, Northwestern University, June 1983.

Journal of International Economics 23 (1987) 377–381. North-Holland

# ENDOGENOUS CHOICE OF TRADE POLICY INSTRUMENTS

Wolfgang MAYER

*University of Cincinnati, Cincinnati, OH 45221, USA*

Raymond G. RIEZMAN*

*University of Iowa, Iowa City, IA 52242, USA*

Received March 1986, revised version received October 1986

Recently developed theories of endogenous trade policy formation have attempted to explain tariffs as the result of economic interest-seeking by individuals or groups. This note demonstrates that tariffs will not emerge as a policy choice if income is redistributed solely through trade policy-induced factor price changes. A production tax cum subsidy will be adopted as both gainers and losers are better off than with a tariff.

## 1. Introduction

Recently developed theories of endogenous trade policy formation are in general agreement that socially suboptimal tariff structures result from the political process in which opposing economic interests compete. The lobbying models of Brock and Magee (1978, 1980), Findlay and Wellisz (1982), and others, as well as the majority voting models of Baldwin (1976) and Mayer (1984), discuss the determination of tariff rates when individuals or groups with different economic interests try to further their own welfare. These writings, however, do not address the question of why tariffs rather than other trade policy measures are chosen through the political process.

This note focuses on the selection of alternative trade policy instruments when participants in the political process can choose among tariffs, production taxes cum subsidies, and consumption taxes cum subsidies and all income redistribution effects are due to policy-induced factor price changes.[1] It is demonstrated that tariffs, which are the subject of study in the current literature on trade policy formation, will not be adopted as production taxes

*We thank Alan Deardorff, Jagdish Bhagwati, Kala Krishna, Neil Wallace, Bob Stern, Jay Wilson, Rick Brecher, and two anonymous referees for many helpful comments on an earlier, more detailed paper on the same subject.

[1]Somewhat different comparisons between tariffs and other trade policy measures are discussed in Bhagwati (1985) and Cassing and Hillman (1985).

cum subsidies are more efficient in redistributing factor income.[2] More efficient means that for every tariff rate there exists some production tax cum subsidy which makes all individuals better off than the tariff does. Consequently, a policy-influencing individual or group will favor production taxes cum subsidies since they lead to larger gains for themselves and smaller losses to, and therefore less political resistance by, opposing individuals or groups.

## 2. Model

Consider an open economy in which two commodities, $X_1$ and $X_2$, are produced, using labor, $L$, and capital $K$, as inputs. Production requires both inputs, production functions are homogeneous of degree one, all markets are competitive, and factors are fully employed, immobile between countries, but mobile between industries. Factor ownership is assumed to differ among the $i=1,\dots,I$ individuals and is described by $(L^i, K^i)$. Preferences, on the other hand, are assumed to be homothetic and identical; they are expressed by the indirect utility function:

$$U^i = U^i(p_c, y_d^i), \quad i=1,\dots,I, \tag{1}$$

where $U^i$ denotes maximum attainable utility, given $P_c$, the price of the first in terms of the second commodity as faced by domestic consumers, and $y_d^i$, the $i$th individual's disposable income. The latter consists of factor income $(wL^i + rK^i)$, minus income taxes paid, $T^i$:

$$y_d^i = wL^i + rK^i - T^i, \tag{2}$$

where $w$ and $r$ stand for returns on labor and capital, respectively.

Three types of commodity taxes, to be imposed on the first good, are considered as potential instruments to enhance individual or group welfare: a production tax (subsidy), $t_p > 0$ ($t_p < 0$), a consumption tax (subsidy), $t_c > 0$ ($t_c < 0$), and an import tariff (subsidy), $\tau > 0$ ($\tau < 0$). The latter is equivalent to an equal-value combination of a production subsidy and consumption tax, such that $\tau = t_c = -t_p$. Furthermore, there is an income tax (transfer), $T > 0$ ($T < 0$), whose sole function is to keep the government's budget balanced. Considering that the tariff is a combination of production subsidy and consumption tax, the budget constraint is written as

$$\pi X_1 t_p + \pi D_1 t_c + T = 0, \tag{3}$$

[2]Essentially, the principles for social welfare maximizing policy choice, as developed by Bhagwati, Ramaswami and Srinivasan (1969), carry over to individually optimal choices.

where $\pi$ is the world price of good 1, and $X_1(D_1)$ stands for aggregate production (consumption) of the first commodity.

Endogenous choice of type and value of policy instruments is based on the decisions of individuals or groups who have the ability to shape the policy selection process. For example, in a majority voting situation the median voter's preferences are decisive; in a lobbying situation, the preferences of the average lobby member may be the determining factor. No matter who makes the final decision, the individual's objective is to maximize its own welfare, as expressed by (1), with respect to $t_p$ and $t_c$. Should the individually optimal values of $-t_p$ and $t_c$ be the same, a tariff $\tau$, represents the optimal policy instrument for individual $i$.

The indirect utility function can be written as

$$U^i = U^i[p_c, \phi_d^i(Y - T)], \tag{1'}$$

where $\phi_d' = (wL^i + rK^i - T^i)/(wL + rK - T)$ is the $i$th person's share of total expenditure and $Y = (wL + rK) = P_p X_1 + X_2$ measures national income, with $P_p$ indicating the price of the first commodity as faced by producers. In order to highlight the redistribution effects of trade policy-induced factor price changes, we assume that the income tax system in neutral in the sense that it does not alter the distribution of income as it results from factor ownership. In other words, the $i$th person's expenditure share, $\phi_d^i$, is the same as its factor income share, $\phi^i$:

$$\phi_d^i = \phi^i, \tag{4}$$

where $\phi^i = (wL^i + rK^i)/(wL + rK)$. After substituting (3) and (4) in (1′) and writing $P_c = \pi(1 + t_c)$ and $P_p = \pi(1 - t_p)$, the individual's objective can be restated as

$$\max_{t_c, t_p} U^i\{\pi(1 + t_c); \phi^i[\pi(1 - t_p)X_1 + X_2 + \pi t_c D_1 + \pi t_p X_1]\}. \tag{5}$$

Assuming that $U^i$ is strictly concave with respect to $t_c$ and $t_p$, necessary conditions for maximizing the $i$th person's welfare are

$$\partial U^i/\partial t_c = (\partial U^i/\partial y_d^i)[-\pi D_1^i + \phi^i \pi D_1 + \phi^i \pi t_c(\partial D_1/\partial t_c)] = 0, \tag{6a}$$

$$\partial U^i/\partial t_p = (\partial U^i/\partial y_d^i)\{(Y - T)(\partial \phi^i/\partial t_p) + \phi^i \pi[t_p(\partial X_1/\partial t_p) + t_c(\partial D_1/\partial t_p)]\} = 0. \tag{6b}$$

In deriving the term $D_1^i$ of (6a), the $i$th individual's consumption of the first commodity, we used Roy's Identity. In the derivation of (6b), we utilized the production efficiency condition $\pi(1-t_p)(\partial X_1/\partial t_p)+(\partial X_2/\partial t_p)=0$.

For homothetic and identical utility functions the $i$th person's share of total consumption of commodity 1 equals the person's expenditure share; that is, $D_1^i/D_1=\phi_d^i$. And since $\phi_d^i=\phi^i$, it is implied that $D_1^i=\phi^i D_1$. Substitution of this expression in (6a) reveals that *the ith person's optimal consumption tax*, $*t_c^i$, *equals zero.* The individually optimal production tax, $*t_p^i$, on the other hand, is generally not zero. It is derived from (6b) after setting $*t_c^i=0$:

$$*t_p^i=-[(Y-T)(\partial\phi^i/\partial t_p^i)]/[\phi^i\pi(\partial X_1/\partial t_p)]. \tag{7}$$

Since $-(\partial X_1/\partial t_p)=(\partial X_1/\partial P_p)\pi>0$, *the ith person's optimal production tax is positive (negative) if an increase in the tax rate raises (lowers) this person's income share.* The tax rate is zero only in the special case of a person's income share remaining unaffected by production taxes. As is shown in Mayer and Riezman (1985), in the Heckscher–Ohlin setting of the present model a person's optimal production tax is positive (negative) if it is relatively poorly (well) endowed with the factor which is intensively used in the good which is to be taxed.

Our conclusion of a zero optimal consumption tax immediately follows from the assumptions that all individuals have homothetic and identical preferences and that individual income and expenditure shares are independent of consumption taxes. Since an individual cannot raise its welfare relative to others through the use of consumption taxes, it is best to opt for the socially optimal consumption tax whose value is zero for a small country with no externalities and distortions. The individually optimal production tax, on the other hand, is generally nonzero, since income and expenditure shares are responsive to production taxes which indirectly alter factor prices. Individual $i$ selects a production tax or subsidy such that the reduction in income due to the tax-induced distortion is just equal to the gain in income from the tax-induced favorable income redistribution, as can be seen by bringing the denominator of (7) to the left-hand side.

When all individuals agree that there should be no consumption tax, each will push for appropriate production taxes or subsidies rather than tariffs in order to attain the desired distribution of income. This conclusion, here derived for a small country, applies to the large country case as well. As is demonstrated in Mayer and Riezman (1985), all individuals are in full agreement on the value of the optimal tariff rate. The tariff's sole purpose is to take advantage of the country's monopoly position. For redistribution of income purposes, on the other hand, individuals again will seek appropriate production taxes or subsidies.[3]

[3]This result is related to Vandendorpe's (1974) findings, who determines the optimal tax structure of a large country which faces noneconomic constraints.

## 3. Concluding remarks

This note suggests that a theory of endogenous tariff formation needs to explain why tariffs are chosen as an instrument through the political process before the question of the value of tariff rates is examined. Although we conclude that tariffs will not emerge through the political process under the assumptions of our model, this model also hints at situations in which tariffs may be more efficient than production taxes cum subsidies to further one's welfare. For example, if both factor endowments *and* consumption preferences varied among people, then there might be some persons that benefit from a combination of production subsidies and consumption taxes; that is, from a tariff. Alternatively, when the income tax system is greatly biased, high income-tax-paying people may prefer tariffs, which lower the need for income tax revenues, to production subsidies, which raise the need for income taxes. Also, tariffs could emerge if the equivalence between domestic taxation and tariffs breaks down, as would be the case when there are different enforcement or collection costs, or if transportation costs are considered. Another direction deserving attention is to enlarge the class of government policies considered and to introduce strategic voting which takes account of the political process [e.g., Rodrik (1986) and Staiger and Tabellini (1986)].

## References

Baldwin, Robert E., 1976, The political economy of postwar U.S. trade policy, The Bulletin (New York University, Graduate School of Business Administration).

Bhagwati, Jagdish N., 1985, Structural adjustment and international factor mobility: Some issues, in: K. Jungenfelt and D. Hague, eds., Structural adjustment in developed open economies (Macmillan Press, London).

Bhagwati, Jagdish N., Ramaswami, V.K. and T.N. Srinivasan, 1969, Domestic distortions, tariffs, and the theory of optimum subsidy: Some further results, Journal of Political Economy 77, 1005–1010.

Brock, William A. and Stephen P. Magee, 1978, The economics of special interest politics: The case of the tariff, American Economic Review 68, 246–250.

Brock, William A. and Stephen P. Magee, 1980, Tariff formation in a democracy, in: J. Black and B. Hindley, eds., Current issues in international commercial policy and diplomacy (Macmillan Press, London) 1–9.

Cassing, James H. and Arye L. Hillman, 1985, Political influence motives and the choice between tariffs and quotas, Journal of International Economics 19, 279–290.

Findlay, Ronald W. and Stanislaw H. Wellisz, 1982, Endogenous tariffs, the political economy of trade restrictions, and welfare, in: J.N. Bhagwati, ed., Import competition and response (University of Chicago Press, Chicago) 223–234.

Mayer, Wolfgang, 1984, Endogenous tariff formation, American Economic Review 74, 970–985.

Mayer, Wolfgang and Raymond G. Riezman, 1985, Endogenous choice of trade policy instruments, Working paper 85-8 (University of Iowa, Iowa City).

Rodrik, Dani, forthcoming, Tariffs, subsidies, and welfare with endogenous policy, Journal of International Economics.

Staiger, Robert W. and Guido Tabellini, 1986, The time inconsistency of free trade, Working paper (Stanford University, Stanford).

Vandendorpe, Adolf L., 1974, On the theory of non-economic objectives in open economies, Journal of International Economics 4, 15–24.

ECONOMICS AND POLITICS 0954-1985
Volume 2 November 1990 No. 3

# VOTER PREFERENCES FOR TRADE POLICY INSTRUMENTS*

WOLFGANG MAYER AND RAYMOND RIEZMAN

We analyze voter preferences for tariffs and production subsidies. The distribution of tax revenues argument shows that voters with high direct tax burdens prefer tariffs to subsidies. The uncertainty argument demonstrates that if actual tariff and subsidy rates are chosen from the set of individually optimal rates then the range of tariff rates is smaller than the range of subsidy rates. Thus, tariffs might be preferred even though they are less efficient. Finally, the large country argument shows that if a country is large then voters whose income shares decline with more protection prefer tariffs to subsidies.

## I. INTRODUCTION

WHEN REDISTRIBUTION of income through commercial policies is considered, which instrument is preferred by voters? This question is of particular interest in an open economy when the choice is between tariffs and production subsidies.[1] Concerning the voters' preferences between these instruments, Mayer and Riezman (1987) have shown that production subsidies dominate tariffs, if people's policy preferences are based on differences in factor ownership.[2] Domination means that every person is better off with a production subsidy than a tariff of the same value, independent of the rate of protection. Consequently, one would expect that neither individual voters nor policy platforms of politicians call for tariffs. Empirical evidence, however, reveals that voters, lobbying groups, and politicians frequently favor tariffs over production subsidies, with the primary objective of redistributing income.

A variety of arguments has been suggested to reconcile theory and practice. Most frequently mentioned is the *transparency argument*.[3] It states that governments prefer tariffs to subsidies because the welfare-reducing effects of tariff intervention are less transparent to individuals. People are less informed about the cost of a tariff, through a loss in consumer surplus, than about the cost of the subsidy, which requires higher taxes to finance it.

[1] Other, potentially more efficient, instruments, such as lump-sum transfers and factor income taxes, are precluded by assumption.

[2] This proposition at the individual's level corresponds to the more basic proposition at society's level that subsidies are better than tariffs in correcting domestic distortions, as demonstrated by Bhagwati and Ramaswami (1963) and Bhagwati (1971).

[3] Hillman (1989) discusses the essence of the argument and refers to its role in the history of Australian tariff formation.

*Comments by Jagdish Bhagwati, Dani Rodrik, and participants in the Columbia Conference on Political Economy and International Economics, as well as by Costas Syropoulos and seminar participants at Pennsylvania State University and the University of Western Ontario are greatly appreciated.

Feenstra and Lewis (1990) also focus on incomplete information in explaining the choice of tariffs. However, it is not the people who are less informed than the government, but the government has incomplete information about the losses of individuals from import competition. A nonlinear tariff becomes the optimal instrument to protect them.

An alternative asymmetry assumption is introduced by Rodrik (1986) in developing what may be called the *public goods argument*. Tariffs, which affect a wider grouping of firms, are more of a public good than subsidies, which tend to be more firm specific. Consequently, the free rider problem is more serious in the case of tariffs and interest groups tend to underpursue them. The public, in turn, wants to minimize injury from trade intervention and pushes politicians into precommitting to the less damaging tariff regime.

Wilson (1990) questions the conclusion of Rodrik's public goods argument and suggests that a given politician should prefer subsidies to tariffs since the former generate higher political contributions. However, he goes on to show that in a political game of several politicians they still may prefer tariffs since the game for subsidies leads to excessive protection.

Staiger and Tabellini (1987) specify a model with fully immobile capital and partially immobile labor in which a terms of trade shock occurs. These adjustment difficulties prevent the government from precommitting to free trade, and tariffs rather than subsidies are likely to be adopted.

Finally, there is a *political process argument*, suggested by Nelson (1987) and elaborated by Mayer and Riezman (1989). It postulates that people differ with respect to more than one feature, in which case multidimensional policy preferences emerge. Even if a tariff is not the ideal point for any person, the social choice process still may yield tariffs as the adopted instrument.

This paper introduces three additional arguments to question the domination of tariffs by production subsidies at the level of voter preferences. The arguments emphasize that the Mayer-Riezman (1987) model, where voters differ with respect to factor ownership only, represents just one polar case. When tax collection and revenue redistribution systems are no longer unbiased, when voters are uncertain about which rates of protection will eventually be adopted, and when the choice is restricted to either tariff or subsidy in case of a large country, subsidies no longer dominate.[4] In each of the three situations at least some individuals consider tariffs superior to production subsidies as an instrument for redistributing income. Given these preferences of voters with respect to policy instruments, this also opens the possibility that society as a whole will choose tariffs rather than subsidies as a regime for protection.

[4] This breakdown of subsidy domination at the level of individual voters is similar to the breakdown of the first-best production subsidy argument at the level of a benevolent government, when there are not just production distortions but also government revenue constraints [Corden (1986, pp. 96–101)], uncertainty [Eaton and Grossman (1985)], revenue-seeking by individuals or groups [Bhagwati, Brecher, and Srinivasan (1984)], or non-economic objectives [Johnson (1965) and Bhagwati and Srinivasan (1969)].

First, we discuss the *distribution of tax revenues argument*. It rests on the assumption that many income tax systems, on which production subsidies draw and to which tariff revenues contribute, are progressive. When a person's tax share is higher than his or her income share, tariffs reduce the individual's direct tax burden while subsidies raise it. There exists an asymmetry with respect to cost, as the cost of a subsidy is borne by a small group of upper-income people while the cost of the tariff, in terms of lost consumer surplus, is spread across the whole population.

Second, there is the *uncertainty argument*. It deals with situations where people must express their preferences for a policy regime, such as tariffs or subsidies, before they know which rates will actually be adopted. It is shown that the potential range of rates is narrower for tariffs than subsidies, under the assumption that actual rates are chosen from the set of individually optimal rates. This implies that individuals consider a tariff regime to be less efficient, but also less risky than a production subsidy regime, and the less risky tariff regime may be preferred.

Finally, there is the *large country argument*. As was indicated in Mayer and Riezman (1987), when a country has control over the terms of trade, each person likes a combination of tariffs and subsidies. All people want the same tariff rate to exploit the country's monopoly position, but individually optimal subsidy rates differ depending on factor ownership. Here, we deal with the more realistic situation that people have to choose between either tariffs or subsidies, excluding the possibility of a combination of the two. It is shown that all people whose income shares decline with more protection of the import industry prefer tariffs to subsidies. Even gainers from the protective measures may be better off with the tariff.

## II. REAL INCOME UNDER TARIFFS AND SUBSIDIES

The economy under consideration is assumed to consist of $I$ risk-neutral individuals who possess homothetic, identical preferences, but differ from each other with respect to their fixed factor endowments. These differences in factor ownership are the underlying cause for people's differences in policy preferences. There are two factors of production which are employed by two competitive industries producing commodities $X_1$ and $X_2$. Unless stated otherwise, the economy under consideration is small.

For the risk-neutral $i$th person, welfare is measured by real income,

$$R^i = y^i_d / e^i(p), \tag{1}$$

where $y^i_d$ is disposable income of individual $i$, $p$ is the domestic price of the second in terms of the first commodity as faced by consumers, and $e^i = e$ is a price index which, under identically homothetic preferences, is the same for all consumers. We also note that $-\partial R^i/\partial p = R^i e_p/e = (\partial R^i/\partial y^i_d)D^i_2 = D^i_2/e$, where $D^i_2$ is the $i$th consumer's demand for the second commodity.

The second commodity, whose world price is $\pi$, is imported. Under a production subsidy, domestic consumers face this world price. Under a tariff, on the other hand, the price becomes:

$$p=\pi(1+t), \tag{2}$$

where $t$ is an *ad valorem* tariff rate on the import good. Disposable income of the $i$th person, $y_d^i$, is income received from factor ownership, $y^i$, adjusted for redistributed tariff revenues received, $\tau^i$, or taxes paid to finance the subsidy, $\sigma^i$:

$$y_{dt}^i=y_t^i+\tau^i \qquad \text{and} \qquad y_{ds}^i=y_s^i-\sigma^i, \tag{3}$$

where subscripts $t$ and $s$ refer to the tariff and subsidy regimes respectively.

It is convenient to define the $i$th person's share of total factor income by $\phi^i=y^i/Y$ and the shares of total tariff revenues received by $\psi_t^i=\tau^i/T$ and of subsidies financed by $\psi_s^i=\sigma^i/S$. In these expressions, $Y=(X_1+pX_2)$ is national income produced (total factor income earned), $X_j$ denotes industry output of commodity $j$, $T=\pi t\,[D_2(p)-X_2(p)]=\pi t M_2(p)$ is total tariff revenues, $S=\pi s X_2\,[\pi(1+s)]$ measures total subsidy payments, $D_2(p)$ is total domestic demand, and $M_2(p)$ expresses import demand for good two at domestic price $p$. Using the share definitions, we express the $i$th person's real income under a tariff and subsidy regime respectively as:

$$R_t^i=[\phi_t^i(Y_t+T)-(\phi_t^i-\psi_t^i)T]/e(p) \tag{4}$$

$$R_s^i=[\phi_s^i(Y_s-S)+(\phi_s^i-\psi_s^i)S]/e(\pi). \tag{5}$$

Each person's real income is proportionate to real national income, $R$, after it has been adjusted by a term which reflects the divergence between factor income and tax shares, whereby real national income under tariff and subsidy respectively equals:

$$R_t=(Y_t+T)/e(p) \qquad \text{and} \qquad R_s=(Y_s-S)/e(\pi).$$

We finally note that, at $t=s$ of a small country, $Y_t=Y_s$, $\phi_t^i=\phi_s^i$, and $(Y_t+T)=(Y_s-S+\pi t D_2)=[Y_s-S]/[1-m_2t/(1+t)]$, where $m_2(p)=pD_2/(Y_t+T)$ is the marginal and average propensity to consume the second good under a tariff.

## III. THE DISTRIBUTION OF TAX REVENUES ARGUMENT

The purpose of this section is to show that in a small economy a person may be better off under a tariff than equal-value production subsidy if the person's shares of taxes paid and of tariff revenues received exceed the share of factor income.[5] In many less developed countries in which a large segment of below-average income people pays no or very little income tax, these conditions are likely to be encountered.

[5] It is explicitly assumed that the choice between tariffs and subsidies is made given the existing income tax system. The model does not explain how the income tax structure has come about and how preferences for various taxes would be determined if the entire tax structure were to be chosen.

We assume that initially, when protection of the import industry is considered, free trade prevails. At issue is whether the $i$th person will fare better with a tariff or an equal-value production subsidy; that is, whether $R_t^i$ is greater or smaller than $R_s^i$, given that $t=s$. Using the earlier stated definitions of real national income, $R_t$ and $R_s$, we subtract (5) from (4) and obtain:

$$R_t^i - R_s^i = \phi^i [R_t - R_s] + [\psi^i - \phi^i] [T/e(p) + S/e(\pi)], \tag{6}$$

where we set $\phi_t^i = \phi_s^i = \phi^i$ and for simplicity's sake assume that $\psi_t^i = \psi_s^i = \psi^i$.[6] The $i$th person's real income change from selecting a tariff rather than production subsidy depends on two effects. First, there is the real income change for the entire country weighted by the person's factor income share. Second, there is the real value of government savings, as it replaces an expenditure-causing subsidization policy by a revenue-generating tariff policy, when weighted by the difference between the person's tax and income shares. Clearly, the second effect is positive (negative) if the $i$th person's tax share is high (low) relative to his or her factor income share.

An interpretation of $(R_t - R_s)$ can be given for situations where policy changes are large. Recalling that $R_t = [Y_t + T]/e(p)$ and $R_s = [Y_s - S]/e(\pi)$, where $Y_t = Y_s$ for $s=t$, and writing $e(p) = e(\pi) + \Delta e$, we obtain:

$$R_t - R_s = \{T + S - [Y_s - S] [\Delta e/e(\pi)]\}/e(p) = [T + S - R_s \Delta e]/e(p), \tag{7}$$

where the change in price index, $\Delta e$, is due to a tariff which, starting from a free trade position, can be expressed as $(\Delta e/\Delta p)\pi t$. For large tariffs, the index change is approximated by:

$$\Delta e/\Delta p \cong [e_p(\pi) + e_p(p)]/2, \tag{8}$$

where we average the price index responses in the neighbourhood of initial and new consumption points respectively. Since $e_p(\pi) = D_2(\pi)/R_s$ and $e_p(p) = D_2(p)/R_t$, we can write:

$$R_s \Delta e = \pi t \{D_2(\pi) + D_2(p) - [D_2(p)/R_t] [R_t - R_s]\}/2. \tag{9}$$

Substitution of $(T+S) = \pi t D_2(p)$, when $t=s$, and of (9) in (7), and using $m_2 = [\pi(1+t)D_2(p)]/[R_t e(p)]$, yields:

$$R_t - R_s = \{\pi t [D_2(p) - D_2(\pi)]\}/\{2e(p)[1 - m_2 t/(2+2t)]\}, \tag{10}$$

which is always negative since $D_2(p) < D_2(\pi)$ for $p > \pi$ and $1 > m_2 t/(2+2t)$. Consequently, no matter what the rate's value, protection of an industry through a tariff makes the nation as a whole always worse off than protection through an equal-rate production subsidy.

[6] This simplification does not affect the argument in a fundamental way.

Knowing that $R_t < R_s$ always, we now return to (6) to draw the following conclusions concerning the *i*th person's welfare effects of a tariff relative to a production subsidy:

(1) If the tax system is unbiased, in the sense that tax shares are the same as income shares, a production subsidy is preferred by every individual independent of factor ownership. This reaffirms the result that tariffs are dominated by subsidies.
(2) If the tax system is biased such that some people's tax shares exceed their income shares, they may find tariffs to be superior to production subsidies as an instrument of protection. The superiority of tariffs is more likely the greater the difference between tax and income shares.

The *distribution of tax revenues argument* rests on the assumption that a country's tax system is such that high-income groups have tax shares which exceed their factor income shares. When high-income people consider protection, they realize that a tariff generates revenues whose distribution would be of primary benefit to them, while production subsidies require higher taxes which fall on them disproportionately. Looked at the two instruments' cost side, subsidization translates into higher income taxes for upper income groups, while tariff costs, in form of reduced consumer surplus, are distributed much more evenly across the population.[7] The argument, therefore, involves an asymmetry concerning the identity of cost bearers; subsidy costs fall on a small group of high income tax payers, while tariff costs are borne by all consumers of the import good.

## IV. THE UNCERTAINTY ARGUMENT

This argument rests on the assumption that the voters' choice between employment of a tariff or subsidy regime has to be made before actual rates of protection are to be selected. For example, in a two-candidate race for political office, candidates may express positions only on the type of instrument but not on the rates to be chosen. What we are going to show is that under this uncertainty about future rates of protection many voters, especially those with moderate preferences for or against protection, may prefer a tariff to a subsidy regime. In presenting the argument, we assume that there is no bias in distributing tariff revenues or collecting taxes to finance the subsidy; that is, we assume that $\psi^i = \phi^i$.

[7] In reality it may not be the case that consumer surplus shrinks in proportion to a person's income, as preferences may not be identical and homothetic. In less developed countries, the share of income spent on imported goods frequently is larger for upper-income than lower-income groups. In such a case, the distribution of tax revenues argument would be weakened.

[8] Nothing is said about the political process itself through which the rate is chosen, as even this process may not be known yet. Loosely speaking, the assumption states that a person considers a certain rate of protection more likely the more people look at it as their best rate.

The uncertainty argument rests on the assumption that the probability of a given rate of protection getting adopted equals the fraction of people which considers this rate to be best.[8] The probability that rate of protection $x$ will be adopted is expressed by $f(x,t)$ and $f(x,s)$ for the alternatives of tariff and subsidy regime respectively. If we define $R^i(x,t)$ and $R^i(x,s)$ as the $i$th person's welfare under tariff and subsidy regimes when rate $x$ prevails, then the person's expected utility under a tariff regime is higher than under a subsidy regime if:

$$B^i = \int_{\underline{x}}^{\bar{x}} R^i(x,t)\,\mathrm{d}F(x,t) - \int_{\underline{x}}^{\bar{x}} R^i(x,s)\,\mathrm{d}F(x,s) > 0, \tag{11}$$

where $F(x,.)$ is the cumulative distribution function under a given policy regime and $\bar{x}$ and $\underline{x}$ are the finite limits on the rates of protection under either policy regime. The values of $\bar{x}$ and $\underline{x}$ are given by the highest and lowest individually optimal rates of protection from all the people of the country.

To evaluate $B^i$, we first add and subtract $\int_{\underline{x}}^{\bar{x}} R^i(x,s)\mathrm{d}F(x,t)$ to obtain:

$$B^i = \int_{\underline{x}}^{\bar{x}} [R^i(x,t) - R^i(x,s)]\,\mathrm{d}F(x,t) - \int_{\underline{x}}^{\bar{x}} R^i(x,s)[\mathrm{d}F(x,s) - \mathrm{d}F(x,t)]. \tag{12}$$

The first term on the RHS of (12) must always be negative when $\psi^i = \phi^i$ since we know from (6) that $R^i(x,t) \leq R^i(x,s)$ for all $x$, with equality holding at $x=0$ only. This term measures the expected loss in utility due to a switch from a subsidy to a tariff regime when the probabilities of tariff rates are employed as weights. Hence, a necessary condition for $B^i$ to become positive is that the second term on the RHS of (12), including the minus sign, is positive.

Using integration by parts, this second term can be rewritten as:

$$-\int_{\underline{x}}^{\bar{x}} R^i(x,s)[\mathrm{d}F(x,s) - \mathrm{d}F(x,t)] = \int_{\underline{x}}^{\bar{x}} R'^i(x,s)\,[F(x,s) - F(x,t)]\,\mathrm{d}x, \tag{13}$$

where $R'^i(x,s)$ is the marginal utility of a subsidy change.[9] For a person whose utility maximizing rate is $\tilde{x}^i$, the term $R'^i$ is positive for $\underline{x} < x < \tilde{x}^i$, whereas $R'^i$ is negative for $\tilde{x}^i < x < \bar{x}$. What we are going to show is that the expression in (13) must always be positive for a voter whose optimal policy is free trade, as the distribution $F(x,t)$ dominates $F(x,s)$[10] in the first-order stochastic sense. For voters whose optimal rate of protection deviates from free trade, the value of this expression becomes smaller with the degree of deviation.

First-order stochastic dominance of $F(x,t)$ over $F(x,s)$ is due to the fact that each person's optimal tariff rate, whether positive or negative, is always less extreme than the same person's optimal subsidy rate. In order to show this, we rewrite (4) and (5) under the assumption that $\phi^i = \psi^i$, as:

$$R^i_t = \phi^i(Y_t + T)/e(p) = \phi^i\{X_1(p) + pX_2(p) + \pi t[D_2(p) - X_2(p)]\}/e(p) \tag{4'}$$

[9] Note that $F(\underline{x},t) = F(\underline{x},s) = 0$ and $F(\bar{x},t) = F(\bar{x},s) = 1$.

[10] See Laffont (1989) for definitions of stochastic dominance.

$$R_s^i = \phi^i(Y_s - S)/e(\pi) = \phi^i\{X_1(p) + pX_2(p) - \pi s X_2(p)\}/e(\pi), \qquad (5')$$

where $p = \pi(1+t) = \pi(1+s)$. The responses of real income to tariff and subsidy rate changes are:

$$\partial R_t^i/\partial t = \pi\phi^i\{\pi t(\partial M_2/\partial p) + [Y_t + T](\partial\phi^i/\partial p)/\phi^i\}/e(p) \qquad (14)$$

$$\partial R_s^i/\partial s = \pi\phi^i\{-\pi s(\partial X_2/\partial p) + [Y_s - S](\partial\phi^i/\partial p)/\phi^i\}/e(\pi), \qquad (15)$$

where $M_2 = (D_2 - X_2)$ is import demand, $(\partial M_2/\partial p) < 0$, $(\partial X_2/\partial p) > 0$, and $(\partial\phi^i/\partial p)$ measures the change in the $i$th person's factor income share as the second good's domestic price rises. Both real income responses reveal that a person can gain from an increase in either tariff or subsidy rate only if his factor income share rises as the domestic price of the import good goes up. Figure 1 portrays the real income curves for two alternative persons, a winner from protection indicated by superscript $w$ and a loser from protection with superscript $L$. The $R^i(t)$ curve is uniformly below the $R^i(s)$ curve except for the free trade point, where $s = t = 0$. Assuming that the second order conditions for a maximum are satisfied, the $i$th individual maximizes real income by choosing a subsidy rate $\tilde{s}^i$ such that:

$$\tilde{s}^i = [(Y_s - S)(\partial\phi^i/\partial p)]/[\pi\phi^i(\partial X_2/\partial p)]. \qquad (16)$$

Clearly, the optimal subsidy rate is positive for a winner from protection, since $\partial\phi^w/\partial p > 0$, and negative for a loser, as $\partial\phi^L/\partial p < 0$. But what is the slope of

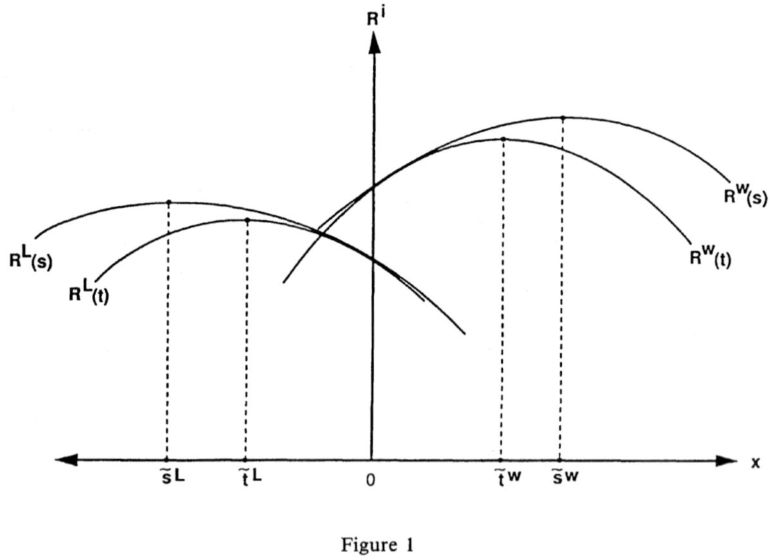


Figure 1

the $R^i(t)$ locus at tariff rate $t=\tilde{s}^i$? If one can show that it is negative at $\tilde{s}^w$, then the individually optimal tariff rate $\tilde{t}^w$ occurs at a lower value than $\tilde{s}^w$, as drawn in the diagram for the winner. And if the slope of $R^L(t)$ is positive at $\tilde{s}^L$ then $\tilde{s}^L<\tilde{t}^L<0$. In demonstrating this we note again that, at a given rate $x$, $Y_s=Y_t$ and $(\partial X_2/\partial p)$ is the same under both regimes. Then, we recall that $(Y_t+T)=(Y_s-S)/[1-m_2t/(1+t)]$. Substituting (16) for $t$ and the expression for $(Y_t+T)$ in (14), one can see after some manipulations that:

$$\partial R^i/\partial t=\frac{\{\pi[Y_s-S][\partial\phi^i/\partial p]\}\{(\partial D_2/\partial p)|_U/(\partial X_2/\partial p)\}}{e(p)[1-m_2t/(1+t)]}, \tag{17}$$

where $(\partial D_2/\partial p)|_U<0$ is the pure substitution effect of the own price change.[11] This implies that, evaluated at $t=\tilde{s}^i$, $\partial R_t^i/\partial t<0$ if $\partial\phi^i/\partial p>0$ and $\partial R_t^i/\partial t>0$ if $\partial\phi^i/\partial p<0$. In words, for people who gain (lose) from protection, real income under the tariff regime is already (still) decreasing (increasing) at the rate where the optimal production subsidy is attained. This means that the optimal import tariff rate is lower than the optimal production subsidy rate for gainers from protection, while the optimal import subsidy (implying a negative value for $t$) falls short of the optimal production tax for losers from protection; that is, $\tilde{s}^i<\tilde{t}^i<0$ for all people with $\tilde{x}^i<0$ and $0<\tilde{t}^i<\tilde{s}^i$ for all people with $\tilde{x}^i>0$.

The fact that the range of individually optimal tariff rates around the free trade point is narrower than the range of subsidy rates furthermore implies that:

$$\begin{aligned}&[F(x,s)-F(x,t)]>0 \text{ for } x<0\\ &[F(x,s)-F(x,t)]<0 \text{ for } x>0,\end{aligned} \tag{18}$$

given our assumption that the probability of a certain rate of protection being adopted equals the fraction of the population which considers this rate to be optimal. As we examine the case of a person whose optimal policies favor free trade, $\tilde{x}^i=0$, such that $R'^i>0$ for $x<0$ and $R'^i<0$ for $x>0$, one can see from (18) that

$$R'^i(x,s)[F(x,s)-F(x,t)]>0 \tag{19}$$

always. Hence, the expression of (13) is positive and the second term in (12), which states the expected utility gain from a subsidy to tariff switch, is positive. Provided the second term's magnitude is sufficient to outweigh the negative first term in the $B^i$ expression, the person will favor a tariff regime.

The case for preferring a tariff regime under uncertainty is weakened when the person's optimal subsidy rate under certainty is not zero. For example, let us consider the case when $\tilde{x}^i=\tilde{s}^i>0$. Then one can rewrite (13) as:

$$\begin{aligned}&\int_{\underline{x}}^{0}R'^i[F(x,s)-F(x,t)]\,\mathrm{d}x+\int_{0}^{\tilde{x}^i}R'^i[F(x,s)-F(x,t)]\,\mathrm{d}x\\ &+\int_{\tilde{x}^i}^{\bar{x}}R'^i[F(x,s)-F(x,t)]\,\mathrm{d}x,\end{aligned} \tag{13'}$$

[11] In deriving this expression we made use of $(\partial M_2/\partial t)/\pi=\partial D_2/\partial p-\partial X_2/\partial p=[(\partial D_2/\partial p)|_U-(\partial X_2/\partial p)]/[1-m_2t/(1+t)]$.

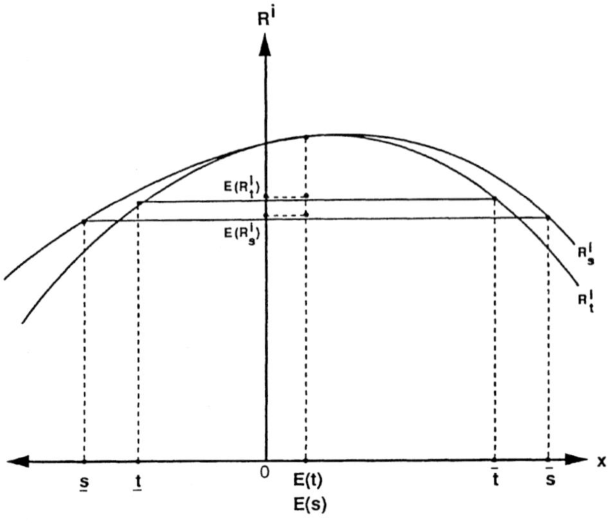


Figure 2

where $R'^i > 0$ for $x < \tilde{x}^i$ and $R'^i < 0$ for $x > \tilde{x}^i > 0$. Using (18), one can see that the first and last terms in (13′) are still positive while the second term becomes negative. The more extreme the optimal subsidy for the individual under consideration, the larger is the impact of this middle relative to the last term and the less likely it is that the person prefers a tariff regime.

Figure 2 provides a simple illustration of the possibility that a person prefers a tariff to a subsidy regime when rates of protection are not known yet. It is assumed that individual $i$ believes that actual trade policy is going to be dictated either by those who strongly favor protection of the second industry, with $\bar{t}$ and $\bar{s}$ as their optimal respective rates, or by those who strongly favor assistance to the first industry, implying $\underline{t}$ and $\underline{s}$ as their choices. Assuming subjective probabilities of 1/2 for each possible outcome, the $i$th person's real income at the expected subsidy rate $E(s)$ exceeds real income at the expected tariff rate $E(t)$. However, expected real income under the tariff regime, $E(R^i_t)$, is larger than expected real income under the subsidy regime, $E(R^i_s)$, making individual $i$ prefer the tariff regime.

## V. THE LARGE COUNTRY ARGUMENT

The earlier made assertion that, at each rate of protection and for each individual, a production subsidy leads to a higher level of welfare than a tariff applies only to the case when world prices are fixed. The purpose of this section is to show that, with variable world prices, all people whose factor income shares shrink with import protection prefer a tariff to a subsidy. Even people whose income shares rise in response to protective action may prefer tariffs to subsidies.

Under variable world prices, equal-valued tariffs and subsidies no longer result in the same domestic prices as faced by producers. The decrease in world excess demand for the second good is larger when a tariff is imposed than when an equal-value subsidy is granted, as can be seen from differentiation of the import functions, $M_2(s)$ and $M_2(t)$, under subsidy and tariff respectively, where:

$$\begin{aligned} M_2(s) &= D_2[\pi, X_1(p) + pX_2(p) - \pi s X_2(p)] - X_2(p) \\ M_2(t) &= D_2\{p, X_1(p) + pX_2(p) + \pi t[D_2(p) - X_2(p)]\} - X_2(p). \end{aligned} \tag{20}$$

These differentiations, assuming that initially $s = t = 0$, yield:

$$\begin{aligned} &\partial M_2/\partial s = -\pi \partial X_2/\partial p < 0 \quad \text{and} \\ &\partial M_2/\partial t = \pi[(\partial D_2/\partial p)|_U - (\partial X_2/\partial p)] < 0. \end{aligned} \tag{21}$$

The import response expression tell us that, evaluated at the initial world price, the decline in world excess demand for the import good is greater in case of a tariff than a subsidy. Consequently, world and domestic prices of the import good will be lower under a tariff than an equal-value subsidy; that is:

$$\pi(s) > \pi(t) \qquad \text{and} \qquad p(s) > p(t) \text{ for } s = t. \tag{22}$$

A second consideration under variable world prices is that each person's optimal instrument use involves now a combination of a tariff and production subsidy rather than use of only one instrument. Independent of factor ownership, all people are in full agreement that the same tariff rate, namely the one which maximizes social welfare for a large country, should be employed. On the other hand, the accompanying optimal subsidy depends on relative factor ownership.[12]

In a situation of instrument choice, a person is not given the option of combining the two instruments. Each individual has to express a preference for either tariffs or subsidies. It is obvious that neither instrument is preferred at all rates and by all people to the other instrument. Some may like tariffs better while others prefer production subsidies. Broadly speaking, however, there exists a bias towards tariffs, as all people whose income shares decline with import protection are better off with a tariff for a large range of protection rates, and even some people whose income shares expand in response to protection are better served by a tariff.

To show this, we express the $i$th individual's real income under instrument use $k = t, s$ as:

$$R_k^i = \phi_k^i R_k, \tag{23}$$

[12] For more details see Mayer and Riezman (1987) and references therein.

where it is assumed that $\psi^i = \phi^i$. Instrument use affects both income share, $\phi^i_k$, and real national income, $R_k$. The latter is maximized when the chosen instrument is a tariff and the rate which is optimal for the whole country, $\tilde{t} = 1/(\epsilon^* - 1)$, is employed, where $\epsilon^*$ is the import elasticity of demand for the foreign country. Furthermore, one can show that real national income under the tariff regime, $R_t$, is larger than real national income under the subsidy regime, $R_s$, for a wide range of rates of protection.[13]

The relationship between a person's income share under a tariff and equal-value subsidy depends on whether the person is a gainer or loser from protection. We first look at people whose income shares are reduced by import protection. As they consider the choice between tariffs and subsidies, tariffs result in smaller losses in income shares, since $p(t) < p(s)$ implies that $(\partial\phi^i_s/\partial p)(\partial p/\partial s) < (\partial\phi^i_t/\partial p)(\partial p/\partial t) < 0$ for all $s = t > 0$. For individuals whose income shares rise with the adoption of protective measures, on the other hand, the gains in income shares are more pronounced in the case of a production subsidy since $(\partial\phi^i/\partial p)(\partial p/\partial s) > (\partial\phi^i/\partial p)/(\partial p/\partial t) > 0$.

Returning to (23), we now examine which instrument is preferred by a given person. If the person's income share is reduced by import protection then, except for some very high rates, $R_t > R_s$ and $\phi_t > \phi_s$ for $t = s > 0$. Consequently, 'losers' from protection are better off with the tariff than the subsidy. If the person's income share rises with import protection then, except for very high rates, $R_t > R_s$ but $\phi_t < \phi_s$ for $t = s > 0$. Hence, 'gainers' from protection are better off with a tariff only if the tariff advantage in raising national income is not offset by the tariff disadvantage in raising one's income share. This is more likely to be the case for small rather than large gainers from protection.

## VI. SOME THOUGHTS ON THE TRANSPARENCY ARGUMENT

Incomplete information is at the core of the *transparency argument*. The argument states that the public can more easily be persuaded to accept a tariff than production subsidy since the detrimental ramifications of the latter are more transparent. The reason for this asymmetry in transparency is, however, not easy to pinpoint. Intuitively, one can argue that tariffs work in a more complicated way than subsidies. In particular, the former require an assessment of how much consumer surplus a person loses while the latter deals with the simpler task of figuring out how much more taxes have to be paid to finance the subsidy. People not only understand the impact of subsidies better than that of tariffs, but they

[13] As long as the rate of protection is less than the socially optimal tariff rate, real national income under a tariff is at least as large as under a production subsidy. This can be seen by adding a consumption tax to a preexisting production subsidy and evaluating the overall welfare change. For very high rates of protection beyond the socially optimal tariff rate, however, it is possible that real national income under the subsidy is higher than under the tariff.

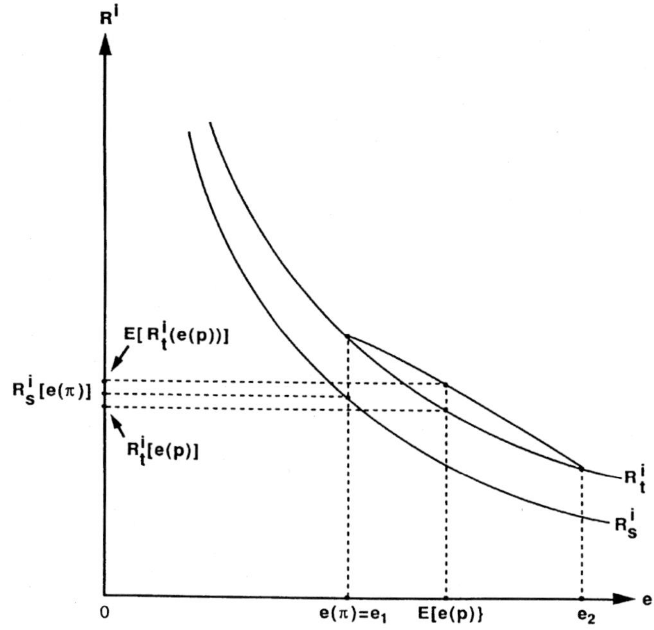


Figure 3

also receive clearer messages from news services and politicians about the costs of these instrument uses.[14]

Let us examine the essence of the transparency argument with more rigor. We return to the earlier made assumption of a small country and employ (4) – (5) to express the *i*th person's real income under tariff and subsidy respectively, assuming that factor income and tax shares are identical; that is, $R_t^i = \phi_t^i (Y_t + T)/e(p)$ and $R_s^i = \phi_s^i (Y_s - S)/e(\pi)$. Now let us assume that the *i*th person is not sure how, starting from an initial free trade position, the tariff would affect his price index $e(p)$. On the other hand, there would be no change in $e(\pi)$ under a subsidy. This uncertainty under the tariff has the following implications for the choice of instruments. As Figure 3 illustrates, $R^i$ is convex in the price index, whereby $R_t^i$ lies uniformly above $R_s^i$ since $(Y_t + T) > (Y_s - S)$ and both disposable incomes are evaluated at the same level of $e$. For a subsidy, real income at $e(\pi)$ would be $R_s^i[e(\pi)]$ which is larger than real income with an equal value tariff

[14] The real complicated question, namely how a given rate of protection affects the factor income of individuals under different protection instruments, does not enter the comparison since in a small country a person's factor income, whatever its value, would be the same under both tariff and subsidy of the same value.

which amounts to $R^i_t[e(p)]$. When $e(p)$ is random, however, then it is possible that $E\{R^i_t[e(p)]\} > R^i_s[e(\pi)]$ since, using Jensen's inequality, $E[1/e(p)] > 1/E[e(p)]$. In the diagram this is illustrated for the case where the person attaches probabilities of ½ to the possible price indices of $e_1$ and $e_2$. The person would prefer a tariff with its unclear effect on consumer surplus over a subsidy with its much more transparent cost.

Unfortunately, the above presented reasoning is flawed. The assumption that people have difficulty in evaluating the price index under the new tariff rate must rest on the premise that people do not know with certainty what their consumption demand would be at the tariff-ridden domestic price. As Drèze (1974), however, points out in his discussion of the foundations of expected utility theory, "uncertainty of the decision-maker about his own tastes at a future date cannot be described through distinct events corresponding to distinct preference structures, since this would violate the condition of interpersonal objectivity."

## VII. CONCLUDING REMARKS

The starting point for this paper was the observation that, with factor ownership the only distinguishing characteristic, tariffs are dominated by production subsidies from an individual's point of view. We added to the growing list of arguments in support of individual preferences for tariffs by allowing for biased income tax systems, by introducing uncertainty about what rates will actually come about, and by doing away with the small country assumption when choice is restricted to one instrument. The objective of the paper was to show that under each of these modifications individuals may indeed express a preference for tariffs. We have talked about individual preferences only and do not want to leave the impression that a given argument automatically explains the social choice of tariffs. One has to add a complete specification of the political process to explain the social choice. However, one could show that for appropriate choices of voter eligibility rules, majority voting can bring about a tariff regime as the social choice under each of the three arguments presented.

WOLFGANG MAYER
*Economics Department*
*University of Cincinnati*
*Cincinnati*
*OH 45221-0371*

RAYMOND RIEZMAN
*University of Iowa*
*Iowa City*
*Iowa 52242*

## REFERENCES

Bhagwati, J. N., 1971, "The generalized theory of distortions and welfare," in J. N. Bhagwati, et al. (eds.), *Trade, balance of payments, and growth*, North-Holland, Amsterdam, 69–90.

Bhagwati, J. N., R. A. Brecher and T. N. Srinivasan, 1984, "DUP activities and economic theory," *European Economic Review*, 24, 291–307.

Bhagwati, J. N. and V. K. Ramaswami, 1963, "Domestic distortions, tariffs and the theory of the optimum subsidy," *Journal of Political Economy*, 71, 44–50.

Bhagwati, J. N. and T. N. Srinivasan, 1969, "Optimal intervention to achieve noneconomic objectives," *Review of Economic Studies*, 36, 27–38.

Corden, W. M., 1986, "The normative theory of international trade," in R. W. Jones (ed.), *International trade: surveys of theory and policy*, Elsevier Science, Amsterdam, 63–130.

Drèze, J. H., 1974, "Axiomatic theories of choice, cardinal utility and subjective probability:" A review, in J. Drèze (ed.), *Allocation under uncertainty*, Equilibrium and optimality, Wiley, New York and Toronto, 3–23.

Eaton, J. and G. M. Grossman, 1985 "Tariffs as insurance: optimal commercial policy when domestic markets are incomplete," *Canadian Journal of Economics*, 18, 258–272.

Feenstra, R. C. and T. R. Lewis, 1990, "Distributing the gains from trade with incomplete information," Mimeo, University of California, Davis.

Hillman, A. L., 1989, *The political economy of protection*, Harwood Academic, New York.

Laffont, J.-J., 1989, *The economics of uncertainty and information*, MIT Press, Cambridge, MA.

Mayer, W. and R. Riezman, 1987, "Endogenous choice of trade policy instruments," *Journal of International Economics*, 23, 377–381.

——, and ——, 1989, "Tariff formation in a multidimensional voting model," *Economics and Politics*, 1, 61–79.

Nelson, D., 1987, "Endogenous tariff theory: A critical survey," Mimeo, Washington University, St Louis.

Rodrik, D., 1986, "Tariffs, subsidies, and welfare with endogenous policy," *Journal of International Economics*, 21, 285–299.

Staiger, R. W. and G. Tabellini, 1987, "Discretionary trade policy and excessive protection," *American Economic Review*, 77, 823–837.

Wilson, J. D., 1990, "On the political choice between tariffs and production subsidies," Mimeo, Indiana University, Bloomington.

*Review of International Economics, 10(4), 657–670, 2002*

# Systematic Political Grass-Root Support for Tariffs

*Wolfgang Mayer**

## Abstract

The leading political-economy-of-trade models are virtually silent on two fundamental questions raised by Rodrik in 1995. Why are trade policies systematically biased against trade? And why are tariffs rather than more efficient production subsidies adopted to redistribute income? This paper shows that systematic political grass-root support for trade-restricting and inefficient tariffs emerges when the government has a revenue goal and collecting taxes is costly. Even if no tax instrument enjoys an advantage with respect to collection costs and the factor ownership distribution is unbiased, more people support tariffs than import or production subsidies. More generally, the presence of tax-collection costs creates a grass-root support bias for taxes over subsidies as instruments to redistribute income.

## 1. Introduction

The political-economy-of-trade-policy literature offers several competing models to explain the wide gap between actually-adopted and socially-optimal policies. Rodrik (1995) surveys these models[1] and asks whether and how they answer truly fundamental questions about the conduct of trade policy: "Why is international trade not free? ... Why are trade policies universally biased against trade? ... What are the determinants of the variation in protection levels across industries, countries, and time?" (p. 1458). Rodrik concludes that these major models provide few, if any, answers and that there is an urgent need for future research to "refocus attention on these fundamental questions."

This paper's primary objective is to address Rodrik's question of "why are trade policies almost always biased against trade, rather than in favor of it?" (p. 1476). In other words, why are countries much more inclined to protect their import-competing industries than promote their export industries?[2] The leading political-economy models provide no satisfactory explanation. They either assume the problem away by limiting policy instruments to tariffs only, or they allow for both tariffs and subsidies but say nothing about any observed bias towards the former. Rodrik (1995, p. 1478) suggests a two-step explanation for this systematic anti-trade bias.[3] The first step is based on the observation that governments of young nations frequently institute trade taxes to satisfy their revenue needs.[4] It is argued that these countries, hampered by limited administrative capabilities, adopt trade taxes because collection costs are lower for tariffs than for other tax instruments. The second step of the explanation concerns the persistence of trade taxes once governments gain the ability to administer other tax instruments that are more efficient than trade taxes. Fernandez and Rodrik (1991) relate this persistence to individuals' uncertainty about gaining and losing from trade-policy changes.

This paper's political-economy explanation of a systematic bias in favor of tariff-restricted trade also hinges on the existence of tax-collection costs. But different from the standard justification used in the tariff-revenue argument, it does not depend on

*Mayer: University of Cincinnati, Cincinnati, OH 45221-0371, USA. Tel: 513-556-2618; E-mail: mayerw@uc.edu.

tariffs having lower collection costs than other tax instruments.[5] In fact, the paper develops its argument under completely unbiased tax-collection costs; financing a dollar's worth of government spending is assumed to be equally costly for trade, income, and production taxes.[6]

Political-economy explanations of actual trade policies are based on the policy preferences of heterogeneous individuals. This paper focuses on the distribution of these trade-policy preferences and the corresponding political grass-root support for tariffs relative to trade subsidies. Clearly, the distribution of trade-policy preferences is strongly influenced by the country's distribution of individual factor ownership. If, for example, in a Heckscher–Ohlin economy with no tax-collection costs, most people own relatively much (little) of the import good's relatively intensive factor, then grass-root support is stronger (weaker) for tariffs than for import subsidies. To avoid any policy bias based on the distribution of factor endowments, I assume this distribution to be symmetric. It follows that, in a Heckscher–Ohlin economy with no tax-collection costs, the number of people favoring a tariff is exactly equal to the number of people favoring an import subsidy. Accordingly, this model eliminates not only the influence of biased tax-collection costs but also the impact of asymmetric distribution of factor ownership. The paper's main conclusion then is that, with tax-collection costs, there exists systematic political grass-root support for tariffs—meaning that more people gain from tariffs than from trade subsidies—even though tariffs have no collection-cost advantage over other taxes and the distribution of factor ownership is symmetric.

The paper's approach sheds light on a second issue raised by Rodrik (1995), namely the *choice of policy instruments* to influence an economy's distribution of income. Specifically, it provides an explanation for the use of inefficient trade taxes relative to more efficient production subsidies as instruments of income redistribution.[7] Again, the major political-economy models pay scant, if any, attention to this issue. Other research, however, has been more successful in addressing this question. One approach, proposed by Rodrik (1986) and Wilson (1990), has been to evaluate the efficiency of political equilibria under tariffs relative to production subsidies rather than the efficiency of the policy instruments themselves. They show that the deadweight loss associated with political equilibrium might be less under tariffs than under production subsidies. A second approach, suggested by Feenstra and Lewis (1991), is to explain tariffs as informationally efficient tools of the government when it wants to protect individuals from terms-of-trade fluctuations but cannot identify winners and losers. Finally, Mayer and Riezman (1990) have shown that individuals might prefer tariffs over production subsidies when either revenue-generating income taxes are progressive or individuals are uncertain about which policy will be adopted through the political process.

This paper argues that the political bias in grass-root support for tariffs relative to both import and production subsidies is the result of an ever-present asymmetry in collection costs when governments have a revenue objective. Given this revenue objective, revenues raised by tariffs replace revenues otherwise generated from income taxes. Under unbiased tax-collection costs, increased costs from tariff collection are exactly offset by reduced costs from income tax collection; there is no net change in the economy's total collection costs. If, on the other hand, subsidies are employed to redistribute income, the government must raise additional revenues through income taxes to pay for the subsidies. The economy, therefore, is subjected to additional collection costs. Hence, redistributing income through tariffs is less costly than redistributing income through subsidies even though collection costs are the same for all tax instruments.

The political bias for tariffs over production subsidies as instruments to redistribute income is not a bias in favor of international over domestic commercial policies. Instead, it is a bias in favor of tax over subsidization instruments in the presence of a revenue objective. Hence, the political-support bias is for tariffs over production subsidies, but for production taxes over import subsidies. Concerning the latter, more people gain from a production tax and, for each beneficiary, the gains from a small production tax exceed the gains from an equally-small import subsidy.

The paper assumes a need for government revenues. Individuals have preferences over both private and public goods and the government finances the provision of the public good. While public-good consumption is added to a standard international trade model, its provision is assumed not to affect the distribution of income. The public good is simply imported and not subjected to tariffs.

The driving force behind the political-support bias for tariffs is the presence of costs in operating the tax system. Two types of costs arise during the collection process. There are administrative costs of the government and there are compliance costs of individual taxpayers. Concerning the income tax in the United States, Blumenthal and Slemrod (1992) have estimated that the government's administrative costs are quite low but that individuals' compliance costs are quite substantial. This author is not aware of any corresponding study concerning administrative and compliance costs for trade taxes. Clearly, they are present as customs officials have to be paid and importers have to prepare documentation for their tariff-subjected imports. Also, there are costs due to inspection-related time delays. Costs arise not only in the collection of taxes but also in the disbursement of subsidies. Governments must spend on administering subsidization programs and individuals incur costs in claiming subsidies.

This paper introduces administrative and compliance costs for both taxes and subsidies in the simplest possible way. These costs are a fixed percentage of taxes to be collected and of subsidies to be disbursed. Clearly, alternative, possibly more realistic, specifications of cost functions could be employed and individuals' preferences for tax instruments would be affected by this choice. The overall thrust of my argument, however, remains valid: a policy instrument that redistributes income and collects revenues has cost advantages over a policy instrument that redistributes income and spends revenues. The motivation behind this specification is to highlight the forces that create a political bias for tariffs.

## 2. The Model

### *The Economy*

Assume a small, open economy whose production structure is characterized by a simple two-by-two Heckscher–Ohlin model. The factors of production, capital and labor, are fully mobile within the country but immobile between countries. Factor markets are perfectly competitive. Firms of industry $j = 1, 2$ employ both factors under a constant-returns-to-scale technology to produce good $j$. Both industries are perfectly competitive.

The economy is inhabited by $L$ people who care for both private and public goods. Their preferences for private goods are homothetic and identical, and their preferences for a single public good, $Q$, are the same. The $i$th person's indirect utility function is assumed to take the form

$$V^i = U(p^d, Y^i) + g(Q), \tag{1}$$

where $p^d = (p_1^d, p_2^d)$ is the vector of prices faced by domestic consumers and $Y^i$ is after-tax income of individual $i$. The $U(.)$-function is continuous in all arguments, strictly increasing in income and nonincreasing in prices. The $g(.)$-function is increasing in $Q$ at a decreasing rate, and $\lim_{Q\to 0} g'(Q) = \infty$. The last assumption assures that there is always some positive amount of demand for the public good.

Individuals differ with respect to factor ownership and, therefore, factor income. Specifically, they are heterogeneous with respect to capital ownership, with person $i$ owning $K^i \geqslant 0$. Ownership of labor, on the other hand, is homogeneous, as each person owns one unit of labor. The $i$th person's factor income before taxes, therefore, is

$$I^i(p^s, K^i) = w(p^s) + r(p^s)K^i, \tag{2}$$

where $w$ is the wage rate, $r$ is the return on capital, and $p^s = (p_1^s, p_2^s)$ is the vector of prices faced by domestic producers. It is convenient to restate an individual's factor income as

$$I^i(p^s, K^i) = \phi^i(p^s, K^i)I(p^s), \tag{2'}$$

where $I(p^s) = [w(p^s)L + r(p^s)\Sigma_{i=1}^L K^i] = p_1^s X_1(p^s) + p_2^s X_2(p^s)$ measures national income and $\phi^i(p^s, K^i)$ denotes the $i$th individual's factor income share. This income share is positively related to person $i$'s ownership of capital. One can show that it rises (declines) with a price increase of the good that is relatively intensive in the factor of which person $i$ owns more (less) than the average person. If, for example, the price of the capital-intensive good rises, income shares of capital-rich people grow and income shares of capital-poor people shrink. We call a person capital-rich (poor) if her capital–labor ownership ratio exceeds (falls short of) the country's capital–labor endowment ratio.

Finally, we measure all goods, private and public, in units such that their respective world prices are equal to one. The first good is exported and the second good is imported, whereby imports can be taxed or subsidized. All of the public good must be imported, but it is not subjected to a tariff.

### *Taxes and the Cost of Administering Them*

The paper considers three tax instruments to raise revenues, namely factor-income taxes, import taxes, and production taxes. In addition, it considers import and production subsidies. Taxes are employed to finance the public good and pay for subsidies. In addition, import and production taxes, as well as import and production subsidies, are employed to alter the distribution of factor income. The collection of taxes and the disbursement of subsidies, however, results in costs: administrative costs to the collecting or disbursing government, and compliance costs to paying or claiming individuals.

The *income tax* is a tax on factor income. Its tax rate is constant, denoted by $0 \leqslant t < 1$. Hence, individual $i$, with factor income $I^i$, pays income tax $tI^i$. The government's administrative costs, in turn, are a constant fraction, $0 \leqslant a < 1$, of the collected tax. Accordingly, only $[1 - a]tI^i$ can be used to finance the public good or to pay for subsidies. The taxpayer, in turn, not only loses $tI^i$ to the government but also incurs compliance costs. The latter are also assumed to be a fraction, $0 \leqslant \alpha < 1$, of the collected tax. Hence, the total loss in income for a tax-paying individual $i$ is $[1 + \alpha]tI^i$, and her after-tax income in equation (1) becomes $Y^i = I^i(.)\{1 - t[1 + \alpha]\}$.

The presence of administrative and compliance costs in collecting income taxes has important financing implications for government spending. Financing one dollar's worth of the public good through an income tax requires the sacrifice of $[1 + \alpha]/[1 - a]$ spending on private goods. Accordingly, the marginal cost of government spending, when financed through an income tax, is $[1 + \alpha]/[1 - a]$. The higher are compliance costs on the part of individuals and administrative costs on the part of government, the higher is the marginal cost of public spending.

A *tariff*, $0 \leq \tau < 1$, can be imposed on imports, $M$, of the second private good. The amount of tariff revenues collected is $\tau M$. The government's administrative costs in running customs are assumed to be a constant fraction of collected tariff revenues, amounting to $m\tau M$, where $0 \leq m < 1$. The taxation of imports, therefore, can finance government spending on the public good or on subsidies in the amount of $[1 - m]\tau M$. The tariff-paying importer, in turn, incurs compliance costs of $\mu\tau M$, where $0 \leq \mu < 1$. The importer's total loss, consisting of tariff payments and compliance costs, therefore becomes $[1 + \mu]\tau M$. Since this finances $[1 - m]\tau M$ in government spending, the marginal cost of government spending, when financed through an import tariff, is $[1 + \mu]/[1 - m]$. The world prices of all goods are set equal to one. An import tariff on the second private good raises its price, as faced by domestic consumers and producers, not only by the amount of the tariff but also by the importer's unit compliance costs; that is:

$$p_2^d = p_2^s = 1 + [1 + \mu]\tau. \tag{3}$$

While some factor owners favor tariffs, others prefer *import subsidies*. The disbursement of subsidies, just as the collection of tariffs, leads to administrative costs for the government and compliance costs for subsidy claimants. The total subsidy payment to importers is expressed by $\sigma M$, where $0 \leq \sigma < 1$ denotes the rate of subsidization. This payment leads to government administrative costs of $e\sigma M$, where $0 \leq e < 1$, and importers' compliance costs of $\varepsilon\sigma M$, where $0 \leq \varepsilon < 1$. Hence, import subsidization costs the government $[1 + e]\sigma M$, but net benefits to subsidized importers are only $[1 - \varepsilon]\sigma M$. The price of the import good, faced by domestic consumers and producers, is then

$$p_2^d = p_2^s = 1 - [1 - \varepsilon]\sigma; \tag{4}$$

the importers' compliance costs reduce the price-lowering effect of the import subsidy.

Finally, consider *production taxes* and *production subsidies*. I discuss them since traditionally they have been viewed as more efficient instruments to redistribute income than import subsidies and tariffs. Again, they are subject to government administrative and taxpayer compliance costs. The *production tax* on the import good raises $hX_2$ in government revenues, where $0 \leq h < 1$ is the production tax rate. The government's administrative collection costs are $bhX_2$, where $0 \leq b < 1$, and the producers' compliance costs are $\beta hX_2$, where $0 \leq \beta < 1$. Hence, the production tax raises $[1 - b]hX_2$ of revenues to finance government spending, but total costs to taxed producers are $[1 + \beta]hX_2$. The marginal cost of government spending, when financed through a production tax, is $[1 + \beta]/[1 - b]$. While the price faced by domestic consumers is $p_2^d = 1$, the producer price becomes

$$p_2^s = 1 - [1 + \beta]h. \tag{5}$$

If, on the other hand, the government pays a *production subsidy*, $z \geq 0$, its total payment to producers is $zX_2$, and its total expense including administrative costs is $[1 + n]zX_2$, where $0 \leq n < 1$. The net subsidy retained by firms, after covering their own compliance costs, is $[1 - v]zX_2$, where $0 \leq v < 1$ denotes the fraction of subsidy payments that is used up for compliance activities. The domestic producer price of the import good, under a "costly" production subsidy, then becomes

$$p_2^s = 1 + [1 - v]z. \tag{6}$$

## 3. Political-Support Bias for Tariff-Restricted Trade

Rodrik's (1995) survey of political-economy models focuses on two important unresolved issues: the widely-observed anti-trade bias of virtually all countries' trade policies, and the systematic use of relatively inefficient trade policies to redistribute income within a country. This section deals with the first issue. It demonstrates the *existence of a political grass-root support bias against trade; more people favor import tariffs than import subsidies even when tax-collection costs are unbiased and the distribution of factor ownership is symmetric.* This grass-root support contrasts with the policy preferences of a benevolent government: it would choose free trade by maximizing the average factor owner's welfare.

Under symmetric factor-ownership distribution, the number of people experiencing a rise in their factor-income share from a small tariff is exactly the same as the number of people experiencing a factor-income share increase from a small import subsidy. In the *absence of tax-collection costs*, symmetric factor-ownership distribution, therefore, implies that the number of people supporting a small tariff is exactly balanced by the number of people supporting a small import subsidy. There is no grass-root political-support bias either against or for trade. This section shows that with *unbiased tax-collection costs*, on the other hand, there are always more people in support of a small tariff than in support of a small import subsidy. Whereas all individuals whose income shares rise with a small tariff continue to gain in welfare, some individuals whose income shares rise with a small import subsidy now lose in welfare. The latter are people who cannot gain from either a tariff or an import subsidy when tax-collection costs are present but unbiased. Consequently, they support free trade. Under unbiased tax-collection costs, there are now three groups with distinctly different trade-policy preferences: supporters of tariffs, free traders, and supporters of import subsidies. Adding the assumption of symmetric factor-ownership distribution, the number of tariff supporters equals the total number of free traders *and* import-subsidy supporters; but it always exceeds the number of import-subsidy supporters alone.

The present section focuses on the choice between import tariffs and import subsidies as instruments of income redistribution. Production taxes and production subsidies are not considered; they are taken up in the next section. The first question raised is whether welfare of individual $i$, with factor income share $\phi^i(p^s, K^i)$, rises when a small tariff is imposed. If it does, the person lends political support to tariff-restricted trade. If it does not, we must further ask whether this person's welfare is raised by a small import subsidy. If it is, she supports trade-expanding import subsidization. If it is not—implying that neither a small tariff nor a small import subsidy enhances the person's welfare—she favors free trade.

The $i$th person's indirect utility function was stated in equation (1). If *an import tariff is imposed*, the government's spending on the public good, $Q$, can be financed through some combination of income and trade taxes; it equals

$$Q = [1 - a]tI(p^s) + [1 - m]\tau M(\tau, t), \tag{7}$$

where $M_\tau(\tau, t) < 0$ and $M_t(\tau, t) < 0$. The $i$th person's individually-optimal income tax and tariff rates are determined by maximizing equation (1) with respect to $t$ and $\tau$, respectively, after substitution of equations (3) and (7), as well as of the expression for after-tax income, $Y^i = I^i\{1 - [1 + \alpha]t\}$ and of equation (2′). Assuming strict concavity of the utility function with respect to both tax instruments, the first-order conditions for individually-optimal income tax and tariff rate choices require that

$$-U_{Y^i}(.)\phi^i(.)[1+\alpha]+g'(Q)\{[1-a]+[1-m]\tau M_t(.)/I(.)\} \leq 0 \quad \text{with equality for } t>0 \quad (8)$$

$$U_{Y^i}(.)[1+\mu]\{-\phi^i(.)M(.)-\phi^i(.)X_2(.)[1+\alpha]t+Y[\partial\phi^i(.)/\partial p_2^s]\}$$
$$+g'(Q)\{[1-a]tX_2(.)(1+\mu)+[1-m][M(.)+\tau M_\tau(.)]\} \leq 0 \quad \text{with equality for } \tau>0. \quad (9)$$

In deriving equation (9), I have made use of Roy's identity and the assumption that consumer preferences are homothetic and identical. This implies that $U_p(.)/U_{Y^i}(.) = -\phi^i(.)D_2(.)$, where $D_2(.)$ denotes the country's aggregate demand for the import good. We also used the symbol $Y = I(p^s)\{1 - t[1 + \alpha]\}$ to express the economy's after-tax income.

Does person $i$ favor trade-restricting import tariffs? The answer is yes if, given her optimal choice of income tax rate, she gains from a small tariff; that is, if, evaluated at $\tau = 0$, the left-hand side of equation (9) is positive. Two situations must be distinguished. One is the case where person $i$ is best off not having an income tax at all. The other is the case of person $i$ adding a tariff to the income tax as a way to raise revenues. For the first case to prevail, the left-hand side of equation (8) must not be positive at $t = 0$. Given the assumption that $\lim_{Q\to 0} g'(Q) = \infty$, this sign restriction is possible only if $Q > 0$ which, in turn, requires that $\tau > 0$. Hence, all people that oppose an income tax must be supportive of a tariff.[8] In the second case, equation (8) holds as an equality, and person $i$ evaluates both equations (8) and (9) at $\tau = 0$. This implies for equation (8) that

$$g'(Q)/U_{Y^i}(.) = \phi^i(.)[(1+\alpha)/(1-a)]. \quad (10)$$

In the absence of a tariff, the $i$th person's marginal rate of substitution between public and private goods equals her marginal cost of acquiring the public good through income-tax financing. The latter, in turn, equals the marginal cost to the economy, $(1 + \alpha)/(1 - a)$, multiplied by her income share. Substitution of equation (10) in equation (9) and setting $\tau = 0$ reduces the left-hand side of (9) to

$$U_{Y^i}(.)[1+\mu]\{\phi^i(.)M(.)[((1+\alpha)(1-m))/((1-a)(1+\mu))-1]+Y[\partial\phi^i(.)/\partial p_2^s]\}. \quad (11)$$

Person $i$ gains from a small tariff, in combination with an income tax, if the braced expression of equation (11) is positive. The sign of this expression crucially depends on two influences: the marginal cost of financing government spending through income taxes relative to tariffs, as measured by the square-bracketed term inside the brace, and the effect of a producer-price change on the person's income share, as expressed by $\partial\phi^i(.)/\partial p_2^s$. The assumption that there is no bias in the collection of taxes implies that the marginal cost of financing government spending is the same for income taxes and tariffs. Hence, $[1 + \mu]/[1 - m] = [1 + \alpha]/[1 - a]$, and the welfare effect of a small tariff depends on the person's income share response alone. As more fully developed in Mayer (1984), the income shares of capital-rich (poor) people rise and of capital-poor (rich) people decline when the producer price of a capital (labor)-intensive import good increases. If the distribution of factor ownership is symmetric, the number of people for whom $\partial\phi^i(.)/\partial p_2^s > 0$ is exactly the same as the number of people for whom $\partial\phi^i(.)/\partial p_2^s < 0$. Accordingly, with no bias in collection costs and symmetric factor-ownership distribution, the number of gainers from a small tariff is exactly balanced by the number of losers from a small tariff. Note also that the average factor owner's income share is not affected by a small tariff. Consequently, *a benevolent government, maximizing welfare of the average person, would oppose a tariff, no matter how small.*[9]

What about the political support by people whose welfare does not rise with a tariff, as $\partial\phi^i(.)/\partial p_2^s < 0$? Do all of them favor an import subsidy? Or do some support free trade, as they cannot gain from either a tariff or an import subsidy? To answer these questions, I examine the *conditions under which individual i gains from an import subsidy*. The analysis proceeds as in the tariff case, with one major difference. Under a tariff choice, the government spends on the public good only and has tariffs and income taxes as instruments to finance it. Under an import-subsidy choice, the government spends on the public good and import subsidies, but has income taxes as its sole financing instrument. Accordingly, spending on the public good equals revenues collected from the income tax, net of government administrative costs, minus the government's total spending on the import subsidy, consisting of the subsidy payment itself plus administrative disbursement costs; that is:

$$Q = [1-a]tI(p^s) - [1+e]\sigma M(\sigma, t), \tag{12}$$

where $M_\sigma(\sigma, t) > 0$ and $p_2^s = p_2^d$ is stated by equation (4). Given the indirect utility function of equation (1), the first-order conditions for utility-maximizing choices of income-tax and import-subsidization rates require that

$$-U_{Y^i}(.)\phi^i(.)[1+\alpha] + g'(Q)\{[1-a] - [1+e]\sigma M_t(.)/I(.)\} \leq 0 \quad \text{with equality for } t > 0 \tag{13}$$

$$U_{Y^i}(.)[1-\varepsilon]\{\phi^i(.)M(.) + \phi^i(.)X_2(.)[1+\alpha]t - Y[\partial\phi^i(.)/\partial p_2^s]\} - g'(Q)\{[1-a]tX_2(.)(1-\varepsilon) + [1+e][M(.) + \sigma M_\sigma(.)]\} \leq 0 \quad \text{with equality for } \sigma > 0. \tag{14}$$

Person *i* gains from a small import subsidy if, at the optimally chosen income tax rate, the left-hand side of equation (14), evaluated at $\sigma = 0$, is positive. Since every person desires some consumption of the public good and the income tax is the only instrument to finance spending, the equality sign must hold in equation (13) for all individuals. At $\sigma = 0$, this again implies the criterion established by equation (10). Substituting (10) into equation (14), and evaluating the latter also at $\sigma = 0$, reduces its left-hand side to

$$U_{Y^i}(.)[1-\varepsilon]\{\phi^i(.)M(.)[1 - ((1+\alpha)(1+e))/((1-a)(1-\varepsilon))] - Y[\partial\phi^i(.)/\partial p_2^s]\}. \tag{15}$$

An individual benefits from an import subsidy if expression (15) is positive. As was the case for tariff choices, there are two crucial influences on the expression's sign: the square-bracketed term inside the brace and the impact of a producer price decrease on the *i*th person's income share, $-\partial\phi^i(.)/\partial p_2^s$; the latter is positive for all individuals who lose from a tariff. The former, on the other hand, is always negative. Different from the tariff case, where the bracketed term vanishes under unbiased tax-collection costs, it must be negative in the import-subsidy case. The reason for this difference between import tariffs and import subsidies lies in their accompanying collection and disbursement costs. Both tariff collection and import-subsidy disbursement are costly. But raising tariffs enables the government to reduce income taxes, while raising import subsidies necessitates an increase in income taxes. The imposition of tariffs, therefore, amounts to substituting the cost of tariff collection for the cost of income-tax collection. With unbiased collection costs, there is no net change in the economy's total collection costs. The imposition of import subsidies, on the other hand, leads to additional costs at both the collection and disbursement stage. Collecting one dollar's worth of import-subsidy payment through the income tax results in total costs of $[1 + \alpha]/[1 - a]$ and disbursing one dollar of the subsidy payment results in total costs of $[1 + e]/[1 - \varepsilon]$. Hence, the term $\{[1 + \alpha][1 + e]\}/\{[1 - a][1 - \varepsilon]\} > 1$ measures the economy's total expense of transferring one dollar of subsidy to an importer.

The presence of costs at both the collection and/or the disbursement stage implies that an import subsidy might raise a person's income share, $-Y[\partial\phi^i(.)/\partial p_2^s] > 0$, but lower her welfare. This person cannot gain from either import subsidization or tariff imposition and, therefore, favors free trade. Consequently, individuals whose income shares rise with an import subsidy belong to one of two groups: free traders or import subsidy supporters.

Earlier I established that, under symmetry of factor ownership and unbiased tax-collection costs, the number of tariff supporters is the same as the number of tariff opponents. The income shares of these opponents rise with an import subsidy. But only some experience a welfare gain from import subsidization, while all others are best off under free trade. Consequently, *political grass-root support is biased in favor of tariff restrictions: there are always more people gaining from a tariff than from an import subsidy*. The presence of administrative and compliance costs is responsible for this political-support bias. Provided no tax instrument possesses a collection-cost advantage, the redistribution of income through tariffs leaves the economy's total collection costs unchanged. The redistribution of income through import subsidies, on the other hand, always raises them.

## 4. Political-Support Bias for Tariffs over Production Subsidies

A second unresolved issue concerns countries' revealed preference for tariffs as an instrument to redistribute income.[10] Why do governments choose relatively inefficient tariffs and not more efficient production subsidies? Both tariffs and production subsidies affect the distribution of income through their impact on producer prices, but production subsidies distort production only while tariffs distort both production and consumption. The objective of this section is to show that the presence of tax-collection costs offers an explanation for this puzzle. Given unbiased tax-collection costs and symmetric distribution of factor ownership, there exists a political grass-root support bias for tariffs over production subsidies as instruments to redistribute income. The number of people gaining from a small tariff is always larger than the number of people gaining from a small production subsidy, and each individual's gain from a small tariff exceeds her gain from a small production subsidy.

This section also shows that the political-support bias is one of taxes over subsidies rather than of international-trade policy over domestic-production policy. While potential beneficiaries from the import good's *price rise* favor a small tariff over a small production subsidy, potential gainers from the import good's *price drop* favor a small production tax over a small import subsidy. Concerning the latter, the number of people gaining from a small production tax is larger than the number of people gaining from a small import subsidy. Furthermore, each beneficiary from a decline in the import good's price gains more if it is accomplished through a small production tax than a small import subsidy.

To establish this political-support bias for taxes over subsidies, I first examine the choice between an import tariff and a production subsidy for individuals whose income shares rise with an increase in the import good's price. The objective function is again stated in equation (1), and there are government administrative costs and individual compliance costs, as discussed in section 2. In the presence of both a tariff and a production subsidy on the import good, its price faced by consumers and producers, respectively, is

$$p_2^d = 1+[1+\mu]\tau \quad \text{and} \quad p_2^s = 1+[1+\mu]\tau+[1-v]z, \tag{16}$$

using equations (3) and (6). Revenues, collected from income taxes and tariffs, in turn, are spent on the public good and production subsidies; hence:

$$Q = [1-a]tI(p^s)+[1-m]\tau M(\tau, z, t)-[1+n]zX_2(p^s). \tag{17}$$

If there were no income tax, tariffs would be the only source of revenues. Hence, all individuals who favor no income tax at all must support a positive tariff rather than production subsidy to provide some $Q > 0$.[11] But what about individuals whose welfare-maximizing choice is to have an income tax? Would they choose a tariff as an income-redistribution tool if production subsidies were available as well? To answer this question, we substitute equations (16) and (17) in equation (1) and differentiate the obtained expression with respect to the income tax rate, $t$, tariff rate, $\tau$, and production subsidy rate, $z$. Given that the person's optimal income tax rate is positive, we determine and compare the gains from a small tariff with the gains from a small production subsidy.

Setting $\tau = z = 0$, the $i$th person's optimal choice of income tax rate implies again that equation (10) is satisfied. Using it, the effect of a small tariff on $i$'s welfare is

$$\partial V^i/\partial\tau = U_{Y^i}(.)[1+\mu]\{\phi^i(.)M(.)[((1+\alpha)(1-m))/((1-a)(1+\mu))-1]+Y[\partial\phi^i(.)/\partial p_2^s]\}, \tag{18}$$

which repeats expression (11). Again, given the assumption of unbiased tax-collection costs, an individual benefits from a rising import-good price if and only if her income share rises. Under symmetric factor ownership distribution, one half of the population supports a small tariff. Also, *a benevolent government maximizing welfare of the average person would not employ a tariff, as the income share of the average factor owner remains unchanged.*

Next, we evaluate the $i$th person's change in welfare from a small production subsidy, again setting $\tau = z = 0$:

$$\partial V^i/\partial z = U_{Y^i}(.)[1-v]\{\phi^i(.)X_2(.)[1-((1+\alpha)(1+n))/((1-a)(1-v))]+Y[\partial\phi^i(.)/\partial p_2^s]\}, \tag{19}$$

again using equation (10). The square-bracketed term inside the brace is always negative, independent of the biasedness of tax-collection costs. Accordingly, some individuals whose income shares rise with a production subsidy do not gain in welfare from a small production subsidy. Furthermore, if the factor-ownership distribution is symmetric, less than half the population supports a production subsidy. Finally, a comparison of equations (18) and (19) reveals that, under unbiased tax-collection costs, each person with a rising income share gains more from a small tariff than a small production subsidy, as

$$\partial V^i/\partial\tau > \partial V^i/\partial z \quad \text{when } (1+\alpha)/(1-a) = (1+\mu)/(1-m). \tag{20}$$

We can therefore conclude that *there exists a political-support bias for tariffs over production subsidies: more people want a small tariff than a small production subsidy, and each beneficiary gains more from a small tariff than from a small production subsidy.*[12]

Individuals whose income shares rise with a declining producer price of the import good consider import subsidization and production taxation as instruments to enhance their welfare. In the presence of both an import subsidy and a production tax, consumer and producer prices of the import good are

$$p_2^d = 1-[1-\varepsilon]\sigma \quad \text{and} \quad p_2^s = 1-[1-\varepsilon]\sigma-[1+\beta]h, \tag{21}$$

respectively. Revenues, collected from income and production taxes, pay for government spending on the public good and on import subsidies. Accordingly:

$$Q = [1-a]tI(p^s)-[1+e]\sigma M(\sigma, h, t)+[1-b]hX_2(p^s). \tag{22}$$

If individual $i$ chooses not to have an income tax, she must favor a production tax to pay for the public good. If, on the other hand, this person supports an income tax, then again equation (10) must hold. Given her optimally chosen positive income-tax rate, can person $j$ gain from a small import subsidy or from a small production tax? And if so, which instrument generates larger gains? To answer these questions, I first state the effect of a small import subsidy on the $j$th person's welfare:

$$\partial V^j/\partial\sigma = U_{Y^i}(.)[1-\varepsilon]\{\phi^i(.)M(.)[1-((1+\alpha)(1+e))/((1-a)(1-\varepsilon))]-Y[\partial\phi^i(.)/\partial p_2^s]\}, \tag{23}$$

which repeats expression (15) as we set $\sigma = h = 0$. Since the bracketed term is again negative, not all individuals with rising income shares, $-\partial\phi^j(.)/\partial p_2^s > 0$, also gain in welfare. The smallest income-share gainers do not support import subsidization; they favor free trade.

The corresponding welfare effect of a small production tax is

$$\partial V^i/\partial h = U_{Y^i}(.)[\beta]\{\phi^i(.)X_2(.)[((1+\alpha)(1-b))/((1-a)(1+\beta))-1]-Y[\partial\phi^i(.)/\partial p_2^s]\}, \tag{24}$$

again setting $\sigma = h = 0$. With unbiased tax-collection costs, the marginal cost of income tax collection, $[1 + \alpha]/[1 - a]$, equals the marginal cost of production tax collection, $[1 + \beta]/[1 - b]$, the bracketed term is zero, and all individuals with rising income shares also gain in welfare. Contrasting this with the effect of an import subsidy, more individuals benefit from a small production tax than from a small import subsidy. Furthermore, each beneficiary of a small production tax gains more than from a small import subsidy since

$$\partial V^i/\partial h > \partial V^i/\partial\sigma \quad \text{when } [1+\alpha]/[1-a] = [1+\beta]/[1-b]. \tag{25}$$

I summarize this section with the observation that political support is stronger for small tariffs than for small production subsidies, but weaker for small import subsidies than for small production taxes. *The political-support bias is in favor of the instrument that is capable of raising taxes relative to the instrument that requires financing*. Financing a subsidy is saddled with costs at the stage of collecting the additional income taxes, as well as at the stage of disbursing subsidy funds. Inevitably, there are losses due to increased government administrative costs and individual compliance costs. Collecting a trade or production tax, on the other hand, substitutes the administrative and compliance costs of income-tax collection for the corresponding costs of production-tax collection. If there is no collection-cost bias, there are no new costs to society.

## 5. Concluding Remarks

Generally, analyses of the welfare effects of various tax instruments do not account for the existence of tax-collection costs. Given the absence of such tax-collection costs, there exists no systematic political grass-root bias in favor of trade-restricting tariffs. At the grass-root level, some individuals gain from tariffs while others gain from import subsidies. When the distribution of factor ownership is symmetric, the number of tariff supporters exactly equals the number of import-subsidy supporters.

A systematic political-support bias in favor of tariffs over import and production subsidies emerges when costs of collecting taxes are accounted for. This bias appears even when the cost of collecting taxes is the same for all tax instruments. With symmetric distribution of factor ownership, more individuals favor a small tariff over a small import subsidy and more individuals favor a small tariff over a small production subsidy. This definite grass-root support for trade taxes stands in contrast to the tax-instrument preferences of a benevolent government. When the collection of tariff revenues is equally costly as the collection of income taxes, a benevolent government would stay clear of tariffs and rely entirely on the use of income taxes. Such a government would opt for tariffs only if, as suggested by the tariff-revenue argument, it is less costly to raise revenues through tariffs than income taxes.

This paper looks at the underlying grass-root political support of individuals only. It compares the fractions of the population gaining from alternative policies, but does not say anything about how the associated policy preferences translate into actual policies through the political process. Clearly, the actual policy choice greatly depends on the political process. One possible political process is majority voting. Since there are two issues over which individuals express their preferences, namely how much of the public good to have and how to pay for it, a voting equilibrium may not exist. If, however, the amount of the public good to be provided had been decided on at an earlier stage, then the voting would be only on the rate at which imports are taxed or subsidized. Given the import good is relatively labor (capital)-intensive, the median voter opts for a tariff if the distribution of capital ownership is such that the median voter is capital-poor. If the distribution of capital ownership is symmetric or the median voter is only modestly capital-rich, majority voting will lead to free trade. Only if the distribution of capital ownership is such that the median voter is quite capital-rich will majority voting result in import subsidization. Given the randomness of factor ownership distributions across countries, majority voting is more likely to result in tariff protection than import subsidization.[13]

## References


Blumenthal, Marsha and Joel Slemrod, "The Compliance Cost of the US Individual Income Tax System: A Second Look after Tax Reform," *National Tax Journal* 45 (1992):185–202.

Corden, W. Max, *Trade Policy and Economic Welfare*, Oxford: Oxford University Press (1974).

Feenstra, Robert C. and Tracy R. Lewis, "Distributing the Gains from Trade with Incomplete Information," *Economics & Politics* 3 (1991):21–40.

Fernandez, Rachel and Dani Rodrik, "Resistance to Reform: Status-Quo Bias in the Presence of Individual-Specific Uncertainty," *American Economic Review* 81 (1991):1146–55.

Findlay, Ronald and Stanislaw Wellisz, "Endogenous Tariffs, the Political Economy of Trade Restrictions, and Welfare," in Jagdish N. Bhagwati (ed.), *Import Competition and Response*, Chicago: University of Chicago Press (1982):223–38.

Gardner, Grant W. and Kent P. Kimbrough, "Tax Regimes, Tariff Revenues and Government Spending," *Economica* 59 (1992):75–92.

Grossman, Gene M. and Elhanan Helpman, "Protection for Sale," *American Economic Review* 84 (1994):833–50.

Hillman, Arye L., "Declining Industries and Political-Support Protectionist Motives," *American Economic Review* 72 (1982):1180–7.

International Monetary Fund, *Government Finance Statistics Yearbook*, vol. 23, Washington, DC: IMF (1999).

Krueger, Anne O., "Asymmetries in Policy between Exportables and Import-Competing Goods," in Ronald W. Jones and Anne O. Krueger (eds.), *The Political Economy of*

*International Trade: Essays in Honor of Robert E. Baldwin*, Cambridge, MA: Basil Blackwell (1990):161–78.

Magee, Stephen P., William A. Brock, and Leslie Young, *Black Hole Tariffs and Endogenous Policy Theory: Political Economy in General Equilibrium*, Cambridge: Cambridge University Press (1989).

Mayer, Wolfgang, "Endogenous Tariff Formation," *American Economic Review* 74 (1984):970–85.

Mayer, Wolfgang and Raymond Riezman, "Voter Preferences for Trade Policy Instruments," *Economics & Politics* 2 (1990):259–73.

Mitchell, Brian R., *International Historical Statistics, The Americas 1750–1993*, New York: Stockton Press (1998).

Rodrik, Dani, "Tariffs, Subsidies, and Welfare with Endogenous Policy," *Journal of International Economics* 21 (1986):285–96.

———, "Political Economy of Trade Policy," in Gene M. Grossman and Kenneth Rogoff (eds.), *Handbook of International Economics*, vol. 3, Amsterdam: Elsevier Science (1995):1457–94.

Wilson, John D., "Are Efficiency Improvements in Government Transfer Policies Self-Defeating in Equilibrium?" *Economics & Politics* 2 (1990):241–58.

## Notes

1. Rodrik discusses five models: "the tariff-formation function approach" of Findlay and Wellisz (1982), "the political-support function approach" of Hillman (1982), "the median-voter approach" of Mayer (1984), "the campaign-contributions approach" of Magee et al. (1989), and "the political-contributions approach" of Grossman and Helpman (1994).
2. This question was also raised by Krueger (1990).
3. The same kind of two-step explanation has been proposed by Krueger (1990, pp. 165–6).
4. In the United States, the percentage of federal revenues collected from customs amounted to more than 90% through much of the first half and more than 50% through much of the second half of the 19th century (Mitchell, 1998). Even in the late 1990s, numerous African countries, such as Ivory Coast, Gambia, Guinea, Lesotho, Madagascar, and Sierra Leone, collected more than 40% of their total revenues from international-trade taxes (International Monetary Fund, 1999).
5. Corden (1974) has pointed out that the choice of tariffs as part of an optimal tax regime is contingent on having lower collection costs. The tariff-revenue argument also takes center stage in Gardner and Kimbrough (1992).
6. Accordingly, if revenues were raised by a benevolent social-welfare-maximizing government of a small country, neither tariffs nor import subsidies would be adopted.
7. As Rodrik (1995, p. 1471) puts it, "there continues to exist a serious gap in our understanding of what makes trade policy so politically efficient, as it must be judged to be by revealed preference, when considerably more direct means of redistributing income certainly exist."
8. One can show that a necessary condition for a person to support a tariff and oppose an income tax is that this person's income share rises with the tariff rate.
9. If collecting trade taxes is less costly than collecting income taxes, as is the case for countries at an early stage of development, then $[1 + \mu]/[1 - m] < [1 + a]/[1 - \alpha]$ and political support for tariffs is even stronger. All individuals with rising income shares, as well as some individuals with moderately declining income shares, gain from a small tariff. Importantly, a benevolent government, maximizing the average person's welfare, chooses a tariff rather than free trade for a small country. While the average person's income share is not affected by the tariff, the square-bracketed term is positive.
10. After reviewing the main political-economy models of international trade, Rodrik (1995, p. 1470) observes that they do not explain why such a highly inefficient tool is chosen to redistribute income. In fact, these models "are largely silent on this issue, since they explicitly rule out recourse to other policies besides trade policy."

11. Again, a necessary condition for giving support to tariffs but opposing an income tax is that the person's income share rises with the tariff rate.
12. Note that this does not imply that only a tariff is chosen. Many individuals will find a combination of a tariff and production subsidy, in addition to a positive income tax rate, to be individually welfare-maximizing. Also, the conclusion that gains are larger from a small tariff than a small production subsidy does not imply that the optimally chosen tariff rate is necessarily larger than the optimally chosen production-subsidy rate.
13. It, thereby, provides an answer to Krueger's (1990, p. 164) question: "Indeed, why should not free trade happen to be the outcome only when exportable and import-competing interests are exactly balanced, in the relevant political sense?"

*Pacific Economic Review*, 1: 2 (1996) pp. 147–167

# AGE AS A DETERMINANT OF LABOR'S TRADE POLICY INTERESTS

JUN LI *CNA Insurance Company, USA*
WOLFGANG MAYER *University of Cincinnati, USA**

*Abstract.* This paper shows that workers with identical innate abilities have heterogeneous trade policy interests, whereby age of the worker and industry of employment are most critical in explaining this heterogeneity. A modified specific factor model, with overlapping generations and a retraining requirement for job switchers, is developed to demonstrate how trade policies affect the economic interests of older workers far more than of younger workers, regardless of whether they gain or lose from the policy. Accordingly, older workers tend to have stronger incentives to become politically active than younger workers.

## 1. INTRODUCTION

The political economy of trade policy formation is frequently modeled as a political game among interest groups whose fortunes are closely tied to the performance of entire industries. The specific factor model (Jones, 1971) has become the preferred vehicle to describe the emergence of opposing factor owner interests on trade policy matters. The seminal work by Findlay and Wellisz (1982), for example, pits capitalists against landowners in a lobbying game to influence trade policies with respect to manufacturing and agriculture. An essential feature of their, as well as other specific factor models is that the trade policy interests of the intersectorally mobile factor, labor, are homogeneous. Regardless of a worker's identity, in terms of age and industry employment, the effects of a given policy are the same for all workers. Furthermore, the effects of policy changes on workers' interests tend to be quite ambiguous, but relatively small in the traditional specific factor model (Ruffin and Jones, 1977); workers may gain or may lose, but either way the effects are not as large as on specific factor owners. This ambiguity and relative smallness of policy effects is the reason why workers do not play much of a role in many models of trade policy formation; for example, Findlay and Wellisz (p. 225) treat workers as "purely passive" in the political process.

The traditional specific factor model's implication that workers have homogeneous trade policy interests runs counter to the observation that many workers of the real world are quite concerned about the choice of trade policies, that this concern makes them politically active, and that their interests are far from homogeneous. One observes that the workers of the export industry have

The authors are grateful for the helpful comments of an anonymous referee.

**Address for correspondence*: Department of Economics, University of Cincinnati, Cincinnati, OH 45221-0371, USA.

views on trade policies quite different from workers in the import industry, and that older workers have much stronger preferences with respect to policy matters than younger workers. Concerning the age characteristic of voters in general, most of whom are workers, there is strong and consistent empirical evidence that older individuals are much more likely to become active in the political process than younger individuals.[1]

Why do older workers become more engaged in the political process than younger workers? The political science literature (Wolfinger and Rosenstone, 1980) argues that the level of political participation rises with a person's knowledge and understanding of the political process, and that education, combined with life experience, fosters this knowledge and understanding. Our paper offers another, complementary explanation for greater political activism of older workers: political activities are driven by economic interests and many forms of trade policies have a greater impact on the economic interests of older than younger workers.

This paper sets up a modified specific factor model in order to highlight the role of age and industry affiliation of workers as determinants of the intensity of their policy interests. Our paper retains the conventional specific factor model assumption that all workers have the same innate abilities and the same potential for work. It differs from the conventional model, however, in a number of important ways:

- Labor is temporarily sector-specific; it is no longer perfectly mobile between industries as a person's employability in a given industry requires that he has received appropriate training prior to work in this industry. There is no job that can be performed before the necessary skills have been acquired. Every person starts training at the beginning of his or her life, in the form of general education and specific-skill learning. A person can change jobs later in life, but job switching necessitates additional training for the new job.
- Our modified specific factor model is dynamic rather than static.[2] It takes time for labor to move from one industry to the other and, during this adjustment process, each person's factor income changes over time.
- Workers are no longer homogeneous; they are differentiated by age. An overlapping generations framework, in which a large number of generations works and consumes at the same time, is added to highlight

[1] Lipset (1960) was the first to provide a systematic explanation of electoral participation at the micro level, in particular in categorizing younger people as low-turnout groups and older people as high-turnout groups. Crewe (1981, p. 258) confirms that "By and large this (Lipset's) summary has stood the test of both time and international comparison." Recent surveys of voters in the United States, reflected in US Bureau of Census (1988) data, reveal that only about one-third of the youngest eligible voters go to the polls in presidential election years, that participation rises monotically with age, and that more than two-thirds of people older than 45 years take part in such elections.

[2] The current literature on factor reallocations within a general equilibrium production economy consists of both dynamic models, developed by Lapan (1976), Mussa (1978, 1982a), and Neary (1982), as well as one-period models, spelled out by Mussa (1982b) and Diamond (1982) and employed by Staiger and Tabellini (1987) and Aizenman and Frenkel (1988).

the effects of trade policies on people at different stages of their lives. Each generation of workers consists of an exogenously given number of people who are homogeneous at birth, begin life with a period of schooling, earn income once employment starts, and finally die after retiring from work some periods earlier.

The main insight provided by this modified specific factor model is that trade policy interests of workers differ not only across industries, but also across generations within the same industry. The key to understanding this heterogeneity of interests among workers is the observation that every trade policy change is followed by a gradual adjustment of the economy, that the adjustment paths of wage incomes differ for workers of different industries, and, most importantly, that workers of different ages are exposed to different phases of this adjustment process. If, for example, a new trade policy lowers the price of manufactured relative to agricultural goods, a wage gap between sectors is opened up. Workers gradually move from manufacturing to agriculture, the movement of labor narrows the wage gap over time, and older workers experience only the front end of the adjustment in wages while younger workers may live through the entire adjustment process. At a given point in time, all workers of a given industry receive the same *current income*, but workers of different age face different *permanent income* levels, as long as their lives cover different spans of the adjustment process.

It is shown that the older and middle-aged workers of the expanding industry benefit the most from a policy change and that the older workers of the contracting industry get hurt the most. The youngest workers, on the other hand, are far less affected by policy changes, regardless of industry of employment, and they, therefore, are prime candidates for remaining passive in the political process of trade policy formation.

Section 2 of the paper formulates the modified specific factor model. Particular emphasis is placed on the choice of each individual's employment, the conditions under which job switching takes place, and the relationship between the benefits from job switching and a person's age. Section 3 provides a detailed analysis of the adjustment process of labor markets in the aftermath of a commodity price change. The focus is on determining the length of the adjustment process, the number of job switchers, the rate of labor reallocation through attrition, and the wage rate adjustments in the two sectors over time. Section 4 highlights the basis for political pressures for trade policy actions, namely the welfare effects of commodity price changes on different types of workers.

## 2. THE SPECIFIC FACTOR MODEL WITH LABOR ADJUSTMENT COSTS

### 2.1. *General assumptions*

The standard two-sector specific factor model assumes that labor is perfectly mobile between industries; labor moves instantaneously and costlessly from one sector to the other, assuring that wage rates are always equalized across sectors. The objective of this section is to replace this restriction by the more realistic assumption that labor encounters adjustment costs in moving between sectors, and that wage rates are not equalized across sectors during the adjustment process set off by some external shock. Labor is temporarily sector-specific as industry-specific training prepares a worker for employment in a given sector. Labor employed in this sector can, however, switch to the other sector if it undergoes retraining.

The economy under discussion is small and open, its two industries are competitive, and their production functions are given by:

$$X_j = f_j(L_j, V_j) \qquad j = 1, 2, \tag{1}$$

where $L_j$ and $V_j$ denote employment of labor and a specific factor in industry $j$, respectively, and the functions are homogeneous of degree one in the two factors. Factor $V_j$ is permanently specific to industry $j$. Labor is mobile in the long run, but sector specific temporarily; labor employed in a given industry has received training specific to this industry and cannot move to the other industry until it has been retrained. Consequently, markets for the two industries' specific factors are completely and permanently separated. For labor, on the other hand, there is only one market in the long run, after all adjustments to a disturbance have been played out, but two separate, though interconnected markets during the adjustment process. The two labor markets are separate during adjustment, as there will be different wage rates, and they are interconnected, as the flow of labor between sectors shapes the convergence of these different wage rates. At any given point in time, $t$, returns on labor and the two specific factors in industry $j = 1, 2$ are given by:

$$w_j(t) = p_j(t)\frac{\partial f_j[L_j(t), V_j(t)]}{\partial L_j(t)} \quad \text{and} \quad r_j(t) = p_j(t)\frac{\partial f_j[L_j(t), V_j(t)]}{\partial V_j(t)} \tag{2}$$

respectively, where $p_j(t)$ is the price of commodity $j$ at time $t$. In the remainder of the paper, we express all prices and incomes in terms of commodity one, setting $p_1(t) = 1$ and $p_2(t) = p(t)$.

The economy's endowment with specific factors is exogenously given. These specific factors are owned by a non-working class of economic agents and they are not transferable among agents.[3] The country's population of workers is given by $N$; but the total number of people actually employed may vary from period to period. At all points in time, the working class population consists of $D$ generations of people, ranging in age from O to $D$. People are born at the instantaneous rate of $n$ and die at the same rate $D$ periods after birth, such that $N = nD$ at all times.

Each working class person's birth is the beginning of an initial training period during which he or she is exposed to general education, as well as

[3] This assumption is introduced in order to focus on the income streams of people whose wellbeing depends exclusively on labor income. Alternatively, one could allow for ownership of specific factors by workers as well. For the special case that all economic agents are workers and each worker's ownership of specific factors is the same, the main conclusion of this paper, namely that trade policy interests of older workers are stronger than of younger workers, remains valid.

specific training for employment in a given industry. Initial training lasts for a fixed number of periods and, for simplicity's sake, we assume that this initial training period is the same in each sector, namely $\underline{\tau}$.

After completion of initial training, a person becomes part of the labor supply in the sector for which specific training was received. A trained worker can always remain in the same job until retirement, $T$ periods after birth and $(T-\underline{\tau})$ periods after starting the first job. A trained worker, however, can also quit his or her current employment and seek work in the other industry.

Prior to starting a job in the other industry, the person must be retrained to learn the skills required in the new industry. The number of time periods a person has to spend in retraining is not constant; it is allowed to vary with the amount of time since the person completed initial training. This initial training had conveyed both general knowledge, useful for work in both industries, and specific knowledge, useful for work in one industry only. It is implicitly assumed that, over time, people tend to forget some of this general knowledge, implying that older workers need more time for retraining than younger workers. If, for example, a worker wants to move from the aerospace to the petrochemical industry, an older person, whose basic training in mathematics and the sciences dates further back, needs more time to acquire the skills required in the petrochemical industry than a younger person.

Concerning these retraining periods, we specifically assume that $\tau_0$ is the minimum amount of time required for a person who has just completed initial training, that the retraining period rises with age, and that this retraining period is always shorter than the initial training period for a newborn person; that is $\tau_0 \leq \tau(s) < \underline{\tau}$ and $d\tau/ds > 0$ for $s > \underline{\tau}$, where $\tau(s)$ denotes the required retraining period for a person of age $\tau$.

Changing careers is not restricted to people who are working already. A person who is not yet employed but is already in the phase of initial training – that is, a person of age $0 < s < \underline{\tau}$ – can switch initial training. Again, the length of required retraining is assumed to depend on a person's age; but for initial trainees, the more general and specific schooling a person has completed already the less time is needed for retraining. The retraining time requirement is shortest for trainees closest to finishing initial training and longest for trainees just starting this training; we have $\tau_0 < \tau(s) < \underline{\tau}$ for $0 < s < \underline{\tau}$, but now $d\tau/ds < 0$.

Figure 1 shows the relationship between a worker's age and the amount of time needed to complete retraining for the other industry. At the beginning of life, the amount of time required is $\underline{\tau}$. The older the initial trainee, the shorter the retraining period becomes until it hits bottom at $\tau_0$ for people who are just starting their first job. Once a person is working, retraining time rises with age, although it always remains less than what it is for an initial trainee, meaning that $\tau(s) < \underline{\tau}$ for $s > 0$.

### 2.2. *The worker's employment decision*

Each person's employment decision is motivated by the objective of maximizing welfare for the remainder of his life. Utility yielded to a representative

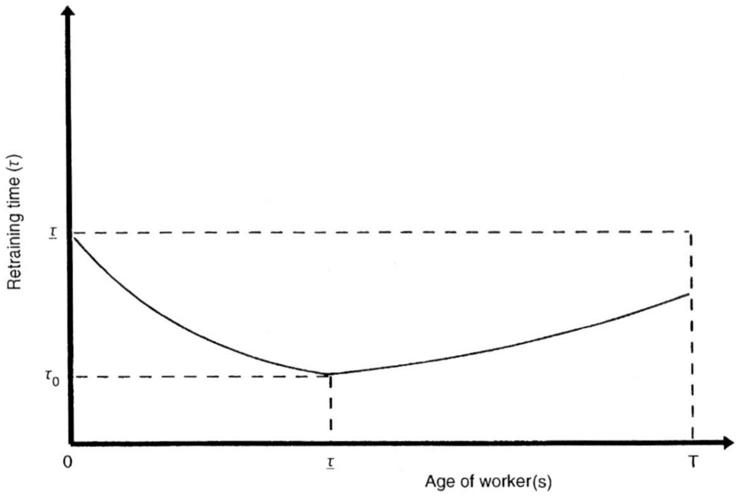


*Figure 1*

individual in period $t$ is given by:

$$U(t) = U[c(t), p(t)], \tag{3}$$

where $c(t)$ is consumption expenditure in terms of good one in period $t$, and utility rises at a decreasing rate with consumption but declines with a rise in the second commodity's price. A person of age $s$ has another $(D-s)$ periods to live, such that his or her cumulative welfare at the current time, $t = 0$, is expressed as:

$$W(s) = \int_0^{D-s} U[c(t), p(t)]\exp(-\beta t)dt, \tag{4}$$

where $\beta$ is the consumer's subjective discount rate. Employment is chosen in a way to maximize $W(s)$. What choice of industry this entails depends, of course, on the anticipated flow of income for the rest of the person's life. In addition, it depends on the ability to borrow and lend. In this paper we assume that each person can borrow and lend at a fixed world interest rate whose value is $r$; we also assume that each individual's personal discount rate equals the world interest rate; that is, $\beta = r$. Finally, we assume that workers do not anticipate any commodity price changes for the remainder of their lives, implying that $p(t) = p$ for $0 \leq t \leq (D-s)$.

Each consumer faces a lifetime budget constraint, permitting no debts at life's end. Denoting personal net wealth at time $t$ by $a(t)$, the lifetime budget constraint states that $a(D) \leq 0$.[4] Also, each worker is assumed to be born

[4] Since each person's utility depends on own consumption expenditure only, there will be no bequest and $a(D) = 0$.

without inherited wealth, such that $a(0) = 0$. For each period between birth and death, there is the constraint that the discounted stream of consumption expenditure plus saving equals the discounted stream of income from factor ownership, $y$, plus interest earned on already accumulated wealth:

$$c(t) + da(t)/dt = y(t) + r(t)a(t). \tag{5}$$

A worker receives factor income during periods of actual employment only; no income is earned during periods of initial training, retraining, or retirement. As we substitute the value of $c(t)$ from (5) into (4), maximize (4) with respect to $a(t)$ subject to the constraints that $a(0) = a(T) = 0$, and employ the restriction that $\beta = r$, Euler's equation implies that $c(t)$ is the same in every period (Kamien and Schwartz, 1991); that is, a person maintains the same consumption level for each period of his or her remaining life, even if no income is earned during some of these periods.

Employment decisions can be made at any age, the criterion being that welfare, as measured by (4), is maximized. With $p(t)$ given and consumption constant over time, this goal is reached by maximizing the instantaneous rate of consumption or what, for simplicity's sake, we just call period consumption. For a person of age $s$, period consumption is denoted by $c(s)$. If, for example, a person was just born, $s = 0$, period consumption is determined by the condition that the discounted stream of consumption expenditures equals the discounted stream of incomes received during the entire lifetime. Consumption starts at the beginning of the newborn's life, at $t = 0$, while income from work is not earned until $\underline{\tau}$ periods later; and consumption terminates at time $D$ while work stops earlier with retirement at time $T$. The lifetime spending constraint states that:

$$c(0)\int_0^D \exp(-\beta t)dt = \int_{\underline{\tau}}^T y(t)\exp(-\beta t)dt \quad \text{or} \quad c(0) = \frac{\int_{\underline{\tau}}^T y(t)\exp(-\beta t)dt}{\int_0^D \exp(-\beta t)dt}. \tag{6}$$

Wages are the only source of income for workers; but they can be earned in either sector. At birth, a person decides on training for the sector in which employment promises the highest attainable period consumption level. In our two-sector model, this means that a newborn worker will start initial training in industry 2 rather than industry 1 if:

$$\int_{\underline{\tau}}^T w_2(t)\exp(-\beta t)dt > \int_{\underline{\tau}}^T w_1(t)\exp(-\beta t)dt. \tag{7}$$

Workers are assumed to have perfect foresight concerning future wage rates, given their anticipation of commodity prices. When constant commodity prices are anticipated and the economy no longer adjusts after an earlier disturbance, wages in each sector will be constant and remain the same over time. When a disturbance occurred more recently and intersectoral reallocations of labor are not yet completed, both sectors' wage rates are still adjusting even if no further changes in commodity prices are anticipated, as discussed in the next section.

A person always retains the option of correcting the initial training decision should economic circumstances change. In particular, a young person in initial training, say for industry 1, may consider the possibility of switching training and eventual employment to industry 2. For a person of age $s$, there exists an incentive to switch initial training if the discounted stream of future income to be earned in industry 2 exceeds that to be earned in industry 1; that is, if:

$$\int_{\tau(s)}^{T-s} w_2(t)\exp(-\beta t)dt > \int_{\underline{\tau}-s}^{T-s} w_1(t)\exp(-\beta t)dt, \qquad (8)$$

where $\tau(s)$, the time it takes a person of age $s$ to retrain, exceeds $(\underline{\tau} - s)$, the time required to complete training already started. No matter what training choice is made, a person of age $s$ has only $(T-s)$ work periods left. If training for industry 1 is continued, then $s$ of the required $\underline{\tau}$ training periods are already completed and income will start to flow after $(\underline{\tau} - s)$ periods; if training is switched to industry 2, the income flow does not start until later, namely $\tau(s)$ periods after the switch.

When a person is already employed, say in industry 1, switching of jobs is a possibility. At age $s > \underline{\tau}$, the choice is based on a comparison of the discounted streams of income in the two industries for the remaining $(T-s)$ periods of work, where staying in industry 1 permits an uninterrupted income flow while employment in industry 2 calls for prior retraining of duration $\tau(s)$. A person of age $s$, already employed in industry 1, will switch to industry 2 if:

$$\int_{\tau(s)}^{T-s} w_2(t)\exp(-\beta t)dt > \int_{0}^{T-s} w_1(t)\exp(-\beta t)dt. \qquad (9)$$

The question of job switching arises when a disturbance to the economy leads to intersectoral wage differentials. Initially the labor market is in equilibrium and workers earn the same wage independent of the sector of employment. When a disturbance raises the price of the second commodity and the labor allocation is constant, the wage in industry 2 will increase relative to industry 1, as can be seen from (2). In view of this wage differential, workers will consider job switching, and the question arises whether one can identify those workers who have the greatest incentive to move to the other industry. With this question in mind, we define $B(s)$, the net benefit of job switching to a worker of age $s$ currently employed in industry 1, as:

$$B(s) = \int_{\tau(s)}^{T-s} w_2(t)\exp(-\beta t)dt - \int_{0}^{T-s} w_1(t)\exp(-\beta t)dt. \qquad (10a)$$

Now,

$$\partial B/\partial s = -w_2[\tau(s)]\exp[-\beta\tau(s)](d\tau/ds) - w_2(T-s)\exp[-\beta(T-s)] + w_1(T-s)\exp[-\beta(T-s)] < 0 \qquad (10b)$$

since $d\tau/ds > 0$ for workers who have completed their initial training, and since the wage in the second industry is at least as high as in the first industry at the time of the workers' retirements $(T-s)$ periods later – and this implies that *the benefits from switching jobs decline with the age of the worker*. This means that, after an unanticipated rise in the wage of the second relative to first industry, young workers of the first industry have greater incentives to switch jobs than middle-aged workers who, in turn, have greater incentives to switch than old workers.

The reasons for young workers to be more inclined to switch are twofold. First, it takes less time to complete retraining as younger workers retain more general knowledge from their initial schooling than do older workers; second, younger workers benefit from the spread between the two industries' wage rates for a longer time than older workers.[5]

## 3. ADJUSTMENTS IN THE LABOR MARKET AFTER A DISTURBANCE

The labor market of this modified specific factor economy is in equilibrium when wage rates are the same in both sectors and are anticipated to remain the same in the future. With $w_1(t) = w_2(t)$ for each worker's relevant decision horizon, none of the current workers or trainees have incentives to switch and new entries to this world are indifferent between the sectors for which they can be trained. In each period there are retirements of the oldest workers who, in turn, are replaced by newly trained young workers.

Any unanticipated change in relative commodity prices – say as the result of a new trade policy – disturbs the long-run equilibrium of the labor market. A rise in the second commodity's price leads to:

$$p\partial f_2(\underline{L}_2, V_2)/\partial L_2 = \underline{w}_2(0) > \underline{w}_1(0) = \partial f_1(\underline{L}_1, V_1)/\partial L_1, \tag{11}$$

where the prevailing long-run equilibrium level of employment in industry $j$ is shown as $\underline{L}_j$. The wage rate in sector $j$ at the new price, but prevailing long-run labor allocation, is denoted by $\underline{w}_j(0)$. If the new commodity price is expected to be permanent, all newborn generations of workers have the incentive to seek initial training in the second industry only.[6] Furthermore, we assume here that the resulting wage differential is sufficiently large that at least some workers of industry 1 want to be retrained for industry 2.

Earlier, we demonstrated that younger workers have a stronger incentive to switch from the low- to the high-paying sector than older workers. There exists a marginally switching generation of age $\sigma$, such that all workers in industry 1 younger than $\sigma$ will switch and all workers older than $\sigma$ will stay in their current jobs.[7] When the second commodity's price increase is sufficiently

[5] A corresponding relationship between the benefits from switching and a person's age is not as clear-cut for people who are still in initial training. The rule that younger trainees have a greater incentive to switch than older trainees holds, however, under the condition that older trainees save relatively little retraining time based on their prior schooling experience.

[6] If a price change is just temporary, in the sense that it will be reversed by the time the current decision makers have reached completion of their training or retraining periods, there will be no adjustments in the labor market. The higher incomes of workers in industry 2 are just temporary, but will not lead to a reallocation of labor between sectors.

[7] One can show that some mild additional restriction also assures that the incentive to switch for initial trainees is greater than for current workers. The restriction is that for older initial trainees the experience from longer training shortens the time required for retraining in the other sector only modestly. For the remainder of the paper we assume that this restriction holds.

large to bring about job switching, the immediate effect on employment in industry 1 is that all its workers of age $\sigma$ or younger, namely $S(\sigma)$, quit their jobs, where

$$S(\sigma) = \int_{\underline{\tau}-\sigma}^{0} \lambda_1(t)dt \tag{12}$$

and where $\lambda_1(t)$ denotes the instantaneous rate of retirement from industry 1 in some past period $t$ which, in turn, measures the instantaneous rate at which the now switching workers had entered the same industry as new workers at that time $t$. For example, the marginal (oldest) generation of job switchers had joined the first industry as new workers $(\sigma - \underline{\tau}) > 0$ periods ago to replace old workers who then were retiring at a rate of $\lambda_1(\underline{\tau} - \sigma)$. Immediately after the disturbance, at $t = 0$, all workers who had replaced retirees of the first industry during the preceding $(\sigma - \underline{\tau})$ periods instantly leave industry 1. This initial loss in manpower by sector 1 through *job switching* is followed by a gradual decline in employment through *attrition*. From the time of the initial shock, $t = 0$, until the adjustment process comes to an end, at $t = z$, workers keep retiring at a rate of $\lambda_1(t)$, but they are no longer replaced; all individuals who were in initial training for industry 1 at the time of the disturbance have switched their training and all newly entering initial trainees receive schooling exclusively for industry 2 employment. Accordingly, the employment level in industry 1, at time $\hat{t}$ is:

$$L_1(\hat{t}) = \underline{L}_1 - S(\sigma) - \int_0^{\hat{t}} \lambda_1(t)dt \quad \text{for} \quad 0 \leqslant \hat{t} \leqslant z. \tag{13}$$

The adjustment process of labor employment in industry 2 is a bit less straightforward. First of all, it must be stressed that industry 2 employment at the time of the disturbance and for some time thereafter remains exactly as it was before the disturbance; none of the existing workers are leaving and there are no net additions to the workforce since the job switchers from the first industry have not yet completed their requisite retraining. It is not until $\tau_0$ periods after the disturbance, when the generation of the most recent industry 1 trainees has been retrained, that the second industry's labor force begins to expand; that is:

$$L_2(\hat{t}) = \underline{L}_2 \quad \text{for all} \quad 0 \leqslant \hat{t} < \tau_0. \tag{14a}$$

After period $\tau_0$, the youngest of the retrained workers, as well as the oldest of the initial trainees for industry 1, are retrained and ready to start work. We define the instantaneous rate of inflow of switching workers and switching trainees by $\mu(t)$ and $\mu^*(t)$, respectively. Switching workers keep flowing into industry 2 until the oldest of them have completed retraining at time $\tau(\sigma)$, and switching trainees keep flowing in until the youngest of them, the generation that had just started school at the time of the disturbance, is retrained at time $\underline{\tau}$, where $\underline{\tau} > \tau(\sigma)$, as we know from Figure 1. It should be noted that the total number of switching workers absorbed by industry 2 at time $\tau(\sigma)$ is equal to the total number of workers that left industry 1 immediately after the disturbance, $S(\sigma)$, and that the total number of switching trainees that become fully absorbed by industry 2 at time $\underline{\tau}$ is exactly the same as the total number of people in initial training for industry 1 at the time of the disturbance. It follows that:

$$L_2(\hat{t}) = \underline{L}_2 + \int_{\tau_0}^{\hat{t}} [\mu(t) + \mu^*(t)]dt \quad \text{for} \quad \tau_0 \leq \hat{t} < \tau(\sigma) \tag{14b}$$

$$L_2(\hat{t}) = \underline{L}_2 + S(\sigma) + \int_{\tau_0}^{\hat{t}} \mu^*(t)dt \quad \text{for} \quad \tau(\sigma) \leq \hat{t} < \underline{\tau}, \tag{14c}$$

where

$$S(\sigma) = \int_{\tau_0}^{\tau(\sigma)} \mu(t)dt = \int_{\underline{\tau}-\sigma}^{0} \lambda_1(t)dt \quad \text{and} \quad \int_{\tau_0}^{\underline{\tau}} \mu^*(t)dt = \int_0^{\underline{\tau}} \lambda_1(t)dt.$$

Finally, there is the interval from the time all retrainees, workers as well as initial trainees, have been absorbed by the expanding industry 2 at time $\underline{\tau}$ and the end of the adjustment process at time $z$. During all that time the economy is fully employed, as there is nobody left in retraining, and industry 2 employment keeps growing at the same rate as workers retire from industry 1 without being replaced, namely at rate $\lambda_1(\tau)$. Hence,

$$L_2(\hat{t}) = \underline{L}_2 + S(\sigma) + \int_0^{\hat{t}} \lambda_1(t)dt \quad \text{for} \quad \underline{\tau} \leq \hat{t} \leq z. \tag{14d}$$

The aim of this paper is to demonstrate how an unanticipated price change affects the *permanent incomes* of an industry's old and young workers in a differential manner while *current incomes* of old and young workers remain the same. Each worker is assumed to own one unit of labor. Hence, current income of a worker in industry $j$ is given by the wage rate received whose value, as indicated by (2), crucially depends on the level of employment in industry $j$; that is $w_j = w_j(L_j)$.

Considering (13) and (14a)–(14d), which describe the level of employment at a given time, Figure 2 traces the paths of the two sectors' wage rates from the time of the shock, $t = 0$, until the adjustment is finished at $t = z$. The pre-disturbance, initial long-run equilibrium wage rate is indicated by $\underline{w}$. A price increase of the second commodity raises the wage, measured in terms of good one, in the second industry to $w_2(0)$ and keeps the wage in the first industry unchanged at $w_1(0) = \underline{w}$, given the long-run allocation of labor at $(\underline{L}_1, \underline{L}_2)$. This long-run labor allocation, however, does not stay in place as job switching instantly reduces employment in industry 1 by $S(\sigma)$ and thereby raises the sector's wage to $w_1'(0) > \underline{w}$. The ensuing gradual outflow of labor from industry 1, all through attrition, raises the first sector's wage over time until it attains the new long-run equilibrium value of $w(z) > w_1'(0)$. In the expanding industry 2, the wage of $w_2(0)$ remains unchanged for the first $\tau_0$ periods after the disturbance, until the first group of job switchers completes retraining and adds to employment in industry 2. From time $\tau_0$ until the end of the adjustment at time $z$ there is a constant inflow of labor to industry 2, first as job switchers and initial training switchers join industry 2 and later as all

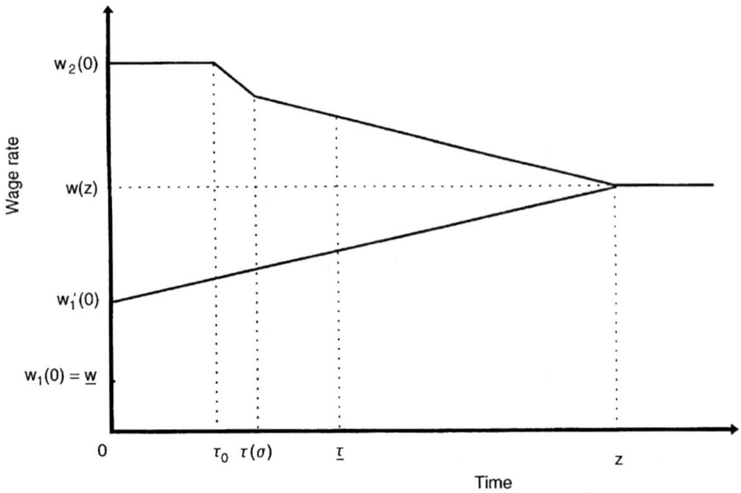


*Figure 2*

new trainees flow into the expanding industry; during this time, the wage rate of sector 2 decreases monotonically until it reaches the new long-run level of $w(z)$.

The description of labor market adjustments introduced two critical variables, namely the length of the adjustment process, $z$, and the age of the marginal job switcher $\sigma$, without providing an explanation of how their values are selected. In fact, those values are determined endogenously. Starting with the value of $z$, the adjustment process is completed when enough labor has been reallocated, through job switching and attrition, that the expanding and contracting sectors' wage rates have again become the same; that is:

$$w_2[L_2(z)] = w_1[L_1(z)], \qquad (15)$$

where $L_1(z)$ and $L_2(z)$ were defined by (13) and (14$d$), respectively.

The age of the marginal job switcher, $\sigma$, on the other hand, is determined by the condition that the person is indifferent between switching jobs and staying in the contracting industry; that is, the value of $\sigma$ is such that:

$$\int_{\tau(\sigma)}^{T-\sigma} w_2[L_2(t)] \exp(-\beta t)dt = \int_0^{T-\sigma} w_1[L_1(t)] \exp(-\beta t)dt. \qquad (16)$$

The left-hand side of the equation expresses the discounted stream of income when job switching to industry 2 takes place; the marginal job switcher is of age $\sigma$, requires $\tau(\sigma)$ retraining periods before work can start, and retires $(T-\sigma)$ periods after the shock. The right-hand side states the discounted stream of income when the same person continues employment in industry 1. Given our earlier finding that benefits from switching diminish with age, all people older than the marginal switcher have no incentive to switch and all people younger than the marginal switcher have positive incentives to switch.

## 4. POLITICAL PRESSURES FOR TRADE POLICIES

The preceding section dealt with labor market adjustments through job switching and attrition in a modified specific factor model. The adjustment process in the labor market was explicitly modeled in order to assess the heterogeneity of workers' interests in trade policies across both industry affiliations and age groups. We consider an economy that initially finds itself in long-run equilibrium, with workers of both sectors receiving the same compensation and no incentives for anyone to change jobs. All workers, independent of sector of employment and age, are equally well off. Although all workers are equally well off to start with, each can improve his wellbeing through a change in trade policies.

The objective of this section is to show that the adoption of commodity price-altering trade policies has a much greater impact on the older workers of an industry than on its younger workers; specifically, that the welfare gap that opens between the older workers of expanding and contracting industries is much larger than the gap that opens between the younger workers of the same industries.

The type of policy proposal supported by a worker and the intensity with which a worker becomes politically active depends on direction and magnitude of welfare effects emanating from such a policy. Anticipating the new trade policy to be permanent, the incentive to become politically active will be strongest for those whose utility per period, measured by $U(c, p)$, is affected the most, in either a positive or negative direction.[8] Our immediate objective is to ascertain how large the welfare effects of a policy are for a worker of a certain age relative to workers of different ages employed in the same industry. Since individuals below working age – all those who are still in initial training for employment in either industry – are typically not eligible to participate in the political process of a country, we look here exclusively at the welfare effects on individuals already employed.

Instantaneous or period utility of a worker of age $s$ employed in industry $j$ and facing price $p_i$ of the second commodity is described by:

$$U[c(s_j), p_i]. \tag{17}$$

Initially, the economy finds itself in long-run equilibrium, the price is $p_0$, all workers are equally well off, and nobody has an incentive to switch jobs between industries. We denote each worker's identical utility level by $\underline{U}$. If the second commodity's price were changed to $p_1 > p_0$ and this change was not anticipated, the gain in welfare to a worker of age $s$ employed in industry $j$

[8] An increase in the second commodity's price raises (lowers) welfare of a worker relative to the status quo if the elasticity of period consumption expenditure with respect to price exceeds (falls short of) the worker's expenditure share on the second good (Ruffin and Jones, 1977, p. 338).

would be:

$$\Delta U(s_j) = U[c(s_j), p_1] - \underline{U}. \tag{18}$$

Since all worker's face the same price $p_1$ at a given time and this price is anticipated to remain unchanged over time, a worker's welfare change per period depends only on how period consumption is related to a worker's age and industry of employment. In the preceding section, we examined the flow of income of workers over time as they are employed in different industries. Here, we consider how income, whatever its source might be, affects period consumption and how this consumption flow varies with age.

Whatever a worker's age, his consumption is limited by his lifetime expenditure constraint. The lifetime expenditure constraint of a worker of age $s$, evaluated at the time of the price change, $t=0$, is:

$$\underline{c}\int_{-s}^{0} \exp(-\beta t)dt + c(s)\int_{0}^{D-s} \exp(-\beta t)dt = \int_{\underline{\tau}-s}^{0} \tilde{y}(t)\exp(-\beta t)dt + \int_{0}^{T-s} y(t)\exp(-\beta t)dt, \tag{19}$$

where $\underline{c}$ denotes past consumption per period from the person's birth until the present, $c(s)$ is newly planned period consumption for a person of age $s$, $\tilde{y}(t)$ is income received in periods up to the present, and $y(t)$ is income anticipated to be received in periods to come. Since the person under consideration is already working at the time of the price change, the first term on the right-hand side is positive, where $(s-\underline{\tau})>0$; this person started consumption $s$ periods ago at a level of $\underline{c}$, started to earn income $(s-\underline{\tau})$ periods ago at a level of $\tilde{y}(t)$ per period, and will consume at the new level of $c(s)$ for the remaining $(D-s)$ periods of his life, anticipating income $y(t)$ in period $t$ of the future. The past level of period consumption, $\underline{c}$, was determined by his lifetime expenditure constraint as viewed at the time of birth, well before the price change, when future period incomes were anticipated to be $\tilde{y}(t)$. At that time, this constraint was:

$$\underline{c}\int_{-s}^{0} \exp(-\beta t)dt + \underline{c}\int_{0}^{D-s} \exp(-\beta t)dt = \int_{\underline{\tau}-s}^{0} \tilde{y}(t)\exp(-\beta t)dt + \int_{0}^{T-s} \tilde{y}(t)\exp(-\beta t)dt. \tag{19'}$$

Using (19′) for substitution in the first term of (19), we can solve (19) for:

$$c(s) = \underline{c} + \int_{0}^{T-s} [y(t) - \tilde{y}(t)]\exp(-\beta t)dt \Big/ \int_{0}^{D-s} \exp(-\beta t)dt. \tag{20}$$

Period consumption of a worker of age $s$ critically depends on his age, in addition to society's accepted retirement age, $T$, the prevailing death age, $D$, and the differential between newly and previously anticipated income flows per period while still working. For a worker, the latter is determined by the new price, which results from a changed trade policy, and the industry of his employment.

The relationship between a worker's future period consumption and age can be shown by differentiating (20) with respect to $s<T$. This yields:

$$dc(s)/ds = -\Bigg\{\big[y(T-s) - \underline{y}\big]$$

$$\left[\exp[-\beta(T-s)]\int_0^{D-s}\exp(-\beta t)\,dt - \exp[-\beta(D-s)]\int_0^{T-s}\exp(-\beta t)\,dt\right]$$

$$+\exp[-\beta(D-s)]\int_0^{T-s}[y(t)-y(T-s)\exp(-\beta t)\,dt]\Bigg/\left\{\int_0^{D-s}\exp(-\beta t)\,dt\right\}^2, \tag{21}$$

where we substituted the constant long-run equilibrium income of the past $\underline{y}$ in place of $\tilde{y}(t)$, and added and subtracted $y(T-s)$ to the integrand of the obtained expression. In interpreting (21), we note that its second bracketed expression of the first term is positive if workers have a retirement period before death, $D>T$, and zero if there is no such retirement period, $D=T$. We also note that a person who is already retired, as $s>T$, will not experience any change in consumption expenditure per period as $c(s \geqslant T) = \underline{c}$.

The simplest situation for evaluating the relationship between age and welfare effects of commodity price changes can be described for the traditional *specific factor model* *without* *adjustment costs.* After the price of the second commodity has increased, labor is reallocated instantaneously, the wage rises from its original value of $\underline{w}$ to the new, unchanging value of $w(t) = w(T-s) = w(z)$, and this wage is the same for workers in both industries. Substituting $w(t)$ for $y(t)$ in (21), this implies that the second term in (21) vanishes while the first term is negative when $D>T$ and zero when $D=T$. This leads to the following proposition.

PROPOSITION 1

*When labor is perfectly mobile between industries and there is a positive-length retirement period, period consumption expenditure and, therefore, period utility is higher for younger workers than older workers regardless of industry of employment.*

In this paper's modified *specific factor model* *with* *adjustment costs*, the welfare effects of a commodity price change vary not only across ages but also across industries. We are starting with an evaluation of the variation of consumption streams across ages in the shrinking industry. Given our assumption that the price of the second commodity rises, the first industry is declining over time and its workers' wage path, traced out in Figure 2, implies that:

$$\underline{w} < w_1(t) \leqslant w_1(T-s) \quad \text{for all} \quad 0<t\leqslant(T-s), \tag{22}$$

with the second inequality holding for at least some $t$. Substitution of $w_1(t)$ for $y(t)$ in (21) implies that the first as well as second term is negative, resulting in the next proposition.

PROPOSITION 2

*When labor is temporarily sector-specific, a trade policy-induced commodity price change results in period consumption expenditure and utility that are lower for older workers of the declining industry than for younger workers of the same industry.*

The reason older workers benefit less than younger workers is twofold. First of all, the declining industry will eventually recover again as the wage gradually moves up to what it will be in both industries after the labor market adjustment is completed at time $z$. The older worker has less opportunity to benefit from the rising wage than the younger worker since he will leave the workforce earlier. Second, older workers will not only earn less per period while they are still working, but they also have fewer periods until they retire. In total, the older worker earns less income, but has to face the same-length retirement period as the younger worker.

For workers in the expanding industry, the interpretation of (21) is a bit more complex. As seen from Figure 2, their wage first jumps at the time of the disturbance, then stays constant, and eventually falls to the new long-run equilibrium level of $w(z)$. The situation is more complex, because age now has both a negative and positive effect on period consumption in the future. On the positive side, the older the worker the higher the pay per work period as older workers get paid during the highest wage periods only, while younger workers remain employed as the wage rate moves down towards its new, lower long-run equilibrium level. On the negative side, the number of work periods relative to retirement periods is less for older than younger workers. Whether the positive effect outweighs the negative effect critically depends on the length of the retirement period. To see this, we first focus on the positive effect, recalling from Figure 2 that:

$$\underline{w} < w_2(T-s) \leqslant w_2(t) \quad \text{for all} \quad 0 < t \leqslant (T-s), \tag{23}$$

with the second equality holding if $(T-s) < \tau_0$, meaning that retirement comes before the newly retrained workers enter the expanding industry. If, for the moment, we assume that workers never retire, such that $D = T$, then the first term on the right-hand side of (21) vanishes, such that the negative effect is eliminated, while the second term on the right of (21) is positive if $(T-s) > \tau_0$, and zero if $(T-s) < \tau_0$; this implies our next proposition.

PROPOSITION 3

*When labor is temporarily sector-specific and there is no retirement period, a trade policy-induced commodity price change benefits the oldest workers of the expanding industry the most. For workers of age $s < (T-\tau_0)$, who will retire after job switchers have completed retraining for work in the expanding industry, the benefits are less the younger the worker; for workers of age $s > (T-\tau_0)$, the benefits are independent of age.*

When there is a retirement period prior to the worker's death, then it is no longer true that the oldest workers in the expanding industry will benefit most from the trade policy change. This can be seen by evaluating (21), after defining the oldest workers as those of age $s > (T - \tau_0)$; the first term in (21) is negative, while the second term is zero since $w_2(T - s) = w_2(t)$ for $s > (T - \tau_0)$. The oldest workers enjoy the higher wage for a very short period only, but have to spread this short-period increase in income over the same number of retirement periods as workers who are not quite as old and can benefit from the higher wage for a longer period of time. This is shown by the $\phi_1$ curve in Figure 3, where $\phi_1 = dc(s; D_1)/ds$ shows the change in period consumption expenditure as a worker's age rises, given an exogenously given retirement age of $D_1$; the slope expression for $\phi_1$ is derived in the Appendix. The diagram marks a value of $s_1$ at which $c(s, D_1)$ is a maximum; $\phi_1$ is negative for workers of age $s > s_1$, meaning that period consumption declines with age for workers older than $s_1$; and $\phi_1$ is positive for workers of age $s < s_1$, meaning that period consumption rises with age as the second commodity's price rises. Workers of age $s_1$ benefit more from the policy change than any other working group in the expanding industry; that is, $\Delta U(s)$ is largest for people of age $s_1$, giving them the greatest incentive to push for a policy change that leads to an expansion of their industry. Figure 3 portrays a second curve, denoted by $\phi_2$, which is drawn for the case that the period between a worker's retirement and death is longer than it was in the construction of the $\phi_1$ curve; that is, $\phi_2$ lies to the left of $\phi_1$

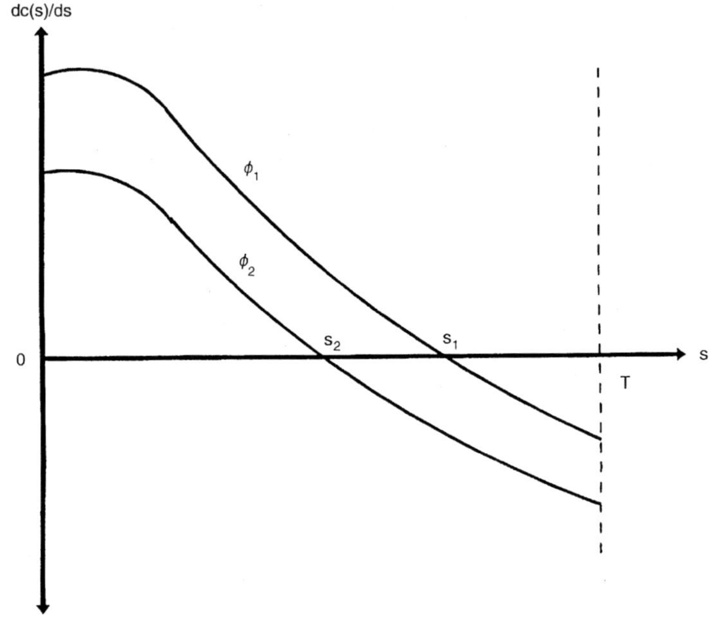


*Figure 3*

for $D_2 > D_1$, as shown in the Appendix. Our next proposition follows from the above discussion and Figure 3.

PROPOSITION 4

*When labor is temporarily sector-specific and there is a positive-length retirement period, older workers of the expanding industry tend to benefit more than much younger workers, but the very oldest workers are never the prime beneficiaries of the trade policy change. The longer the workers' retirement period, the lower is the age of the prime beneficiary in the expanding industry.*

The above proposition suggests that the incentive to push for a trade policy favorable to one's industry is greatest at an age well before retirement in economies where people enjoy rather lengthy retirement periods. The middle-aged worker might be in the best position for getting a significant lift in welfare through a change in policy. In economies where people don't retire until they are close to the time of death, on the other hand, the older groups of workers gain most from a favorable policy change. In general, the youngest workers in the expanding industry will never benefit as much from the change in policy as the middle-aged workers and older workers, unless retirement periods become extremely long.

So far, we have compared the effects of trade policy changes on period consumption expenditure for different age groups employed in the same industry. Figure 4 goes one step further, as it provides a picture of these welfare effects across both age groups and industry employment. First, it must

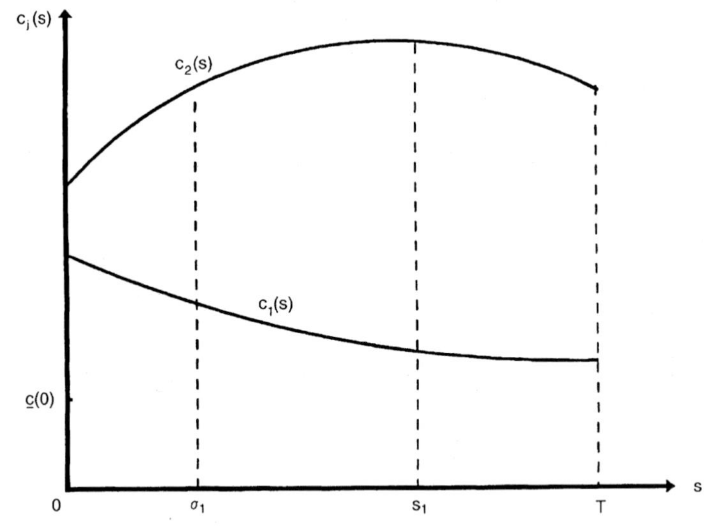


*Figure 4*

be noted that our measure of comparison, consumption per period, is expressed in terms of the first good and that the price increase of the second good raises period consumption for every worker regardless of age and industry employment. Given an institutionalized retirement period of $D_1$, the main beneficiary of the second commodity's price increase is a worker of age $s_1$ who is employed in the second industry. The main losers from the price increase of the second commodity are the very oldest workers in the contracting first industry.

It should be noted that the diagram also marks the value of $\sigma_1$, the age of the marginal job switcher, moving from industry 1 to industry 2. Workers younger than the marginal job switcher, $s < \sigma_1$, must always be better off than workers of the contracting industry that did not switch; the former could have stayed on in the second industry and they would have been better off than older non-switchers of the same industry, but they found it to their advantage to switch. Although we can definitely conclude that job switchers are better off than those older workers who remain in the declining industry, one cannot draw the same conclusion among different age groups of those workers who do switch; it is not necessarily the case that a younger switcher is always better off than an older switcher.

Finally, we point out that the gap in period consumption, and therefore utility, between people of the same age tends to be smallest among the young people and far more substantial among middle-aged and older workers. This implies that, if utility rises for some people and falls for other people when the price of the second commodity rises, the strongest push for a price increase comes from middle-aged and older workers of the second industry while the strongest opposition comes from the older workers of the first industry. It follows that alternative policy positions of competing politicians concern the youngest workers far less than middle-aged and older workers. Consequently, political activism among younger workers tends to be less than among older workers.

## 5. CONCLUDING REMARKS

A country's actual trade policies reflect the economic interests of different individuals and groups that have the ability to influence the political process. Concerning these economic interests, both the traditional specific factor model and the Heckscher–Ohlin model suggest that all workers, independent of industry of employment and age, have the same economic interests with respect to trade policy formation. Empirical evidence, on the other hand, suggests that the economic interests of workers with respect to trade policies are far from homogeneous. The objective of this paper was to modify the traditional specific factor model such that heterogeneity of economic interests across age groups and industries of employment emerges. There are two key assumptions in this modification of the traditional model: one is that there are adjustment costs for workers that want to move between industries, the other is that the lives of workers are finite. The first of these assumptions leads to a divergence of interests on the basis of industry employment; the second, when combined with the first, brings out the importance of age among otherwise identical people.

This paper contains a rather detailed model of labor reallocation between industries. These details are essential in order to understand why a given disturbance to the economy has different implications for individuals of different age. The repercussions of a disturbance, described by the adjustment process and a new long-run equilibrium, are played out over an infinite period of time. The lives of individuals, however, are finite and a person of a certain age will experience only a small part of these repercussions. Although we do not explore this issue explicitly, the model suggests that a policy may lead to long-term losses for certain factor owners after an initial period of temporary gains. In such a situation, older generations of people might support such a policy, even if it is detrimental to the factor they own in the long run.

Our modified specific factor model focuses on the welfare effects of a trade policy change on workers only. We did not say anything about what happens to specific factor owners as a result of the increase in price of the second commodity. It is relatively simple to show that age again plays an important role in determining their economic interests but, in contrast to labor, the youngest specific factor owners are affected more than the older ones. The reason for the reversal in the role of age is that the youngest specific factor owner experience the full reallocation of labor which raises the specific factor return of the expanding industry and lowers that of the declining industry over time. Accordingly, the youngest specific factor owners of the expanding (declining) industry benefit (lose) the most and the oldest factor owners of the expanding (declining) industry benefit (lose) the least.

## APPENDIX

### A. *Slope of the $\phi(s)$ function*

Defining $\phi(s) = dc(s)/ds$, we differentiate (21) with respect to $s$ to obtain:

$$\frac{dc^2(s)}{ds^2} = \frac{dy(T-s)}{dt}\left[\exp[-\beta(T-s)]\Big/\int_0^{D-s}\exp(-\beta t)dt\right]$$
$$+\frac{dc(s)}{ds}\left\{\beta+\left[2\exp[-\beta(D-s)]\Big/\int_0^{D-s}\exp(-\beta t)dt\right]\right\}.$$

Income, $y(t)$, recieved by workers in the second industry is $w_2(t)$ and, from Figure 2, we know that $dw_2(T-s)/dt$ is non-positive. Accordingly, $dc(s)/ds$ is downward sloping whenever $dc(s)/ds<0$. Also, there is a unique value of $s^*$, where $dc(s^*)/ds=0$, provided $dw_2(T-s)/dt<0$. The later expression holds for all age groups for which $s>T-\tau_0$.

### B. *Shifts of the $\phi(s)$ function*

The value of $s^*$, at which $dc(s^*)/ds=0$, depends on the value of $D$, as can be seen from (21). Accordingly, $dc[s^*(D), D]/ds=0$ determines the value of $s^*$

at which $\phi(s^*) = 0$. Differentiating this expression with respect to $D$ yields:

$$\frac{ds^*(D)}{dD} = -\frac{\partial^2 c[s^*(D), D]}{\partial s \partial D} \Bigg/ \frac{\partial^2 c[s^*(D), D]}{\partial s^2} < 0,$$

where the denominator has been shown to be negative for a unique value of $s^*$ and

$$\frac{\partial^2 c[s^*(D), D]}{\partial s \partial D} = -\Bigg\{[y(T-s) - \underline{y}] \exp[-\beta(T-s)]$$

$$\times \left[ \exp[-\beta(D-s)] \int_0^{D-s} \exp(-\beta t)\, dt \right] \Bigg\} \Bigg/ \left\{ \int_0^{D-s} \exp(-\beta t)\, dt \right\}^2 < 0.$$

Accordingly, the $\phi(.)$ schedule shifts to the left as $D$ increases relative to $T$.

## REFERENCES


Aizenman, J. and J. A. Frenkel (1988) "Sectoral Wages and the Real Exchange Rate," *Journal of International Economics* 24, 69–91.

Crewe, I. (1981) "Electoral Participation," in D. Butler, H. R. Penniman, and A. Ranney (eds), *Democracy at the Polls*, Washington, DC: American Enterprise Institute for Public Policy Research.

Diamond, P. A. (1982) "Protection, Trade, Adjustment Assistance, and Income Distribution," in J. N. Bhagwati (ed.), *Import Competition and Response*, Chicago: University of Chicago Press, 123–145.

Findlay, R. and S. Wellisz (1982) "Endogenous Tariffs, the Political Economy of Trade Restrictions, and Welfare," in J. N. Bhagwati (ed.), *Import Competition and Response*, Chicago: University of Chicago Press, 223–234.

Jones, R. W. (1971) "A Three Factor Model in Theory, Trade, and History," in J. N. Bhagwati *et al.* (eds), *Trade, Balance of Payments, and Growth*, Amsterdam: North-Holland, 3–21.

Kamien, M. I. and N. L. Schwartz (1991) *Dynamic Optimization*, Amsterdam: North-Holland.

Lapan, H. E. (1976) "International Trade, Factor Market Distortions, and the Optimal Dynamic Subsidy," *American Economic Review* 66, 335–346.

Lipset, S. M. (1960) *Political Man*, Garden City, NY: Doubleday.

Mussa, M. (1978) "Dynamic Adjustment in the Heckscher–Ohlin–Samuelson Model," *Journal of Political Economy* 86, 775–791.

—— (1982a) "Government Policy and the Adjustment Process," in J. N. Bhagwati (ed.), *Import Competition and Response*, Chicago: University of Chicago Press, 73–120.

—— (1982b) "Imperfect Factor Mobility and the Distribution of Income," *Journal of International Economics* 12, 125–141.

Neary, P. (1982) "Intersectoral Capital Mobility, Wage Stickiness, and the Case of Adjustment Assistance," in J. N. Bhagwati (ed.), *Import Competition and Response*, Chicago: University of Chicago Press, 39–69.

Ruffin, R. and R. W. Jones (1977) "Protection and Real Wages: The Neoclassical Ambiguity," *Journal of Economic Theory* 14, 337–348.

Staiger, R. W. and G. Tabellini (1987) "Discretionary Trade Policy and Excessive Protection," *American Economic Review* 77, 823–837.

United States Bureau of the Census (1988) "Voting and Registration in the Elections of November, 1988," *Current Population Reports*, Series P-20. No. 440.

Wolfinger, R. E. and S. J. Rosenstone (1980) *Who Votes?*, New Haven: Yale University Press.

ECONOMICS AND POLITICS 0954-1985
Volume 6 March 1994 No. 1

# INTEREST GROUPS, ELECTORAL COMPETITION, AND PROBABILISTIC VOTING FOR TRADE POLICIES*

WOLFGANG MAYER AND JUN LI

Current models of trade policy formation in representative democracies lack the microfoundations from which the political actions of voters, interest groups, and policy makers can be deduced. This paper provides microfoundations for the most influential of representative democracy models, the Magee-Brock-Young (MBY) model. Probabilistic voting is formally introduced, the conditions for active lobbying are examined, uniqueness of lobbying equilibrium is established, and the responses of different groups' lobbying to exogenous changes are discussed. Finally, the existence of tariff equilibria is studied when, different from MBY, both parties share a common strategy space.

## 1. INTRODUCTION

ENDOGENOUS TRADE policy formation has been analyzed in direct and representative democracy frameworks.[1] Direct democracy models (Baldwin 1976 and Mayer 1984) emphasize the role of individual voters who choose policies through majority voting; lobbies have no influence on the outcome and the government's function is that of a voting rule. Representative democracy models (Brock and Magee 1978 and Findlay and Wellisz 1982) focus on the role of interest groups that influence vote-maximizing politicians with the goal of shaping policies favorable to their group members. Lobbying groups can gain influence over politicians since individual voters are incompletely informed and rationally ignorant.

Representative democracy models have been criticized for their lack of microfoundations of the political process (Austen-Smith 1991, Nelson 1988, and Weck-Hannemann 1991). In particular, these models are not explicit about who the general voters are and how they participate in the political process;[2] they frequently do not state whether lobbying consists of campaign contributions or

*An earlier version of this paper was entitled "Reevaluating the Magee-Brock-Young Analysis when Probabilistic Voting is Formally Specified". Comments by two anonymous referees, participants at the 12th Annual Conference on International Trade at the University of Western Ontario, and members of the trade workshop at the University of Florida are greatly appreciated.

[1] For a survey of these models, see Hillman (1989).

[2] In the first part of MBY's book, where a specific factor model is postulated, the mobile factor's owners presumably are the general voters; in the second part of the book, where a Heckscher-Ohlin framework with labor and capital lobbies is assumed, general voters apparently do not own any factors.

information transmission, even though different forms of lobbying generate significantly different lobbying functions;[3] and they make no attempt to relate the assumption of parties maximizing their probability of getting elected to the formal probabilistic voting literature.[4]

The purpose of this paper is to provide explicit microfoundations for the political process in a representative democracy model when voting is probabilistic. The actions of the three major agents, namely political parties, interest groups, and general voters, are fully described. We provide the microfoundations for the most influential of representative democracy models, namely the Magee-Brock-Young (1989) or MBY model. A comparison of our findings with their major theorems suggests a need for laying out these microfoundations for other reduced-form political economy models as well.[5]

To accomplish our objective, this paper retains the basic structure of the MBY model and adds new features only in its probabilistic voting formulation and in establishing logical consistency. In particular, we adopt the MBY assumption that trade policies are chosen by the winner of a two-party election and the party policy platforms are influenced by both interest groups and voters. Also, we keep the assumption that interest groups exert influence through campaign contributions and that campaigning by parties uses up income directly rather than certain types of resources.[6] Our paper changes the MBY model in regard to probabilistic voting by replacing MBY's ad hoc formulation with a formally structured probabilistic voting model, based on Hinich, Ledyard, and Ordeshook (1972), Hinich (1977), Enelow and Hinich (1984), Coughlin (1986, 1992), Austen-Smith (1987), Lindbeck and Weibull (1987), Mueller (1989), and Coughlin, Mueller, and Murrell (1990a, 1990b).[7] Furthermore, this paper explicitly describes the identity of general voters and their incentives to vote for a certain party in the election.

The next section lays out the model's economic and political structure. The economy's production is described by a two-industry specific factor model in which labor is mobile between industries. In the political arena, only the owners of specific factors have the ability to form lobbying groups, whereas both workers

[3] The importance of distinguishing between the two forms of lobbying has been pointed out by Austen-Smith (1991). Lobbying functions for trade policies, when lobbying consists of information transmission about voter characteristics, are examined in Mayer (1992).

[4] This is the main issue raised by Austen-Smith (1991). Munger (1991) also pointed out that maximizing the probability of winning elections in the MBY model has little to do with the theory of probabilistic voting. A recent survey of the probabilistic voting literature, initiated by Hinich, Ledyard, and Ordeshook (1972), Hinich (1977), Enelow and Hinich (1984) and others, can be found in Coughlin (1992).

[5] Grossman and Helpman (1992) develop the microfoundations for a different type of political economy model, namely one in which lobbying groups offer contributions to incumbent officeholders. Riezman and Wilson (1993), on the other hand, build the structure of a model with electoral competition which is to examine the effects of partial restrictions on political competition.

[6] In contrast, Bhagwati (1982) and Findlay and Wellisz (1982) assume that resources are directly employed in the production of lobbying activities.

[7] Probabilistic voting models are not free of serious shortcomings. In particular, the existence of equilibrium requires stringent restrictions on the models, as Slutsky (1986) showed.

and specific factor owners are voters. Policies are chosen by the winner of a two-party election, voting is probabilistic, and lobbying takes the form of campaign contributions. In this model, we examine whether interest groups engage in lobbying, to whom they make lobbying contributions, and how the intensity of lobbying by one relative to the other group is affected by the tariff platforms of competing parties, the size and ideology of interest groups, and the number of general or non-interest group voters. In contrast to MBY and Findlay and Wellisz (1982), uniqueness of the lobbying equilibrium is not assumed but examined. Finally, the political parties' choices of tariff platforms are determined. Although uniqueness of policy choices cannot be assured, one possible equilibrium is shown to be identical tariff platforms for both parties.

## 2. REFORMULATING THE MBY MODEL

### 2.1 *The Economy*

The economy is made up of two competitive industries whose firms employ an industry-specific factor $H = 1,2$ and intersectorally mobile labor to produce final commodity $X_H$.[8] Industry production functions are homogeneous of degree one in labor and the relevant specific factor, and there are no distortions and externalities. The economy is open and small,[9] and factors of production are inelastically supplied by the country's $N$ people, of which $N^0$ own one unit of labor and $N^H$ own one unit of factor $H$ such that:

$$N^0 + N^1 + N^2 = \mathrm{N}. \tag{1}$$

All factors are completely immobile between countries, and the second industry is import competing.

Each factor-supplying individual is a consumer in economic markets, and a voter as well as potential lobby member in political markets. Person $i$, owning one unit of factor $j = 0,1,2$, has the indirect utility function:

$$U^{iJ} = U(p, y^{iJ}), \tag{2}$$

where $p$ is the price of the second or import good in terms of good one and $y^{ij} = (w^J + T^{iJ} - c^{iJ})$ is income spent on consumption. In the income expression, $w^J$ denotes the return on factor J, $T^{iJ}$ is tariff revenues received, and $c^{iJ}$ is campaign contributions made by person $i$ owning factor $J$. Campaign contributions can be made to either political party,

[8] This model is also employed by Findlay and Wellisz (1982) and, in less specific form, in the first part of MBY.

[9] For a large economy, with unbiased tariff revenue redistribution, the political pressures for trade policies remain unchanged; each person's optimal tariff is what it would be in a small economy when added to the large country's optimal tariff rate which is common to all people (Mayer and Riezman 1987).

$$c^{iJ} = c_1^{iJ} + c_2^{iJ}, \tag{3}$$

where subscript $g$ in $c_g^{iJ}$ refers to party $g = 1,2$ receiving the contribution.

Factor returns respond to changes in ad valorem import tariffs, t, as derived in Jones (1971), Mayer (1974), or Mussa (1974):

$$\frac{dw^1}{dt}\frac{(1+t)}{w^1} < 0 < \frac{dw^0}{dt}\frac{(1+t)}{w^0} < 1 < \frac{dw^2}{dt}\frac{(1+t)}{w^2}. \tag{4}$$

A tariff increase on good two definitely lowers factor income for owners of specific factor one, while raising labor income less than proportionately and income of specific factor two more than proportionately.

Receipt of tariff revenues by person $i$ of factor group $J$ is assumed to depend on the prevailing tariff rate: $T^{iJ} = Tp^{iJ}(t)$ where $\partial T^{iJ}/\partial t > 0$ at least for low tariffs.[10] Considering the dependence of $w^J$, $T^{iJ}$, and $p = \pi(1+t)$, where $\pi$ is the constant world price of good two, on tariff rate $t$, the indirect utility function for a representative owner of factor J can be restated as:

$$\Psi^J(t,c^J) = U[\pi(1+t), w^J(t) + T^J(t) - c^J], \tag{2'}$$

where utility depends on the tariff rate, chosen by the winning political party, and campaign contributions by the owner of factor $J$. Superscripts $i$ are deleted since all owners of the same factor have the same utility functions, receive the same tariff revenues, and pay the same lobbying expenditures.

MBY (p. 268) do not employ the general indirect utility function of (2′); instead they use:

$$\Psi^J(t,c^J) = w^J(t) - c^J. \tag{2''}$$

This simplified utility function implies that both the price effect on real income and the tariff redistribution influence on money income are disregarded. In addition, the marginal utility of income is one, making factor owners risk neutral in income.

As our goal is to build microfoundations for the MBY model, we retain as many of its features as possible. We, therefore, adopt the MBY specification for the utility functions of specific factor owners – who may form lobbying groups – as stated in (2″). On the other hand, the utility function of workers – who make up the group of general voters – must be changed to accommodate lobbying in the form of campaign contributions.[11] We, therefore, postulate that

[10] When the revenues distribution formula is given, individual tariff receipts depend on total tariff revenues collected which, in turn, are positively related to tariff rates when the latter are small.

[11] MBY do not tell us what the general voter's utility function is. However, if lobbying takes the form of campaign contributions, and these contributions are used by political parties to clarify their positions to uncertain voters, clarification will be effective only if general voters are risk averse (Schepsle 1972).

each worker's utility function is given by (2′), with the additional restriction of $\Psi^0_{tt}<0$, making general voters risk averse in tariff rates.

Voting and lobbying decisions are driven by the welfare effects of tariffs on the three factor-owning groups. Given the utility function of (2″) and the factor income responses of (4), a tariff increase always improves (lowers) welfare of specific factor owners in the import (export) industry. For the working general public, on the other hand, a tariff's welfare effect is far less obvious, as differentiation of (2′) with respect to t and use of Roy's identity reveals:

$$\Psi^0_t = [\partial U/\partial y^0]\,[-\pi D^0_2 + (\mathrm{d}w^0/\mathrm{d}t) + (\mathrm{d}T^0/\mathrm{d}t)]. \tag{5}$$

The first term inside the parenthesis, where $D^0_2$ is the representative worker's demand for good two, is negative, whereas the second and third terms are positive. Given the assumption that $\Psi^0_{tt}<0$, the optimal tariff rate for workers, $\tilde{t}^0$, can be determined. Workers lose (gain) from a tariff increase if the actual tariff exceeds (falls short of) $\tilde{t}^0$.

### 2.2 The Political Process

Two political parties compete in an election whose winner gains the right to set the country's tariff rates. Each party maximizes its probability of getting elected, parties may receive campaign contributions from lobbying groups, and voting is probabilistic. The model departs from MBY in that it attempts a complete specification of probabilistic voting in the presence of campaign contributions. Following Austen-Smith (1987), we assume uncertainty on the part of both voters and political parties. Voters are uncertain about the parties' tariffs to be adopted, and political parties are uncertain about the voters' non-policy preferences. Voter uncertainty can be reduced through policy-clarifying campaign activities of parties provided voters are risk averse in tariffs, and lobbies gain influence on parties by funding the required campaign expenditures. Political party uncertainty, on the other hand, comes from parties not knowing voter preferences for non-policy considerations such as ideology of and personalities in the party. The assumption of random non-policy voting preferences justifies the introduction of probabilistic voting.

Each party's goal is to maximize the probability of getting elected. The election of party $g=1,2$ affects a voter's utility through the economic impact of its tariff platform, $t_g$, and its non-policy characteristics. Voters are uncertain about tariff platforms, but fully cognizant of the party's non-policy characteristics. Stated more precisely, expected utility of individual $i$ with factor ownership $J$ yielded by the election of party $g$, $V^{iJ}_g$, consists of expected utility from the tariff policy to any member of group $J$, $E[\Psi^J(t_g,c^J)]$, plus utility from the non-policy characteristics, $\zeta^{iJ}_g$; that is:

$$V^{iJ}_g = E[\Psi^J(t_g,c^J)] + \zeta^{iJ}_g. \tag{6}$$

The expected tariff policy effect, $E[\Psi^J(t_g,c^J)]$, which both political parties are assumed to know fully, is the same for all owners of factor $J$, making superscripts for individual $i$ superfluous. The non-policy effect of getting party g elected, $\zeta_g^{iJ}$, on the other hand, varies among people with the same factor ownership, and these personal non-policy voting preferences are not fully known to the parties.

The $i$th person's vote is based on the value of:

$$V_1^{iJ} - V_2^{iJ} = z^J - \beta^{iJ}, \tag{7}$$

where $z^J = \{E[\Psi^J(t_1,c^J)] - E[\Psi^J(t_2,c^J)]\}$ measures the expected *economic gains* from having the first rather than second party elected and $\beta^{iJ} = (\zeta_2^{iJ} - \zeta_1^{iJ})$ is the *personal preference bias* of the $i$th person of group $J=0,1,2$ in favor of party 2. The probability that person $i$ of group $j$ votes for party one is:

$$\phi^{iJ} = \begin{cases} 1 \text{ if } z^J > \beta^{iJ} \\ 0 \text{ if } z^J \leqslant \beta^{iJ} \end{cases}, \tag{8}$$

making each individual's choice deterministic, as each person has full knowledge of the value of $\beta^{iJ}$. The political parties, on the other hand, are unable to observe $\beta^{iJ}$ and do not know each individual's value of the non-policy bias term. The parties do, however, possess some information about the distribution of the biases over all individuals of group J, expressed by a twice continuously differentiable distribution function $F^J(\beta^J)$ with everywhere positive density $f^J(\beta^J)$. The density functions are assumed to be unimodal and symmetric.

Parties tend to have more information about the voting preferences of interest groups than about the voting preferences of general voters. Accordingly, we assume that each party knows the density functions $f^1(\beta^1)$ and $f^2(\beta^2)$. Concerning general voters (workers), both parties are assumed to know the density function for a given mean value of $\beta^0$, denoted by $\mu^0$, but they do not know with certainty what this mean value is. More precisely, the density function of the general voter's non-policy preference biases, $f^0(\beta^0|\mu^0)$, is assumed to be translate symmetric,[12] meaning that at each value of $\mu^0$ the density function is a *translate* of a common symmetric density; both parties know this common density and they share common beliefs about the probabilities of $\mu^0$ occurring, given by the twice continuously differentiable distribution function $G(\mu^0)$ with density $g(\mu^0)$ and supports $(\underline{\mu},\overline{\mu})$. The density function of $\mu^0$ is symmetric around a single mode of $\mu^0=0$, implying that parties expect general voters to be unbiased on average.

For a given mean value of the non-policy bias $\mu^J$, the fraction of factor $J$ owners voting for party 1 is given by:

$$\Pr(\beta^J < z^J) = F^J(z^J|\mu^J), \tag{9}$$

[12] The same assumptions about unimodal, symmetric, and translate symmetric density functions are made in Lindbeck and Weibull (1987).

where symmetry of $f^J(\beta^J|\mu^J)$ implies that $F^J(\mu^J|\mu^J)=1/2$, $[\partial F^J(z^J|\mu^J)/\partial z^J] = f^J(z^J|\mu^J)$, and $[\partial f^J(z^J|\mu^J)/\partial z^J]$ has the sign of $(\mu^J - z^J)$. In words, if $z^J=\mu^J$ – such that, on average, neither party has a net advantage among group J voters – then each party gets half of the group's voters; and the fraction of group $J$ voting for party 1 increases as group $J$'s economic gains from the first party's platform rise, at an increasing (decreasing) rate when a minority (majority) of the group favors the first party at prevailing tariff platforms and non-policy preferences.

The expected vote for the first party, with both parties having the same expectations, is:

$$N^0 \int_{\underline{\mu}}^{\bar{\mu}} F^0(z^0|\mu^0)g(\mu^0)d\mu^0 + N^1F^1(z^1|\mu^1) + N^2F^2(z^2|\mu^2); \tag{10}$$

while parties know how many votes they will get from the interest groups, they are not sure about how many votes they will receive from the general public.

Before we examine the lobbying equilibrium in the next section, we have to discuss the values of $z^J$, the expected economic gains to a member of group $J$ from getting the first party elected. Starting with workers, who make up the general public, they are uncertain about the parties' trade platforms to be adopted, and they are risk averse in tariffs. For each of them,

$$z^0 = E[\Psi^0(t_1)] - E[\Psi^0(t_2)], \tag{11}$$

where $c^0$ does not appear in the $\Psi^0$-function since, by assumption, mobile workers do not engage in lobbying for one or the other industry. The true value of $z^0$ is approximated through a second-order Taylor expansion of the indirect utility function $\Psi^0(t_g)$. The stochastic tariff, $t_g = \tau_g + \epsilon_g$, is assumed to have a mean of $\tau_g$ and a variance of $(s_g)^2$, with higher moments of $t_g$ negligible compared to $(s_g)^2$. Using such a Taylor expansion, one can show that:

$$E[\Psi^0(t_g)] \approx \Psi^0(\tau_g) + (s_g)^2\Psi^0_{gg}(\tau_g)/2 = \Psi^0(\tau_g) - xS_g(C_1,C_2), \tag{12}$$

where $S_g(C_1,C_2)=(s_g)^2$ and $x = -\Psi^0_{gg}/2 = -(\partial^2\Psi^0/\partial\tau_g^2)/2>0$ is assumed to be approximately constant for all $\tau_g$. According to (12), expected utility yielded to a worker by the gth party's tariff policy depends on the expected tariff rate, $\tau_g$, and the workers' faith in the announced policy, as expressed by the variance term $S_g$. Faith in an announced policy can be strengthened through clarification of the party's policy position. Expenditure on policy clarification by party $g$, defined as $C_g$, consists of the sum of contributions made to party $g$ by the $N^1$ members of the first and the $N^2$ members of the second lobby; that is:

$$C_g = N^1c^1_g + N^2c^2_g. \tag{13}$$

The effects of expenditure on policy clarification are assumed to be given by:

$$S_g' = \partial S_g/\partial C_g < 0, \quad S_g'' = \partial^2 S_g/\partial C_g^2 > 0, \quad \text{and } \partial S_j/\partial C_g = 0 \tag{14}$$

for $g \neq j = 1,2$; campaigning by party $g$ reduces voter uncertainty about the party's own policies at a decreasing rate, but has no effect on the voters' beliefs about the other party's policies; that is, negative campaigning is not part of this model.

Returning to (11), a worker's expected net gain from electing the first party can be expressed as:

$$z^0(\tau_1,\tau_2;C_1,C_2) = \Psi^0(\tau_1) - \Psi^0(\tau_2) - x[S_1(C_1) - S_2(C_2)], \tag{11'}$$

using (12) and (13). The first party can increase its advantage among general voters by raising (lowering) the expected tariff, $\tau_1$, if the latter is lower (higher) than the general voter's optimal tariff rate, $\bar{t}^0$, or by spending more on campaign clarification, $C_1$; the second party can raise its advantage in a corresponding way.

Owners of specific factor $H = 1,2$ were assumed to be risk neutral in tariffs; based on (2″), their expected net economic gain from the election of the first party is:

$$z^H(\tau_1,\tau_2) = w^H(\tau_1) - w^H(\tau_2). \tag{11''}$$

It should be noted that, in contrast to the workers' net economic gain function of (11′), $z^H$ depends on tariff platforms only, as members of lobby-forming factor groups are risk neutral.

## 3. CAMPAIGN CONTRIBUTIONS BY INTEREST GROUPS

### *3.1 Goals of Interest Groups*

The objective of each lobby is to maximize expected utility from the election outcome for all its members. Potentially, there are three distinct lobbies, namely specific factor owners of the first and the second industry, and workers. We follow Findlay and Wellisz (1982), as well as MBY, and assume that workers never form a lobby. For the two groups of specific factor owners, on the other hand, the decisions to form a lobby and to choose a certain level of campaign contributions are endogenously determined. Any operating and free-rider containment costs of the lobby are assumed away, as is done in MBY and much of the relevant literature.

Expected utility from the election outcome to person $i$, owning factor $H$, is:

$$E(V^{iH}) = \rho V_1^{iH} + (1-\rho) V_2^{iH} = \rho(z^H - \beta^{iH}) + V_2^{iH}, \tag{15}$$

where $0 \leqslant \rho \leqslant 1$, the probability of party one winning the election, is discussed later.[13]

Expected utility from the election outcome for the entire group of factor $H$ owners, $E(V^H)$, is obtained by integrating (15) over the "large number" of factor $H$ owners, yielding:

$$E(V^H) = N^H \int_{-\infty}^{\infty} \rho(z^H - \beta^H) f^H(\beta^H | \mu^H) d\beta^H + \int_{-\infty}^{\infty} [\Psi^H(\tau_2, c^H) + \zeta_2^H] h^H(\zeta_2^H) d\zeta_2^H = N^H [\rho(z^H - \mu^H) + \Psi^H(\tau_2, c^H) + \bar{\zeta}_2^H], \tag{16}$$

where $f^H(\beta^H|\mu^H)$ and $h^H(\zeta_2^H)$ denote the fraction of people in group $H$ with non-policy preference bias, $\beta^H$, and expected utility from the second party's non-policy characteristics, $\zeta_2^H$, respectively; $\mu^H$ and $\bar{\zeta}_2^H$ are the known mean values of $\beta^H$ and $\zeta_2^H$, respectively, and $\Psi^H$ had been defined in (2″).

### *3.2 The Probability of Getting Elected*

In the absence of any abstentions, the probability of party one getting elected, $0 \leqslant \rho \leqslant 1$, is equal to the probability that party one gets at least one half of the votes; that is:

$$\rho = \Pr(R \geqslant N/2), \tag{17}$$

where $R = \Sigma_0^2 N^J F^J(z^J|\mu^J)$ is the total number of votes received by party one when $\mu^J$ prevails. As stated before, the actual value of the general public's $\mu^0$ is not known and may take values between $\underline{\mu}$ and $\bar{\mu}$, whereas the values of $\mu^1$ and $\mu^2$ are known by both parties. Let us define the value of $\tilde{\mu}^0$, for which:

$$N^0 F^0(z^0|\tilde{\mu}^0) + N^1 F^1(z^1|\mu^1) + N^2 F^2(z^2|\mu^2) = N/2; \tag{18}$$

$\tilde{\mu}^0$ is the average general voter's non-policy bias in favor of party two at which, given the parties' tariff platforms and interest groups' non-policy preferences, each party receives exactly one half of all votes. If, *ceteris paribus*, the general voters' bias for party two were less than $\tilde{\mu}^0$, then party one would win the election as more of the general voters favored party one than is required to win; that is, for any $\underline{\mu} \leqslant \mu^0 \leqslant \tilde{\mu}^0$, $R \geqslant N/2$; consequently, the probability of party one winning the election is:

[13] In an earlier version of this paper, the probability of party one getting elected was incorrectly equated with the party's expected vote. We thank a referee for directing us to the discussion by Calvert (1986) on why the two concepts cannot be equated. The probability of getting elected, as introduced here, is discussed as an election goal by Aranson, Hinich, and Ordeshook (1974, 139).

$$\rho = \Pr(R \geqslant N/2) = \Pr(\mu^0 \leqslant \tilde{\mu}^0) = G(\tilde{\mu}^0), \tag{19}$$

where $G(\mu^0)$ is the previously defined cumulative distribution function of $\mu^0$, with symmetric density function $g(\mu^0)$ whose mean was assumed to be zero. $\tilde{\mu}^0$ can be interpreted as the maximum allowable non-policy bias of general voters for the second party under which party one will not lose; in the future, we simply refer to $\tilde{\mu}^0$ as the "general public's criticial bias value". The larger this critical value, the greater is the probability that party one will win. As can be seen from (18), this critical value, and therefore the probability of winning, can be influenced through campaign contributions and tariff policies; it also depends on the size of the various voter groups and the known average non-policy preference biases of the interest groups.

### 3.3 *Lobbying Equilibrium*

The objective of each lobby $H = 1,2$ is to have each member contribute that amount, $c_g^H$, to party $g = 1,2$ which maximizes $E(V^H)$ in (16). Parties spend all contributions on clarifying their own tariff positions, the latter being taken as given by interest groups. Provided $E(V^H)$ is strictly concave in $c_1^H$ and $c_2^H$, the first-order conditions for a maximum of (16) imply that:

$$\frac{\partial E(V^H)}{N^H \partial c_g^H} = (-1)^g g(\tilde{\mu}^0)\,[z^H - \mu^H]\, S_g' N^H x - 1 \leqslant 0, \quad \text{for } g = 1,2; H = 1,2 \tag{20}$$

where an equality holds if $c_g^H > 0$, and the steps of the derivation are outlined in the Appendix. The Appendix also contains explanations for four propositions which follow from (20):

**Proposition 1:** A necessary condition for a group to contribute to either party is that, at prevailing tariff platforms, the group is not indifferent between the two parties.

**Proposition 2:** If, on average, a group has a net preference for a given party, it will never contribute to the other party. If a group makes any contributions at all, it makes them to its favored party only.

**Proposition 3:** Both interest groups may contribute to the same party.

**Proposition 4:** A rise in the number of general voters makes it more likely that both interest groups make campaign contributions if, on average, general voters favor the same party at the critical value of their non-policy bias irrespective of whether the impact of tariff platforms is accounted for.

Proposition 1 states that lobbying is driven by the interest groups' overall preferences for candidates, made up of policy and non-policy considerations.

Even if both parties propose the same tariff platform, the groups might still have an incentive to lobby provided their non-policy preferences for certain parties are quite strong. This finding differs from the MBY conclusion that there will be no lobbying if both parties propose the same tariff platform, as the MBY model of probabilistic voting does not account for any non-policy biases.

Proposition 2 corresponds to the MBY campaign contribution specialization theorem, with the difference that net rather than pure policy preferences matter for the choice of parties to whom contributions are made. The critical assumption behind the campaign contribution specialization theorem is risk neutrality on the part of interest group members. If these members were risk averse, interest groups may gain from contributing to both parties (Li, 1992).

Proposition 3 raises the possibility that both interest groups support the same party, a situation that is quite likely when both groups have strong non-policy preference biases for the same party. This possibility cannot occur in MBY due to their a priori restriction that there is a proexport lobby that supports a proexport party and a protectionist lobby that supports a protectionist party.

Proposition 4 tells us that, under certain restrictions, a larger general voting public makes a better target for interest groups and, therefore, will lead to more lobbying. Campaign contributions are more likely the more effective they are in raising the probability of the interest group's preferred party getting elected. This effectiveness is raised by an increase in the size of the general population when, evaluated at the critical value of their non-policy bias, the party preference of the majority of general voters is not changed by the suggested party platforms. In the important case of both parties supporting the same tariff platform – which later is shown to be a possible tariff equilibrium – this restriction is always satisfied.

Based on (20), it is possible that neither group, one group only, or both groups engage in lobbying; and in the last case, lobbies may contribute to the same or to different parties. The equilibrium configuration which has drawn the most attention in the representative democracy literature is the one where each party receives positive contributions from one of the two interest groups. Our next objective is to examine uniqueness of equilibrium for this scenario of each interest group lobbying and each party receiving campaign contributions. We describe a specific lobbying structure by assuming that non-policy preference biases of the two groups and the tariff platforms of the two parties are such that group one has a net preference for party 1, $(z^1-\mu^1)>0$, group two has a net preference for party two, $(z^2-\mu^2)<0$, and each group has an incentive to lobby in the absence of lobbying by the other group.[14] The resulting lobbying equilibrium is portrayed in Figure 1, where $R^H_H R^H_H$ denotes the lobbying reaction curve of group $H=1,2$. Expressions for the slopes of these reaction curves are contained in the Appendix.

[14] In Figure 1, each reaction curve has a positive intercept on its own lobbying expenditure axis.

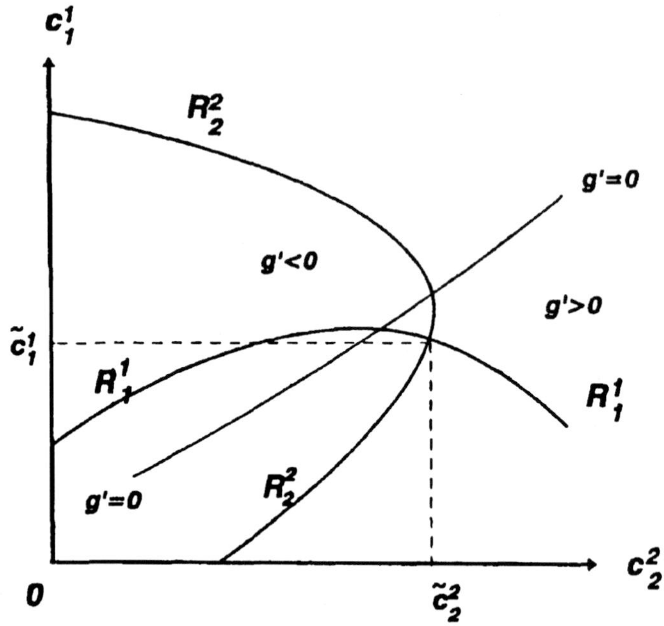


Figure 1.

The action of the first (second) lobby is the contribution level by each of its members to party one (two). Recalling the assumption that density function $g(\mu^0)$ is symmetric with a single mode at $\mu^0 = 0$, the first lobby's reaction curve is positively (negatively) sloped if general voters have a non-policy preference for the second (first) party at the critical value of $\tilde{\mu}^0$; that is, if $\tilde{\mu}^0 > 0$ or $g' < 0$ the slope is positive and if $\tilde{\mu}^0 < 0$ or $g' > 0$ the slope is negative, as indicated in Figure 1. Stated differently, if the first party can win even if general voters have on average a non-policy preference for the second party, then increases in expenditures by the second lobby will be countered by expenditure increases of the first lobby; but if the first party can win only if general voters have on average a non-policy preference for the first party, then increases in the second lobby's expenditures result in a decline in expenditures by the first interest group. Correspondingly, the reaction curves of the second interest group slope in the opposite direction of the first interest group's reaction curves, since the second group also reacts positively (negatively) to increases in the first group's lobbying when it can (cannot) win even if on average general voters favor the first party. Figure 1 reveals that the two groups' reaction curves intersect only once, making the equilibrium unique. As drawn, both interest groups engage in lobbying. However, it also is possible that only one of them lobbies.

### *3.4 Which Interest Group Spends More On Lobbying?*

Retaining the assumption that both interest groups engage in lobbying, we next examine which group spends more on lobbying and how relative lobbying expenditures, the expenditure by one relative to the other group, adjusts when some of the exogenous variables change. These questions are answered by taking the first-order conditions of (20) for ($g=1, H=1$) and ($g=2, H=2$), writing them as equalities, and dividing the first by the second equation, to obtain:

$$\frac{S_1'(C_1)}{S_2'(C_2)}=-\frac{(z^2-\mu^2)N^2}{(z^1-\mu^1)N^1}=\frac{(\mu^2-z^2)N^2}{(z^1-\mu^1)N^1}>0, \tag{21}$$

where $C_g$ is total campaign expenditure by party $g$, all paid by a single lobby. As shown in the Appendix, the next two propositions follow from (21).

**Proposition 5:** The interest group that gains more from its favored party's election, spends more on lobbying.

**Proposition 6:** Lobbying expenditure of a group rises relative to expenditure by the other group, if the former expands in size relative to the other group, if its non-policy preference biases move even stronger in favor of the already preferred party, or if a tariff change results in a greater gain from having its favored party elected relative to the opposing group's gain from having its favored party elected.

Both propositions are obtained under the assumption that the policy clarification function, $S_g(C_g)$, is the same for both parties. Proposition 5 holds in general; proposition 6, on the other hand, is derived for the specific policy clarification function $S_g=C_g^{-\alpha}$, where $\alpha>0$. The above propositions tell us that, for the specific function chosen, a group's relative lobbying expenditures are directly related to the total benefits it receives relative to the other group from having its favored party elected. The more people are in a group, the stronger the bias in favor of one's favored party, and the more a tariff change makes the group's favored party attractive relative to the attractiveness of the other party to the opposing lobby, the larger the group's total lobbying expenditures. Although one can draw these conclusions about relative total expenditures of the two groups, one generally cannot determine how absolute expenditures at the individual's level are affected by the mentioned exogenous changes.

## 4. ENDOGENOUS TARIFF EQUILIBRIUM

Political parties choose their tariff platforms with the objective of maximizing their probability of getting elected. Party one selects $\tau_1$ to maximize $\rho$ and party two selects $\tau_2$ to minimize $\rho$ which, defined in (19), can be expressed as:

$$\rho=\rho[\tau_1,\tau_2;C_1(\tau_1,\tau_2),C_2(\tau_1,\tau_2)], \tag{22}$$

considering (19), (18), (11′), and (11″), as well as the relationship between $C_g$ and $\tau_g$ implicit in (20). A party's tariff platform affects its chances of getting elected in two ways: directly, through changing the benefits from the expected policy to all voters, and indirectly, through influencing the magnitude of campaign funds made available for clarification of the parties' tariff platforms.

The Appendix states the necessary conditions for a tariff equilibrium. Considering the complexity of the model, with three different factor owners, heterogeneity of non-policy preferences, and two interest groups, it is not surprising that, at least for general functions, one cannot establish uniqueness of the tariff equilibrium. It is possible, however, to examine the much narrower question of existence of an equilibrium in which both parties select the same tariff rates. Existence of such an equilibrium is of interest since MBY explicitly preclude it when they assume that the protectionist party's choice is limited to import tariffs and the proexport party's choice is limited to export subsidies.[15]

The two parties' expected tariff platforms are the same when $\tau_1 = \tau_2$. As can be seen from (11′) and (11″), neither $z^0$ nor $z^1$ and $z^2$ will change when both parties adjust their commonly chosen tariff platforms. This, in turn, implies that the critical value of the general voters' non-policy preferences, $\tilde{\mu}^0$, which determines the probability of getting elected, also does not change directly when the common tariff platform varies. Hence, the only way the probability of getting elected could change is if variations in the common tariff altered the two lobbies' campaign contributions which indirectly would affect $z^0$. To check this possibility, we reexamine the lobbies' optimal levels of campaign contributions, as determined in (20); it reveals that neither $C_1$ nor $C_2$ are affected by the tariff change since *ceteris paribus* changes in the common tariff rate do not alter any of the variables in that equation. It follows:

**Proposition 7:** When both parties choose the same tariff platform, the probability of getting elected is independent of the level of the common tariff.

The finding that a change in the common tariff rate does not affect the value of $\rho$ means that $[(\partial\rho/\partial\tau_1)+(\partial\rho/\partial\tau_2)]=0$ for all $\tau_1=\tau_2$. Considering the entire range of possible values of tariff rates, if $(\partial\rho/\partial\tau_1)>0$ for some values of $\tau_1=\tau_2$ and $(\partial\rho/\partial\tau_1)<0$ for other values of $\tau_1=\tau_2$, then continuity of the $\rho$-function assures that there must be at least one value of $\tau_1=\tau_2$ for which $(\partial\rho/\partial\tau_1)=(\partial\rho/\partial\tau_2)=0$. For this value of $\tau_1=\tau_2$, the necessary conditions for maximizing the probability of getting elected are satisfied.

**Proposition 8:** If a party can raise its probability of getting elected for some range of common tariff values by unilaterally raising its tariff and for another range of

[15] Austen-Smith (1991, pp. 74–5) argues that "if the effective options confronting one party differ from those available to another, this is necessarily part of the phenomena to be explained and not something to be assumed."

tariff values by unilaterally lowering its tariff, then there exists at least one equilibrium in which both parties choose the same tariff.

For an economy that is greatly distorted by either very high tariffs or very high import subsidies, it generally (although not inevitably) is the case that the party which proposes a lowering of this extreme tariff or import subsidy enhances its probability of getting elected. A tariff equilibrium in which both parties advocate the same policy exists in such a case. The MBY assumption that the two parties' policy choices are not overlapping precludes such an endogenous solution.

## 5. CONCLUDING REMARKS

This paper developed the microfoundations for a representative democracy model of tariff determination and presented its findings through several propositions. In building the microfoundations, the MBY framework was retained to the extent it could be reconciled with probabilistic voting theory. This allows us now to examine the sensitivity of various MBY theorems to a more detailed specification of their own model.

Broadly speaking, our paper supports the thrust of the various MBY theorems. However, there are substantial differences in details due to the introduction of non-policy preferences, and there are more significant differences in substance due to the elimination of the MBY restrictions on parties' strategy spaces. The MBY "contribution specialization theorem" states that each lobby contributes to at most one political party; it is supported in principle through our Proposition 2, but is modified through Proposition 3 as both lobbies may contribute to the same party. The MBY "polarized policies generate greater contributions theorem" requires more significant modifications. First of all, it is generally not possible to determine changes in the absolute levels of lobbying expenditures as tariff platforms change; at best, one can determine expenditure of one relative to the other lobby when the two parties' tariff platforms become more different. Second, making a tariff platform more beneficial to one interest group brings forth lobbying responses by both interest groups and not just by the benefiting group as in MBY. Third, if one does not restrict the effect of campaigning on policy clarification to the functional description of the text, it is quite possible that the lobby that benefits from a widening of tariff positions responds less than the other lobby.

The MBY theorem that "interest groups refrain from lobbying when both parties propose the same tariff" holds when interest groups on average have no non-policy preferences for either party, but breaks down when there are significant non-policy biases. Finally, and most importantly, the MBY restrictions on the parties' tariff choice space eliminates one possible tariff equilibrium, namely the one in which both parties choose the same platform.

WOLFGANG MAYER
*Department of Economics, University of Cincinnati*
*Cincinnati, Ohio 45221-0371*

## REFERENCES

Aranson, P. H., M. J. Hinich, and P. C. Ordeshook, 1974, Election Goals and Strategies: Equivalent and Nonequivalent Candidate Objectives. *American Political Science Review* 64, 135–152.

Austen-Smith, D., 1987, Interest Groups, Campaign Contributions, and Probabilistic Voting. *Public Choice* 54, 123–152.

Austen-Smith, D., 1991, Rational Consumers and Irrational Voters: A Review Essay on "Black Hole Tariffs and Endogenous Policy Theory" by Stephen Magee, William Brock and Leslie Young, Cambridge University Press, 1989. *Economics and Politics* 3, 73–92.

Baldwin, R. E., 1976, Political Economy of Postwar US Trade Policy. *Bulletin 1976-4* (New York Graduate School of Business Administration, Center for the Study of Financial Institutions, New York).

Bhagwati, J. N., 1982, Directly-Unproductive, Profit-Seeking (DUP) Activities. *Journal of Political Economy* 90, 988–1002.

Brock, W. A. and S. P. Magee, 1978, The Economics of Special Interest Politics: The Case of Tariffs. *American Economic Review*, Proceedings 68, 246–250.

Calvert, R. L., 1986, Models of Imperfect Information in Politics, Vol. 6 of *Fundamentals of Pure and Applied Economics* (Harwood Academic Press, Chur).

Coughlin, P. J., 1986, Probabilistic Voting Models, in: S. Kotz, N. Johnson, and C. Read, eds., *Encyclopedia of Statistical Sciences*, Vol. 7 (Wiley, New York) 204–210.

Coughlin, P. J., 1992, *Probabilistic Voting Theory* (Cambridge University Press, Cambridge).

Coughlin, P. J., D. C. Mueller, and P. Murrell, 1990a, A Model of Electoral Competition with Interest Groups. *Economics Letters* 32, 307–311.

Coughlin, P. J., D. C. Mueller, and P. Murrell, 1990b, Electoral Politics, Interest Groups, and the Size of the Government. *Economic Inquiry* 28, 682–705.

Enelow, J. M. and M. J. Hinich, 1984, *The Spatial Theory of Voting* (Cambridge University Press, Cambridge).

Findlay, R. and S. Wellisz, 1982, Endogenous Tariffs, the Political Economy of Trade Restrictions, and Welfare, in: J. N. Bhagwati, ed., *Import Competition and Response* (University of Chicago Press: Chicago) 223–234.

Grossman, G. M. and E. Helpman, 1992, Protection for Sale (*NBER Working paper, no. 4149*, Cambridge).

Hillman, A. L., 1989, The Political Economy of Protection, Vol. 32 of *Fundamentals of Pure and Applied Economics* (Harwood Academic Press, Chur).

Hinich, M. J., 1977, Equilibrium in Spatial Voting: The Median Voter Result is an Artifact. *Journal of Economic Theory* 16, 208–219.

Hinich, M. J., J. O. Ledyard, and P. C. Ordeshook, 1972, Nonvoting and the Existence of Equilibrium under Majority Rule. *Journal of Economic Theory* 4, 144–153.

Jones, R. W., 1971, A Three-Factor Model in Theory, Trade and History, in: J. N. Bhagwati et al., eds., *Trade, Balance of Payments and Growth: Essays in Honor of C. P. Kindleberger* (North Holland: Amsterdam) 3–21.

Li, J., 1992, *Will Tariff Lobbies Contribute to More than One Candidate*? (mimeo, Southern Methodist University).

Lindbeck, A. and J. Weibull, 1987, Balanced-Budget Redistribution as the Outcome of Political Competition. *Public Choice* 52, 273–297.

Magee, S. P., W. A. Brock, and L. Young, 1989, *Black Hole Tariffs and Endogenous Policy Theory* (Cambridge University Press, Cambridge).

Mayer, W., 1974, Short-Run and Long-Run Equilibrium for a Small Open Economy. *Journal of Political Economy* 82, 955–967.

Mayer, W., 1984, Endogenous Tariff Formation. *American Economic Review* 74, 940–985.

Mayer, W., 1992, *Lobbying for Tariff Policies* (mimeo, University of Cincinnati).

Mayer, W. and R. G. Riezman, 1987, Endogenous Choice of Trade Policy Instruments. *Journal of International Economics* 23, 377–381.
Mueller, D. C., 1989, *Public Choice II, A revised edition of Public Choice* (Cambridge University Press: Cambridge).
Munger, M. C., 1991, Book Review of Stephen P. Magee, William A. Brock and Leslie Young, "Black hole tariffs and endogenous policy theory". New York: Cambridge University Press, 1989.xx + 438 pages. *Public Choice* 70, 108–110.
Mussa, M., 1974, Tariffs and the Distribution of Income: The Importance of Factor Specificity, Substitutability, and Intensity in the Short and Long Run. *Journal of Political Economy* 82, 1191–1204.
Nelson, D., 1988, Endogenous Tariff Theory: A Critical Survey. *American Journal of Political Science* 32, 796–837.
Riezman, R. and J. D. Wilson, 1993, *Political Reform and Trade Policy* (mimeo, Indiana University).
Shepsle, K., 1972, The Strategy of Ambiguity: Uncertainty and Electoral Competition. *American Political Science Review* 66, 551–568.
Slutsky, S., 1986, Elections with Incomplete Information: Comments on the Papers of Coughlin and Ferejohn. *Public Choice* 50, 105–129.
Weck-Hannemann, H., 1991, Institutional Analysis of Protectionism, in: H. J. Vosgerau, ed., *European Integration in the World Economy* (Springer: Heidelberg).

## APPENDIX

### *1. Derivation of Equation (20)*

Differentiating (16) with respect to $c_g^H$ yields:

$$[\partial E(V^H)/\partial c_g^H] = N^H [(z^H - \mu^H)(\partial \rho/\partial c_g^H) + (\partial \Psi^H/\partial c_g^H)]. \tag{A.1}$$

Since $(\partial \Psi^H/\partial c_g^H) = -1$ from (2″) and $(\partial \rho/\partial c_g^H) = g(\tilde{\mu}^0)(\partial \tilde{\mu}^0/\partial c_g^H)$ from (19) and $(\partial \tilde{\mu}^0/\partial c_g^H) = (\partial z^0/\partial c_g^H) = (-1)^g x S_g' N^H$ from (18), (11′), (13), and (14), appropriate substitutions in (A.1) yield: $[\partial E(V^H)/\partial c_g^H] = N^H [(-1)^g g(\tilde{\mu}^0)[z^H - \mu^H] S_g' N^H x - 1]$ to obtain (20).

### *2. Arguments in Support of Propositions 1–4*

**Proposition 1:** For $(-1)^g g(\tilde{\mu}^0)[z^H - \mu^H] S_g' N^H x < 1$, it must be that $c_g^H = 0$. If $z^H = \mu^H$, such that group $H$ is indifferent between the two parties, the left-hand side of this relation is zero, and $c_g^H = 0$.

**Proposition 2:** If $(-1)^g (z^H - \mu^H) < 0$ for some $g = H = 1,2$ and sufficiently large that $c_g^H > 0$, then it cannot be that $(-1)^g (z^H - \mu^H) < 0$ for $g \neq H = 1,2$.

**Proposition 3:** If $(z^1 - \mu^1)$ and $(z^2 - \mu^2)$ have the same signs, which is quite possible if the two groups have non-policy preferences for the same party, then it is possible that $c_g^1 > 0$ and $c_g^2 > 0$ for either $g = 1$ or $g = 2$.

**Proposition 4:** When $c_H^g = 0$, an increase in $N^0$ has no effect on any of the variables in (20) except for $\tilde{\mu}^0$; from (18):

$$\partial\tilde{\mu}^0/\partial N^0 = [F^0(z^0|\tilde{\mu}^0) - 1/2]/[N^0 f^0(z^0|\tilde{\mu}^0)], \tag{A.2}$$

noting that $N = N^0 + N^1 + N^2$. Consequently, for $g = H = 1,2$:

$$\begin{aligned}&\partial\{(-1)^g g(\tilde{\mu}^0)[z^H - \mu^H] S_g' N^H x\}/\partial N^0\\ &= (-1)^g [z^H - \mu^H] S_g' N^H x g'(\tilde{\mu}^0)(\partial\tilde{\mu}^0/\partial N^0).\end{aligned} \tag{A.3}$$

Assuming that $(-1)^g[z^H - \mu^H] < 0$, such that there exists, at least, the potential for lobbying of party $g$ by group $H$, the sign of (A.3) is positive if $g'(\tilde{\mu}^0)(\partial\tilde{\mu}^0/\partial N^0) > 0$ or, using (A.2), if $g'(\tilde{\mu}^0)[F^0(z^0|\tilde{\mu}^0) - 1/2] > 0$ which, in turn, requires that $g'(\tilde{\mu}^0)$ and $[F^0(z^0|\tilde{\mu}^0) - 1/2]$ have the same sign. Recalling the assumption that $g(\mu^0)$ is symmetric around the single mode of $\mu^0 = 0$, the sign of $g'(\tilde{\mu}^0)$ is positive (negative) if $\tilde{\mu}^0 < 0(\tilde{\mu}^0 > 0)$; that is, if, at the critical value of general voters' non-policy preferences, the majority favors party one (two). $[F^0(z^0|\tilde{\mu}^0) - 1/2]$, on the other hand, is positive (negative) if $[F^0(z^0 - \tilde{\mu}^0|0) - 1/2]$ is positive (negative) which, in turn, requires that $(z^0 - \tilde{\mu}^0)$ is positive (negative). The condition for (A.3) to be positive reduces to the requirement that $\tilde{\mu}^0$ and $(\tilde{\mu}^0 - z^0)$ have the same sign. The requirement, therefore, is that the general voters' party preference at the critical value is not changed by adding the influence of policy platforms.

### 3. *Slopes of the Reaction Curves*

The reaction curve of members of *the first interest group*, $R_1^1(c_2^2)$, is defined by the identity:

$$-g\{\tilde{\mu}^0[R_1^1(c_2^2), c_2^2]\}\{z^1 - \mu^1\} x N^1 S_1'[N^1 R_1^1(c_2^2)] - 1 \equiv 0, \tag{A.4}$$

where $R_1^1(c_2^2)$ is the solution to (20) for $g = H = 1$. Differentiating (A.4) with respect to $c_2^2$ yields:

$$-[z^1 - \mu^1] x N^1 \left\{ g(\tilde{\mu}^0) S_1'' N^1 \frac{dR_1^1}{dc_2^2} + S_1' g'(\tilde{\mu}^0) \left[ \frac{\partial\tilde{\mu}^0}{\partial R_1^1} \frac{dR_1^1}{dc_2^2} + \frac{\partial\tilde{\mu}^0}{\partial c_2^2} \right] \right\} \equiv 0,$$

where it was shown before that $\partial\tilde{\mu}^0/\partial R_1^1 = -x S_1' N^1$ and $\partial\tilde{\mu}^0/\partial c_2^2 = x S_2' N^2$. Substitution of these terms yields:

$$\frac{dR_1^1}{dc_2^2} = \frac{-N^2[x S_2' g'(\tilde{\mu}^0)]}{N^1\{[S_1'' g(\tilde{\mu}^0)/S_1'] - x S_1' g'(\tilde{\mu}^0)\}}, \tag{A.5}$$

where the denominator is negative from the second-order conditions of a maximum and the numerator is positive (negative) when $g'(\tilde{\mu}^0)$ is positive (negative) which, in turn, is the case when $\tilde{\mu}^0$ is negative (positive). In a similar fashion one can derive and interpret the slope of the reaction curve of the second lobby. The $R_2^2R_2^2$ curve, as drawn in Figure 1, is described by:

$$\frac{dc_1^1}{dR_2^2}=\frac{N^2\{[S_2''g'(\tilde{\mu}^0)/S_2']+xS_2'g'(\tilde{\mu}^0)\}}{N^1xS_1'g'(\tilde{\mu}^0)}, \tag{A.6}$$

with the numerator being negative and the denominator negative (positive) for $g'(\tilde{\mu}^0)$ positive (negative).

### 4. *Arguments in Support of Propositions 5 and 6*

It is assumed that $S_g(C_g)$ is the same for both parties. Concerning Proposition 5, since $S_g'<0$ and $S_g''>0$, it follows that $c_1>C_2$ if $S_2'(C_2)<S_1'(C_1)$; that is, if $S_1'(C_1)/S_2'(C_2)<1$. To establish Proposition 6, we employ the specific function $S_g(C_g)=C_g^{-\alpha}$, where $\alpha>0$. For this special form, (21) reduces to:

$$\frac{C_2}{C_1}=\left[\frac{(\mu^2-z^2)N^2}{(z^1-\mu^1)N^1}\right]^{\frac{1}{1+\alpha}}. \tag{A.7}$$

If the second lobby's non-policy preference shifts more in favor of party two ($\mu^2$ rises) or its membership goes up then $C_2$ rises relative to $C_1$. The same happens if the first lobby's non-policy preference shifts away from party one ($\mu^1$ rises) or its membership declines. Finally, one can show that for a tariff change:

$$\frac{d(C_2/C_1)}{d\tau_g}>0 \text{ if} -\frac{dz^2}{d\tau_g}/(\mu^2-z^2)>\frac{dz^1}{d\tau_g}/(z^1-\mu^1), \tag{A.8}$$

where $dz^H/d\tau_g$ is obtained from (11″).

### 5. *Necessary Conditions for a Tariff Equilibrium*

Using (19), necessary conditions for a Nash equilibrium in tariff rates are that: $\partial\rho/\partial\tau_g=g(\tilde{\mu}^0)[(\partial\tilde{\mu}^0/\partial\tau_g)+(\partial\tilde{\mu}^0/\partial C_1)(dC_1/d\tau_g)+(\partial\tilde{\mu}^0/\partial C_2)(dC_2/d\tau_g)]=0$ for $g=1,2$, where the effects of $\tau_g$, $C_1$, and $C_2$ on $\tilde{\mu}^0$ can be derived from (18) and the effects of the tariff on lobbying expenditure of the two respective groups can be obtained from (20). In general, one cannot sign the various terms; however, if $\tau_1=\tau_2$ change at the same rate, then neither $\tilde{\mu}^0$ nor $C_g$ will be affected, leaving the probability of getting elected unchanged.

# PART IV

# Designing Conditional Assistance Programs

*Review of Development Economics, 9(4), 449–466, 2005*

# The Political Economy of IMF Conditionality: A Common Agency Model

*Wolfgang Mayer and Alexandros Mourmouras**


## Abstract

The paper models the relationship between an aid-providing international financial institution (IFI) and an aid-receiving government whose economic policy choices are influenced by a domestic interest group. Two assistance schemes are evaluated: conditional aid in which the IFI makes assistance contingent on less-distorting economic policies and unconditional aid which is provided without such conditions. Conditional aid is shown to raise welfare of the receiving country and the world as a whole relative to unconditional aid. The paper also examines how conditional and unconditional aid schemes are influenced by the IFI's opportunity cost of providing assistance and the receiving government's political dependence on a domestic interest group.


## 1. Introduction

Recent years have witnessed an explosion of interest in the political economy of the International Monetary Fund (IMF) and other International Financial Institutions (IFIs). To a significant extent, this reflects the failure of some developing and transition countries to tackle long-standing economic problems despite extensive financial involvement by the IMF, the World Bank and other IFIs, and despite significant expansion of IMF conditionality. It is now widely recognized that the success of IMF-supported reforms hinges critically on the domestic ownership of programs which, in turn, depends on the political economy of recipient countries. The IMF's conditionality review, conducted during 2000–2002, agreed that conditionality had over-reached and called for a reversal of the Fund's mission creep to strengthen ownership and improve the record of implementation of IMF-supported programs.

Organized opposition to IMF-supported reforms varies, depending on the nature of the reforms themselves and the political economy of the recipient countries. Some macroeconomic stabilization programs, including those primarily aimed at taming hyperinflation, provide large and immediate benefits to every citizen and are relatively uncontroversial. Although distributional politics can be responsible for delayed macroeconomic stabilization, as Alesina and Drazen (1991) suggest, in practice, the IMF (2001) has been able to mobilize broad-based support for such programs, including from the government, opposition parties, the legislature and other stakeholders. Fernandez and Rodrik (1991) point out that building pro-reform coalitions is more difficult when the reform outcomes are uncertain and when change threatens the rents of politically powerful groups. This tends to be the case for programs with structural orientation. IMF policy recommendations call for the elimination of trade barriers, preferential loans and subsidies to large and politically connected firms, and for reduc-

*Mayer: University of Cincinnati, Cincinnati, Ohio, USA. Tel: 513-556-2618; Fax: 513-556-2669; E-mail: mayerw@uc.edu. Mourmouras: amourmouras@imf.org. Mourmouras: IMF Institute, International Monetary Fund, Washington, DC, 20431, USA. Tel: 202-623-5402; Fax: 202-589-5402; E-mail: amourmouras@imf.org.
We appreciate helpful comments on an earlier version of this paper by Pat Conway, Jim Boughton, Tim Lane, and Anna Ivanova. Any errors are our responsibility.

tions in transfers to middle- and upper-income groups. These reforms are sometimes resisted by labor and business interests, the intelligentsia, and by governments whose political support depends not only on social welfare, but also on the patronage of interest groups.

This paper examines the impact of IMF-supported reform programs on domestic politics using the theory of special-interest politics as laid out in Grossman and Helpman (2001). According to this theory, the political influence exerted by organized interest groups is essential for understanding why inefficient policies and instruments are used in practice.[1] Organized interest groups exert their influence by producing information and analysis that is useful for politicians and by making contributions to electoral campaign war-chests. The power of interest groups stems in large part from imperfections in political systems, including in countries supported by the IMF. According to Olson (1965), these imperfections enable interest groups to push for favored policies at the expense of unorganized opposition, often over the objections of technocratic economists.

The pernicious power of interest groups and the countervailing influence of the IMF can be analyzed with the help of a common-agency model. Common agency is a strategic situation in which a decision-maker (the agent) selects actions under the influence of competing principals. The common-agency setup was first proposed by Bernheim and Whinston (1986) and was later applied to political-economy issues by Grossman and Helpman (1994) and Dixit, Grossman and Helpman (1997). In our model, a sovereign government chooses economic policies under the influence of a domestic interest group and the IFI.[2]

This model highlights the role of IMF assistance as an incentive scheme in the spirit of Dixit (2000). The IMF is an institution that has been set up to promote world welfare, defined as a weighted sum of welfare in creditor and debtor countries. The IMF employs its financial leverage to enhance the government's willingness to pursue welfare-improving policies.[3] In equilibrium, IMF loans encourage recipient governments to adopt less-distorting policies than would result from the political interactions between government and interest group alone.

The terms and conditions of IMF loans are in reality determined in negotiations with the authorities. For the sake of simplicity and tractability, however, this analysis abstracts from issues related to bargaining. We follow the common-agency literature in assuming that the IFI and the interest group make simultaneous, take-it-or-leave-it offers to the government. The IFI tenders a truthful assistance schedule and the interest group tenders a political contributions schedule to the government. The government then selects its policy actions to maximize its overall political support, taking as given the interest group's and the IFI's respective contribution and assistance schedules. The outcome of the common-agency game is a pair of truthful Nash equilibrium contribution and assistance schedules and the corresponding equilibrium levels of economic policy distortions, IMF assistance and interest group contributions. Truthfulness means that equilibrium contribution and assistance schedules accurately reflect the principals' valuations of the government's choices of policy distortions.

Our main result is that truthful equilibria in the common-agency model of IFI conditionality are constrained Pareto-optimal for the world as a whole. This is an instance of the standard result in common-agency games stating that political trades are efficient for the set of active participants. If there were unexploited gains to be made from political trades, the interest group or the IFI could revise its contribution or assistance schedule to take advantage of them. In this model, the IFI is effectively a "lobby" that was organized to promote world welfare. Since it represents the interests of all the citizens of the world, the IFI and the recipient government exhaust all mutually advantageous gains in their strategic interaction.

The second major result concerns the distributional impacts of conditional lending on IFI creditor and IFI debtor countries. While some of the specific results depend on the timing and other features of the model (only one lobby, perfect information, ability to make take-it-or-leave-it offers, simultaneous moves, etc.), it is instructive to compare the equilibrium payoffs of the participants in the common-agency game with their payoffs under unconditional assistance or with no IFI assistance.

Truthful equilibria will feature positive IFI assistance if a conditional resource transfer from creditors to debtors raises world welfare as evaluated by the IFI. The IFI is selective in its lending in the sense that it will not offer conditional assistance if the opportunity cost of the transfers to creditors is very high or if the improvement in economic policy distortions in recipient countries is small. But if truthful equilibria feature positive conditional assistance, then they also result in reduced policy distortions when compared either to no assistance or to unconditional assistance. Conditional assistance is superior to no assistance or unconditional assistance from the perspective of the IFI. The general public in the recipient country is also better off with conditional assistance than with unconditional or no assistance. Economic policy distortions are lower and the level of assistance is higher, both of which raise welfare. The loser from adopting a conditional assistance scheme is the domestic interest group. It is hurt by the entry of another principal with opposing interests. Finally, the recipient domestic government is indifferent to the adoption of conditional assistance. The IFI offers the government just enough to assure its willingness to accept conditional aid.

Specification of the IFI's assistance schedule, the level of distortions, and payoffs to IFI, interest group, and government depend on the economic and political features of the assistance-receiving country and the IFI's opportunity costs of securing assistance. In particular, countries differ from each other with respect to the government's representativeness (the extent of the general public's influence on the government's political support). The paper shows that governments whose political support is more dependent on the wellbeing of the general public do not necessarily receive more assistance from the IFI. While unconditional assistance is definitely higher when the government is more responsive to the general public, the same conclusion does not necessarily hold for conditional assistance. Changes in the opportunity costs of IFI assistance, on the other hand, affect the flow of aid in a definite manner. Both unconditional and conditional assistance shrink when aid-giving becomes more costly.

## 2. The Model

Consider the domestic economy of an assistance-receiving country whose economic policies are shaped by the interactions of three different players. First, there is an incumbent domestic government ($G$) that makes the actual policy choices. Second, there exists a domestic interest group ($V$) that favors policies that benefit its members but have distorting effects on the economy. Third is an international financial institution (IFI) that acts as gatekeeper of the world's welfare and thereby opposes distorting policies. The aid-receiving country's welfare is measured by its national income, $Y$. National income, in turn, depends on the country's labor force, stock of capital, and state of technology, as well as on the severity of economic distortions. The latter is measured by a distortion index, $\omega$.

The aided economy's labor force and state of technology are given. Its capital stock, $K$, on the other hand, varies with the amount of aid received; and the degree of economic distortions, $\omega$, is the result of the government's policy choices. The country's national income, therefore, can be described by the function:

$$Y = y(K, \omega) \tag{1}$$

where $y_K > 0, y_{KK} < 0, y_\omega < 0, y_{\omega\omega} \leq 0$, and $y_{K\omega} \leq 0$. We also assume that $\lim_{\omega \to 0} y_\omega(K, \omega) > -\infty$. National income increases with capital at a decreasing rate but declines with the degree of policy distortions at a constant or increasing rate. Also, the marginal product of capital does not increase with the degree of distortions. The $y$-function is assumed to be strictly convex in its arguments.[4] For the discussion at hand, foreign assistance is restricted to be non-negative, $T \geq 0$, and is assumed to take the form of a capital transfer. Hence,

$$K = \underline{K} + T \tag{2}$$

where $\underline{K}$ is the domestic country's stock of capital in the absence of IFI assistance. The IFI provides assistance in form of a grant. Accordingly, there is no repayment.

Assistance is allocated by an IFI whose operations are financed by the rest of the world (ROW). Given the ROW's labor force and state of technology, $t^*$, its income, $Y^*$, is determined by the production function:

$$Y^* = t^* y^*(K^*) \tag{3}$$

where $K^*$ is the rest of the world's capital stock and where $y_K^* > 0$ and $y_{KK}^* < 0$. The rest of the world is assumed to pursue economic policies with negligible distortions. Accordingly, its own distortion index, $\omega^*$, is not explicitly stated in its output function.[5] The technology parameter $t^*$ is introduced to show the impact of changing productivity of inputs in the ROW—and therefore of changing opportunity cost of foreign aid—on the design of the IFI's assistance programs. It is assumed that $t^* = 1$ initially.

The ROW finances the IFI's operations. It gives up capital that otherwise would have been employed in the ROW's production. Given its initial capital endowment, $\underline{K}^*$, financing the assistance program reduces the ROW's capital stock to:

$$K^* = \underline{K}^* - T. \tag{4}$$

Each of the three decision makers has a well-defined objective. The assistance-receiving country's *government* aims at maximizing its political support. As in Grossman and Helpman (2001), political support is measured by a weighted average of financial contributions from the interest group, $C$, and welfare of the general public, measured by national income $Y$. The government's instrument to maximize political support is its economic policies. Distortions of the economy, caused by these policies, are measured by a distortion index $\omega$. In choosing economic policies, the government faces a conflict between interest group and general public. The type of policies that benefits the interest group creates distortions that hurt the general public. The interest group tenders a financial contribution schedule, $C(\omega)$, to the government, making more financial support contingent on the adoption of more distorting economic policies. The government's political support function is written as:

$$G(T, \omega; \lambda) = (1 - \lambda)C(\omega) + \lambda y(\underline{K} + T, \omega) \tag{5}$$

where $0 < \lambda < 1$ is a parameter that reflects the government's concern for the general public' welfare. It is explicitly recognized that the government values both contributions from the interest group and support from the public. If a country's political institutions are weak, then $\lambda$ tends to be small. The value of $\lambda$, therefore, varies across countries.

There is one *interest group* in the aid-receiving country. It is the beneficiary of distorting economic policies and, therefore, pressures the government to adopt them. The interest group's net welfare, $V$, is utility obtained from the distorting policies, $U$, minus the financial contribution made to the government, $C$; that is,

$$V(\omega) = U(\omega) - C(\omega) \tag{6}$$

where the group's welfare before contributions is assumed to rise at a decreasing rate with the distortion index, such that $U_\omega > 0$ and $U_{\omega\omega} < 0$. It also is assumed that $\lim_{\omega \to 0} U_\omega(\omega) = \infty$, assuring that the economy is always distorted as long as an interest group exists. The nature of the contribution schedule will be discussed later.

The *international financial institution* (IFI) is portrayed as a costless, public-interest institution that cares about total welfare of both assistance-receiving country, $Y$, and assistance-financing rest of the world, $Y^*$. The IFI's objective function is:

$$I(T, \omega; t^*) = y(\underline{K} + T, \omega) + t^* y^*(\underline{K}^* - T). \tag{7}$$

As mentioned, the transfer consists of capital. The IFI has been set up with the explicit understanding of facilitating transfers between countries to raise world welfare. It is implicitly assumed that imperfections in capital markets result in a market-based allocation of capital such that, in the absence of transfers and distortions, the marginal product of capital is higher in the receiving country than in the *ROW*; that is $y_K(\underline{K}, 0) > t^* y_K^*(\underline{K}^*)$ in the small neighborhood of $t^* = 1$.

## 3. Unconditional Aid

Aid is unconditional if the IFI, with the objective of maximizing world welfare, provides assistance to a country without imposing explicit conditions on the government's choice of economic policies. Although the IFI does not impose conditions, its choice of the aid level recognizes that world welfare depends on the magnitude of distortions in the receiving country. Accordingly, the amount of unconditional aid transferred by the IFI is an optimal response to the adoption of economic policies in the receiving country. Correspondingly, the receiving country's government cares about the amount of assistance received from the IFI. More assistance means more national income; and a larger national income means stronger political support from the public. The government's policy choice, therefore, accounts for the amount of assistance received even if there are no policy-choice conditions attached.

This *unconditional aid scheme* can be described as a Nash game in which the political support-maximizing government chooses policies that result in distortion index $\omega^u$ and the world welfare-maximizing IFI chooses an assistance level $T^u$. Superscript "$u$" indicates equilibrium values when aid is unconditional. Economic policies and economic assistance are chosen simultaneously. Furthermore, the domestic government's policy is influenced by a domestic interest group. The latter views the government as its agent, as described in Grossman and Helpman (1994, 2001). The interest group tenders a contribution schedule, $C(\omega)$, that explicitly makes its financial support of the government contingent on the adoption of the type of policies that entail more distortions. In offering its contribution, the interest group must ensure that the government is willing to accept it. This means that an acceptable contribution must make the government at least as well off with the contribution as without it.

More precisely, the government's policies are the outcome of a two-stage game in which the government chooses the distortion index (economic policy) in the second stage given the financial contribution schedule tendered by the interest group in the first stage. This outcome describes an equilibrium that is truthful; that is, an equilibrium for which the contribution schedule of the interest group is truthful relative to the equilibrium welfare level of the players. In a general common-agency framework, the conditions for a truthful equilibrium are explicitly stated in Proposition 3 of Dixit, Grossman, and Helpman (1997). Adapting these conditions to our situation of a political game in which there is only one principal, namely the interest group, and one agent, namely the government, the truthful political equilibrium consists of a truthful financial contribution schedule, $C^T$, and a distortion index, $\omega^u$, that is characterized by two conditions: First, the government's choice of $\omega^u$ must be such that it gains the highest attainable political support; that is,

$$\omega^u = \text{argmax}_{\omega \geq 0}(1-\lambda)C^T(\omega, V^u) + \lambda y(\underline{K} + T^u, \omega) \tag{8}$$

where $V^u$ denotes the interest group's net welfare in equilibrium when aid is unconditional and $T^u$ is the amount of unconditional aid in Nash equilibrium. Second, the interest group's influence-seeking must keep the government no worse off than it would be in the absence of influence-seeking; that is,

$$(1-\lambda)C^T(\omega^u, V^u) + \lambda y(\underline{K} + T^u, \omega^u) = 0 + \lambda y(\underline{K} + T^{-V}, \omega^{-V}) \tag{9}$$

where $\omega^{-V}$ is the distortion index the government would choose in the absence of influence-seeking by the interest group and $T^{-V}$ is the amount of unconditional aid received if there is no interest group. Since gains to the government come at a loss to the interest group, the latter has no interest to contribute more to the government than it has to, and (9) holds as an equality. Hence, in equilibrium, the interest group's truthful contribution is just enough to make political support for the government with influence-seeking the same as it would be without influence-seeking. The government would choose distortion-free economic policies in the absence of an interest group. Consequently, it must be that $\omega^{-V} = 0$ and that $T^{-V}$ is the amount of aid received by a distortion-free economy.

One can see from (6) that $C^T(\omega, V^u) = U(\omega) - V^u$. It follows that the first of the above conditions requires that $\omega^u$ is chosen to satisfy:

$$(1-\lambda)U_\omega(\omega^u) + \lambda y_\omega(\underline{K} + T^u, \omega^u) \leq 0, \tag{10}$$

with equality holding for $\omega^u > 0$. Given that $\lim_{\omega \to 0} U_\omega(\omega) = \infty$ and $\lim_{\omega \to 0} y_\omega(K, \omega) > -\infty$, it must be that (10) holds as an equality, and there exists some positive level of distortions in equilibrium. The second equilibrium condition implies that the interest group's equilibrium contribution is such as to satisfy:

$$(1-\lambda)[U(\omega^u) - V^u] + \lambda y[\underline{K} + T^u, \omega^u] = \lambda y[\underline{K} + T^{-V}, 0]. \tag{11}$$

Equation (10) reveals that the degree of distortions, $\omega^u$, depends on both the amount of unconditional assistance received from the IFI, $T^u$, and the government's concern for the general public's welfare, measured by $\lambda$. The more unconditional aid is received and the more the government cares for the public's welfare, the less distorting policies are adopted. This optimal response of the government to different assistance levels is traced out in Figure 1 of the next page as the $R_G R_G$ curve. The slope of the government's reaction curve, $R_G R_G$, is given by:

$$\left.\frac{dT}{d\omega}\right|_G = -\frac{(1-\lambda)U_{\omega\omega} + \lambda y_{\omega\omega}}{\lambda y_{\omega K}}. \tag{12}$$

Provided distortions diminish capital's marginal product, $y_{\omega K} < 0$, the $R_G R_G$ curve is negatively sloped. In the extreme case that capital's marginal product is independent of the distortion index, the $R_G R_G$ locus is a vertical line.

The position of the $R_G R_G$ schedule depends on parameter $\lambda$ that describes the political conditions of the receiving country. A rise in the value of $\lambda$ signifies the government becoming less captive to the country's influential interest group and more responsive to the general public's preferences. As can be seen from (10), an increase in the value of $\lambda$ shifts the $R_G R_G$ curve to the left; at the same level of assistance, the government adopts less-distorting economic policies.

In stage two of the above-described game, when the government chooses its economic policies, the IFI simultaneously determines how much *unconditional aid* it makes available. Its goal is to determine the value of $T^u$ that maximizes world welfare $\{y(\underline{K} + T, \omega) + t^* y^*(\underline{K}^* - T)\}$. A necessary condition for this optimizing choice is that:

$$y_K(\underline{K} + T^u, \omega) - t^* y_K^*(\underline{K}^* - T^u) \leq 0, \tag{13}$$

with equality holding for $T^u > 0$. Our assumption that $y_K(\cdot) > t^* y_K^*$ at $\omega = 0$ assures that (13) holds as an equality for at least some distortion levels. This means that, for sufficiently low distortions, it is in the interest of the IFI to give some aid even if it cannot impose conditions.

The IFI's reaction curve is based on (13) and is marked by $R_I R_I$ in Figure 1. Provided $y_{\omega K} < 0$, it also is negatively sloped. It is in the best interest of the IFI to lower assistance when the receiving country's government adopts more-distorting economic policies. Its slope is given by:

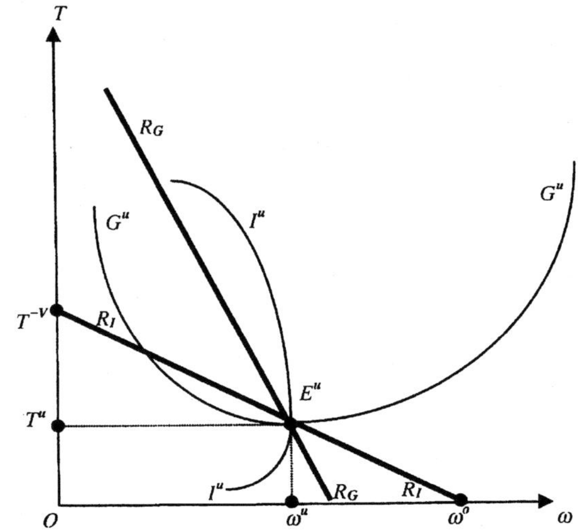


*Figure 1. Unconditional Assistance Equilibrium*

$$\left.\frac{dT}{d\omega}\right|_I = -\frac{y_{K\omega}}{y_{KK} + t^* y^*_{K^*K^*}} \leq 0. \tag{14}$$

In the special case of the marginal product of capital being independent of the level of distortions, $y_{\omega K}$ equals zero and the IFI's reaction curve is a horizontal line. But even if $y_{\omega K} > 0$, it can easily be ascertained that the $R_I R_I$ curve is flatter than the $R_G R_G$ curve given our assumption that the domestic economy's aggregate production function is strictly convex in $K$ and $\omega$.

Two points on the $R_I R_I$ curve deserve special mention. Point $T^{-V}$ indicates the amount of assistance that maximizes world welfare if the receiving country is free of policy-induced distortions. This would be the case in the absence of influence-seeking by the interest group. The earlier-made assumption that $y_K(\underline{K}, 0) > t^* y^*_K(\underline{K}^*)$ implies that $T^{-V} > 0$. When $y_{K\omega} < 0$, the IFI offers less assistance as policy-induced distortions in the receiving country rise. Point $\omega^o$ then marks the level of distortions in the receiving country at which the IFI stops all assistance. For any level of distortions exceeding $\omega^o$, moving capital from the ROW to the receiving country reduces world welfare; that is, $y_K(\underline{K}, \omega) < t^* y^*_K(\underline{K}^*)$ for $\omega > \omega^o$. Given such severe distortions, world welfare can be enhanced only by a reverse transfer from the country with high distortions to the ROW. Since the IFI is not authorized to reverse the direction of assistance, we have the restriction that $T^u \geq 0$. This, in turn, implies that, beyond $\omega^o$, the IFI's reaction curve, $R_I R_I$, coincides with the $\omega$ axis. Finally, we note that the position of the $R_I R_I$ curve depends on the rest of the world's technology parameter $t^*$. Initially, $t^*$ is assumed to be equal to one. An increase in the productivity of capital in the ROW shifts the IFI's reaction curve down. At a given level of distortions, the IFI offers less assistance if capital becomes more productive in the ROW. Stated differently, higher opportunity costs of providing aid reduce the IFI's willingness to assist.

Figure 1 shows equilibrium for the unconditional aid program as the intersection of $R_G R_G$ and $R_I R_I$ curves at point $E^u$. As drawn, the equilibrium unconditional aid level is denoted by $T^u > 0$ and the corresponding equilibrium distortion index is $\omega^u > 0$. We also mark the IFI's level of welfare by $I^u I^u$ and the government's political support contour by $G^u G^u$. Concerning this unconditional aid equilibrium, it must be noted that the level of assistance is not necessarily positive. It is quite possible that $R_G R_G$ and $R_I R_I$ intersect at a value of $\omega \geq \omega^o$. In this case $T^u = 0$ and (13) is stated as an inequality. In examining the impact of changing political conditions in the receiving country and changing opportunity costs for providing assistance in the rest of the world, we will allow for both possibilities, $T^u > 0$ and $T^u = 0$.

We now focus on the influence of a receiving country's political situation on the unconditional assistance package received from the IFI. The importance of the general public relative to special interests in shaping a government's economic policies is captured by the parameter $\lambda$. A smaller value of $\lambda$ describes a government that is more captive to special interests and less concerned about the policy's impact on the general public. Dictatorships whose survival depends more on support from special groups than from the general public fall into this category. Since a lower value of $\lambda$ shifts the $R_G R_G$ curve to the right, while leaving the $R_I R_I$ curve's position unchanged, $T^u$ declines and $\omega^u$ rises. This leads to:

PROPOSITION 1. *The less a government's political support depends on the general public's wellbeing, the less unconditional assistance is provided by the IFI and the more distorting policies are adopted by the receiving country's government.*

More precisely, differentiation of (10) and (13), written as equalities, with respect to $\lambda$ yields:

$$\frac{\partial \omega^u}{\partial \lambda} = \frac{(U_\omega - y_\omega)(y_{KK} + t^* y^*_{K^*K^*})}{\Delta} < 0 \quad \text{and} \quad \frac{\partial T^u}{\partial \lambda} = -\frac{(U_\omega - y_\omega) y_{K\omega}}{\Delta} > 0, \tag{15}$$

where $\Delta = [(1 - \lambda)U_{\omega\omega} + \lambda y_{\omega\omega}][y_{KK} + y^*_{K^*K^*}] - \lambda(y_{K\omega})^2 > 0$ since $y(\cdot)$ is strictly convex in $K$ and $\omega$.

Next, we evaluate the impact of changing opportunity costs of assistance on the receiving country's aid program. As mentioned, a rise in opportunity costs is the result of an increase in the ROW's technology parameter $t^*$. Higher opportunity costs shift the IFI's reaction curve down, while the position of $R_G R_G$ remains unchanged. Clearly, this lowers the value of $T^u$ and raises the value of $\omega^u$, resulting in:

PROPOSITION 2. *When the opportunity costs of providing aid increase, the IFI's unconditional assistance declines and the level of distortions in the receiving country rises.*

The precise relationships are obtained from differentiation of (10) and (13) with respect to $t^*$, yielding:

$$\frac{\partial \omega^u}{\partial t^*} = \frac{-y^*_{K^*} \lambda y_{\omega K}}{\Delta} > 0 \quad \text{and} \quad \frac{\partial T^u}{\partial t^*} = \frac{y^*_{K^*}[(1-\lambda)U_{\omega\omega} + \lambda y_{\omega\omega}]}{\Delta} < 0. \tag{16}$$

Propositions 1 and 2 were derived under the assumptions that the two reaction curves intersect at a value of $T^u > 0$. If the initial unconditional equilibrium occurred at $T^u = 0$, then a small decline in $\lambda$ would raise $\omega^u$ but have no impact on $T^u = 0$, whereas a small increase in $t^*$ would leave both $T^u = 0$ and $\omega^u$ unchanged.

## 4. Conditional Aid

Aid is conditional when it is based on a contractual agreement that makes the IFI's aid payments contingent on the government's adoption of less-distorting economic policies. The IFI presents its aid proposal in form of an explicit economic assistance schedule. The domestic government is fully aware that promised assistance will be rescinded if its policies do not live up to the conditions imposed. This conditional aid is offered on top of any unconditional aid the IFI might choose to provide. Hence, a complete aid package has two components: conditional aid and unconditional aid.

Conditional aid is offered to a government that already is influenced by a domestic interest group. Different from the unconditional aid model in which the IFI simply hands out aid, conditional aid comes as a quid-pro-quo proposal: more aid for better economic policies. In both conditional and unconditional aid models, the IFI and domestic interest group have opposing objectives with respect to policies. The IFI favors lower distortions in order to enhance world welfare. The interest group wants more of those distortions that advance the group's welfare. In both models, the IFI offers aid which indirectly enhances political support for the government. More aid means more capital, more capital means more national income, and more national income strengthens political support. And in both models, a domestic interest group seeks influence through financial contributions to the government. This type of payment enhances political support directly.

The conditional aid scenario is conveniently modeled within the political-economy, common-agency framework developed by Grossman and Helpman (1994) and further expanded in Dixit, Grossman, and Helpman (1997). The government is the common agent for both IFI and interest group who act as principals. Each principal presents the government with a payment schedule: The IFI's is an economic assistance schedule that makes more assistance contingent on lower distortions; the domestic interest group's is a financial contribution schedule that makes higher contributions contingent on more distortions. The government chooses economic policies, and thereby the distortion index, fully accounting for the interest group's push for more and the IFI's urging for fewer distortions.

The interactions between domestic interest group, IFI, and domestic government can be described as a two-stage game. The government chooses policies in the second stage given the contribution schedule of the interest group and the assistance schedule of the IFI. Both payment schedules are offered to the government in the first stage. As was the case in the preceding section, where the interest group was the only principal, we are in search of an equilibrium in which both contribution schedule, $C^T$, and conditional assistance schedule, $A^T$, are truthful. In addition to this conditional assistance, $A$, there might be unconditional assistance, $T^u$. To describe this equilibrium, we return to Proposition 3 of Dixit, Grossman, and Helpman (1997), which characterizes such a *truthful equilibrium*, and adapt their conditions of equilibrium to our circumstances. We employ superscript $c$ to indicate conditional equilibrium values of the relevant variables.

The first of the Dixit–Grossman–Helpman requirements for a truthful *conditional assistance equilibrium* states that the government chooses a policy that, given the truthful contribution schedule offered by the interest group, $C^T(\cdot)$, and the truthful assistance schedule offered by the IFI, $A^T(\cdot)$, maximizes its political support; that is, the government's policy choice, $\omega^c$, is such that:

$$\omega^c = \text{argmax}_{\omega\geq 0}(1-\lambda)C^T(\omega, V^c) + \lambda y[\underline{K} + A^T(\omega, I^c) + T^u(\omega^{-I}), \omega] \tag{17}$$

where $V^c$ and $I^c$, respectively, denote the interest group's net welfare and the entire world's (IFI's) welfare evaluated at the conditional assistance equilibrium, and where $T^u(\omega^{-I})$ is the amount of unconditional aid that would be forthcoming if only the interest group lobbied. The symbol $\omega^{-I}$, in turn, indicates the value of the distortion index that comes about if the IFI does not provide conditional aid but does give unconditional aid.

A second requirement for a truthful conditional assistance equilibrium is that the equilibrium contribution of the interest group keeps the government's political support at the same level as it would be in the absence of the contribution, evaluated at the equilibrium welfare level of the IFI; that is,

$$\begin{aligned}(1-\lambda)C^T(\omega^c, V^c) + \lambda y[\underline{K} + A^T(\omega^c, I^c) + T^u(\omega^{-I}), \omega^c]\\ = \lambda y[\underline{K} + A^T(\omega^{-V}, I^c) + T^u(\omega^{-V}), \omega^{-V}]\end{aligned} \tag{18}$$

where $\omega^{-V} = 0$ is again the government's choice of the distortion index when the interest group does not contribute, $C = 0$, and where $T^u(\omega^{-V})$ equals $T^{-V}$ as defined in Section 3. While the left-hand side indicates equilibrium political support when the interest group lobbies and the IFI gives conditional aid, the right-hand side expresses the same level of support when the interest group does not lobby but the IFI gives both conditional and unconditional aid.[6]

The third requirement for a truthful equilibrium is that the IFI's equilibrium assistance payment is such that political support for the government is as strong when it assists as it would be if it made no conditional assistance payments, evaluated at the equilibrium welfare level of the interest group. This requires that:

$$(1-\lambda)C^T(\omega^c, V^c)+\lambda y[\underline{K}+A^T(\omega^c, I^c)+T^u(\omega^{-I}), \omega^c] \\ =(1-\lambda)C^T(\omega^{-I}, V^c)+\lambda y[\underline{K}+T^u(\omega^{-I}), \omega^{-I}] \tag{19}$$

where the right-hand side measures political support when the interest group lobbies, but conditional aid from the IFI is zero. There remains unconditional aid in this situation.

Recalling again that $C^T(\omega, V^c) = U(\omega) - V^c$, a necessary condition for meeting the first of the three requirements for a truthful equilibrium is that $\omega^c$ satisfies:

$$-\frac{(1-\lambda)U_\omega(\omega^c)+\lambda y_\omega(\cdot)}{\lambda y_K(\cdot)}=\frac{\partial A^T(\cdot)}{\partial \omega} \tag{20}$$

where $y(\cdot) = y[\underline{K} + A^T(\omega^c, I^c) + T^u(\omega^{-I}), \omega^c]$ and $y^*(\cdot) = y^*[\underline{K}^* - A^T(\omega^c, I^c) - T^u(\omega^{-I})]$. The left-hand side of (20) reflects the slope of the government's political-support indifference curve between aid ($A$) and distortions ($\omega$), derived from (5) after substitution of $C(\omega) = U(\omega) - V$. It states the rate at which the government is willing to accept more economic assistance for fewer distortions. The right-hand side of (20), on the other hand, expresses the slope of the IFI's world-welfare indifference curve. The value of its slope can be explicitly derived from (7):

$$\frac{\partial A^T}{\partial \omega}=\frac{y_\omega(\cdot)}{t^* y^*_{K^*}(\cdot)-y_K(\cdot)}. \tag{21}$$

This expression states the rate at which the IFI is willing to offer more assistance for reduced policy distortions. Consequently, the political-support-maximizing choice of the distortion index, $\omega^c$, implies that the IFI's and government's welfare contours are tangent to each other, as drawn in Figure 2. For a given level of interest group welfare, $V^c$, the combination $\omega^c$ and $A^T(\omega^c, I^c)$ maximizes joint welfare of government and IFI.

The second condition for a truthful equilibrium can be restated as:

$$(1-\lambda)[U(\omega^c)-V^c]+\lambda y[\underline{K}+A^T(\omega^c, I^c)+T^u(\omega^{-I}), \omega^c] \\ =\lambda y[\underline{K}+A^T(0, I^c)+T^u(0), 0] \tag{18'}$$

where we substituted $C^T(\omega^c, V^c) = [U(\omega^c) - V^c]$ and $\omega^{-V} = 0$. Correspondingly, the third condition for a truthful equilibrium is expressed as:

$$(1-\lambda)U(\omega^c)+\lambda y[\underline{K}+A^T(\omega^c, I^c)+T^u(\omega^{-I}), \omega^c] \\ =(1-\lambda)U(\omega^{-I})+\lambda y[\underline{K}+T^u(\omega^{-I}), \omega^{-I}] \tag{19'}$$

where $\omega^{-I}$ is the government's choice of distortions when the IFI does not provide conditional aid.

Figure 2 portrays the equilibrium choice of total economic assistance, $T^T = T^u + A^T(\omega^c, I^c)$, and economic distortions, $\omega^c$, when the IFI assistance package has both unconditional and conditional components. The diagram highlights the interactions between IFI and government while keeping the role of the interest group in the background. As in Figure 1, the diagram shows the reaction curves of government and IFI when a domestic interest group influences economic policy choices through conditional financial contributions. The unconditional aid equilibrium is again portrayed by point $E^u$, whereby $T^u$ indicates the unconditional aid payment.

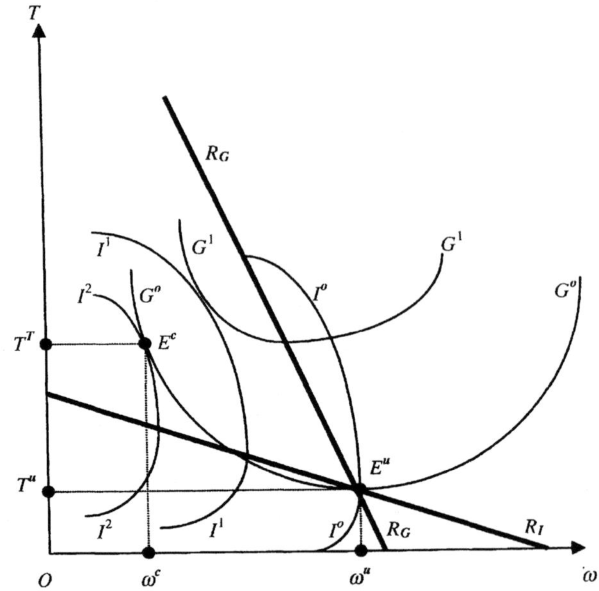


*Figure 2. Conditional Assistance Equilibrium*

The conditional aid equilibrium requires that equations (18′), (19′), and (20) be satisfied. Equation (20) states that the rate at which the IFI is willing to offer conditional aid for lower policy distortions is equal to the rate at which the domestic government is willing to accept conditional aid for lower distortions. This condition is met at all tangency points between the government's political support contours, $G^iG^i$, and the IFI's welfare contours, $I^iI^i$, whereby higher superscripts $i$ express higher levels of political support and IFI welfare, respectively. Equation (19′), in turn, pins down at which of an infinite number of tangency points the conditional aid equilibrium is established. It states that, given the interest group's equilibrium welfare $V^g$, the government must receive as much political support in conditional aid equilibrium as it does in unconditional aid equilibrium. Accordingly, the conditional equilibrium is situated on the government's welfare contour $G^oG^o$ which runs through the unconditional aid equilibrium. The conditional aid equilibrium is given at point $E^c$, where the government's political support is just as strong as it is when the IFI limits itself to paying aid unconditionally. The unconditional aid equilibrium was at point $E^u$. Note that $\omega^{-I}$ of equations (18′), (19′), and (20) expresses the distortion index in the absence of conditionality on the part of IFI assistance and, therefore, equals $\omega^u$ in Figure 2.

The total amount of equilibrium aid provided by the IFI is denoted by $T^T$. It consists of unconditional aid, $T^u$, and conditional aid $A^T = T^T - T^u$. The corresponding levels of policy distortions under conditional and unconditional aid are $\omega^c$ and $\omega^u$, respectively. Comparing the conditional with the unconditional aid equilibrium, we state:

PROPOSITION 3. *The introduction of a conditional aid program enlarges the total volume of assistance payments and reduces the level of policy distortions in the receiving country.*

A key issue raised by the introduction of conditional aid programs is who gains and who loses from offering conditional aid. To answer this question, we recall that welfare contours with higher superscripts in Figure 2 indicate greater welfare for the party involved; and we also recall that $T^T > T^u$ and $\omega^c < \omega^u$. This enables us to state:

PROPOSITION 4. *Conditional aid programs raise welfare of the general public in the receiving country, as well as of the world as a whole. Conditional aid programs accomplish these welfare gains without weakening political support for the receiving country's government. They lower welfare of the domestic interest group.*

Welfare of the general public in the receiving country is measured by $y(\underline{K} + T^T, \omega)$, where $y_K > 0$ and $y_\omega < 0$. Since conditional aid programs raise $T^T$ and lower $\omega$, the general public's welfare must always rise. Second, the IFI, representing the interests of the world as a whole, becomes better off since the equilibrium $E^c$ on welfare contour $I^2I^2$ represents higher welfare than the equilibrium $E^u$ on welfare contour $I^oI^o$. Third, the government's welfare remains unchanged since both $E^c$ and $E^u$ are points on the same welfare contour $G^oG^o$. Finally, the interest group loses from the granting of conditional aid, as demonstrated in the Appendix.

## 5. Determinants of Total Aid

Propositions 1 and 2 of the preceding section relate the amount of unconditional aid, $T^u$, to the IFI's opportunity costs of providing aid, $t^*$, and the receiving government's concern for its general public, $\lambda$. It was concluded that higher opportunity costs lower unconditional aid, but that the government's greater concern for the general public enlarges unconditional aid. The next task is to explore whether these relationships remain valid with respect to total aid provided by the IFI; that is, we want to determine the effects of $t^*$ and $\lambda$ on $T^T$.

Let us recall that the conditional aid equilibrium was described by equations (18′), (19′), and (20), after substitution of (21) in the latter. The endogenous variables were the distortion index, $\omega^c$, welfare of the IFI, $I^c$, and welfare of the domestic interest group, $V^c$. Next, we note that one can substitute $T^T = T^u(\omega^c) + A^T(\omega^c, I^c)$ in the above-mentioned equations and rewrite (19′) and (20), after substitution of (21) and some simplifications as:

$$(1-\lambda)U(\omega^c) + \lambda y(\underline{K} + T^T, \omega^c) = (1-\lambda)U(\omega^{-1}) + \lambda y(\underline{K} + T^u, \omega^{-1}) \tag{22}$$

$$(1-\lambda)U_\omega(\omega^c)[t^* y^*_{K^*}(\underline{K}^* - T^T) - y_K(\underline{K} + T^T, \omega^c)] + \lambda y_\omega(\underline{K} + T^T, \omega^c) t^* y^*_{K^*}(\underline{K}^* - T^T) = 0. \tag{23}$$

Equations (22) and (23) can be solved for $\omega^c$ and $T^T$ in terms of $t^*$ and $\lambda$, where we further note that $T^u$ is a function of $\lambda$ and $t^*$, as stated in (15) and (16), and that $\omega^u = \omega^{-1}$. Accordingly, one can determine the relationship between total IFI assistance, $T^T$, on the one hand, and the IFI's opportunity cost parameter, $t^*$, and the aid-receiving government's responsiveness to its general public, $\lambda$, on the other hand.

Starting with the impact of changing opportunity costs, differentiation of (22) and (23) with respect to $t^*$ yields:

$$\partial T^T/\partial t^* = \left\{ y^*_{K^*}[(1-\lambda)U_\omega(\cdot) + \lambda y_\omega(\cdot)]^2 + [\Omega_{11}\lambda y_K(\cdot)(\partial T^u/\partial t^*)] \right\} / \Omega \tag{24}$$

where we made use of (10) and (22). First, we note that $\Omega = \lambda y_K(\cdot)\Omega_{11} - [(1-\lambda)U_\omega(\cdot) + \lambda y_\omega(\cdot)]\Omega_{12} < 0$, as follows from the second-order conditions of the government's optimal choice of $\omega^c$. Next, we state that $\Omega_{11} = \{[1-\lambda]U_{\omega\omega}(\cdot)[t^*y^*_{K^*}(\cdot) - y_K(\cdot)] + \lambda y_{\omega\omega}(\cdot)t^*y^*_{K^*}(\cdot) - [1-\lambda]U_\omega(\cdot)y_{K\omega}(\cdot)\}$ and $\Omega_{12} = -\{[1-\lambda][t^*y^*_{K^*K^*}(\cdot) + y_{KK}(\cdot)]U_\omega(\cdot) + \lambda t^*y^*_{K^*K^*}(\cdot)y_\omega(\cdot) - \lambda t^*y^*_{K^*}(\cdot)y_{\omega K}(\cdot)]\}$. For sufficiently small values of $y_{K\omega}(\cdot) < 0$, it must be that $\Omega_{11} < 0$ and $\Omega_{12} > 0$. Finally, it should be noted from (16) that, if $T^u > 0$ initially, then $(\partial T^u/\partial t^*) < 0$ in (24). This implies:

Proposition 5. *If initially there is no unconditional aid, higher opportunity costs of giving aid always reduce conditional aid. If initially there is unconditional aid, this response is reinforced as long as the value of $y_{K\omega}(\cdot)$ is sufficiently small.*

The first part of Proposition 5 holds because the first term in the numerator of the RHS of (24) is always positive whereas the second term is zero since $(\partial T^u/\partial t^*) = 0$, and $\Omega$ is negative. The second part of the proposition follows from the observation that the second term in the numerator of the RHS of (24) is also positive since $(\partial T^u/\partial t^*) < 0$ and $\Omega_{11} < 0$ if $y_{K\omega}(\cdot) < 0$ is sufficiently small.

When the assistance-receiving country's government becomes more independent of the influence of the interest group and its political support is more sensitive to the well-being of the general public, the value of $\lambda$ rises. Differentiating equations (22) and (23) with respect to $\lambda$ yields:

$$\begin{aligned}\partial T^T/\partial\lambda = &-\{U_\omega(\cdot)[t^*y^*_{K^*}(\cdot) - y_K(\cdot)] - y_\omega(\cdot)ty^*_{K^*}(\cdot)\}/\Omega \\ &+ \{\Omega_{11}[\mu + \lambda y_K(\cdot)(\partial T^u/\partial\lambda)]\}/\Omega,\end{aligned} \tag{25}$$

where $\mu = [U(\omega^c) - U(\omega^{-l}) - [y(\omega^c) - y(\omega^{-l})] < 0$ since $\omega^c < \omega^{-l}$, $U(\omega)$ is increasing in $\omega$ and $y(\omega^c) > y(\omega^{-l})$ based on Proposition 4. The first term on the RHS of (25) is always positive since $[t^*y^*_{K^*}(\cdot) - y_K(\cdot)] > 0$ in equilibrium, $U_\omega(\cdot) > 0$, $y_\omega(\cdot) < 0$, and $-\Omega > 0$. The second term on the RHS of (25) can have either sign since, based on (15), expressions $\mu$ and $\lambda y_K(\cdot)(\partial T^u/\partial\lambda)]$ have opposite signs. Without further restrictions, one cannot preclude the possibility that the second term overpowers the first term, implying:

Proposition 6. *When political support for the government becomes more dependent on the state of welfare of the general public, total assistance from the IFI does not necessarily increase. In contrast, unconditional assistance always rises in this situation as had been stated in Proposition 1.*

## 6. Concluding Remarks

The conditional loans extended by the IMF and other IFIs, and the economic reform programs they support, have not always achieved intended results. Efforts to improve our understanding of what lies behind several failed IFI-supported reform programs point to the recipient countries' domestic political economy and to weak ownership of reforms. This paper presented a framework for thinking about conditional lending based on the theory of special interest politics. This theory focuses on the role of distributional conflicts in recipient countries and helps shed light on the role of IFI assistance as an incentive scheme. Although the analysis should be viewed primarily as a framework for dealing with issues surrounding IFI economic assistance provision and less so as a compendium of definite findings, it offers several conclusions.

Conditionality can steer the domestic political equilibrium in the direction of more efficient policies, but its power is constrained by imperfections in the political systems of recipient countries. These imperfections permit organized special interest groups to influence governments at the expense of the general public and limit the extent to which IFIs can leverage their financial clout to improve policies in recipient countries.

The effectiveness of conditionality is limited by the competition between IFIs and interest groups in the political-influence game. Even though IFI assistance helps reduce interest group power and wealth, the IFI cannot afford to ignore the government's outside value—the political support the politicians can obtain from their interaction with domestic interest groups. If foreign assistance does not match the government's outside value, IFI policy advice and financial assistance are likely to be ineffective.

IFI financial involvement raises the government's outside value in its interaction with interest groups. This forces these groups to adjust their political contributions so as to not be ignored in equilibrium, which lowers their payoffs. The weakening of special interest groups may promote longer-term institutional reform, especially if lobby formation is endogenous, requiring, say, a fixed cost as in Mitra (1999). It may then be possible for IFI assistance to be designed in such a way that it pushes interest group payoffs below the threshold consistent with organized lobbying.

Conditionality has certain limitations as a political influence device, depending on the different ways in which the IFI and domestic interests exert their weight on the government. Whereas the interest group's contributions directly raise the government's political support, the IFI's conditional loans do so only indirectly, by alleviating financial constraints and raising national welfare, which is typically felt with long and variable lags. In addition, economic outcomes are the result of shocks and luck, as well as skillful and timely policy implementation. To the extent that voters in recipient countries are myopic or remain uninformed about the causes and effects of economic policies—the political market imperfection again—they may have a difficult time appreciating the long-term benefits of IFI-supported reforms. They may also scapegoat the IMF—blame foreign intervention for all that goes wrong. The IMF needs to provide economic information to the public about the intended goals of IMF-supported reforms and explain the outcomes of reform programs.

The ownership of "property rights" to economic assistance funds is important for the design and impact of conditionality. In this paper the authors have assumed, as is usually done in the principal-agent literature, that the principals make take-it-or-leave-it offers to the agent. In this case, conditional assistance leads to higher payoffs for the IFI, but leaves the government's political support at the same level as when there was no assistance. The equilibrium payoffs would be different if, instead, the government had a "right" to present proposals for assistance to the IFI in exchange for reductions in its domestic policy distortions. This change in the power to set the agenda (make moves) would not change the result that allocations are Pareto Optimal for the world economy. It would, however, alter equilibrium payoffs in favor of the recipient government, with fewer reductions in distortions per dollar of IFI loans and more generous assistance payments. More broadly, payoffs resulting from games in which both parties alternate in making moves, as in a bargaining solution, would still be on the contract curve, but would leave the players with payoffs that are in between the two extremes.

Our framework can accommodate a variety of adjustments that add more realism at the cost of greater complexity. The simplest changes are in modifying the objective functions of the government, interest group, and IFI, while retaining the static, perfect information setup. The IMF may have narrowly bureaucratic objectives, as argued by

Vaubel (1996) and others. It could also be excessively influenced by financial interests in industrial countries, as maintained by Stiglitz (2002). The IFI could even be likened to a sympathetic social worker, as emphasized by Mussa (2002, pp. 67–69), or could even be influenced by northern or southern NGOs concerned about the plight of the poor in the developing world. Each of these perspectives leads to a different specification of the IFI's utility function, which are natural extensions of the Benthamite framework.

Additional realism could be gained by relaxing the perfect information assumption and allowing for two-sided incomplete information. The IFIs rely on member governments' cooperation to collect the country-specific information they need to make conditionality decisions. The IFIs know less than domestic actors about the effectiveness of economic assistance, the government's concern for (dependence on) the general public, and the influence-wielding ability of interest groups. On the other hand, IFIs have an advantage in analytical and cross-country knowledge of what works and what doesn't, which is useful in designing economic reform programs. This model can accommodate all these modifications. And as they are expected to lead to new insights, the authors will look at some of them in future research.

Conditionality has a role to play that is different from the one highlighted in this paper if national economic policy choices generate significant cross-border externalities. National governments do not always internalize the impact of their policy actions on neighboring countries and world welfare. Examples of such beggar-thy-neighbor policies abound: tariffs and other trade protection in developing countries, industrial-country agricultural subsidies that lock out producers from low-income countries, and so on. Being custodians of world economic welfare, the IFIs are mandated to use their policy advice and financial resources to avoid inefficient policies from being adopted in member countries. The IFIs' inherent internationalist orientation may thus generate conflicts of interest with recipient governments. This is likely to be an important consideration in thinking about conditionality *vis-à-vis* regionally or systemically important countries. Modifying this model to incorporate conditionality aimed at mitigating beggar-thy-neighbor policies is straightforward, as Mayer and Mourmouras (2002) show. The IFI's conditional assistance schedule then reflects in part its desire to ameliorate the international externalities resulting from distortionary national policies while taking into account the cost of transfers to the creditors.

The IMF and other IFIs have long recognized that the effectiveness of their assistance is intimately related to domestic political, social and economic conditions. The IMF's conditionality guidelines—in particular Guideline 4, IMF Guidelines on Conditionality, 1979, reproduced in IMF (2001)—have long called for the institution to pay "due regard to the domestic social and political objectives, the economic priorities, and the circumstances of members, including the causes of their balance of payments difficulties" But the Fund has not always paid due attention to the need to ensure greater country ownership. It overextended its mandate in areas that were not critical to its core mission.

The Fund has internalized these lessons and has moved to address the criticisms. The new conditionality guidelines, issued in September 2002, call for streamlining and refocusing of the conditions attached to IMF loans, with the aim of strengthening country commitment to reforms and raising program effectiveness. The focusing and streamlining of conditionality should help clarify the Fund's core objectives and reduce opposition to programs. The guidelines also seek to improve the Fund's interactions with borrowing countries and to tailor programs to the needs of member countries. The greater openness and transparency should help explain to the public why the IMF adopts the views it does and catalyze public debate. In the process, one hopes that the level of economic debate will rise as will the support for reforms that benefit silent, unorganized majorities in recipient countries.

## Appendix: Impact of Conditional Aid on the Interest Group's Welfare

Equation (9) indicates the equilibrium contribution of the interest group when it tries to influence the policy choices of a government that receives unconditional aid from an IFI. Equation (11), which restates this condition, can be expressed as:

$$(1-\lambda)U(\omega^u)+\lambda y[\underline{K}+T^u,\ \omega^u]=(1-\lambda)V^u+\lambda y[\underline{K}+T^{-V},\ 0). \tag{A1}$$

Equation (18) expresses the equilibrium contribution of the interest group when it competes with conditional aid from an IFI for influence on the government's policy choices. Its restatement of (18′) can be written as:

$$\begin{aligned}&(1-\lambda)U(\omega^c)+\lambda y[\underline{K}+A^T(\omega^c,\ I^c)+T^u(\omega^{-I}),\omega^c]\\ &\quad=(1-\lambda)V^c+\lambda y[\underline{K}+A^T(0,I^c)+T^u(0),0].\end{aligned} \tag{A2}$$

Solving (A1) for $V^{-I}=V^u$ and (A2) for $V^c$, setting $\omega^u=\omega^{-I}$ and $T^u=T^u(\omega^{-I})$, and using equation (19′) implies that:

$$V^{-I}>V^c \quad \text{if} \quad y[\underline{K}+A^T(0,I^c)+T^u(0),0]>y[\underline{K}+T^{-V},\ 0). \tag{A3}$$

Clearly, $V^{-I}>V^c$ since $T^u(0)=T^{-V}$ and $A^T(0,I^c)>0$.

## References

Alesina, Alberto and Allan Drazen, "Why Are Stabilizations Delayed?" *American Economic Review* 81 (1991):1170–88.

Bernheim, B. Douglas and Michael D. Whinston, "Menu Auctions, Resource Allocation, and Economic Influence," *Quarterly Journal of Economics* 101 (1986):1–32.

Dixit, Avinash, "IMF Programs as Incentive Mechanisms," manuscript, IMF, June 2000.

Dixit, Avinash, Gene M. Grossman, and Elhanan Helpman, "Common Agency and Coordination: General Theory and Application to Government Policy Making," *Journal of Political Economy* 105 (1997):752–69.

Drazen, Allan, "Conditionality and Ownership in IMF Lending: a Political Economy Approach," *IMF Staff Papers* 49 (2002):36–67.

Fernandez, Rachel and Dani Rodrik, "Resistance to Reform: Status Quo Bias in the Presence of Individual Specific Uncertainty," *American Economic Review* 81 (1991):1146–51.

Grossman, Gene M. and Elhanan Helpman, "Protection for Sale," *American Economic Review* 84 (1994):833–50.

———, *Special Interest Politics*, Cambridge: MIT Press (2001).

International Monetary Fund, "Conditionality in IMF-Supported Programs—Policy Issues," http://www.imf.org/ (2001).

Mayer, Wolfgang and Alexandros Mourmouras, "Vested Interests in a Positive Theory of IFI Conditionality," IMF Working Paper, Washington, D.C.: International Monetary Fund (2002).

Mitra, Devashish, "Endogenous Lobby Formation and Endogenous Protection: a Long Run Model of Trade Policy Determination," *American Economic Review* 89 (1999):1116–34.

Mussa, Michael, *Argentina and the Fund: From Triumph to Tragedy*, Washington D.C.: Institute for International Economics (2002).

Olson, Mancur, *The Logic of Collective Action*. Cambridge: Harvard University Press (1965).

Stiglitz, Joseph, *Globalization and its Discontents*, New York: W. W. Norton (2002).

Vaubel, Roland, "Bureaucracy at the IMF and the World Bank," *The World Economy* 19 (1996):195–210.

## Notes

1. Dixit, Grossman and Helpman (1997) develop a positive model of taxation and redistribution that extends Ramsey's classical theory.
2. Whereas this paper views the government as a unitary actor subject to pressure by *private* interest groups, in Drazen's (2002) paper the government must contend with veto players *within* the government.
3. This is consistent with the IMF's mandate (Article I.v of its Articles of Agreement) but is not the only possible description of its motivations. To cite an extreme public choice position, Stiglitz (2002, p. 18) argues that the IMF does not represent the interests of developing countries, having been captured by financial and commercial interests in industrial countries.
4. This means that additional capital required for keeping national income constant increases with the level of distortions.
5. The aid-receiving country's distortion index, $\omega$, on the other hand, might also be considered an argument in the ROW's national income function. A more distorted, less prosperous economy may lower welfare of its trading partners. We ignore this potential effect since the aid-receiving country is assumed to be small.
6. Note that unconditional aid in the presence of the interest group, $T^u(\omega^{-I})$, is different from unconditional aid in the absence of an interest group, $T^u(\omega^{-V})$.

ECONOMICS & POLITICS DOI 10.1111/j.1468-0343.2008.00339.x
Volume 21 March 2009 No. 1

# INTERNATIONAL FINANCIAL ASSISTANCE: A LOAN MECHANISM-DESIGN APPROACH

ALEX MOURMOURAS* AND WOLFGANG MAYER[1]

International Financial Institutions (IFIs) tie resource transfers to capital-scarce countries to improvements in their economic policies and institutions. The objective of this assistance is twofold: to augment the recipient's capital base and to improve its allocation of resources. This paper offers a political-economy explanation for the limited success of some of these loan programs. In our model, governments select policies under the influence of interest groups. Their capacity to absorb IFI loans and their reform efforts are both unobservable to the IFI. An optimally designed loan mechanism must create sufficient incentives – in the form of rewards and punishments – to counter the influence of interest groups on economic policy choices. The loan mechanism is, however, constrained in two ways: it cannot punish a country so severely as to threaten its political stability and it must remain affordable to the IFI. Whenever reform incentives are inadequate, a government will accept the loan but cheat on the implementation of reforms. If, on the other hand, the mechanism design is optimal, it might be so costly to the IFI that a well-entrenched interest group can block the reform program. Nonetheless, the availability of properly designed loan mechanisms will push governments to implement partial reforms even if the optimal mechanism is too costly for the IFI.

## 1. INTRODUCTION

INTERNATIONAL ASSISTANCE programs, such as loans and grants administered by official bilateral creditors and International Financial Institutions (IFIs), are appealing because they potentially raise the recipient country's welfare in two mutually reinforcing ways. First, they represent a direct resource transfer that adds to the recipient's capital stock (broadly construed), thereby expanding its production possibilities. Second, by calling for productivity- and welfare-enhancing policy and institutional reforms, these programs improve the efficiency with which a country's resources are employed. The IFIs' role is especially important in countries whose marginal product of IFI capital, evaluated at existing policies, is low relative to the international cost of funds, and that are cut off from private international

*Corresponding author: Alex Mourmouras, European Division, IMF Institute, International Monetary Fund, 700 19th Street, NW, Washington, DC 20431, USA. E-mail: amourmouras@imf.org

[1]Earlier versions of this paper were presented at the IMF and the Federal Reserve Bank of Minneapolis.

capital markets. By linking capital transfers to domestic reforms, countries are able to receive the double dividend of more resources and greater efficiency. In practice, however, international assistance has a mixed record in delivering these two dividends. While policy reform has been strong in some countries receiving international assistance, it has been weak in others.[2]

For the IMF, linking assistance to reform "conditions" has evolved over time. Until the mid-1970s, conditions were primarily macroeconomic ones, aiming to build up a country's official international reserves, curb excessively large government budget deficits, limit the growth of money and credit aggregates, and facilitate real exchange rate adjustments. Beginning with the oil shocks of the 1970s, and especially following the debt crisis of the 1980s and the admission of transition countries in their ranks, the IMF and other IFIs began to augment macroeconomic conditions with first- and second-generation structural reforms.[3] The reform agenda focused on liberalizing pricing and trade regimes, restructuring and privatizing state enterprises and banks, and reforming financial and corporate systems and governance.[4] In light of its member countries' needs at the time, the IMF aimed to boost the supply side of the economy, improve the efficiency of economic institutions, and raise exports and growth performance. In the 1990s, the IMF also used structural conditionality in response to financial crises in emerging economies, including Mexico and Asia, which revealed the need to address structural weaknesses in these countries.

The conditions attached by the IMF, when it extends financing to sovereigns, were originally motivated by the need to safeguard its own resources, i.e. ensure that IMF loans get repaid, and the related objective of ensuring that countries in need of economic adjustment and reform avoid the adoption of trade protectionism and other inefficient policy measures. Conditionality also provides guarantees to borrowers, who are reasonably confident that they can obtain IMF financing if they meet the conditions stipulated in the agreement.[5]

[2]On the record and effectiveness of IFI-supported programs, see Dollar and Svensson (2000), Ivanova et al. (2005), and Mussa and Savastano (1999).

[3]On the evolving focus of World Bank conditions, see World Bank (2005, p. 52). On the trends in structural conditionality in IMF-supported programs, see IMF (2001a, 2001b, pp. 8–13). World Bank (2006) is an example of the sorts of structural fiscal reforms advocated by international assistance providers.

[4]The IMF established the *Extended Fund Facility* in September 1974 to help member countries address balance of payments difficulties that arise from "structural maladjustments in production and trade and widespread cost and price distortions." In 1976, the IMF established the *Trust Fund* to assist low-income developing countries. This was succeeded by the *Structural Adjustment Facility* in 1986 and the *Enhanced Structural Adjustment Facility* in 1987. The IMF has also participated in the *Heavily Indebted Poor Countries Initiative* since 1996. In 1999, the ESAF was restructured and renamed the *Poverty Reduction and Growth Facility*. This facility has made poverty reduction and growth more central in the IMF's lending operations to the poorest member countries.

[5]The Conditionality Guidelines (IMF, 2002) state that "Conditions on the use of Fund resources are governed by the Fund's Articles of Agreement and implementing decisions of the Executive Board. Conditionality – that is, program-related conditions – is intended to ensure

Consistent with the mechanism-design approach, it has long been recognized that IMF-supported programs must be effective incentive mechanisms.[6] These programs are designed to incorporate sufficient rewards and punishments to ensure a reasonably good chance of delivering needed policy adjustments. What the formal mechanism-design theory emphasizes is the need to consider carefully participation, incentive compatibility, limited liability, and financial viability constraints.

The uneven success of some loans that incorporate structural reforms has been attributed to two major impediments: information frictions and acute political economy constraints associated with them.[7] Many structural reforms are complex and not easily quantifiable, making monitoring by an IFI or third parties quite difficult. A simple listing of reform measures – which were beneficial in and of themselves – frequently did not lead to meaningful reforms unless they were "owned" by the recipient country's key stakeholders. In addition, IFI programs sometimes faltered because they ignored or overestimated the recipient's capacity to administer the loans and to implement the reforms. This was particularly the case in some IFI programs with newly installed but untested administrations, and in some situations in which the payoffs of technical assistance investments did not meet initial expectations.

The objective of this paper is to formulate a theoretical model that captures the essential features of IFI loans with structural reform conditions and to assess the strengths and weaknesses of such loan programs. The model highlights the influence of information asymmetries, as well as the political constraints under which governments operate. It thereby addresses IFI loans to developing countries as a mechanism-design problem in a political-economy setting.[8] In this asymmetric information model of special-interest politics, loan decisions and economic policy choices are shaped

that Fund resources are provided to members to assist them in resolving their balance of payments problems in a manner that is consistent with the Fund's Articles and that establishes adequate safeguards for the temporary use of the Fund's resources."

[6]For an introduction to mechanism-design theory, see the survey and references in http://nobelprize.org/nobel_prizes/economics/laureates/2007/ecoadv07.pdf. Issues of optimal monitoring of international assistance programs are set aside. Dixit (2000) advocates using mechanism-design theory to analyze IMF-supported programs and presents a thoughtful informal discussion.

[7]Rodrik (1996, p. 31) emphasizes the information frictions present in official creditor–debtor relationships. Dixit (2002, 2003) stresses the agency costs associated with informational asymmetries, special-interest politics, and the public sector nature of recipients.

[8]The formal literature on conditional lending analyzes political economy models of IFI–debtor country interactions under complete and perfect information, in which reforms are observable by all actors. See Boughton and Mourmouras (2004), Drazen (2002), Mayer and Mourmouras (2005), and the references therein. Recently, some papers in this tradition have begun to examine issues of asymmetric information. Ivanova (2006) presents a common agency model of IFI lending but does not consider the possibility of political instability or sovereign default. See also Drazen and Isard (2004), who present an analytically informed discussion of the role of public debate in disseminating information about the objectives of reform programs and overcoming informational frictions.

through the interactions of three risk-neutral agents: a political-support-seeking government, an altruistic IFI, and a domestic interest group that benefits from distorting policies.[9] All agents observe the recipient economy's actual performance, which depends on the state of nature, the choice of economic policies, and the impact of the IFI loan. Economic reforms raise the probability of the economy performing well, but the actual implementation of reforms cannot be observed by the IFI. This creates a moral hazard situation. The loan-granting IFI also cannot observe a government's competency in executing a loan program. This leads to an adverse selection problem. Whereas the IFI does not observe the competency of the government and its implementation of reforms, the domestic interest group does. The interest group in the recipient country negotiates rent-creating policies in exchange for financial contributions to a government that maximizes its political support *à la* Grossman and Helpman (1994, 2001). The model also allows for the possibility of the government defaulting on the loan.

The design of a loan mechanism is significantly constrained by three critical considerations: assuring political stability of the loan-receiving country,[10] maintaining financial viability of the IFI,[11] and overcoming the power of an interest group. First, a country's political stability is threatened if the public perceives that a bad state of nature is exacerbated by a government arrangement with a foreign institution. Political and economic chaos is the likely consequence. Such political instability is all but inevitable when the IFI designs loan mechanisms without limited liability constraints. Second, even though the IFI is altruistic and cares for the recipient country's welfare, it cannot afford to ignore its own financial viability. While the IFI might end up with losses on some loans and gains on others, on average it has to break even. The IFI will not lend if its expected return on the loan is negative. And finally, the loan contract offered by the IFI is shaped by the interest group's

[9]For earlier work on this topic, see Mayer and Mourmouras (2004, 2005, 2008).

[10]Obviously, IFIs care about instability in that it reduces repayment prospects and substantially raises the probability of default. An alternative to linking instability to excessive repayment and the violation of limited liability constraints would be to model how instability is related to reforms and repayment prospects. The IFI might risk some political instability in order to increase the probability of generating reforms. It is beyond the scope of this paper to examine these connections, but progress can be made along the lines suggested by Acemoglu and Robinson (2006).

[11]The IMF's financial viability has come into sharper focus in recent years because of the dramatic increase in official reserves holdings in many emerging market countries and a significant decline in the volume of IMF loans to its member countries. An eminent persons committee was established to review the sustainability of the IMF's finances that included Alan Greenspan and other eminent policy-makers and financiers. Their report is available on http://www.imf.org/external/np/oth/2007/013107.pdf. Also note that the IMF's Articles of Agreement [Article I(v)] and the IMF's more detailed Conditionality Guidelines (IMF, 2002, 2005), which outline the general rules governing its lending activities, both emphasize the "temporary" nature of IMF loans and the need for "adequate safeguards" to ensure repayment by countries who make use of Fund credit. These concerns are motivated by the need to guarantee that these resources are available for other countries when they are in a balance-of-payment need.

power in the country of the loan-seeking government. The deal that the government can potentially negotiate with the interest group represents its best alternative to the IFI loan contract.

The paper highlights the precarious nature of loan mechanisms that incorporate reform conditions. Asymmetric information requires the design of suitable incentives for loan-receiving governments to implement reforms. To create such incentives, loan repayments are made contingent on the observable state of the economy.[12] The drawback of creating an incentive mechanism is that it calls for punishment when the economy performs poorly, making a badly performing economy even worse off than it would be without the loan and thereby threatening the political stability of the country. If the IFI is sensitive to its borrower's political stability, it has to limit the severity of punishment for underperforming. The price of granting limited liability constraints, in turn, is that it diminishes the expected return for the loan-granting IFI.

The paper demonstrates that an IFI's ability to break even on a loan with reform strings depends on the strength of a country's interest group, as well as on the country's expected income gains from the loan. A strong interest group can effectively block the IFI from making a profitable loan with reforms. However, blocking an IFI loan does not eliminate the IFI's influence. It is shown that the mere existence of an IFI – as long as it is willing to make a loan to a weaker interest group – pushes the government into partial reforms. Our model also addresses the question of which type of loan, with or without reforms, the IFI will offer if both loan types earn positive returns. We show that a sufficiently altruistic IFI – one that cares at least as much for the recipient country as for the loan-providing donors – will always choose the loan with reforms.

The model provides answers to two kinds of questions. First, will the IFI be willing to make a loan? And, if so, how large will the loan be? Second, what economic policies will be chosen? In our model, the decision of making a loan is made by the IFI. A country's economic policies, on the other hand, are chosen by a government. When the IFI does not call for policy reforms – either because no IFI exists, the loan has no reform strings attached, or the interest group is able to block the IFI's loan with reforms – then the policy choice is based on a policy-for-contributions deal the government negotiates with special interests. It is assumed to result from an asymmetric Nash-bargaining game. When the IFI does strike a loan deal with the government,

[12]Formally speaking, IFI loans are standard fixed-rate contracts, often incorporating some grant element. De facto, however, these loans are renegotiated ex post, when economic times in recipient countries have turned out to be weak. IFIs have rescheduled their loans and provided debt relief, along with bilateral official donors. Hence, repayments of IFI loans to sovereigns vary de facto with the strength of the recipient's economy. Gelb (cited in Isard et al., 2006, p. 23) and other knowledgeable observers acknowledge the "quasi-like" features of IFI loans. Chamon and Mauro (2005) have proposed issuing "GDP-indexed sovereign debt" that would make the connection a part of the formal contract.

the IFI requests the government to reform completely. This would eliminate the privileged position of the interest group. But it remains up to the government to decide whether it wants to implement those reforms or set its own policy and thereby retain support from its interest group.

The remainder of this paper is structured as follows. Section 2 provides a brief overview of conditionality practices at the IMF. Section 3 sets up the basic model. Section 4 describes the interactions between interest group and government. Section 5 lays out the time line of events and decision-making. After describing the possibility of default in section 6, section 7 presents the optimal mechanism with no limited liability constraints. Section 8 does the same assuming limited liability. Sections 9 and 10 describe the main results – the circumstances under which the IFI will be able to offer loans with or without reform incentives and the influence of the IFI's latent presence on reforms. Section 11 concludes.

## 2. CONDITIONALITY AT THE IMF

As mentioned, conditionality has evolved over time. The expansion of structural conditionality in the 1980s and 1990s was well intentioned and a necessary response to criticism that IMF-supported programs relied excessively on short-term austerity measures; it did, however, produce some unintended consequences. The language of mechanism-design theory is useful in illustrating these consequences. When conditionality became overly ambitious and complex, it certainly undermined *incentive constraints*: domestic ownership for reforms weakened as cash-strapped governments sometimes agreed to conditions mainly to secure international loans. Lack of ownership hindered the implementation of reforms. As programs expanded beyond its core areas, the IMF was spread thin. Some countries backtracked on promised reforms and even misreported information to the Fund in order to secure the approval or the continuation of IMF funding (IMF, 2000). Violation of *participation constraints* was also an issue as some countries that needed IMF financing were reluctant to come to the negotiating table. Countries procrastinated and only sought IFI assistance at a late stage, when their economic problems had become very acute. *Uncertainty* about the effectiveness of governments in administering IMF and other loans was also an issue, especially when dealing with well-meaning, newly elected democratic governments deserving to be supported. In these situations, in which IFIs were inclined to help, *inadequate tailoring* of loans to government type caused results to fall short of expectations.

These concerns led the IMF and other IFIs to give high priority to streamlining and focusing its conditionality and strengthening national ownership. Starting in the spring of 2000, the IMF initiated an extensive review of its conditionality principles and practices. Following several discussions at its Executive Board, the IMF issued new Conditionality

Guidelines in September 2002, replacing an earlier set that dated from 1979. A review of the implementation of these guidelines was concluded in the spring of 2005 as part of the IMF's biennial review of conditionality.[13] The guidelines encourage the Fund to help countries build broad support for sound policies, including through public discussion and, potentially, the adoption of participatory processes (see also Drazen and Isard, 2004). IMF staff is encouraged – if the member country desires – to assist through seminars, meetings with parliamentary committees, trade unions, business groups, and the media. IMF resident representatives are to play a key role in this.[14]

The guidelines limit conditionality to measures that are critical to program goals or are needed for monitoring. *Prior actions* (conditions that must be met before the disbursement or continuation of IMF financing) are to be used parsimoniously as they cannot offset lack of country ownership. Adding conditions at any stage in an IMF program's life cycle requires clear justification as to why the new measures have become critical to program objectives. Conditions can be set on economic targets and objectives rather than policy actions (outcomes-based conditionality). These outcomes must be controllable by the authorities and should not be achieved through inefficient measures.

The IMF revisited the conditionality guidelines in 2004–2005. This review concluded that structural conditionality had shifted to the Fund's core areas and been reduced in scope, and that clarity of conditionality had improved (see IMF, 2005). But whereas permanent program interruptions had declined, the implementation of structural conditionality had not improved. The IMF continued to issue many waivers for conditions that were not met, probably because their implementation time frames are overly ambitious. The IMF Board encouraged IMF operational staff to strive for ambitious but realistic timetables, especially when judging implementation capacity is difficult, and to explore the potential of floating tranches.

## 3. THE MODEL

The recipient economy's total output, $X$, depends on the economy's state of nature, as reflected in the value of $y$ and on the output-expanding effect of

[13]The 2002 guidelines set out five principles to guide IMF conditional lending. These principles are: (i) national ownership of programs; (ii) parsimony in conditionality; (iii) tailoring of programs to borrowing country circumstances; (iv) coordination with other multilateral institutions; and (v) clarity in conditionality.

[14]The guidelines state that "the Fund will encourage members to seek to broaden and deepen the base of support for sound policies in order to enhance the likelihood of successful implementation." But while intended to help build ownership, IMF help to countries adopt participatory processes is not without controversy. Many developing countries have complained that such processes may effectively weaken ownership by circumventing their democratically elected executive branch.

the IFI loan, $T$. The country's aggregate production function is

$$X = g(T)y, \tag{1}$$

where the function $g(T)$ expresses the magnifying influence of the loan, $T$, on the economy's performance and where $g(0) = 1$, $g'(T) > 0$, and $g''(T) < 0$ for $T > 0$. The value of $y$, in turn, is stochastic and depends on the economy's state of nature. The economy is "strong" when $y = \bar{y}$ and "weak" when $y = \underline{y}$; $\Delta y = (\bar{y} - \underline{y}) > 0$ measures the *economy's output volatility* due to exogenous changes in the state of nature.

Ex post, all decision-makers can observe and verify the value of $y$. Ex ante, none of them knows whether output, absent of loan effects, will be $\bar{y}$ or $\underline{y}$. It is common knowledge, however, that a strong economy is more likely the smaller economic policy distortions are, as measured by the distortion index $0 \leq \omega \leq 1$. The probability of a strong economy is expressed by $0 \leq \pi(\omega) \leq 1$, where $\pi'(\omega) < 0$ and $\pi''(\omega) < 0$; that is, more distorting policies reduce the probability of good performance, and they do so at an increasing rate. A value of $\omega = 0$ indicates that distortions have been completely removed: $\omega = 0$ is therefore the first-best policy that delivers complete reform. We denote the probability of a strong economy under complete reforms by $\pi(0) = \underline{\pi}$. Subsequently, we will encounter the expression $[\underline{\pi} - \pi(\omega)] = \Delta\pi(\omega) > 0$ for all $\omega > 0$; it is a measure of the *effectiveness of complete reforms* in bringing about a strong economy relative to initial policy distortions of $\omega > 0$.

There are three decision-makers: the government of the loan-seeking country, an interest group of the same country, and an IFI, which is the sole source of loans for the country in question. The government chooses its policies either directly in a deal with the interest group or indirectly as part of an IFI loan mechanism. The IFI is assumed to aim for complete reform. The government's objective is to maximize its political support, which derives from the general public and the interest group. Support from the public is directly related to the economy's performance; support from the interest group comes in the form of political contributions that are determined through negotiations. Alternatively, the government accepts an IFI-designed loan program, which specifies the size of the loan, the economic reforms the government must carry out, and the amount it has to repay. One possibility is to refrain from calling for economic reforms.

The *government's* objective function, following Grossman and Helpman (1994), is

$$G = C + aV, \tag{2}$$

where $G$ is a measure of political support for the government, $C$ denotes the interest group's financial contributions, and $V$ stands for the country's net income. Parameter $a \geq 0$ expresses the degree to which the net income of the entire country translates into the general public's political support for the government.[15] The greater the public's influence on the government, the larger the value of $a$. Hence, $a$ can be interpreted as the extent of the encompassing interest of the state in the economy, as defined by Mancur Olson.

The country's net income is $V = X - Z - \theta T$, where $X$ is the economy's output as defined in (1), $Z \geq 0$ denotes the government's contractual repayment of loan $T$, and $\theta \geq 0$ stands for the government's unit cost of administering the loan. Repayments, $Z$, are spelled out in the loan offer and are contingent on the economy's state at the loan due date. The loan package – defined by $(T, Z)$ – might also be affected by the government's effectiveness in administering the loan program. For a cost-effective or a "good" government, the unit cost of administering the loan, $\theta_G$, is lower than for a cost-ineffective or a "bad" government, with unit cost $\theta_B$.

The *interest group* makes a contribution, $C$, to the government in return for the adoption of policies, indexed by $\omega$. The group's goal is to maximize its expected net income

$$H = R(\omega) - C, \tag{3}$$

where $R(\omega)$ denotes expected economic rents created by policy distortion $\omega$, and where $R(0) = 0$.[16] Economic rents are assumed to rise with policy distortions at a decreasing rate, such that $R'(\omega) > 0$ and $R''(\omega) < 0$. While distorting policies benefit the interest group, they lower the probability of a strong economy and thereby reduce the economy's expected income and corresponding expected political support from the public. The contribution, $C$, is determined through bargaining between the interest group and the government.

The *IFI* is portrayed as a public-interest institution that cares about the welfare of both loan-receiving and loan-financing (donor) countries. Its objective, $W$, is to maximize a weighted average of the recipient country's expected net income, $E(V)$, and the IFI's expected net return on the loan, $E(I)$:

$$W = \beta E(V) + (1 - \beta)E(I), \tag{4}$$

where $0 \leq \beta \leq 1$ and $E(I) = E(r) - T$. The term $E(r)$ denotes the expected loan repayment that depends on the state of the economy at the loan due date. Repayments are either the contractually agreed amount or a renegotiated smaller amount in case the country threatens to default.

## 4. INTEREST GROUP AND GOVERNMENT

The influence of special interests on economic policies can be direct or indirect. It is direct when the government chooses policies that benefit the group in return for financial contributions. The interest group and the

[15] See Grossman and Helpman (2001, p. 119, n. 5) for a discussion of the size restrictions on $a$.
[16] We are not explicitly modeling the type of distortions that bring about the rent.

government bargain over what the contribution will be for a certain policy and the government, anticipating this bargain, chooses the policy that maximizes its political support. The outcome might be influenced by the presence of an IFI that offers loans in return for reforms.

Special interests retain an indirect influence on the government even when the government accepts and implements an IFI loan that incorporates reform incentives. Although the interest group disbands under complete reforms, the threat of its re-emergence indirectly shapes the content of the loan mechanism designed by the IFI. The IFI loan must make the government at least as well off when it accepts the loan and reforms as it would be if it continued its cooperation with the group. Specifically, the IFI, in designing such a loan program, must account for the government's alternative action of cheating on economic reform implementation and, in return for not reforming, of continuing to receive support from the interest group. Accordingly, IFI loan mechanisms that aim at delivering reforms are indirectly shaped by the group's latent ability to benefit from distorting economic policies.

The outcome of bargaining between government and interest group is the solution to an asymmetric Nash-bargaining game. Critical for the solution is the government's expected political support and the group's expected welfare when bargaining succeeds relative to what it would be if it broke down. To illustrate, consider the case of government and interest group bargaining when there is *no IFI at all.* If they strike a bargain, the interest group's welfare is $\{R(\omega) - C\}$ and the government's expected political support is $\{C + a[\pi(\omega)\bar{y} + (1 - \pi(\omega))\underline{y}]\}$. Should bargaining break down, the government is best off completely reforming on its own, such that $\omega = 0$ and expected political support is $a[\underline{\pi}\bar{y} + (1 - \underline{\pi})\underline{y}]$. The interest group, on the other hand, fades away as $R(0) = 0$. The bargaining solution is that the value of $C$ that maximizes

$$\{[C + a[\pi(\omega)\bar{y} + (1 - \pi(\omega))\underline{y}] - a[\underline{\pi}\bar{y} + (1 - \underline{\pi})\underline{y}]\}^{\tau}\{R(\omega) - C\}^{1-\tau},$$

where $0 \leq \tau \leq 1$ is a measure of the government's bargaining power. The maximizing choice of $C$ depends on the distortion index $\omega$, such that

$$C(\omega) = \tau R(\omega) + (1 - \tau)a\Delta y\Delta\pi(\omega). \tag{5}$$

For any bargaining to take place, it must be that $R(\omega) > a\Delta y\Delta\pi(\omega)$. Hence, ceteris paribus, the contribution rises with the bargaining power of the government, $\tau$, with the size of rents at a given level of distortion, $R(\omega)$, and the country's expected gain in income when it reforms, $\Delta y\Delta\pi(\omega)$.

Given the *contribution function* of (5), the government adopts economic policies, $\omega^*$, to maximize its expected political support, $\{C(\omega) + a[\pi(\omega)\bar{y} + (1 - \pi(\omega))\underline{y}]\}$. This implies that

$$-R'(\omega^*)/\pi'(\omega^*) = a\Delta y. \tag{6}$$

The value of $\omega^*$ states the government's political-support maximizing level of distortions in the absence of the IFI and the pair $[\omega^*, C(\omega^*)]$ describes the corresponding *policy-for-contributions deal*; the government gives the group $\omega^*$ and receives $C(\omega^*)$ in return. Because $R''(\omega) < 0$ and $\pi''(\omega) < 0$, (5) and (6) imply:

**Proposition 1.**

(i) Economic policies are less distorted and interest group contributions are larger, the more influence the general public has on the government, $a$, and the greater the economy's output volatility, $\Delta y$.

(ii) Greater bargaining power on the part of the government results in higher interest group contributions but has no effect on the choice of policies.

## 5. TIME LINE OF EVENTS AND DECISION-MAKING

The government's search for a loan from the IFI starts at $t_1$, at which time it chooses policy $\omega^*$ in return for interest group contributions $C(\omega^*)$.

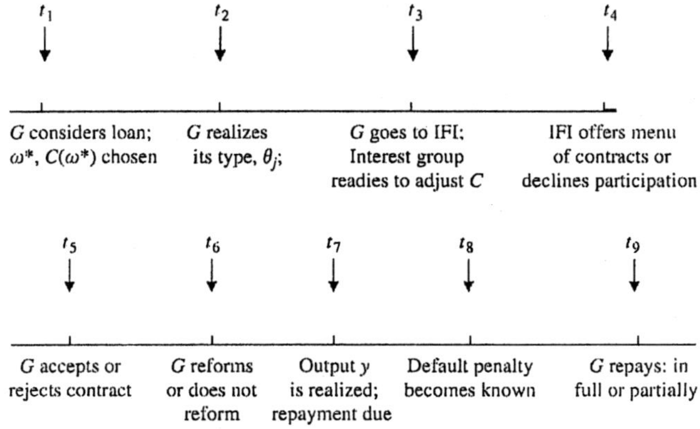


At $t_2$, the government realizes its effectiveness in administering a loan program. At $t_3$, the government goes to the IFI, which does not know whether it has been approached by a cost-effective, *good*, or cost-ineffective, *bad*, government. The IFI, however, is aware of the interest group's relationship with the government and, in particular, of the best political-support-yielding deal the government could negotiate with the interest group. Whatever its best *potential* response, the interest group's actual contribution will be adjusted in one of two ways: either it stops all contributions, as the IFI insists on complete reforms, or it raises them sufficiently to block the IFI from offering a loan with incentives to reform. If, at

$t_4$, such a loan cannot be blocked, then the IFI offers a menu of stochastic loan contracts from which the government can choose. Each contract spells out the amount to be disbursed and the corresponding repayment at the due date. The contracts are stochastic because creating the necessary incentives for economic reforms calls for linking the amount of repayment to the state of the economy at the due date. In addition, each contract accounts for the possibility of default; should the government have an incentive to default at repayment time, the IFI is prepared to renegotiate the repayment.

The government decides on whether to accept the contract intended for its type at $t_5$. If accepted, the government faces, at time $t_6$, the decision of implementing economic reforms; it has an incentive to implement and enforce reforms if the relevant moral hazard incentive constraints are satisfied. At $t_7$, both the IFI and the government observe the economy's performance and they learn about the level of repayment as set in the contract. Before repaying, the government considers the possibility of defaulting. At $t_8$, both the IFI and the government find out about the penalty the government has to pay if it defaults on the loan repayment. Finally, at $t_9$, the government either repays the amount stipulated in the initial loan contract for the realized state of the economy or it accepts a renegotiated lower payment to avert default.

## 6. ACCOUNTING FOR THE POSSIBILITY OF DEFAULT

For any loan, the IFI must allow for the possibility of default. We model the possibility of rational default in the simplest possible way, following Eaton and Gersovitz (1995). The government is assumed to face a penalty for defaulting whose severity, at the time the loan is made, is not known to either the IFI or the government. They do know, however, the distribution of penalties. More specifically, let $P$ denote the penalty a country incurs if it defaults on an IFI loan. The idea is that default triggers several reactions that are costly to the country, such as trade sanctions, the inability to borrow from other IFIs, and loss of (or more restricted access to) private capital markets. At the loan due date, the government compares the contractually agreed-upon repayment amount, $Z$, with the size of the penalty, $P$, and defaults if

$$Z \geq P. \tag{7}$$

Both the government and the IFI do not learn the realization of the penalty until the due date for repayment. At the stage of designing the loan contract, their knowledge is limited to the density function, $f(p)$, where $p = P/y$ measures the penalty per unit of $y$. Given contractual repayment $Z$, the probability of government default, meaning that $z = Z/y \geq P/y = p$, equals $F(z)$.

When the IFI designs its menu of loan contracts, it is fully aware that the government might default. Should the latter threaten default, the IFI can either accept default without repayment or offer an amended contract that reduces the repayment to an amount equal to the penalty. Because the IFI is always better off with partial repayment than no repayment, each initial contract contains such a default repayment clause. Given a contractual repayment $Z$ and a penalty distribution function $f(p)$, the expected repayment from the government to the IFI, $E(r)$, equals

$$E(r) = \int_0^z Pf(p)dp + \int_z^\infty Zf(p)dp. \tag{8}$$

For $p \leq z$, repayment is adjusted to $P = py$; for $p \geq z$, repayment is the negotiated amount of $Z = zy$. After substitution and integration by parts, equation (8) can be restated as

$$E(r) = y\int_0^z pf(p)dp + yz\int_z^\infty f(p)dp = y\left[z - \int_0^z F(p)dp\right]. \tag{8'}$$

The expected repayment, $E(r)$, is smaller than the negotiated repayment, which equals $Z = yz$, but it exceeds what the IFI expects to be repaid if it received nothing under default, which is $yz[1 - F(z)]$. The expected repayment depends on whether the economy is strong, $\bar{y}$, or weak, $\underline{y}$, as well as on whether the government is good or bad. Accordingly, expected repayments by a government of type $j = G, B$ are denoted as $E(\bar{r}_j)$ when $y = \bar{y}$ and $E(\underline{r}_j)$ when $y = \underline{y}$.

## 7. LOAN MECHANISM DESIGN WITHOUT LIMITED LIABILITY

The IFI's goal is to design a loan program that maximizes its objective of accommodating the interests of both recipient and donor countries, as stated in (4). The interests of the recipient country with the $j$th-type government are captured by its expected net income, $E(V_j)$. The donors' interests are reflected in the IFI's expected return, $E(I)$, which equals expected repayment minus the loan's cost. The IFI does not offer a contract unless it expects at least to break even.

We assume that the IFI has all the bargaining power in its relationship with the recipient country. It alone determines the design of the loan mechanism and it makes a take-it-or-leave-it offer to the government. However, asymmetric information on both the government's effectiveness in administering the loan and on the implementation of economic reforms calls for careful crafting of the loan mechanism. The IFI's inability to assess the government's competence to administer the loan puts it into an adverse selection situation; its inability to observe the government's implementation of reforms creates moral hazard. In the presence of both adverse selection and moral hazard, each government must have the incentive to accept the contract designed for its type and each type government must have the incentive to implement the called-for economic reforms. Furthermore, two additional conditions must be satisfied. First, at the time of the contract signing, *expected* political support must be at least as strong as without the loan. Second, after the state of the economy becomes known, the country must *actually* be at least as well off as it would be without the loan. The former condition imposes the usual ex ante participation (or individual rationality) constraint. The latter adds an ex post limited liability constraint. The purpose of this section is to show that, without limited liability constraints, loan mechanisms call for such punishments in the weak state of the economy that the general public becomes worse off than without the IFI loan, thereby endangering the country's political stability. The discussion of loan mechanisms with limited liability constraints follows in section 7.

As already mentioned, at the time it designs its loan mechanism, the IFI is unable to judge the government's ability to administer the loan. Administering a loan is costly, whereby the cost depends on both the size of the loan, $T$, and a cost-effectiveness parameter, $\theta_j$. For a cost-effective or good government, the cost of administering one unit of the loan is $\theta_G > 0$; for a cost-ineffective or bad government, it is $\theta_B > 0$, where $\theta_B > \theta_G$. Each government, as well as its interest group, knows whether it is efficient or inefficient, but the IFI does not. The latter does know, however, that the government is efficient with probability $0 < \gamma < 1$.

The IFI loan mechanism consists of two stochastic contracts $[T_j, \overline{Z}_j, \underline{Z}_j]$, for $j = G, B$: one intended for a good government, $G$, and one intended for a bad government, $B$. Each contract states the loan amount, $T_j$, as well as repayment in a strong and weak economy, indicated by $\overline{Z}_j$ and $\underline{Z}_j$, respectively. Each contract also contains a clause stating that repayment is reduced to the default penalty, $P$, whenever $Z_j > P$. Not knowing the government's type, the IFI's expected net return from the loan is

$$E(I) = \gamma[\underline{\pi} E(\bar{r}_G) + (1 - \underline{\pi})E(\underline{r}_G) - T_G]$$
$$+ (1 - \gamma)[\overline{\pi} E(\bar{r}_B) + (1 - \overline{\pi})E(\underline{r}_B) - T_B], \quad (9)$$

where $E(\underline{r}_j)$ and $E(\bar{r}_j)$ denote expected repayment by government type $j$ in a weak and strong economy, respectively, as defined in (8′).

The IFI maximizes its objective function of (4) by choosing the size of the loan and corresponding repayment subject to the following set of constraints: a pair of *participation constraints* to ensure that each government type is willing to accept the loan contract; a set of *adverse selection incentive constraints*, so that each government selects the contract designed for its type; and a pair of *moral hazard incentive constraints*, so that each government type has the incentive to reform the economy.[17] It will also be recalled from section 1 that, in all this, we explicitly assume that the IFI insists on complete reform as a condition for the loan, reducing distortions to $\omega = 0$ and raising the probability of a strong economy to its maximum value of $\underline{\pi}$.

Before stating the constraints formally, we calculate the recipient country's expected net income, evaluated at $t_7$ on our time line, as a function of its government type $j = G, B$. At this loan due date, output $y$ has been observed and contractual repayments are due, but the default penalty remains unknown. At that time, the country's expected net incomes in a strong and weak economy, respectively, are

$$\begin{aligned} \overline{V}_j &= [g(T_j)\bar{y} - \theta_j T_j - E(\bar{r}_j)] \\ \underline{V}_j &= [g(T_j)\underline{y} - \theta_j T_j - E(\underline{r}_j)]. \end{aligned} \tag{10}$$

In (10), expectations are taken with respect to the probability distribution of default $F(z)$. We will use these expected net income measures to describe the constraint set faced by the IFI as well as later when we restate (9), the expected net return for the IFI.

For each type government, the *participation constraint* is satisfied if its expected political support under full implementation of the loan mechanism (that is, with receipt and repayment of the loan and implementation of first-best reforms) is at least as strong as it would be without the IFI loan and without complete reforms. As a preliminary, it is important to consider what policies the government would select if it entered negotiations with the interest group knowing that it can get a loan with certain strings attached from the IFI in case these negotiations break down. Appendix A.1 shows that the presence of a loan-offering IFI pushes the government to adopt partial reforms even if the loan is not taken out: the government would choose policies $\omega_j' < \omega^*$ and receive interest group contributions $C(\omega_j')$.[18] As the IFI does not know whether it is dealing with a good or a bad government, the participation constraint must hold for each government type:

$$a[\underline{\pi}\overline{V}_G + (1-\underline{\pi})\underline{V}_G] \geq C(\omega') + a\{\pi(\omega')\bar{y} + [1-\pi(\omega')]\underline{y}\}, \tag{11}$$

$$a[\underline{\pi}\overline{V}_B + (1-\underline{\pi})\underline{V}_B] \geq C(\omega') + a\{\pi(\omega')\bar{y} + [1-\pi(\omega')]\underline{y}\}. \tag{12}$$

In (11) and (12), the LHS states expected political support if the loan was accepted and reforms were implemented, whereas the RHS states expected political support when no loan is accepted and the best alternative policy is chosen under a policy-for-contributions deal with the interest group, in full knowledge of the IFI's loan conditions.

[17]For a modeling approach in which there is both adverse selection and moral hazard, see Laffont and Martimort (2002, ch. 7).

[18]Appendix A.1 also shows that this best alternative policy choice to implementing reforms is independent of the type of government, implying that $\omega_G' = \omega_B' = \omega'$.

The *adverse selection incentive constraints* require that each government type have an incentive to select the loan contract designed for its type. Hence, the contract designed for the good (bad) government must be at least as favorable to the good (bad) government as the loan contract designed for the bad (good) government. In addition, because the good (bad) government's acceptance of the bad (good) government contract allows the former either to implement reforms or to cheat and keep the economy distorted, there are two adverse selection incentive constraints for each type of government. Letting $\Delta\theta = \theta_B - \theta_G > 0$, the adverse selection constraints require that[19]

$$[\underline{\pi}\overline{V}_G + (1-\underline{\pi})\overline{V}_G] \geq [\underline{\pi}\overline{V}_B + (1-\underline{\pi})\underline{V}_B + T_B\Delta\theta], \tag{13}$$

$$a[\underline{\pi}\overline{V}_G + (1-\underline{\pi})\underline{V}_G] \geq C(\omega') + a\{\pi(\omega')\overline{V}_B + [1-\pi(\omega')]\underline{V}_B + T_B\Delta\theta\}, \tag{14}$$

$$[\underline{\pi}\overline{V}_B + (1-\underline{\pi})\underline{V}_B] \geq [\underline{\pi}\overline{V}_G + (1-\underline{\pi})\underline{V}_G - T_G\Delta\theta], \tag{15}$$

$$a[\underline{\pi}\overline{V}_B + (1-\underline{\pi})\underline{V}_B] \geq C(\omega') + a\{\pi(\omega')\overline{V}_G + [1-\pi(\omega')]\underline{V}_G - T_G\Delta\theta\}. \tag{16}$$

Each government type's loan contract must also satisfy a *moral hazard incentive constraint*. The contract must create incentives for the government not only to accept it as designed for its type but also to fully implement economic reforms. Accordingly, the government's expected political support must be at least as strong when it accepts and implements the IFI contract and economic reforms as it would be if it accepted the loan and its repayment conditions but did not implement the reforms. This requires for each type government that

$$a[\underline{\pi}\overline{V}_j + (1-\underline{\pi})\underline{V}_j] \geq C(\omega') + a\{\pi(\omega')\overline{V}_j + [1-\pi(\omega')]\underline{V}_j\}$$

or, stated differently, that

$$a\Delta\pi(\omega')[\overline{V}_G - \underline{V}_G] \geq C(\omega'), \tag{17}$$

$$a\Delta\pi(\omega')[\overline{V}_B - \underline{V}_B] \geq C(\omega'), \tag{18}$$

where $\Delta\pi(\omega') = [\underline{\pi} - \pi(\omega')] > 0$. The moral hazard incentive constraints assure the voluntary adoption of reforms. The gap between the country's

[19]To illustrate how these expressions are obtained, we fully write out the constraint that leads to equation (13) as

$$\underline{\pi}[g(T_G)\overline{y} - \theta_G T_G - E(\overline{r}_G)] + (1-\underline{\pi})[g(T_G)\underline{y} - \theta_G T_G - E(\underline{r}_G)$$
$$\geq \underline{\pi}[g(T_B)\overline{y} - \theta_G T_B - E(\overline{r}_B) + (1-\underline{\pi})[g(T_B)\underline{y} - \theta_G T_B - E(\underline{r}_B)$$

and substitute (10).

expected net income when the economy is strong, $\overline{V}_j$, and when it is weak, $\underline{V}_j$, must be sufficiently large to entice the government to reform and, thereby, raise the probability of a strong economy.

At the time the IFI offers an incentive-compatible loan, equations (11)–(18) must be satisfied. If the participation constraint for the bad government, (12), the adverse selection constraint of (13) for the good government, and both moral hazard constraints, (17) and (18), are binding, the remaining four constraints are satisfied as well. From the binding constraints one can solve for expected net income of each type country when the economy is strong and when it is weak. To highlight the political damage caused by punishments under an IFI contract that delivers reforms but does not impose limited liability constraints, we solve for expected net income of both country types in the weak state of the economy:

$$\underline{V}_B = \underline{y} - \pi(\omega')[C(\omega') - a\Delta y\Delta\pi(\omega')]/[a\Delta\pi(\omega')], \tag{19}$$

$$\underline{V}_G = \underline{y} - \pi(\omega')[C(\omega') - a\Delta y\Delta\pi(\omega')]/[a\Delta\pi(\omega')] + T_B\Delta\theta, \tag{20}$$

where $[C(\omega') - a\Delta y\Delta\pi(\omega')] > 0$.[20] In a weak economy, countries with both good and bad government types will be punished.[21] A weak economy's expected net income, at the time output is realized, is *always less* with the loan than without the loan if the government is bad and it *might also be less* if the government is good.

**Proposition 2.** The rewards and punishments incorporated into IFI loan mechanisms that are designed to deliver reforms but impose no liability limits on punishments violate the goal of securing the recipient country's political stability.

The IFI designs its loan mechanism to be an incentive system – that is, to reward strong economic outcomes, whose prospects are promoted by economic reforms, and to punish weak economic outcomes, which are more likely if no reforms are implemented. Hence, the government and its people are severely punished when the economy turns out to be weak and they are generously rewarded when the economy turns out to be strong. Getting punished when the economy is already weak is a recipe for disaster. Social unrest, rioting, and the complete collapse of the country's political system could follow. The IFI, therefore, has to modify the incentive system by adding *limited liability constraints* that assure political stability. We next turn to this modified incentive mechanism.

[20]This must always be the case as long as bargaining with the interest group generates more political support for the government than reforming on its own.

[21]The punishment is equal to $\pi(\omega')[C(\omega') - a\Delta y\Delta\pi(\omega')]/[a\Delta\pi(\omega')]$. It rises with the size of the interest group's maximum contribution, $C(\omega')$, and the probability of the good state, $\pi(\omega')$, and it declines with the public's influence on its government, $a$.

## 8. LOAN MECHANISM DESIGN WITH LIMITED LIABILITY

In order to secure political stability, the IFI's mechanism must guarantee that repayment of the loan in any state of the economy makes the general public no worse off with the loan than it would be without it. Hence, political stability requires that

$$\overline{V}_G \geq \bar{y}, \tag{21}$$

$$\underline{V}_G \geq \underline{y}, \tag{22}$$

$$\overline{V}_B \geq \bar{y}, \tag{23}$$

$$\underline{V}_B \geq \underline{y}. \tag{24}$$

With limited liability, the two stochastic loan contracts offered by the IFI, $[T_G, \overline{Z}_G, \underline{Z}_G]$ and $[T_B, \overline{Z}_B, \underline{Z}_B]$, must satisfy the 12 constraints (11)–(18) and (21)–(24). If the *adverse selection incentive constraint* for the good government, as stated in (13), the *moral hazard incentive constraints* for both types of government, (17) and (18), and the *limited liability constraint* for the bad government in a weak economy, (24), are binding, then all other constraints are satisfied as well.[22] Solving the four binding constraints for expected net income of the two types of countries in the two possible states of the economy yields:

$$\begin{aligned} &\underline{V}_B = \underline{y} \\ &\overline{V}_B = \bar{y} + [C(\omega') - a\Delta y\Delta\pi(\omega')]/[a\Delta\pi(\omega')], \end{aligned} \tag{25}$$

$$\begin{aligned} &\underline{V}_G = \underline{y} + T_B\Delta\theta \\ &\overline{V}_G = \bar{y} + T_B\Delta\theta + [C(\omega') - a\Delta y\Delta\pi(\omega')]/[a\Delta\pi(\omega')] \end{aligned} \tag{26}$$

for countries with a bad and a good government type, respectively.

Equations (25) and (26) reveal that, in every state of the economy, a country's expected income, independent of the cost-effectiveness of its government in administering the IFI loan, is at least as high as it would be

[22]In order to check whether (11)–(18) and (21)–(24) are satisfied when (13), (17), (18), and (24) are binding, we first note that adding (13) and (15) implies that $(T_G - T_B) > 0$. That (11) is satisfied can be seen after substitution of binding (17), writing $[\pi(\omega')\bar{y} + (1-\pi(\omega')\underline{y}] = \underline{y} + \pi(\omega')\Delta y$, and using $[R(\omega') - a\Delta y\Delta\pi(\omega')] > 0$ as well as (22). To show that (12) holds, substitute binding (18) and (24), and again use $[\pi(\omega')\bar{y} + (1-\pi(\omega')\underline{y}] = \underline{y} + \pi(\omega')\Delta y$ and $[R(\omega') - a\Delta y\Delta\pi(\omega')] > 0$. That (14) holds as well, one can see after substituting the RHS of binding (13) on the LHS of (14), and using binding (18). Equation (15) is satisfied, as one can see from substituting binding (13) and using $(T_G - T_B) > 0$. The same is the case for (16), after substituting binding (13) and using binding (17), as well as $(T_G - T_B) > 0$. Equation (22) is satisfied, after substituting binding (17), (18), and (24) in (13). Equations (21) and (23) are satisfied, using binding (17) and (18), as well as (22) and (24).

without the loan. This outcome is due to the limited liability constraints, which assure that punishments under the moral hazard incentive system do not cause political turmoil. The worst possible outcome occurs for a country run by a bad government type when the economy turns out to be weak. Its expected net income is $\underline{V}_B = \underline{y}$, making it equally well off as without the loan. If the economy is weak in a country run by a good government, expected net income, $\underline{V}_G$, is raised above the no-loan level of $\underline{y}$ due to an *adverse selection information rent* of $T_B\Delta\theta > 0$. The IFI has to pay this information rent to a good government so that it will not opt for the contract designed for the bad government. It represents one form of information cost faced by the IFI, a cost that reduces the repayment it expects.

A second form of rent gained by the loan-seeking government is a *limited liability rent*. It is a consequence of the IFI's and government's desire to avoid political instability. As mentioned in footnote 21, if there were no *limited liability constraints*, the punishment of a government in a weak economy would be $\{\pi(\omega')[C(\omega') - a\Delta y\Delta\pi(\omega')]/[a\Delta\pi(\omega')]\}$.[23] The need for political stability rules out this punishment. Eliminating the punishment raises the country's expected net income not only in a weak economy but also in a strong economy. This is so because the incentives for implementing economic reforms, as reflected in the binding *moral hazard constraints* of (17) and (18), require that a gap in expected net income of $C(\omega')/[a\Delta\pi(\omega')]$ be maintained between a strong and a weak economy. Hence, the limited liability constraints raise the level of expected net income by $\{\pi(\omega')[C(\omega') - a\Delta y\Delta\pi(\omega')]/[a\Delta\pi(\omega')]\}$ not only under the worst possible scenario of a bad government in a weak economy, but for all types of governments and in all states of the economy. For the IFI this implies that limited liability constraints create an across-the-board reduction in loan repayment receipts for all types of government and in all states of the economy.

The size of loans is determined by the IFI, as it chooses $T_G \geq 0$ and $T_B \geq 0$ with the goal of maximizing its objective function as stated in (4). In that equation,

$$\begin{aligned} E(V) &= \gamma[\underline{\pi}\overline{V}_G + (1-\underline{\pi})\underline{V}_G] + (1-\gamma)[\underline{\pi}\overline{V}_B + (1-\underline{\pi})\underline{V}_B] \\ &= \underline{E}(y) + \gamma T_B\Delta\theta + \underline{\pi}[C(\omega') - a\Delta y\Delta\pi(\omega')]/[a\Delta\pi(\omega')] \qquad (27) \end{aligned}$$

is the expected net income of the loan-receiving country as viewed by the IFI at the time it offers its menu of stochastic contracts and

$$\begin{aligned} E(I) &= \gamma[g(T_G)\underline{E}(y) - (1+\theta_G)T_G] \\ &\quad + (1-\gamma)[g(T_B)\underline{E}(y) - (1+\theta_B)T_B] - E(V) \qquad (28) \end{aligned}$$

[23]It should be noted that the moral hazard problem does not lead to information rents when the government is risk neutral, as has been assumed, and there are no limited liability constraints.

is the expected return of the IFI, obtained after substitution of (10) into (9). We also recall that $\underline{E}(y) = [\underline{\pi}\bar{y} + (1 - \underline{\pi})\underline{y}]$ is the expected national income of a fully reformed economy without any loan effects and that $0 < \gamma < 1$ is the probability of dealing with a good government. Substitution of (27) and (28) into (4) enables us to state the IFI's expected welfare as

$$E(W) = \{1 - \beta\}\{\gamma[g(T_G)\underline{E}(y) - (1 + \theta_G)T_G] + (1 - \gamma)[g(T_B)\underline{E}(y) - (1 + \theta_B)T_B]\} + (2\beta - 1)E(V). \quad (4')$$

From (27) one can see that $\partial E(V)/\partial T_G = 0$ and $\partial E(V)/\partial T_B = \gamma\Delta\theta$. Hence, the values of $T_G^c$ and $T_B^c$ that maximize $E(W)$ in (4′) satisfy

$$g'(T_G^c)\underline{E}(y) = (1 + \theta_G), \quad (29)$$

$$g'(T_B^c)\underline{E}(y) = (1 + \theta_B) + [(1 - 2\beta)\gamma\Delta\theta]/[(1 - \beta)(1 - \gamma)], \quad (30)$$

where superscript $c$ indicates that these are optimal loan choices *conditional* on reforms being implemented.

The size of the loan to a good government is efficient and the same as it would be under symmetric information. The marginal gain in expected gross income of the reformed economy, $g'(T_G^c)\underline{E}(y)$, equals the marginal cost of spending and administering another dollar on the loan, $(1 + \theta_G)$. The optimal loan size designed for a bad government, on the other hand, is different from what it would be if the IFI knew that the government was bad. Its deviation from the efficient size crucially depends on the weight of the country's welfare in the IFI's objective function. If the IFI cares only about its own expected return and not at all about the loan-receiving country, then $\beta = 0$ and (30) reduces to $g'(T_B^c)\underline{E}(y) = (1 + \theta_B) + \gamma\Delta\theta/(1 - \gamma)$. In this case, the marginal gain in expected gross income must cover not only the marginal cost of spending and administering another loan dollar, but it must also cover the marginal information cost of $[(\gamma\Delta\theta)/(1 - \gamma)]$. In this case, the size of the loan offered to a bad government is less than it would be if the IFI knew that the government was indeed bad. If, on the other hand, the IFI cares for the welfare of the recipient country more than for its own wellbeing, then $\beta > \frac{1}{2}$ and the RHS of (30) is always less than $(1 + \theta_B)$. The effect of such strong caring for the borrowing country is overinvestment. The IFI's loan to the bad government will be larger than is efficient. Only in the special case that the IFI attaches equal weights to its own expected return and the recipient country's expected welfare, in which case $\beta = \frac{1}{2}$, is the loan designed for the bad government efficient. We summarize these findings in:

**Proposition 3.** In the context of an optimal IFI loan mechanism designed to achieve complete reform while ensuring political stability, loans designed for a good government type are always efficient. Such loans designed for a bad government result in either underinvestment or overinvestment depending on whether the IFI cares more for its own welfare or for the borrowing country's welfare.

## 9. OPTIMAL LOAN MECHANISMS AND THE IFI'S FINANCIAL CONSTRAINTS

The section relates the properties of the optimal loan mechanism to the financial constraints faced by the IFI. The informational and political realities earn the government various rents, while generating costs to the IFI. If the optimal loan mechanism becomes too costly, the IFI will not offer a loan.

The IFI has to cope with several information problems. It lacks complete information on the government's effectiveness to administer the loan, on the government's effort to implement reforms, and on the default penalty if the government does not repay. While the first two information problems add costs to the IFI's expected return calculation, the possibility of default does not, given our assumption of a risk-neutral government.[24] Added information costs manifest themselves as reduced loan repayments for the government and lower expected returns for the IFI. The IFI, as an institution, cannot survive unless it expects to do no worse than break even on each loan. It works with many potential borrowers and while, ex post, it might show losses on some loans and gains on others, on average it has to break even. Consequently, the IFI operates under the constraint that its expected returns be non-negative. If it cannot meet this constraint, the IFI is unwilling to offer a loan program that incorporates reform incentives.

The following proposition relates the IFI's willingness to offer a loan with reform incentives to the power of a borrowing country's interest group:

**Proposition 4.** The larger the interest group's ability to make a contribution and the smaller the gains in expected net income due to the loan, the more likely it is that the IFI is not able to offer a loan mechanism that incorporates reform incentives.

To establish this proposition, we first return to (28), substitute (27) for $E(V)$, and determine that level of policy distortion, denoted by $\underline{\omega}$, at which the IFI's expected return is zero. Setting $E(I) = 0$ yields

$$C(\underline{\omega})/[a\Delta\pi(\underline{\omega})\Delta y] = 1 + [E\Delta X(T) - \gamma T_B^c \Delta\theta]/[\underline{\pi}\Delta y], \tag{31}$$

where $C(\underline{\omega})/[a\Delta\pi(\underline{\omega})\Delta y]$ measures the government's tradeoff between interest group contributions and support from the public as a result of income gains from complete reforms, when evaluated at the IFI's break-even

[24]If the probability of default were zero, the IFI's expected return would remain unchanged. The IFI avoids any default costs by raising repayments when there is no default in order to offset the shortfall in repayments when there is default.

distortion level of $\underline{\omega}$. The term

$$E\Delta X(T) = \gamma\{[g(T_G^c) - 1]\underline{E}(y) - (1+\theta_G)T_G^c\} + (1-\gamma)\{[g(T_B^c) - 1]\underline{E}(y) - (1+\theta_B)T_B^c\}, \quad (32)$$

in turn, expresses the IFI's expectation of the country's gain in net output due to the loan alone, evaluated at the full-reform probability of a strong economy.

As shown in Appendix A.2, the value of $C(\omega)/\Delta\pi(\omega)$ is inversely related to the value of $\omega$. This has the following implication. If, as an alternative to a loan mechanism that incorporates reform incentives, the government and the interest group can negotiate a policy-for-contributions deal $[\omega^o, C(\omega^o)]$ for which $\omega^o < \underline{\omega}$, then the IFI is not able to offer a mechanism that could bring about reforms. Such a deal between the government and the interest group to block the IFI mechanism will be arrived at whenever $\omega'$, the lowest distortion level the interest group would agree to, is less than $\underline{\omega}$. This will be the case if the interest group's rent evaluated at $\underline{\omega}$ exceeds the contribution it must make to the government to block the IFI from offering a loan mechanism that incorporates reform incentives. The larger the interest group's rent from given policies, as expressed by the value of $R(\omega)$, and the smaller the expected net output gain from the IFI's reform-compatible mechanism, as reflected in the value of $E\Delta X(T)$, the more likely it is that the IFI is unable to offer such a loan mechanism.

The IFI's inability to offer a loan mechanism that incorporates reform incentives will, however, not eliminate the influence of the IFI on the government's policy choice. The reason the IFI retains some influence is the following: its mere presence as a potential source of funds that could bring about reforms at sufficiently high policy distortion levels alters the interest group's bargaining position, the amount of contributions it must make, and the policies it obtains in exchange. Recall from (5) and (6) that, in the absence of the IFI, the government and the interest group arrive at a policy-for-contributions deal $[\omega^*, C(\omega^*)]$. Now, when the IFI is present as a potential source of loans, its refusal to offer a mechanism that aims at reforms comes into play only if the government is able to choose $\omega < \underline{\omega}$. Consequently, blocking the IFI's involvement requires that the adopted policy, denoted by index $\omega^o$, is such that $\omega^o \leq \underline{\omega} < \omega^*$, which implies partial policy reforms.[25]

**Proposition 5.** Even if the interest group can block a loan mechanism that incorporates reform incentives, the prospect of such a mechanism is sufficient to bring about partial reforms.

[25]As shown in Appendix A.2, bargaining between the interest group and the government results in a policy-for-contributions deal $[\omega^o, C(\omega^o)]$, for which $\omega^o < \underline{\omega}$ as long as $\omega' < \underline{\omega}$. In other words, the government will reform more than is necessary to block IFI loans aiming at bringing about reforms.

Partial reform means that $0 < \omega^o < \omega^*$, where $\omega^*$ is the policy-created distortion index in the absence of the IFI and $\omega = 0$ means complete reforms. With the IFI ready to make loans aiming at reforms under the "right" circumstances, the interest group would rather settle for partial than complete reforms. And the government would be no worse off receiving interest group support under partial reforms than obtaining a loan aiming at complete reforms and no interest group support.

## 10. LOAN MECHANISMS THAT RELAX INCENTIVE-COMPATIBILITY CONSTRAINTS

The preceding section demonstrated that a loan mechanism designed to bring about full reforms will not be forthcoming if the interest group can afford a policy-for-contributions deal that prevents the IFI from breaking even. The IFI could counter, of course, by designing a mechanism that relaxes some of the constraints. Relaxing or removing the *limited liability constraints* would be most effective in raising the IFI's expected return. The risk of doing so is that the economy turns out to be weak at the time of repayment and the country experiences political turmoil. A second possibility is to ignore the *moral hazard incentive constraints*, with the result that the loan mechanism's reform incentives disappear. A mechanism designed without reform in mind will still benefit the recipient country, by raising its stock of productive capital. But, under the circumstances, the IFI cannot realize the potential of a second dividend from the effect of improved policies on output.

This section analyzes the consequences of IFI loan mechanisms designed without full reform incentives in mind. As before, the IFI does not know the effectiveness of the government in administering its loan, there again is the possibility of default, and the terms of the loan must be consistent with the maintenance of political stability. We first set up the model under the assumption that IFI loans do not aim at reforms. We then show that there exists a range of best-alternative policy choices for the government under which a loan mechanism designed to deliver full reform yields a positive return for the IFI, but that this return is less than for a mechanism that does not incorporate reform incentives. Second, we establish general conditions under which the IFI continues to offer a loan mechanism that incorporates reform incentives even if it is less profitable than the mechanism that does not implement reforms.

The IFI's goal when it designs a loan mechanism without reform incentives is again to maximize a weighted average of the borrowing country's expected welfare and the IFI's own expected return. However, the mechanism no longer aims to deliver reforms and, therefore, policies are adopted in return for contributions from the interest group. The IFI again chooses the size of the loan, as well as the repayment conditions for different types of borrowers in different states of the economy. The IFI maximizes its objective function subject to *participation constraints*, (33) and (34), *adverse selection constraints*, (35) and (36), and the previously stated *limited liability constraints* of (21)–(24). We now attach superscript $n$ to all endogenous variables to indicate that the loan mechanism does *not* aim to deliver reforms.

The participation constraints require that each type government is at least as well off with the IFI loan and the negotiated policy-for-contributions deal $[\omega_j^n, C(\omega_j^n)]$, as it would be in the absence of such a loan, when it negotiates the deal $[\omega^*, C(\omega^*)]$, as shown in (5) and (6):

$$C(\omega_G^n) + a\{\pi(\omega_G^n)\overline{V}_G^n + [1-\pi(\omega_G^n)]\underline{V}_G^n\}$$

$$\geq C(\omega^*) + a\{\pi(\omega^*)\bar{y} + [1-\pi(\omega^*)]\underline{y}\}, \tag{33}$$

$$C(\omega_B^n) + a\{\pi(\omega_B^n)\overline{V}_B^n + [1-\pi(\omega_B^n)]\underline{V}_B^n\}$$

$$\geq C(\omega^*) + a\{\pi(\omega^*)\bar{y} + [1-\pi(\omega^*)]\underline{y}\}. \tag{34}$$

The corresponding adverse selection incentive constraints require that each type government receives at least as much political support by taking the loan program designed for its type as from the program designed for the other type:

$$\{\pi(\omega_G^n)\overline{V}_G^n + [1-\pi(\omega_G^n)]\underline{V}_G^n\} \geq \{\pi(\omega_G^n)\overline{V}_B^n + [1-\pi(\omega_G^n)]\underline{V}_B^n + T_B^n\Delta\theta\}, \tag{35}$$

$$\{\pi(\omega_B^n)\overline{V}_B^n + [1-\pi(\omega_B^n)]\underline{V}_B^n\} \geq \{\pi(\omega_B^n)\overline{V}_G^n + [1-\pi(\omega_B^n)]\underline{V}_G^n T_G^n\Delta\theta\}. \tag{36}$$

The limited liability constraints are the same as for a loan program that aims at reforms, (21)–(24), with the modification that expected net income values are now marked with superscript $n$.

The IFI chooses the loan size and corresponding repayment, thereby determining the expected net income of each government's economy, $\overline{V}_j^n$ and $\underline{V}_j^n$. Each government, in turn, takes these net income values as given and negotiates a contributions-for-policy deal with the interest group, as more fully explained in Appendix A.3.

One can show that for the net income values of

$$\underline{V}_B^n = \underline{y} \qquad \overline{V}_B^n = \bar{y}, \tag{37}$$

$$\underline{V}_G^n = \underline{y} + T_B\Delta\theta \qquad \overline{V}_G^n = \bar{y} + T_B\Delta\theta \tag{38}$$

for the country with a bad and a good government, respectively, all constraints stated in (33)–(36) and (21)–(24) are satisfied, and that the participation constraint for the bad government type, (34), the adverse selection constraint for the good government type, (35), and the two limited liability constraints for the bad government type, (23)–(24), are binding. The solution values of (37) and (38) also imply that $(\overline{V}^n_G - \underline{V}^n_G) = (\overline{V}^n_B - \underline{V}^n_B) = (\bar{y} - \underline{y})\Delta y$.

Comparing loan mechanisms that aim at bringing about reforms with those that do not, there exists an important difference with respect to their eventual impact on economic reforms. As shown in the preceding section, the availability of loan mechanisms that aim at reforms always leads to *some* reform: the reforms are complete when the mechanisms are financially viable for the IFI and are therefore proposed and adopted and they are partial if offering a loan mechanism is financially not viable for the IFI. On the other hand, mechanisms that do not incorporate reform incentives lead to no reforms.[26] As shown in Appendix A.3, under mechanisms without reforms, each government type chooses the same level of distortions which, in turn, is exactly the same as the distortion level in the complete absence of the IFI, namely $\omega^n_G = \omega^n_B = \omega^*$.

Comparing the *size of loans* aiming at reforms relative to those that do not incorporate reform incentives leads to the following proposition, which is analogous to the one obtained for mechanisms designed to facilitate reforms.

**Proposition 6.**

(i) Loans offered in mechanisms that do not incorporate reform incentives are smaller than loans under mechanisms designed with reforms in mind.
(ii) Loans offered in mechanisms that do not incorporate reform incentives and designed for a good government are efficient, whereas such loans for a bad government result in over- (under-)investment if the IFI cares more (less) for the borrowing country than for itself.

To prove this proposition, we again maximize the IFI's objective function, $E(W^n) = \beta E(V^n) + (1 - \beta)E(I^n)$, with respect to $T^n_G$ and $T^n_B$, where

$$E(V^n) = \gamma\{\pi(\omega^*)\overline{V}^n_G + [1 - \pi(\omega^*)]\underline{V}^n_G\} + (1 - \gamma)\{\pi(\omega^*)\overline{V}^n_B + [1 - \pi(\omega^*)]\underline{V}^n_B\} = E^n(y) + \gamma T^n_B \Delta\theta, \tag{39}$$

$$E(I^n) = \gamma[g(T^n_G)E^n(y) - (1 + \theta_G)T^n_G] + (1 - \gamma)[g(T^n_B)E^n(y) - (1 + \theta_B)T^n_B] - E(V^n), \tag{40}$$

[26]The conclusion does not hold if the IFI offers an unconditional loan because, at prevailing strength of the interest group, it is not willing to offer a conditional loan. With the conditional loan a potential threat, the government has to reform sufficiently to keep this threat at bay.

and where $E^n(y) = \{\pi(\omega^*)\bar{y} + [1 - \pi(\omega^*)]\underline{y}\}$ is the country's expected net income in the complete absence of the IFI. Maximizing $E(W^n)$ with respect to $T_G^n$ and $T_B^n$ requires that

$$g'(T_G^n)E^n(y) = (1 + \theta_G), \tag{41}$$

$$g'(T_B^n)E^n(y) = (1 + \theta_B) + [(1 - 2\beta)\gamma\Delta\theta]/[(1 - \beta)(1 - \gamma)]. \tag{42}$$

A comparison of (41)–(42) with (29)–(30) reveals that the criteria for the choice of loans that do not aim at reforms are the same as for loans that do, except that the terms $g'(T_j)$ are multiplied by $E^n(y)$ for the former and by $\underline{E}(y)$ for the latter. Because $E^n(y) < \underline{E}(y)$ and $g''(T_j) < 0$, it must be that $g'(T_j^n) > g'(T_j^c)$ and $T_j^n < T_j^c$.

We now turn to examining the choice of mechanism when both mechanisms, those that incorporate reform incentives and those that do not, yield positive expected returns to the IFI. The choice depends on the kind of mechanism that is more profitable. Begin by letting $\omega^n$ be that distortion level at which expected returns from the two kinds of mechanism are the same. More precisely, we determine the value of $\omega^n$ that equates $E(I)$ with $E(I^n)$. To do so, we first take (28), substitute (27) for $E(V)$, and use the expression of (32) to obtain

$$E\Delta X(T) - \gamma T_B\Delta\theta - \underline{\pi}\{C(\omega^n)/[a\Delta\pi(\omega^n)] - \Delta y\} = E(I^n). \tag{43}$$

Then, we substitute (31) into (43) and solve for

$$C(\omega^n)/[a\Delta\pi(\omega^n)] = C(\underline{\omega})/[a\Delta\pi(\underline{\omega})] - E(I^n)/\underline{\pi}. \tag{44}$$

Because $C(\omega^n)/[\Delta\pi(\omega^n)] < C(\underline{\omega})/[\Delta\pi(\underline{\omega})]$, it must be that $\omega^n > \underline{\omega}$. The distortion level at which expected returns from the two types of mechanisms are the same is larger than the distortion level at the break-even point for the IFI.

If both loans with reforms and loans without reforms yield a positive expected return for the IFI, which type of loan will be chosen? In order to answer this question, we return to (27) and (28) and note that $E(I^c)$ rises with $\omega'$ – which, as shown in (A1), is the government's best alternative policy choice if it does not accept the loan with reforms – because $E(V^c)$ is negatively related to $\omega'$. Which type of loan yields the higher return then depends on the size of $\omega'$ relative to $\omega^n$.

**Proposition 7.** If $\omega^n > \omega'$, loan mechanisms that do not incorporate reform incentives yield a higher expected return to the IFI than mechanisms that aim at reform. If $\omega' > \omega^n$, mechanisms that aim at reform are more profitable than the ones that do not contain reform incentives.

When a loan mechanism designed to bring about reform yields a lower positive IFI expected return compared with one that does not, offering the former might still be the best course of action for the IFI. Recall that the IFI is altruistic: its objective is not merely to earn a high return on its loans but also to help the borrowing country reform its policies. Hence, the type of mechanism the IFI selects depends on its preference for the welfare of its creditors relative to that of its borrowers. This leads to:

**Proposition 8.** If the IFI cares at least as much for the borrowing country as for itself, the IFI will always offer a positive return-yielding loan mechanism with reforms, regardless of the expected return on mechanisms that do not aim at reform.

To prove this result, we first state the IFI's expected welfare under the two mechanisms:

$$E(W) = (1-\beta)\{E\Delta X(T)\} + \beta\{\underline{E}(y)\} + (2\beta - 1)\{\gamma T_B \Delta\theta + [R(\omega') - a\Delta y \Delta\pi(\omega')][\underline{\pi}/(a\Delta\pi(\omega'))]\}, \quad (45)$$

$$E(W^n) = (1-\beta)\{E\Delta X(T^n)\} + \beta\{E^n(y)\} + (2\beta - 1)[\gamma T_B^n \Delta\theta], \quad (46)$$

using (4′) and (27) for $E(W)$ and (4), (39), and (40) for $E(W^n)$. Comparing each of the three braced terms on the RHS of the expressions, it should be noted that $T_j > T_j^n$, $E\Delta X(T) > E\Delta X(T^n)$, $\underline{E}(y) > E^n(y)$, and $[R(\omega') - a\Delta y\Delta\pi(\omega')] > 0$. Consequently, each of the three braced terms on the RHS is larger in (45) than in (46). If the IFI cares at least as much for the recipient country as it does for itself, such that $\frac{1}{2} \leq \beta \leq 1$, then it must always be that $E(W) > E(W^n)$.

## 11. CONCLUSION

This paper developed a theoretical framework to shed light on the mixed success of IFIs providing loans with reform strings attached. It highlights three features that play a significant role in the real world: first, loan-seeking governments typically choose policies under the influence of domestic interest groups. Second, the loan-providing IFI has less information than the government and its supporting interest groups on both the government's ability to administer a loan program and its willingness to implement economic reforms. Third, two types of constraints restrict any mechanism designed to overcome the IFI's information shortfall. The IFI cannot punish the loan-receiving country so much as to create political turmoil and it cannot pay such high information rents as to endanger its financial viability.

The paper demonstrated that the success of a loan program with reform critically depends on the strength of the receiving country's interest group. If an interest group is very powerful, in the sense that it earns high economic rents from the economic policies it promotes, then it might have the ability to completely block the loan with reform strings attached. To overcome the power of the interest group, the IFI would have to offer the government such favorable loan conditions that its own financial viability would be jeopardized. Nonetheless, the presence of an IFI that would be willing to make a loan to a government that is less dependent on an interest group is sufficient to bring about some internal reforms. The IFI's preparedness to make loans that allow it to break even strengthens the government's bargaining position vis-à-vis the interest group. It enables the government to receive more financial contributions from the interest group while initiating partial reform. Even if no loan is actually made, the country's expected income will be higher.

The paper also points out that, even if the IFI earns a positive expected return from a loan with reform incentives, it might be able to do better if it issued a loan without any reform strings. This will be the case if the interest group is unable to block the loan with reforms but is sufficiently strong to make the IFI pay heavily for creating the necessary incentives for implementing them. Only when interest groups are relatively weak will the IFI be better off imposing reform conditions than granting a loan without reforms.

The strength of the interest group is only one important influence on the expected profitability of the loan with reforms. The other influence of note is the loan's expected impact on the economy's performance. The larger the expected gain in net output due to the loan, as viewed by the IFI, the more likely it is that the IFI's financial viability is not compromised.

Although the IFI's expected return might be higher from a loan without reforms than with reforms, the receiving country's general public will be worse off. Not only will the public forego the dividend from reforms, it will also have to do with a smaller loan. The benefits of different types of loans will come into play when the IFI is concerned not only about its own (and indirectly its donors') welfare but also about the recipient country's welfare. The paper shows that an IFI that cares as much for the loan recipient as for itself will always issue loans with reform incentives, as long as it breaks at least even.

Our analysis comes with an important caveat. In the model presented, the IFIs are uninformed principals whose role as financiers is decoupled from their function as trusted advisors of sovereigns. In some important respects, however, IFIs may be better informed than recipient governments. They are "knowledge banks" that can advise governments on what policies work in practice and how to set up and organize various institutions of economic management. It is natural then that IFIs tie their loans to the implementation by sovereigns of key policy and institutional recommendations. IFIs are well placed to play this role of providers of information and analysis. They are constitutionally mandated to provide regular surveys of national, regional, and global economic conditions and provide specialized technical assistance services to their member countries. These activities give IFIs preferential access to valuable information about the economic conditions and challenges facing member countries. Surveillance and technical assistance are justifiable IFI activities because they concentrate in areas with economy- or sector-wide spillovers that do not crowd out the private sector (see Rodrik, 1995, p. 8). The readiness of IFIs to commit financing, in turn, can raise the credibility of IFI policy advice and could make it easier for recipients to implement reforms that may be costly in the short run. The design, monitoring, and agency cost of international assistance programs that tie together the provision of financing with that of information, analysis, and advice is an important agenda for future research.

## APPENDIX A

### *A.1 The Government's Best Alternative to IFI Loans with Reform Objectives*

Section 4 determined the government's choice of policies, $\omega^*$, when there is no IFI as a potential source of a loan that aims at bringing about reform. In the current situation, there is an IFI that is willing to make such loans. Borrowing from the IFI and reforming presents an alternative to negotiating a policy-for-contributions deal with the interest group. It will make the government choose a different policy even if it does not accept the loan that it would have chosen in the complete absence of the IFI.

Given the IFI's offer of a loan contract, $[T_j, \overline{Z}_j, \underline{Z}_j]$, the expected net income for a country with type $j$ government will be $\overline{V}_j$ and $\underline{V}_j$ in a strong and weak economy, respectively. If the government is willing to strike a bargain with the interest group, it will accept the loan contract but not implement the accompanying reforms. In that case, its expected political support will be $\{C(\omega_j) + a[\pi(\omega_j)\overline{V}_j + (1 - \pi(\omega_j))\underline{V}_j]\}$, where $\omega_j > 0$. If, on the other hand, bargaining breaks down, then the government takes the loan and reforms completely, yielding expected political support of $a[\underline{\pi}\overline{V}_j + (1 - \underline{\pi})\underline{V}_j]$. When bargaining succeeds, the contribution level will maximize

$$\{C(\omega_j) + a[\pi(\omega_j)\overline{V}_j + (1 - \pi(\omega_j))\underline{V}_j] \\ - a[\underline{\pi}\overline{V}_j + (1 - \underline{\pi})\underline{V}_j]\}^{\tau}\{R(\omega_j) - C\}^{1-\tau},$$

yielding the contribution function

$$C(\omega_j) = \tau R(\omega_j) + (1 - \tau)a\Delta V_j \Delta\pi(\omega_j), \tag{A1}$$

where $\Delta V_j = (\overline{V}_j - \underline{V}_j)$. As before, the government chooses its policy, $\omega_j'$, to maximize its political support, given the contribution function of (A1). This yields:

$$-R'(\omega_j')/\pi'(\omega_j') = a\Delta V_j. \tag{A2}$$

In equilibrium, the spread between expected net income in the good and bad state of the economy is set by the binding moral hazard incentive constraints of (17) and (18), which require that $a\Delta V_j = C(\omega_j')/\Delta\pi(\omega_j')$.

Substitution yields the condition for the government's policy choice in the presence of an IFI, $\omega_j'$, as

$$-R'(\omega_j')/\pi'(\omega_j') = C(\omega_j')/\Delta\pi(\omega_j'). \tag{A3}$$

Two results follow from the above three equations. First, $\omega_G' = \omega_B' = \omega'$ since the optimal policy choice criterion is independent of $\theta_j$. Second, $\omega' < \omega^*$; that is, the best alternative economics policy to an IFI loan with reform conditions, $\omega'$, entails partial reforms relative to the policy that prevailed in the absence of any IFI, $\omega^*$. This can be seen by comparing the RHS of (A3) with the RHS of (6) and noting that the value of $-R'(\omega_j)/\pi'(\omega_j)$ declines as $\omega$ rises. The RHS of (A3) is always larger than the RHS of (6), since $\{C(\omega') - a\Delta y\Delta\pi(\omega')\} = \{C(\omega') + a[\pi(\omega')\overline{y} + (1 - \pi(\omega'))\underline{y}] - a[\underline{\pi}\,\overline{y} + (1 - \underline{\pi})\underline{y}]\} > 0$. If this inequality did not hold, the government would have an incentive to fully reform on its own.

### *A.2 Bargaining when IFI Loans can be Blocked by Interest Groups*

Section 9 determined $\underline{\omega}$ as the policy choice at which the IFI expects to break even. Whenever $\omega' < \underline{\omega}$, no loan aiming at reforms will be offered, and the government is back to actual bargaining with the interest group.

Define $\overline{V}_j(\underline{\omega})$ and $\underline{V}_j(\underline{\omega})$ as the expected net income in a strong and weak economy, respectively, when the government's policy choice is $\underline{\omega}$. In that case, the $j$th government's gain in expected political support from bargaining with the interest group, rather than accepting the IFI loan with complete reforms, is $\{C_j - a\Delta\pi(\omega_j)[\overline{V}_j(\underline{\omega}) - \underline{V}_j(\underline{\omega})]\}$ and the interest group's gain is $\{R(\omega_j) - C_j\}$. Following the steps taken in deriving (5), the solution to the asymmetric Nash-bargaining game is

$$C(\omega_j) = \tau R(\omega_j) + (1 - \tau)\{a\Delta\pi(\omega_j)[\overline{V}_j(\underline{\omega}) - \underline{V}_j(\underline{\omega})]\}, \tag{A4}$$

where $a[\overline{V}_j(\underline{\omega}) - \underline{V}_j(\underline{\omega})] = C(\underline{\omega})/\Delta\pi(\underline{\omega})$ from (17) and (18). Given the contribution function of (A4), the $j$th government chooses $\omega_j^o$ to maximize its expected political support $G_j = \{C(\omega_j) + a[\pi(\omega_j)\overline{V}_j(\underline{\omega}) + (1 - \pi(\omega_j))\underline{V}_j(\underline{\omega})]\}$. From the first-order conditions, it follows that

$$-R'(\omega_j^o)/\pi'(\omega_j^o) = C(\underline{\omega})/\Delta\pi(\underline{\omega}). \tag{A5}$$

First, note that the RHS of (A5) is independent of the type of government and, therefore, $\omega_G^o = \omega_B^o = \omega^o$. Second, it follows from (A4) that $C(\omega)/\Delta\pi(\omega)$ decreases with $\omega$ if $R(\omega)/\Delta\pi(\omega) > R'(\omega)/\pi'(\omega)$, where we now drop the subscript $j$. This inequality holds for all values of $\omega$ for which $\omega > \omega'$ since the value of $R(\omega)/\Delta\pi(\omega)$ reaches a maximum at $\omega'$, where $R(\omega')/\Delta\pi(\omega') = R'(\omega')/\pi'(\omega')$, and is declining for all $\omega$ larger than $\omega'$. Consequently, in the relevant range of policy choices negotiated with the interest group, it must be that $C(\omega)/\Delta\pi(\omega)$ is decreasing with $\omega$. Finally, one can show that $\omega^o < \underline{\omega}$. Using (A4), one can restate (A5) as

$$-C'(\omega^o)/\pi'(\omega^o) = C(\underline{\omega})/\Delta\pi(\underline{\omega}). \tag{A6}$$

Since $C(\omega)/\Delta\pi(\omega)$ decreases with $\omega$, it must be that, at $\underline{\omega}$, $-C'(\underline{\omega})/\pi'(\underline{\omega}) < C(\underline{\omega})/\Delta\pi(\underline{\omega})$ and that $\omega^o < \underline{\omega}$ in order to establish the optimality condition of (A6).

### *A.3 Bargaining when IFI Loans Do Not Incorporate Reform Incentives*

When the loan is not designed to bring about reform and loan conditions generate expected net incomes of $(\overline{V}_j^n, \underline{V}_j^n)$, expected political support to the government becomes $\{C_j + a[\pi(\omega_j^n)\overline{V}_j^n + (1 - \pi(\omega_j^n)\underline{V}_j^n]\}$ and the interest group ends up with $[R(\omega_j^n)C_j)]$. If, on the other hand, bargaining breaks down, then the government's best course of action is to take the loan and reform completely on its own, yielding political support of $\{a[\underline{\pi}\overline{V}_j^n + (1 - \underline{\pi})\underline{V}_j^n]\}$. In that case, the interest group ends up with nothing. Hence, the gain to striking a bargain is $\{C_j + a\Delta\pi(\omega_j^n)[\overline{V}_j^n - \underline{V}_j^n]\}$ for the government of type $j$ and $[R(\omega_j^n) - C_j]$ for the interest group. From (37) and (38), we know that $[\overline{V}_j^n - \underline{V}_j^n] = \Delta y$ for both types of government and, therefore, that receiving a loan that does not aim at reform results in that level of interest group contributions to the government that maximizes $\{[C_j + a[\Delta\pi(\omega_j^n)\Delta y]\}^\tau\{R(\omega_j^n) - C_j\}^{1-\tau}$. This yields

$$C(\omega_j^n) = \tau R(\omega_j^n) + (1 - \tau)a\Delta y\Delta\pi(\omega_j^n). \tag{A7}$$

The expression is the same as in (5), where we derived the contribution level in the complete absence of the IFI. Consequently, when the government maximizes its political support, given (A7), it chooses policies with a distortion index $\omega_j^n = \omega^*$. Both types of government select those policies that would have been adopted in a world without an IFI.

ACKNOWLEDGMENTS

We thank Ales Bulir, Enrica Detragiache, Len Erickson, Andy Feltenstein, Patrick J. Kehoe, V. V. Chari, the editor, and two anonymous referees for many useful comments on earlier drafts. The views expressed in this paper are ours and do not necessarily represent those of the IMF or IMF policy.

ALEX MOURMOURAS
*The IMF Institute*

WOLFGANG MAYER
*University of Cincinnati*

REFERENCES

Acemoglu, D. and J. A. Robinson, 2006, *Economic Origins of Dictatorship and Democracy* (Cambridge University Press, New York).

Boughton, J. M. and A. Mourmouras, 2004, Whose program is it? Policy ownership and conditional lending, in: D. Vines and C. L. Gilbert, eds., *The IMF and its Critics* (Cambridge University Press, Cambridge) pp. 225–253. Available online at: http://www.imf.org/external/pubs/ft/wp/2002/wp0272.pdf

Chamon, M. and P. Mauro, 2005, Pricing growth-indexed bonds. IMF Working Paper No. 05/216, International Monetary Fund, Washington, DC. Available online at: http://www.imf.org/external/pubs/ft/wp/2005/wp05216.pdf

Dixit, A., 2000, IMF programs as incentive mechanisms. Unpublished, International Monetary Fund, Washington, DC. Available online at: http://www.princeton.edu/~dixitak/home/wrkps.html

——, 2002, Incentives and organizations in the public sector: an interpretative review. *Journal of Human Resources* 37, 696–727.

——, 2003, Some lessons from transaction cost politics for less-developed countries. *Economics and Politics* 15, 107–133. Available online at: http://www/bsos.umd.edu/umccc/olson_memorial_lecture_series_schedule.htm

Dollar, D. and J. Svensson, 2000, What explains the success or failure of structural adjustment programmes? *Economic Journal* 110, 894–917.

Drazen, A., 2002, Conditionality and ownership in IMF lending: a political economy approach. *IMF Staff Papers* 49(Special Issue), 36–67. Available online at: http://www.imf.org/External/Pubs/FT/staffp/2001/00-00/pdf/ad.pdf

—— and P. Isard, 2004, Can public discussion enhance program "ownership"? Paper presented at the IMF Conference in Honor of Guillermo Calvo, Washington, DC, April 15–16. Available online at: http://www.imf.org/external/np/res/seminars/2004/calvo/pdf/drazen.pdf

Eaton, J. and M. Gersovitz, 1995, Some curious properties of a familiar model of debt default. *Economics Letters* 63, 367–371.

Grossman, G. M. and E. Helpman, 1994, Protection for sale. *American Economic Review* 84, 833–850.

—— and ——, 2001, *Special Interest Politics* (MIT Press, Cambridge, MA).

International Monetary Fund, 2000, Report of the Acting Managing Director to the International Monetary and Financial Committee on Strengthening Safeguards on the Use of Fund Resources and Misreporting of Information, April 10. Available online at: http://www.imf.org/external/np/omd/2000/msreport.htm

——, 2001a, *IMF Conditionality* (IMF, Washington, DC).

——, 2001b, Conditionality in fund-supported programs – policy issues. Available online at: http://www.imf.org/external/np/pdr/cond/2001/eng/policy/021601.pdf

——, 2002, *Guidelines on Conditionality*, September 25. Available online at: http://www.imf.org/External/np/pdr/cond/2002/eng/guid/092302.pdf

——, 2005, Review of the 2002 conditionality guidelines – selected issues. Available online at: http://www.imf.org/External/np/pp/eng/2005/030405.htm

Isard, P., L. Lipschitz, A. Mourmouras, and B. Yoncheva, 2006, *The Macroeconomic Management of Foreign Aid* (International Monetary Fund, Washington, DC).

Ivanova, A., 2006, Outcomes-based conditionality: its role and optimal design. *IMF Staff Papers* 53(Special Issue), 76–91. Available online at: http://www.imf.org/External/Pubs/FT/staffp/2006/03/pdf/ivanova.pdf

——, A. Mourmouras, W. Mayer, and G. Anayiotos, 2005, What determines the implementation of IMF-supported programs?, in: A. Mody and A. Rebucci, eds., *IMF-Supported Programs: Assessing Program Design, Implementation, and Effectiveness* (International Monetary Fund, Washington, DC) pp. 160–188. Available online at: http://www.imf.org/external/pubs/ft/wp/2003/wp0308.pdf

Laffont, J.-J. and D. Martimort, 2002, *The Theory of Incentives* (Princeton University Press, Princeton, NJ).

Mayer, W. and A. Mourmouras, 2004, The political economy of conditional and unconditional foreign assistance: grants versus loan rollovers, in: D. Mitra and A. Panagariya, eds., *The Political Economy of Trade, Aid and Foreign Investment Policies* (North-Holland, Amsterdam) pp. 249–276.

—— and ——, 2005, The political economy of IMF conditionality: a common agency model. *Review of Development Economics* 9, 449–466.

—— and ——, 2008, On the viability of conditional assistance programs, in: E. Dinopoulos, P. Krishna, A. Panagariya, and K. Wong, eds., *Trade, Globalization and Poverty* (Routledge, New York) pp. 206–229.

Mussa, M. and M. Savastano, 1999, The IMF's approach to economic stabilization. IMF Working Paper No. 99/104, International Monetary Fund, Washington, DC.

Rodrik, D., 1995, Why is there multilateral lending? NBER Working Paper No. 5610, National Bureau of Economic Research, Cambridge, MA.

——, 1996, Understanding economic policy reform. *Journal of Economic Literature* 34, 9–41.

World Bank, 2005, Experience with World Bank conditionality, in: S. Koeberle, H. Bedoya, P. Silarszky, and G. Verheyen, eds., *Conditionality Revisited: Concepts, Experiences, and Lessons* (World Bank, Washington, DC) pp. 45–56.

——, 2005, *Turkey Public Expenditure Review*. World Bank Report No. 36764-TR, Europe and Central Asia Region, December 18. Available online at: http://siteresources.worldbank.org/INTTURKEY/Resources/361616-1173282369589/tr_per_cr.pdf